FOREIGN POLICY
AND
DEMOCRATIC POLITICS

The American and British Experience

FOREIGN POLICY
AND
DEMOCRATIC POLITICS

The American and British Experience

Kenneth N. Waltz

Brandeis University

LITTLE, BROWN AND COMPANY
BOSTON AND TORONTO

This book was jointly sponsored by the Institute of War and Peace Studies, School of International Affairs, Columbia University, under whose auspices it was begun, and the Center for International Affairs, Harvard University, under whose auspices it was completed.

FIRST PRINTING

*Published simultaneously in Canada
by Little, Brown & Company (Canada) Limited*

PRINTED IN THE UNITED STATES OF AMERICA

PREFACE

Seven years ago, I set out to write a little book on the domestic politics of foreign policy. I believed then, and still do, that the foreign-policy capabilities of democratic states are unduly disparaged. Not having previously studied or taught in the realm of domestic or comparative politics, I underestimated the extent of the task undertaken. Adding the internal to the external dimension of foreign policy makes for many complications, especially since few books have been written on the domestic politics of foreign policy. If the job was bigger than I had realized, it was also more fascinating.

With the sponsorship of Columbia University's Institute of War and Peace Studies and the generous support of the Rockefeller Foundation, I was able to spend a year in London. The Institute's director, William T. R. Fox, gave me his counsel and criticism throughout. Equally important, he did not try to hurry me unduly but instead waited patiently for my thoughts to take form. While in England, I talked with students and teachers of politics, with journalists and governmental officials, with MP's and party workers. Their conversation was indispensable to my gaining an understanding of British politics, and their hospitality was an unfailing delight. The research departments of both major parties assisted me greatly. Dr. Henry Durant, director of the British Institute of Public Opinion, which is now called Social Surveys and is frequently referred to as the Gallup Poll, generously placed at my disposal data that span thirty years. Unless otherwise noted, all information on British opinion is from this source. Vivian Chapman completed for me the record of British opinion for the years following my stay in London.

Thomas Schelling invited me to spend a year at Harvard University's Center for International Affairs just at the time when I felt overwhelmed by a mass of materials and lost in a confusion of inchoate ideas. I am deeply in his debt for, among other things, the endless number of provocative ideas his conversation unfailingly supplies. Much of the draft of this book was written during the year I spent at the Center, and I want to thank its director, Robert Bowie, for the support he gave me. Stephen Graubard, editor of *Daedalus*, has kindly permitted me to use in this book passages from an article, "The Stability of a Bipolar World," written while I was at the Center, which first appeared in the Summer, 1964, issue of *Daedalus*. Ann Mostoller, my secretary for a year, applied to my great benefit her knowledge of politics, her skills as a secretary, and her mastery of Harvard's library system. Robert Ferguson, now of the Harvard Law School, did research for me on Britain's relations with Europe, on matters of social security, and on public opinion in the United States. For the use of materials on American opinion, I should like to thank the Roper Public Opinion Research Center at Williams College and its director, Philip K. Hastings.

It is demanding enough to read and make comments on the draft of a manuscript that is on the brink of publication. It is even harder on the reader to criticize a rough draft, but the author thereby gains more. The following persons read an early draft of the manuscript and did me the invaluable service of criticizing it thoroughly and bluntly: Robert Erwin, William T. R. Fox, Charles E. Gilbert, Morton H. Halperin, Donald Hellmann, Samuel P. Huntington, J. Roland Pennock, and Richard Rose. They will notice that usually their criticisms have led me to correct errors and modify conclusions. Occasionally, however, their comments stimulated me to express contrary ideas more strongly and to explain them more fully. In both ways, the book has gained, and my gratitude is boundless. Others made a number of helpful comments, for which I am grateful, either on a later version of the manuscript or on a smaller portion of it. They are: Bernard C. Cohen, M. D. Feld, Stanley Hoffmann, Robert Keohane, Roy Macridis, Nelson Polsby, and Enid Bok Schoettle.

Faithfully and expertly throughout her senior year at Swarthmore College, Cynthia Grant checked and amended my text; Helen Heusner, a veritable H. W. Fowler, combed the manuscript for literary infelicities, which she discovered in abundance. I am grateful to the Swarthmore Faculty Research Fund for making their employment possible.

Robert Erwin of the Center for International Affairs, who combines the qualities of academic critic and professional editor, caused me time and again to define and reorder my thoughts and helped me to present them more clearly. Without his keen mind and skilled hand the manuscript would be much inferior. As always, my wife aided me in many ways, specifically by undertaking research on the parties in London and generally by criticizing my pages. The editorial staff at Little, Brown was nicely responsive to my many requests, which they met with remarkable speed. A portion of the text, drawn mainly from Chapter 10, appears as an essay in a book edited by James Rosenau and published in 1967 by the Free Press under the title, *Domestic Sources of Foreign Policy*. The essay was discussed in the spring of 1965 at a conference sponsored by the Foreign Policy Association and by Princeton University's Center of International Studies.

It is a pleasure to acknowledge these many debts, for incurring them was also a joy.

Kenneth N. Waltz

CONTENTS

Chapter 10

OPINION AND CRISES
IN AMERICAN FOREIGN POLICY   267

Chapter 11

FOREIGN POLICY
AND DEMOCRATIC POLITICS   298

LIST OF TABLES AND FIGURES

Tables

Figures

xii

FOREIGN POLICY
AND
DEMOCRATIC POLITICS

The American and British Experience

Chapter I

INTRODUCTION

The purpose of this book is to measure the capabilities of democracies in the realm of foreign policy by looking closely at the politics and institutions of two of the oldest and most prominent of democratic states. The foreign policy of a country is formed by its political institutions, tempered by its experiences and traditions, and shaped by the pressure of other states upon it. It is well at the outset to compare the ways in which international political forces have borne upon British and American foreign policies. Once this is done, we shall, in this preliminary chapter, review some common opinions on the relation of internal politics to external policy in order to identify the difficulties that are thought especially to beset democratic states.

International Conditions and National Responses

The United States, it is often said, now holds the place in the world long occupied by Britain.[1] The proposition is erroneous, but because it has been influential, there is reason to examine the similarities of the old British role and the new American one before drawing attention to the differences. Britain in the nineteenth century, greater in power than her principal competitors, was smaller in expanse and in population than most of them. She controlled vast numbers of distant natives by winning some of them to her side—Hindu potentates or tribal chieftains—in order to use them as the instruments of her rule. The United States, small in

[1]Cf. Lionel Gelber, *America in Britain's Place* (New York: Praeger, 1961).

1

population as compared to the People's Republic of China and much less spacious than the Soviet Union, exceeds both of them in material capability by margins that are wide without being comfortable. Like Britain earlier, the United States has had its client states, some of which remain in a condition of bondage. Relations of control and dependence developed, inadvertently in both cases, as British and American citizens or their governments sought such other ends as commercial advantage and defensive strength. Britain depended, as Rome had before her and as any world power must, on the ability to move rapidly in order to deliver military force to distant and widely separated points.

Inferior to the combined might of European states, Britain nevertheless long enjoyed the splendors of isolation by limiting her goals on the Continent to preventing its union rather than seeking to exercise direct control over some of its people. England's security through most of her history has depended on the operation of a balance of power in Europe. Always some Englishmen have missed the point. Charles James Fox, for example, at the time of the French Revolution argued that what France might do on the Continent of Europe was not properly the concern of England. Some Liberals in Gladstone's day could assert that "it would be a crime to shed the blood of Englishmen in an insane attempt to protect Belgium against France or any other power." [2] England's proximity to the Continent, however, made disregard of the distribution of power in Europe a comparatively minor theme in England's political history. Sir Eyre Crowe, in a classic statement of England's interest in relation to Europe, expressed fear of the power and purpose of Germany's new navy. He drew attention at the same time to the dangers for England of the French and Russian ascendancy that would follow upon a drastic reduction of Germany's power.[3] Through four centuries of modern European history, fluidity in the identification of possible enemies and likely friends was an enduring characteristic of Britain's policy.

In a world of three or more great powers, to play off one state against another was the requisite art, which, from the reign of the First Elizabeth to the Second, England persistently practiced. Britain's role as the fulcrum in Europe's classical balance of power rested firmly upon her interest in preventing any one state from becoming so powerful in Europe that it would be able to mass its strength and, unharried by Continental

---

[2] James Headlam-Morley, *Studies in Diplomatic History* (London: Methuen, 1930), p. 177.
[3] "Memorandum by Sir Eyre Crowe on the Present State of British Relations with France and Germany, January 1, 1907," in G. P. Gooch and H. Temperley, eds., *British Documents on the Origins of the War, 1898–1914* (London: HMSO, 1928), III, 417.

opponents, mount an attack upon the British Isles. Britain's interests were worldwide. Those of her interests that centered in Europe were always negatively defined. They lay not in securing control of territory or other tangible advantages but rather in preserving a political condition. From the Congress of Vienna to the London Conference of 1913, England tried to promote political settlements that would remove the occasions for war in Europe. Her aim was to contain the powerful and ambitious by suspending them in a semi-self-regulating system of equilibrium rather than by seeking to suppress them. The eloquent protest of John Maynard Keynes against the harsh economic terms of peace inflicted upon Germany by the Treaty of Versailles, for example, reflected not only his righteous indignation but also, consciously or not, the political interests of England.[4] It takes force to repress the powerful. Germany, temporarily weakened by war and with her economy constricted by the terms of the Peace Treaty, nevertheless remained *potentially* powerful. Her discontent would make her restless, and her artificial weakness would render France dominant and quite possibly troublesome. The double error of the Peace Settlement, in the eyes of its British critics, was to unbalance power on the Continent while sowing seeds of dissatisfaction whose bitter harvest would be reaped in the future.

Neither before nor after World War I was it always possible to avoid war by accommodating nationalist aspirations and economic demands. In preparing for war and in waging it, England sought allies who would bear the main burdens of Continental fighting.[5] England's military strategy was often—and in Winston Churchill's view should always have been—a simple extension of the principles upon which her foreign policy was based. The military precepts, whose validity was constant while application varied with circumstance, were: (1) to strike at the enemy where he is weak, rather than meet and seek to destroy the main body of his forces; (2) to gain allies, keep them in good heart, and assist them in their campaigns; (3) to guard Britain's influence jealously, while being careful to husband her resources.

The imbalance of Britain's own forces, an imbalance intentionally maintained in peacetime, would in time of war be righted most easily and efficiently by allying with countries equipped to fight on land as Britain was on the sea. The outbreak of war should not bring an end to the

---

[4]Keynes, *The Economic Consequences of the Peace* (London: Macmillan, 1920).
[5]Cf. Prime Minister Macmillan's description of Britain's traditional alliance policy. National Union of Conservative and Unionist Associations, *Report of the 81st Annual Conference*, October 10 to October 13, 1962, Llandudno (London, 1962), p. 147.

3

quest for auxiliaries. In World War I, the ill-fated expedition to Gallipoli was, in Churchill's view, an effort to weaken one of the enemies' allies and awaken among others doubts that might lead them to take up arms against the Central Powers. The secret treaties, by which the fruits of war were distributed before they were gathered, would help to keep one's own allies in good spirit.[6] In itself, the absence of positive war aims permitted Britain to pursue a peripheral strategy in both world wars of this century. The strategy, however, was no longer as effective as it had been in the days when England's relative power was greater. It was difficult in World War I to sustain a strategy that called for nibbling at the edges of the major foe's power when it seemed possible that in the meanwhile he would score decisive victories in the central theater of war. In World War II, Churchill committed more British troops to the Mediterranean than did the United States and carefully maintained equality of numbers in the invasion of Normandy. It was nevertheless impossible to establish and maintain the ascendancy of Britain's influence over the American ally she had so expertly wooed.

The present obsolescence of British strategy in foreign policy should not obscure its success over a period of centuries. Its long serviceability should in turn remind us, first, of the conditions upon which the strategy depended and, then, of the national habits of mind and procedure that its success helped to inculcate.

Britain could play the role of balancer among the great powers of Europe only so long as certain conditions prevailed. The first of them was that the margin of power on the side of the aggressor not be so large that British strength added to the weaker side would be insufficient to redress the balance. If the states of the Continent were themselves nearly in balance, Britain could act with effect. The second was that Britain's ends remain negative, for positive ends help to determine alignments. A state that wishes to secure a piece of territory will ordinarily have to ally with those states that do not already possess it. The goals of the state will then lessen the scope of its diplomatic maneuver. Finally, to be effective in the role of balancer, Britain required a status in power at least equal to that of the mightiest. British weakness vis-à-vis European countries has to the present day always meant entanglement with them. Only when strong has Britain been able to remain aloof until the moment arrived when her commitment could be diplomatically decisive.

[6]Winston S. Churchill, *The World Crisis: 1915* (New York: Scribner, 1929), pp. 178–80. On the second point, see his *Aftermath* (New York: Scribner, 1929), pp. 125–28.

Only when strong has she been able to enjoy the luxury of pursuing a peripheral strategy in order to husband her resources. Only when strong has she been able to enter alliances while retaining control of her policy. For Britain, these conditions no longer exist.

If the similarities exceed in importance the differences between the present American and the previous British condition, then ideas for policies that will serve America well can, with appropriate geographic and other adjustments, be drawn from the long and, as the world goes, quite happy history of Britain. Because of changes in the configuration of world power, however, comparisons between the old role of Britain and the part now played by the United States are seriously misleading. Though similarities abound, the differences are overwhelming both in weight and in number. Britain was the leading power when all of the world's great powers were Western. Though none was stronger than Britain, other states were approximately as strong. Britain could be challenged by combinations formed among states that were her peers and was occasionally threatened by one of them acting alone, for centuries by France and then by Germany for decades. The international system was one in which more than two powers of comparable magnitude sought to safeguard their interests and occasionally contended for mastery. The United States is not now in the position, as Britain once was, of being first among equals in a world of seven or eight great powers. It is instead the leading power in a world in which two states outstrip all others. Since World War II, only the United States and the Soviet Union have been able to extend their influence globally and compete at all levels of power.[7] The principal lessons to be learned from Britain's diplomatic experience are relevant only if the new world of the mid-twentieth century is Britain's old world geographically writ large. Appropriately enough, those who have thought of the United States since 1945 as occupying Britain's former place—and for the sake of simplicity Walter Lippmann can represent them—think of bipolarity as perpetually in the process of rapidly passing away.[8]

Lippmann has consistently written as though he has learned the lessons of Britain's experience. In peacetime, Britain had never kept troops on

---

[7]Cf. Kenneth N. Waltz, "The Stability of a Bipolar World," *Daedalus*, XCIII (Summer, 1964), 881–909.

[8]Lippmann, "Breakup of the Two-Power World," *Atlantic Monthly*, CLXXXV (April, 1950), 30. Cf., e.g., his column "NATO Crisis—and Solution: Don't Blame De Gaulle," *Boston Globe*, December 5, 1963, p. 26. "The paramount theme of this decade, as we know it thus far, is that we are emerging from a two-power world and entering one where there are many powers."

the Continent. Lippmann urged upon the makers of American foreign policy the wisdom, indeed the necessity, of a similar course. "We cannot," he advised, "organize military coalitions inside the Eurasian continent which require the presence or the immediate availability of large American land forces." [9] But in fact the United States has done precisely that, and more. The United States has been since the war the creator of Western European stability economically, and by indirection politically. The United States, by brandishing a nuclear deterrent, has been the guarantor of Western Europe's security. It has also been the largest military power in the area by virtue of the presence of its troops. Western Europe has become, to use the terminology of the 1930's, a "consumer of security," which has borne a made-in-America label.

In a bygone age, Britain at times supplied money and equipment in order to avoid having to commit her meager manpower resources to battle. The United States has committed troops along an extended periphery and has supplied money and materiel to boot. Britain sought allies in order to gain their assistance. The United States has sought allies, and subsidized and equipped them, so that they would become willing to accept American military guarantees and stable enough to merit receiving them. The important objective has not been to lighten burdens by sharing them but has instead been to strengthen the non-Communist world against possible Russian aggression by extending the network of defenses. Before World War II, so long as European states were poised against each other, Britain was safe, and so, incidentally, was America. The disunity of Europe was England's guarantee of security; any state that became too powerful thereby became England's enemy. Since World War II, only one state has been powerful enough to threaten America. The United States has not been in the British position of the nineteenth century and earlier; rather, her situation is more like that of France between the two world wars. In French eyes, Germany was the ultimate danger, whether or not she was at the moment resurgent. The potential enemy and the source of all serious danger was apparent to France then as it has been to the United States since the war. The obsessing problem for each of them, to the sometime annoyance of their associates, was to rally other countries against the danger which, though sometimes latent, was nevertheless passionately believed to be common and constant.

Britain found more pleasure and more profit in dealing with weak peoples abroad than in coming to grips with European states, who if bal-

[9] "Breakup of the Two-Power World," p. 30.

anced against each other would provide out of their own insecurity the condition of England's safety. The United States has wanted unity in Europe, just as France wished for and worked to establish a united front against Germany. In one way, America's tasks are more complicated than those of France used to be, for the arenas in which the two principal adversaries contend now cover the globe. In the middle 1950's, the Soviet Union, having recuperated from the war and with a firm and imaginative hand newly on the helm, began to behave as a global great power rather than as a merely regional one. The wider and more varied demands that have been placed on the power and policies of the United States illustrate and support the proposition that the bipolarity of the postwar world, instead of eroding, has merely more fully matured. In another way, however, the problem of American foreign policy is simpler than Britain's ordinarily was, for the bipolar structure of the world makes the country of principal concern in America's foreign policy constantly easy to identify. The requirements of policy are then easier to comprehend. In the last analysis, what the United States must do in the world is determined not by calculation of how to gain new allies or please old ones but by gauging the power and disposition of the Soviet Union. A foreign policy adequate to American interests must be more closely responsive to the capabilities and intentions of the Soviet Union than to those of any other country, for allies can do comparatively little to augment America's strength or to lessen that of the Soviet Union. Whether or not such a statement is pleasing, it expresses the requirements of logic and safety in a world in which two states overshadow all others in power. It also points to the immensity of the difference between the tasks that confront America now and those that Britain faced in the era of her greatness.

The ground upon which Britain's international role had rested, gradually worn away in the late years of the nineteenth century, finally disappeared in two world wars. A hard residuum of national habits and of deep-set attitudes toward international affairs has remained. The aim of Britain's foreign policy was always to bring about a devolution of international burdens. Fluidity of commitment was her one constant principle. The manner of foreign policy that Britain developed was suitable to her international situation and consonant with her domestic political habits, consonance between the two being required if greatness is to be attained. To proceed by a sidling movement rather than move directly toward an object, to underplay one's hand, to dampen conflicts and depreciate dangers, to balance parties off against each other, to compromise rather than fight, to postpone decisions, to obscure issues rather than confront them, to move as it were by elision from one position in policy to another: such habits, anciently engendered and long crystallized, form the style of British foreign policy. American habits, reinforced by postwar experience, are drastically different. Much more so than England's, the American style of politics and especially of foreign policy is to dramatize differences in order to clarify issues, to confront problems in order to solve them, to assume burdens in order to be able to say that duties have been discharged, to exaggerate dangers in order to justify action, and to draw policies out of a series of collisions between ideas in opposition.

The difference in national styles is often sensed, yes, but wrongly described as the difference between empirical British procedures and the doctrinaire stance of the United States. In reality more pragmatic than doctrinaire, the United States has pursued a foreign policy of confrontation and settlement in response to the bipolar condition of the world, which has rendered largely inappropriate the older British habits, attuned to a world of many great powers, of manipulation and adjustment. The worrisome question of the past was often: Would Britain summon soon enough the will to stand firm? The question that will often be crucial in the future is this: Will the United States, as the arenas of major contention multiply, develop sufficient flexibility of policy while continuing to keep its eye steadily on the main source of potential danger?

Internal Politics and External Policy

Do the institutions and processes of democracy make excellence in foreign policy difficult to achieve? Many have thought so, including de Tocqueville.

> Foreign politics demand scarcely any of those qualities which are peculiar to a democracy; they require, on the contrary, the perfect use of almost all those in which it is deficient. . . . a democracy can only with great difficulty regulate the details of an important undertaking, persevere in a fixed design, and work out its execution in spite of serious obstacles. It cannot combine its measures with secrecy or await their consequences with patience.[10]

This conclusion, reached by de Tocqueville in 1835, was not a statement about the past but a guess about the future. Seldom has political prophecy achieved so fully the prestige of frequent quotation and the honor

[10]Alexis de Tocqueville, *Democracy in America* (New York: Knopf, 1945), I, 234–35.

8

of general belief. In the nineteenth century, an oligarchic era, de Tocqueville's opinion was widely reflected. Bismarck, questioned on his foreign policy in the Reichstag, exploded with a bluntness and crudity that are wrongly thought to be the inventions of twentieth-century politics. The conduct of policy, he told members of the lower house, is difficult enough without "three hundred asses" trying to interpose their ill-formed opinions.[11] If the voice of the popularly elected assembly could not be stilled, then an active foreign policy would simply become impossible. In the case of England, Lord Salisbury's policy of "splendid isolation" reflected less an estimate of what was desirable in policy than a conviction that with increasing Parliamentary control long-term commitments could not be made. German governments of the 1890's doubted the value of an executive agreement with England. Parliamentary ratification was necessary to give some assurance of continuity. Even so, Salisbury thought, assurance of continuity would not be achieved. There was another hazard: the next Parliament might undo what the last had done. To any treaty, whether with Germany, France, Russia, or Japan, there would be dissent in Parliament; and its open expression might impair the value a treaty would otherwise have. The Liberal Sir Edward Grey, first Foreign Secretary to sit in the House of Commons since 1865, was caught between the traditions of the Foreign Office and increasing pressures from within his party to conduct his diplomacy openly. He largely evaded the issue by eschewing formal commitments while achieving their substance in the form of gentlemen's agreements with France and Russia. Parliament and most of the Cabinet remained uninformed of arrangements that effectively, if informally, bound England to fight a future war against the Central Powers. In the process he came to be the first Foreign Secretary charged with being a prisoner of his permanent officials.[12] Secretary of State Hay in America, like Salisbury and Grey in England, chafed under the difficulties of pleasing the popular assembly while trying to do what the international situation seemed to require.[13] The untrammeled conduct of Cabinet diplomacy had become impossible, and yet a foreign policy democratically made and conducted was not thought possible either.

The foreign policy of a democratic country, theorists have repeatedly said, is necessarily isolationist or quiescent. Alongside this cautious assessment and forbearing conclusion runs a seemingly contradictory aspir-

[11]Erich Eyck, *Bismarck and the German Empire* (New York: W. W. Norton, 1964), pp. 191–92.
[12]A. J. P. Taylor, *The Trouble Makers* (London: Hamish Hamilton, 1957), p. 97.
[13]See below, Chapter 5, p. 97.

9

ation. To be democratic, foreign policy must be controlled by the people, and control by the people will bring peace. Far from being defective government, democracy in foreign as in domestic affairs is seen to be the only form of government that provides a promise of decent policy. The conviction gathered strength throughout the nineteenth century. It found its early expression among Liberals and especially Radicals and Socialists, its efflorescence in the Peace Movement at the turn of the century, its supposed partial fulfillment in the two Hague Peace Conferences, and its culmination in England in the Union of Democratic Control and generally in the policies and prophecies of Woodrow Wilson and the establishment of the League of Nations. Was de Tocqueville then to be examined and found in error? Not at all. His dictum was addressed to the problem of making democratic foreign policy viable in a world of power politics. Can a few democracies play the game that the many oligarchic countries are engaged in? The answer continued to be "no," or at best "not very well." De Tocqueville was not refuted. He was to be transcended, and this by a double process: improvement in the tone and temper of international relations as more and more states joined the charmed circle of democracy, and growth in the capacities of the ordinary citizen to understand and thus to regulate the world about him. For years the discussion of democratic capabilities in the world of foreign policy fastened upon these two points.

In nineteenth-century England, as political participation spread downward from the classes to the masses, voices of warning were raised. According to "respectable" opinion, the many poor and improvident, devoid of a knowledge of political economy, would use their franchise to vote themselves a share of the nation's wealth that they had not earned. Nor could they enrich themselves without destroying the capital treasures, accumulated by the industrious and thrifty, upon which the continued health of the economy was solemnly avowed to depend. The many, it was feared, would seek to control an intricate economy which their educations had not fitted them to understand. Convinced of the danger, some sought devices to mute or modulate the voice of the masses, as did John Stuart Mill in espousing Hare's system of proportional representation. On questions of domestic policy, the edge of doubt was gradually dulled, though not deadened. In matters of foreign policy, comparable worries endure.

Almost fifty years ago, A. F. Pollard in *The Evolution of Parliament* drew attention to the uneven impact of public opinion. Should the government of the day propose to limit the number of public houses, popular opposition would be immediate, deep, and effective. On the other hand, Lord Lansdowne in 1903–4 was able to initiate a foreign-policy line of supreme importance without anyone thinking that a general election should be fought about it. Whole categories of public policy were decided without reference to the electorate. The uncertain dividing line between questions that are left to the government and questions with which the public will be actively concerned is fixed at any moment by the electors themselves, not consciously but through the influences to which their minds are subjected. Like Bryce and many others, Pollard saw ignorance as the temporary enemy of popular control. Temporary only, for "education automatically widens the legitimate sphere of popular judgement; and when the mass of the voters comprehend the conditions of foreign policy there is no reason why they should not claim its control." [14]

This remains one of the major themes of foreign-policy commentaries. The people and their representatives need, according to Lord Bryce then and Robert Dahl more recently, a greater knowledge of the outside world, a better understanding of the minds of other people. Even with knowledge and understanding enlarged, the people will not be fitted to regulate the details of great undertakings, but they will be able to perform the principal function of peoples and assemblies: to select the ends of policy and determine broadly the lines along which it should proceed.[15] Still, it is difficult to shake loose from the idea, long prominent, that in the jungle of international relations democracies are inherently at a disadvantage. Ideological differences between countries easily give rise to passions within them. Such questions as reparations, disarmament, foreign aid, the rights of ethnic minorities, military budgets, the drawing of boundaries, and the diplomatic recognition of states easily lend themselves to domestic political dispute and historically have often done so. The internal pressures of politics may foment a policy that conflicts with the supposed necessities of the state in relation to the outside world. If foreign policy is not a major issue in a modern-day British or American election, there is lamentation. The world may be at the brink of disaster, certain earnest men will be quick to complain, yet the democratic citizen is concerned only with his creature comforts, the bread-and-butter or cake-and-jam issues. If foreign policy *does* become prominently a subject

[14]Pollard, *The Evolution of Parliament* (London: Longmans, Green, 1920), pp. 348–49.
[15]James Bryce, *Modern Democracies* (London: Macmillan, 1921), II, 419–20; Robert Dahl, *Congress and Foreign Policy* (New York: Harcourt, Brace, 1950), pp. 70–84.

of popular debate, however, many will deplore the fact that the voice of the mass is attempting to pronounce on matters that it does not understand. Foreign affairs, including the problem of the "dollar gap," were practically excluded from the British election campaign of 1950. H. G. Nicholas, writing of the campaign, was disturbed by this omission. Yet he was equally disturbed by Churchill's attempt, in his February speech at Edinburgh, to introduce foreign-policy issues that were not thought to be fit subjects of electoral decision.[16] In all fairness, such views are not simply contradictions; they are legitimate and important worries.

Public opinion at times is merely something the pollster discovers. At other times it is an active political force, the yelp emitted by the man in the street when his shoe pinches. One need not be an economist to fear unemployment, a pedagogue to resent poor state schools, a sociologist to worry about juvenile delinquency. The citizen can know that something is wrong and impress his concern upon politician and party without knowing or even pretending to know just how to set things right. Matters of foreign policy have most often been considered in a separate category. They are once further removed from the daily experience of the citizen. It takes little wit to relate the level of taxation and the quality of social services (though the connection is often not made). It is supposedly more difficult to appreciate the relation between defense spending and the possible prevention of war in the future.[17] One may conclude, as many have, that foreign policy is properly left in the hands of the governors. But can it be made to stay there? From time to time, matters of foreign policy become major issues in domestic politics whether or not political leaders want them to. More and more often in and after World War I, the foreign-policy shoe has pinched. And of course public figures may themselves make an issue of foreign policy where the people at large would not otherwise have seen one, as did Hearst and Pulitzer preceding the Spanish-American War. Thus the dilemma was long ago produced: the people may aspire to influence foreign policy while being unable to do so intelligently.

If the free play of opinion on international questions is harmful to a state's foreign policy, one may be driven to the conclusion that even in democracies élite control of foreign policy is necessary. A generation ago, Carl Friedrich seeing this as certainly undesirable and probably impossible, found hope in the thought that "Democracy will march forward

[16]Nicholas, *The British General Election of 1950* (London: Macmillan, 1951), pp. 304–5, 101–3.

[17]Cf. Bryce, *Modern Democracies*, II, 405.

toward international organization." [18] International conditions, supposedly transitory, have proved to be of long endurance, and characteristics of democracy once described as temporary disadvantages are now more often thought of as being permanent. Neither the education of the citizenry nor the international organization of the world has changed essentially the problem of democracy's survival in an undemocratic world. Where does one go from here? One way is the old route, followed by Walter Lippmann and others. Mr. Lippmann is a democratic skeptic who doubts the virtues and values of a general and active popular control, especially in foreign policy but also in domestic matters. His criticism of democratic foreign policy, in *The Public Philosophy*, joins hands with an enduring aristocratic distrust of mass electorates. One wonders, however, whether he has correctly described the workings of democracy. And even if he were right, could anything be done about it? In a happier world, a world in which the democracies were not so sorely tried, Mr. Lippmann's critique of democracy would still have point and purpose. Others have shortened their philosophic reach to concentrate more closely upon problems of the moment. Engaged in mortal combat with a monster, one must become a monster himself. Thinking of the disadvantages of democracy as merely temporary has suddenly, in the space of two decades for America and perhaps twice as long a time for the democracies of Western Europe, ceased to give comfort, for the fear has grown that disadvantages even of short duration may be fatal. America's potential opponents in war and her adversaries in day-to-day competition are garrison states, tightly organized and closely controlled. If this does give them a clear advantage, then democracies are encouraged to adopt similar methods. Competitors, by the force of their struggle, are made to become alike; the one less well equipped for the contest must imitate the other or fall by the wayside.

On several counts, democracies have time and again been faulted in the conduct of their foreign affairs. First in the minds of many critics is the thought that democratic foreign policy is unstable. In order to pursue effectively the objectives of a state in world affairs, a steady gaze and an unflagging will are required. With the ends and execution of policy dependent upon a shifting majority, the policy of today may be rejected tomorrow. Woodrow Wilson fathered the League of Nations and was then unable to get his own country to adopt the child. Ramsay MacDonald

[18] Carl Joachim Friedrich, *Foreign Policy in the Making* (New York: W. W. Norton, 1938), pp. 88–89.

worked hard to close the gaps in the League Covenant only to have his efforts disavowed in 1924 by the succeeding Conservative Government. Yet there is no magic in mere continuity, for it is continuity of a good policy that is wanted. Doubt about which policy is good may increase the instability of policy. Where doubt exists or can be created, politicians and parties seeking to gain or to hold office may use foreign-policy issues as domestic political weapons. The canons of reason would hold that argument should be on the merits of policy. The pressures of politics may cause foreign-policy issues to be used as a means to discredit the other party. The right policy and the popular policy may not coincide. Good policies may be discontinued as readily as bad ones. In any event the fear remains, and this is often thought to be the second great weakness of democracies, that not only will policy be unstable but that its changing directions will be determined by internal pressures that have little to do with the state's situation in the world.

Related to the second difficulty is a third worry. Even an ill-informed and inattentive legislature will occasionally be aroused by a foreign issue or incident. Even a peaceful and prosperous people will occasionally be frightened or angered by a seeming threat to the state's position or by an injustice suffered abroad. The worry that peoples and parliaments know and care too little about events abroad now often gives way to a concern that popular demands and legislative interventions destroy the basis for a steady administration of policy. Because he may be harried and hounded at home, the foreign-affairs official may be unwilling to risk the action abroad he would otherwise deem desirable. Having risked it, he may find his work undone, which will serve as a caution to his successors. The difficulty is thought to be greater in the United States than in England, though in England there are examples enough. Because it was unpopular domestically, the attempt by Sir Samuel Hoare and Pierre Laval to satisfy the hunger of Mussolini by feeding him pieces of African territory went unsupported in the Cabinet, and Hoare lost not only his policy but also his position as Foreign Secretary.

Evidence of similar difficulties in the Parliamentary and Presidential systems does not mean that there are no important differences in capabilities between them. To weigh the differences in order to assess the foreign-policy merits of the two systems has long been an academic sport. The outcome of the game has varied. Bryce and Friedrich, in the works already cited, noted with approval both the greater stability of American foreign policy and the opportunity of the President, certain of at least

14

four years in office, to pursue a policy without fear that the legislature might seize upon it to overturn the government. Herbert Hoover, in his *Memoirs*, was more impressed with the abilities of an English party in power to control the Parliamentary majority and thus ensure legislative support for its policy. The Parliamentary system permits the active playing of the power-political game; the Presidential system, and in Hoover's view this was fortunate, does not.[19] With the possibility of governments being defeated in Parliament much diminished and with American foreign policy more dependent upon dollars and thus upon Congress, the weight of opinion has come more nearly to rest on the side of Herbert Hoover. Was he largely correct? Are there major disabilities in the Presidential system that the Parliamentary system does not suffer? And if so, what are the implications at a time when, disabilities not withstanding, the United States must play a major part in the world?

The Characteristics of Policies and Institutions

Worries about the continuity, content, and execution of policy will be taken up in the chapters that follow. To deal with them requires comparing national political performances, lest measurement be made against an unattainable ideal, and defining, if only roughly, the characteristics of a good foreign policy.

Success in foreign policy depends upon the ability of political leaders to set sensible goals for their nation: to figure out what interest requires and resources permit. In a Hobbesian world, national interest is easy to define. Concern for self-preservation is necessarily paramount, though it may often be difficult to see just what policies will best serve that primary interest. In all but the most exceptional instances, political leaders have evinced a deep and abiding concern for the preservation of their states. The predictable minimum aim of a government is to deter potential attackers and to defend the state should deterrence fail. An admirably successful defense may have been necessary only because policies of deterrence were applied without skill, foresight, and sophistication. Britain's successes in World War II represented the horrible price that had to be paid for the failures of her policy in the 1930's. The success of a policy may be occasion for lamenting the government's failure to follow a different course or the previous government's disinclination to

---

[19]Hoover, *Memoirs* (New York: Macmillan, 1951), pp. 476–77. The judgment appears in the portion of his memoirs written in the early 1920's.

do so. Beyond deterrence or defense, the ends of a state—its definition of the interests to be served by its policies—may range from the grandiose goal of world conquest to the simple desire to turn international circumstance to national advantage. If the preservation of the state is not in question, national goals easily fluctuate between the grandiose and the frivolous. A state may set as its goal the conquest of another state or even the subjugation of all other states. It may seek to shape the world order or to fabricate a new one by persuading its friends and allies to render assistance and so enhance its strength that enemies will be won over or overawed. Whether or not consciously on the part of the government, the foreign policy of a state may serve mainly to provide pleasurable feelings of international honor and influence to its citizens. Governments may indulge themselves with foreign policies of moral pronouncement, justify an expedient policy of isolation on the ground of high principle, or pretend to be too good to fight. Conversely, they may treat war against the weak as though it were a sport, build military establishments more for prestige than for safety, follow a line of diplomacy in order to gain popularity at home, or, at the extreme, fashion for the state a foreign policy that will help to maintain internal political stability whether or not it serves the interests of the nation abroad.

Policy should ideally be responsive, in fine balance, both to internal constituents and to external conditions. What is wanted in foreign policy is not a set of simple attributes but instead a nice balance of qualities: realism and imagination, flexibility and firmness, vigor and moderation, continuity of policy when policy is good and the ability to change direction when international conditions make new departures desirable, adaptability of policy without destruction of its coherence or dependability. Given intricate tasks to perform in a dangerous world, it is all the more important to ask what the likelihood may be, in one system as compared with another, that competent politicians and officials will be first produced and then elected or hired. Are public servants encouraged to consider a wide range of choices in policy, or are they constrained by the impact of opinion to measure policies mainly in terms of their domestic acceptability? Do the different branches and departments of government stimulate each other to alert performance, or do they drive the system to stalemate?

Blame for the frequent disappointments of policy and praise for the successes sometimes enjoyed are normally assigned to the most vulnerable or visible parts of a political system. Where the political structure of a country permits the representative assembly to wield autonomous power, the legislature becomes a conspicuous target for criticism. It does many things, and therefore many things wrong. Virtues and vices become difficult to separate. Where the political habits of a country, supported by the arrangement of offices, encourage competition and bring criticisms to the surface and errors to the public's attention, features of the political system that facilitate its self-correction are easily taken to be weaknesses. The question of democracy's capacities in the realm of foreign policy requires comparison with the political characteristics and performance of nondemocratic political systems. Such a comparison is suggested in the concluding chapter. Meanwhile it is sufficient to say that in the foreign policy of every country disappointments abound, and after the event errors are easy to identify. Criticism of British and American policies and evaluation of the democratic political systems that produce them can be made without any necessary implication that authoritarian governments can be expected to do better. Democratic states have often suffered unduly when compared with authoritarian governments, and for reasons that are broadly similar, so has the American government when compared with the British.

In the chapters that follow, efforts are persistently made to achieve objectivity in analyses and significance in comparisons by examining the parts of each government always in relation to the country's political structure. A state's foreign and domestic policies are in many ways alike. Parties and the public, politicians and representative assemblies, Prime Ministers or Presidents—the institutions for making domestic policy are for the most part the same as those charged with responsibility for foreign policy. Beyond this, the controversial proposition that policy in the two different realms has become substantively more similar will, in Chapter 4, be affirmatively argued. The similarities of internal and external policy enable the student who is interested in the foreign-policy capacities of democracy to learn by examining purely domestic politics, an opportunity of which use has been made in the pages that follow. The principal purpose of the book remains, however, to determine the ways in which the internal politics of democracies affect their external policies.

Departing from current fashion, the question most often asked is not how do national processes compare but how do political structures differ and, in their differences, affect the processes and policies of governments. In Chapters 2 through 6, various characteristics of the British and American political systems are examined and compared; in each of the following four chapters an extended case study is presented. No effort has been made to preserve formal symmetry. Rather than superficially balancing the account, I have dealt with the characteristics of each political system that are crucial for it and have taken up, as case studies for each country in turn, situations and problems that are thought to be most difficult for that country to meet or to manage: for the United States, the foreign-aid program and reactions to crises; for Great Britain, military policy and relations with Europe. For reasons that are easily understood, aid policy has not been a problem in Britain; to examine its making and execution would reveal little not already known about the British political system. While it would be fruitless to examine British aid policy at length, it would be inexcusable not to do so for the United States. I have, in sum, taken up hard cases only and from among them tried to choose those that would be politically most revealing.

Chapter 2

POLITICAL PERFORMANCE

England is a majoritarian democracy. The party that wins more seats than its rivals in a general election forms a government. Given the electoral system, however, a mere plurality of votes may give a majority in the House of Commons to one party. Indeed, in only one general election since 1918 has a party gained more than half of the popular vote, and that was in 1935.[1] Still, in the last seven elections, the governing party's majority over all other parties in Parliament has ranged from 4 to 148 seats. With a majority as small as the former figure, a government may be led to caution and will surely suffer pain. The Labour Governments elected in 1950 and in 1964 brought Members to Westminster by ambulance in order to insure victory in crucial divisions. Nevertheless, in such a system there is an electoral winner and loser; and the winner takes all, so long as third parties are minor. The winning party, having taken its positions on issues and having explained or obscured them in a three-week campaign, can supposedly legislate a coherent program and govern effectively. Such has been the conventional interpretation of British Parliamentary government.[2] A British government, with a disciplined party

---

[1]The election of 1931, when a coalition of Liberal National, National Labour, and Conservative candidates received 67.1 percent of the popular vote, is excluded. D. E. Butler, *The Electoral System in Britain, 1918–1951* (Oxford: Clarendon Press, 1953), p. 173.

[2]See, for example, Samuel H. Beer, "New Structures of Democracy: Britain and America," in William N. Chambers and Robert H. Salisbury, eds., *Democracy in the Mid-Twentieth Century* (St. Louis, Mo.: Washington University Press, 1960), pp. 30–59; James MacGregor Burns, *The Deadlock of Democracy* (New York: Prentice-Hall, 1963); and William H. Riker, *Democracy in the United States* (New York: Macmillan, 1953).

backing it in the House of Commons, puts its program into effect. With the prospect of up to five years of office it can seemingly do what the future requires instead of listening with the ear of political expediency to every murmur of public discontent. Prime Minister, Cabinet, and Parliamentary party are locked in a close embrace. This fusion of the executive with its party in Parliament produces a situation in which he who wills the end thereby wills the means. The policy of the government receives the support it may need from the legislative assembly. Programs do not go financially unsupported. Their application cannot be obstructed by assembly investigation, vitiated by unwillingness to approve the appointment of suitable persons to office, or reduced to inanition by contradictory legislation pushed through by a party or group in the assembly. Democracy is realized, for the elector has a choice of at least two parties whose leaders are known and whose programs are advertised. Accountability is preserved, in this interpretation of the system, for at the next general election the citizen can compare promise with performance and reward or punish parties by the casting of his vote.

The case often made for the American democracy is similarly impressive.[3] In the absence of discipline, individuals and groups from the two parties can come together in some points of policy without having to agree on all. Dissension is muted; class and other cleavages are lessened; and responsiveness to majority wishes is increased to a maximum. Because the individual member of Congress can have a direct influence upon policy, abler and more vigorous men are recruited for the representative assembly. With checks and balances built into the system of government, more than a simple majority may be required to give force and effect to a piece of legislation. This is doubly fortunate, so those who make the case claim. With disciplined parties a majority of the majority may prevail. The preferences of less than half of the electorate will then be reflected in the government's program. With a wider consensus required there is less tendency for the next government to undo what the present government has accomplished. A system of concurrent majorities thus provides measured progress, increased social cohesion, responsiveness, and full play for individual initiative in and through representative bodies.

In such evaluations, quite characteristically, the executive function or

---

[3]See, for example, J. Roland Pennock, "Responsiveness, Responsibility, and Majority Rule," *American Political Science Review*, XLVI (September, 1952), 790–807; Ernest S. Griffith, *The Impasse of Democracy* (New York: Harrison-Hilton, 1939); and Pendleton Herring, *The Politics of Democracy* (New York: Rinehart, 1940).

branch of government tends to be slighted. Beyond this, what is most bothersome is the difficulty of finding in the arguments just summarized the practice of the government that is being criticized. Apologists of the American system caricature British government and then with considerable glee knock over the straw man they have built. The faults of the American system, on the other hand, are made to disappear by means of a close and subtle analysis, or are at least shown to be the price wisely paid for a more than compensating virtue. The British parties tend to be pictured as monoliths, with the party in power enacting a program that at least half of the people oppose. By those convinced of the superiority of the British system, American parties are seen as no parties at all but rather as jumbled heaps of interest, unguided by principle and incapable of sustained or coherent activity whether in power or in opposition. The government—checked, bound, and balanced—acts, when it acts at all, in response to pressures randomly generated and indiscriminately applied. The rolling log rather than the reasonable program is its symbol.

Problems and Policies

It is safe to say, without benefit of statistics, that at least until recently a majority of those American political scientists who concern themselves with such comparisons have argued the superiority of the Parliamentary system in its British version. They have agreed with their English colleagues. Superiority in form and process should, of course, produce a superior result. National accomplishments are seldom compared when one makes judgments about the merits of political systems. Comparisons are not wholly instructive unless "other things remain equal." Though they seldom do remain equal, it is nevertheless insupportable to proceed without attempting to weigh and compare national performances; for the political forms and processes of a nation directly affect its policies, which are the most tangible evidence of excellence or deficiency. In the pages that immediately follow, mainly domestic problems and policies come up for examination. The United States and Great Britain have been more similar to each other in their internal conditions than in their international political situations. Each of them is a long-established, highly stable democracy. That both of them have predominantly two-party systems, highly literate societies, and heavily industrialized economies facilitates useful comparison. Important foreign-policy questions are often best treated as a series of reactions to crises. Domestic problems display a

21

greater continuity, and data bearing upon them are more copiously and more easily available. Comparability, extent, and plenitude of data make it desirable to concentrate on domestic questions. The benefits of doing so will ultimately become evident when we relate political structure to policy in general, whether domestic or foreign.

William Riker, a notably skillful partisan of the majoritarian cause, once asked his readers to compare Great Britain's success in preventing inflation in the decade of the 1940's with America's failure to do so. "By 1951," he noted, "prices in England had risen about 53 per cent over 1939, while in this country they had risen to about 85 per cent over the same base year." How, he wondered, can one account for the difference? England's public policy, he answered, is a bundle of compromises conditioned by pressure groups, "but the compromises are rationally formulated among the great national interests, not accidentally thrown together at the behest of interests great and small."[4] Maybe so. But one cannot help thinking that the difference between 85 and 53 percent can also be accounted for in other ways. The United States entered the war later and, perhaps for that reason, applied price control after the rise of prices had gained a greater momentum. Receiving foreign loans and aid reduces the pressure on prices to rise. The United States gave and did not receive, while Britain received more than she gave. Britain must export. Unless her prices are competitive, she dies. Price control may bring benefits, but it also bears costs. The United States could more easily forego the benefits in order to avoid paying for them. That the government gave in to anti-price control pressures and, in effect, scrapped the program in 1947, demonstrates that the President has difficulty getting his program accepted and not, as Riker suggests, that one system produces a program or policy superior to that of the other, which is quite a different proposition. If we remember that the British economy has long been more conditioned to control, we may conclude that the explanation of differences of policy lies outside the realm of the wholly political. Finally, if we look at performance in these matters over different periods of time, we may even conclude that the movement of prices lies, in part, beyond the control of the best of political systems. From 1953 to 1963, consumer-goods prices rose by 30 percent in Britain, by 13 percent in the United States.[5] Do the British compromises, "rationally formulated" though they may be, result in a policy more appropriate to conditions than American policy "thrown

[4]Riker, *Democracy in the United States*, p. 332.
[5]*New York Times*, June 30, 1963, p. E-1.

together at the behest of interests great and small"? Even if the description of process is accurate, the answer is not immediately discernible.

Perhaps a more helpful answer can be found by taking a wider and longer view. The Great Depression of the 1930's would seem to have provided a chance for any system to demonstrate its superior worth. But who would argue that the governments of MacDonald, Baldwin, and Chamberlain showed more imagination or produced a better result than did the American government of the period? That may have been an exceptional time and Franklin Roosevelt an exceptional man, but in this case at least, it would be difficult to say that the exceptions proved the rule. The British economy failed to recover from World War I. In the years from 1921 to 1938, the unemployment rate never fell below the 9.6 percent "enjoyed" in 1927, and in 1932 it was as high as 21.9 percent. Unemployment in the United States first exceeded 10 percent in 1931, touched a high of 24.9 percent in 1933, and stood at 17.2 percent when the war began in 1939.[6] In each country, the performance of the economy was bleakly unimpressive. Among many English journalists and academic commentators, however, among politicians at least leftward from Harold Macmillan (who was then a Conservative MP highly critical of his party's performance), there was widespread agreement that the British system had failed to produce governments of sufficient enterprise and zeal. And, many of them added, the United States was more nearly rising to the difficult occasion.[7]

Now, after another great war, it may all look different. Just in case it does, we should consider some important features of postwar politics in the two countries. Nationalization is a policy that will immediately come to mind. Whatever its merits, must one not say that the program was broadly conceived and designed to work a major change in the economy? Nationalization, many would argue, amounted to a controversial policy that broke boldly with the past and yet was implemented without a long series of legislative battles and the addition of amendments that would have destroyed the integrity of the government's program. Actually, by 1945 proposals to nationalize certain sectors of the economy were less controversial than such a summary of views would indicate. Eight enter-

[6]William H. Beveridge, *Full Employment in a Free Society* (London: Allen & Unwin, 1944), p. 47; U.S. Bureau of the Census, *Statistical Abstract of the United States: 1960* (Washington, D.C.: GPO, 1960), p. 205.

[7]See Harold Macmillan, *Reconstruction: A Plea for a National Policy* (London: Macmillan, 1934), and *The Middle Way* (London: Macmillan, 1938). For leftist Labour reactions and changes of mind about British-American comparisons customarily unfavorable to the latter, see Henry Pelling, *America and the British Left* (London: Black, 1956).

23

prises were nationalized. Three of them—the Bank of England, Cable and Wireless, Civil Aviation—were previously controlled, regulated, or subsidized to an extent that made nationalization little but a change in form. Of the other five enterprises, one, the iron and steel industry, barely underwent the beginnings of nationalization; another, coal, had long been seen as a sick industry curable only by shock treatment; and three fell into the utility-transportation category where the question of ownership is less important than the general agreement that extensive regulation and control are necessary.

Geoffrey Crowther, speaking to the Economic Club of New York in 1949, reported a British planner as saying, "British industry is now divided into two sections: privately owned industry, over which the Government has a fair degree of control; and publicly owned industry, over which the central organs of the Government have no control at all." [8] A compatible conclusion has been more cautiously and more recently suggested by the British economist Alan Day. "It is not clear," he wrote, "whether the Government's control over the nationalised industries since the war has or has not been greater than its control over the private sector." It is clear, he added, that nationalization has not given much extra power to the government.[9] That many members of the Labour movement have developed grave doubts about the economic purpose and political desirability of nationalization lends force to such judgments. The effectiveness of minority pressures in pushing the Labour Government in 1965 toward re-nationalizing steel makes one wonder what the word "coherent" so commonly applied to British policy may mean, a question to which we shall shortly return.

Nationalization, seen in perspective, appears to be only a moderate departure in policy and thus cannot be said to demonstrate the British government's ability to innovate controversial programs while keeping them coherent. Recalling the length and depth of the interwar depression, followed by the upheaval of war itself, may indeed cause one to think of Britain's postwar economic measures as modest to the point of timidity. It hardly takes one's breath away to learn that a party that had pressed for a program through nearly three decades of national adversity was finally given the chance to apply it, especially when the form of its measures was broadly in accord with customary national procedures. In Britain, it has been governmental policy to let monopolies develop and

[8]Crowther, "British Socialism on Trial," *Atlantic Monthly*, CLXXXIII (May, 1949), 27.
[9]Day, "The Economic Setting," *Political Quarterly*, XXXI (July–September, 1960), 266.

then to control them, whether paternalistically by a Conservative Government persuasively offering subsidies and other favors or formally by a Labour Government imposing public ownership and regulation. In the United States, since the Sherman Antitrust Law of 1890, governments have sought to break up large units so that they will, by competition, regulate each other. Despite different national inclinations, both countries depend increasingly on a system of regulation, subsidy, and control. The United States has gone somewhat farther in enforcing standards in foods, drugs, and the stock market; Britain has favored detailed supervision of credit, control of investment, and regulation of the money market. Belatedly feeling the trauma of two decades of widespread joblessness, British governments since the war have taken pains to maintain consistently full employment. Keynesian measures have been relied upon heavily, even though the practice of frequently making money dear has impeded the growth of the economy. Englishmen of the 1950's often remarked incredulously that the American government had not yet understood and accepted the Keynesian revolution in economics and somehow interpreted this supposed failure of comprehension as evidence of the stalemate that results from the separation of powers. One may as easily point out that England, in her devotion to Keynesian measures, has reflected her deep-seated inclination to avoid problems rather than confront them, in this case, to meet each threat of inflation and each balance-of-payment crisis by financial regulation and fiscal adjustment. The fiscal manipulations of British governments, though they have served to keep the economy going, have postponed the structural changes that would have been forced if fiscal policy were less supple. Differences in national attitude and style have been more impressive than differences in the quality of governmental performance.

In welfare policies, as in the management of the economy, differences between the two nations are commonly thought to be great. On both sides of the water, a stereotype exists of England as a country that redistributes the wealth by taxing at high rates and by spending large sums on health, public housing, and a system of cradle-to-grave security. An American who visits England for any length of time is likely to be impressed by the amount of slum clearance, the quantity of public housing, and the comprehensiveness and efficiency of national medical care. He may thereupon conclude that England is a welfare state, that the United States is not, and that the postwar achievements of England are a demonstration of its more effective public concern for social equality and justice and of its political ability to inaugurate programs that are at once broad in purpose and sensibly composed.

Some parts of the picture that is customarily drawn correspond to reality; others do not. In 1954, 1 percent of American and British adults owned, respectively, 24 and 43 percent of their countries' personal net capital.[10] The narrower concentration of wealth in Britain may in itself make large public welfare programs more highly desirable. Furthermore, taxation in the United States has probably been more progressive, though the difficulties of measurement are immense. In the higher income brackets, both countries have lowered the ceiling, with England generally more severe in taxing the middle reaches and more lenient with the very rich. Prior to the Labour Government's 1965 budget, capital gains were almost entirely untouched; death duties are often avoided. The United States relies much more heavily than Britain upon taxes collected directly from individuals and corporations.[11] Though the British have often spoken of themselves as the most heavily taxed people in the Western world, taxation, national and local, bears more lightly in Britain than it does in West Germany and not so very much more heavily than in the United States. In 1957, for example, West Germany collected 35.3 percent of the gross national product in taxes, the United Kingdom 31.5 percent, and the United States 28.2 percent.[12]

To provide out of government funds more services to citizens than is customary in the United States, England must tax more heavily or skew her expenditure to favor this one type of state activity. By doing a little of both, she is able to meet, in relation to resources available, a markedly larger yearly bill for social services, as Table 1 makes clear.

The difference in any one year is large. The pattern over the six-year period is interesting. That Britain in 1961 spent, in proportion to gross national product, about 50 percent more on social welfare than did the United States may be said to support the statement that Britain is a wel-

---

[10]H. F. Lydall and D. G. Tipping, "The Distribution of Personal Wealth in Britain," *Bulletin of the Oxford University Institute of Statistics*, XXIII (February, 1961), 93.

[11]The 1957 ratio of direct to indirect taxes collected by central and local governments was 1.61 in the United States and 0.93 in Britain. Counting social-security contributions as direct taxes, the ratios become 2.01 and 1.10, respectively. William Fellner, "Attaining High Employment and Adequate Growth Rates Without Inflation," *Congressional Record,* CVII, Pt. 11 (87th Cong., 1st sess., 1961), 14601–4. For 1961, Jacob A. Stockfish of the U.S. Treasury Department has calculated that indirect taxes account for 42.7 percent of total tax yield in the U.S. and 50.0 percent in the U.K. Committee on Ways and Means, *Compendium of Papers on Excise Tax Structure* (Washington, D.C.: GPO, 1964), Pt. I, p. 115.

[12]Fellner, "Attaining High Employment," p. 99.

fare state and America is not. But if one compares British spending in 1955 with American spending in 1961, most of the difference disappears. During these years, both countries increased their spending by about 3 percentage points. The United States may be following the path that Britain has trod. Britain's social welfare program was not a sudden creation of the Labour Government after World War II. Rather, it has taken

TABLE 1 AMERICAN AND BRITISH SOCIAL WELFARE EXPENDITURES BY ALL LEVELS OF GOVERNMENT

	UNITED STATES			GREAT BRITAIN		
Year	Gov. Expenditure on Social Services[a]	Percent of Total Gov. Expenditure	Percent of GNP	Gov. Expenditure on Social Services[a]	Percent of Total Gov. Expenditure	Percent of GNP
	in millions of dollars			in millions of pounds		
1955	32,019	31.6	8.5	2665	48.7	13.7
1956	34,607	32.5	8.5	2886	48.4	14.7
1957	38,796	33.2	9.0	3077	49.9	14.8
1958	44,909	36.4	10.2	3371	51.9	15.6
1959	49,202	35.7	10.5	3606	52.3	15.9
1960	52,330	37.5	10.6	3821	52.2	16.0
1961	57,862	39.1	11.5	4171	51.8	16.6

Sources: United States statistics are taken from *Statistical Abstract of the United States: 1963*, p. 282. British statistics are compiled from: Central Statistical Office, *National Income and Expenditure: 1962* (London: HMSO, 1962), Tables 11, 44, pp. 12, 46–49.

[a]Social Services include social insurance, public aid, health services, other welfare services, veterans' programs, education, and public housing for the United States; and National Insurance, National Health Service, child care, school meals, welfare foods, war pensions and service grants, education, and housing for the United Kingdom.

its present form by a combination of old programs growing almost of their own accord and new ones introduced by governmental decision. Asquith and Lloyd George before World War I laid the foundations of the present social-security system, whereas in the United States comparable action was not taken until the 1930's. The National Health Service, new in the sweep of its coverage, nevertheless built on extensive medical programs that had long been in existence.[13] The British government entered the welfare business earlier than the United States and has carried it further. If Britain deserved to be described as a welfare state in

[13]Practically all low-income workers were automatically insured by the Health Insurance Act of 1911. By the early 1940's, those with an annual income of £420 or less were eligible, and the cost to the employee was $8\frac{1}{2}d$. weekly. Only those who had paid were covered, but for those insured, medical benefits continued until death. By the middle 1940's about one-half of the population of Great Britain was insured under the program, in which more than two-thirds of all doctors participated. Almont Lindsey, *Socialized Medicine in England and Wales: The National Health Service, 1948–1961* (Chapel Hill: University of North Carolina Press, 1962), pp. 5–6.

1955, however, it might well be thought that the United States should be now. Looked at in this way, the difference between the two countries has frequently been overstated.

If the figures are examined closely, one finds that England spends relatively more public money than does the United States but spends it primarily on two programs, health and public housing. The National Health Service, in 1961, took 3.7 percent of GNP. In the United States, 0.9 percent of GNP was spent by governments at all levels on health and medical services. For public housing the respective figures are 1.6 percent and 0.04 percent.[14] One may be struck by America's spending about as large a proportion of GNP as does England on all programs other than the two mentioned and wonder either why the Americans have been slow to follow on health and housing or why the English have led. The United States spends proportionately as much of its GNP on education as the United Kingdom does—more, in fact, if one adds the large amount of private money given to colleges and universities. Are the different directions of governmental spending in the two societies appropriate to needs and conditions, or is the pattern that of mere responses to whatever pressures have developed the greatest thrusts?

In the United States, spending for education has been more popular than governmental spending for individual health services. The American Medical Association, powerful and tenacious, found allies among other anti-spending interests. It raised the bugbear of socialism and argued that a national health service would destroy the professional relation of doctor to patient. The pressure had effect, though the argument is strange, for in England the relation of doctor to patient *is* professional. In America it is often replaced by a cold, cash nexus, whose absence in England may make a freer choice among doctors possible. Sustained and strident opposition delayed the inauguration of a general health program; it also helped to make the cost of medical care a prominent public issue, caused substitute programs to be more diligently sought, and hastened the introduction of special programs, of which Medicare is both the outstanding example and the undoubted precursor of more general programs. It can perhaps be said that, with a higher per capita income, leaving medical care in America largely to the individual makes some sense. The policy and the need must be considered in conjunction with others. It also makes some sense to say that in England, with a less productive

[14]*Statistical Abstract of the United States: 1963,* p. 282; *National Income and Expenditure: 1962,* Tables 11, 36, 44, pp. 12, 37, 46–49.

economy, with a housing deficit accumulated over two decades and intensified by the destruction of war, and with a lower average per capita income, the immediate needs of housing and health properly came before the far-reaching revision of a narrow educational system.

To understand the welfare programs of the two countries, amounts spent in dollars or pounds must be looked at along with percentage figures. The American population in 1960 was about three and one-half times the British; the American GNP was about eight times as large. Spending the same percentage of GNP enables the United States to finance benefits at a much higher level for the individual recipients. In social-security programs, benefits are appropriately related to customary wage and standard of living. Education is a different matter. While in the United States it is necessary to ask why relatively so much is spent on education and so little on health and public housing, in Britain the question must be reversed. Each country has responded to pressures and reflected public preferences and prejudices in governmental programs. In Britain, the smallness of expenditure on education is reflected in the results achieved. They have been found tolerable, at least until recently.

Political Structure and Governmental Responsiveness

Whether or not it is well for a country to have a comprehensive and costly welfare system is a matter of controversy that turns upon individual values and is influenced by the experiences and conditions of a nation. Insofar as governmental programs embody national preferences and prejudices it is impossible to say that, because one country narrowly preceded another in constructing welfare programs, the first country's political system more easily permits innovation without loss of coherence in policy. Among the important questions to be asked in assessing the merit of a democratic system are these: Does it effectively serve the public interest, and does it permit the identification by the electorate of those who are responsible for the policies and acts of government? In attempting to evaluate governmental performance, it is difficult to circumvent problems posed by the incommensurability of national traditions and values and correspondingly easy to slip into applying purely formal criteria of excellence. Harold Laski once argued that coherence is achieved if the direction of policy is easily discernible and if responsibility for it is clearly affixed. In the role of defender of British institutions, which he sometimes assumed, he rested the case for British political excellence

29

upon the features ensuring easy identification of those who are formally responsible. Thus in Britain, he noted, "there is little difficulty in concluding that our protective tariff was a wreath deposited by the Tory party, through the agency of Mr. Neville Chamberlain, on the tomb of his distinguished father." In the United States, he added, it is all quite different, for no one can lay responsibility for such an act as the Hawley-Smoot Tariff on a particular party or group.[15] By placing such importance on "responsibility," Laski was able to praise the British political system while deploring its performance. He did not think that British policy between the wars was innovative, bold where meeting foreign and domestic challenges required courage and careful where caution was needed. Instead he was pleased that the British people, if they found the government's policy incoherent, unimaginative, ill-attuned to their mood and to the condition of the country, would at least know which party to vote against. The test of coherence, he implied, is not the content of policy but the reaction of the electorate to it.

The widespread habit of applying such a formal test makes comprehensible what is otherwise odd to the point of absurdity: namely, that the protracted ill performance of Britain's government so little influenced the warm admirers of her Parliamentary system. Surely Britain's foreign policies were badly conceived and executed in the 1930's. Yet Herman Finer took the British political system as the standard by which to measure and condemn the similar failures of the American government in foreign affairs. Having found "a want of alert coherence" between the President and the relevant departments and agencies, a "lack of solidarity at the center," and "fumbling in the formation of policy," he heavily scored America's "incoherence and mismanagement of foreign policy from 1933 to Pearl Harbor." The description of political process and the criticism of it are reasonable. He then argued, in contrast, that "Pearl Harbors, domestic as well as foreign, may be avoided where a collective fifteen are responsible, and where the Congressional five hundred badger them with relentless questions." He added that "the unintermittent merging of executive and legislature, the ever-continuing life in each other's physical presence," as in Britain or even in France, "is some assurance of the unison of mind which leads to a unison of guesswork, and therefore to a sharing of responsibility for policy."[16] But in the management of their

[15]Laski, "The Parliamentary and Presidential Systems," *Public Administration Review,* IV (Autumn, 1944), 349, 357.

[16]Finer, *The Theory and Practice of Modern Government* (rev. ed.; New York: Henry Holt, 1949), pp. 679–80, 703.

foreign affairs the two systems produced similar results. Since both failed, it becomes difficult to use failure to argue the inherent inferiority of one to the other. Without at all wishing to defend American foreign policy between the wars, one might say that the British failures were the more glaring. England had a closer familiarity with European politics and a tradition of some involvement. She was more immediately and directly threatened by the rising power and ambition of Hitler than was the United States. Both countries nevertheless staggered and fumbled and displayed more incoherence than "unison of guesswork."

The time lag in adjusting scholarly opinion to political performance is apparently accounted for less by excellence of accomplishment than by the strong aesthetic appeal of a system that provides direct electoral confrontation of disciplined parties, orderly and literate debates in the Commons, and the clear affixing of responsibility. Whether or not coherence is formally preserved may be an interesting question, but other questions would seem to be more important. Does the political structure that permits a formal test of coherence produce any corresponding and more or less predictable results? The tendencies of a system are sharply revealed by the great challenges of depression, war, racial strife, economic growth, and social inequality. Does the political system, one may ask, encourage imaginative responses to needs, whether or not the needs are widely acknowledged? How sensitively, in short, does the system respond? Is the political framework so constructed as to bring forth alert and vigorous leaders? It is now common to investigate policy in relation to process. In the present analysis, both process and policy are considered in relation to political system.

Give us a "doctor's mandate"—the slogan of Britain's National Government seeking electoral approval in the depth of depression—was deeply different in tone from the notion of a "New Deal." "Weather the storm while preserving old values" was the emphasis of the one; "We can build a new and good life without repudiating the old" was the message of the other. One must bear in mind that it may sometimes be well to evade challenges or postpone meeting them, to temper zeal for reform by showing some regard for the merit of perpetuating old ways. Two decades of ineffective response and uncertain leadership, both in foreign and domestic affairs, may, however, be taken as revealing the inherent tendencies of a political system. Within the British system strong leadership is not easily and surely not often provided. The movement of policy is customarily steady but slow; governments promote compromise and contrive adjustments between interests in conflict rather than meeting problems head on; ministers calculate carefully before giving even the appearance of leading. Continuity of policy is impressive; coherence has often been confused with it.

Do conclusions that are borne out by the experience of the 1920's and 1930's hold true three decades later? Again the performance of governments indicates that they do. In recent years, concern over the effects of England's narrow educational system has mounted, as is made clear by the appointment of the Crowther, Newsom, and Robbins Committees to report on the condition of education in Britain, and by the writings and statements of John Vaizey and C. P. Snow among others. General concern that a narrow system of education is no longer adequately serving the interests of a commercial and industrial country in an age of rapidly increasing scientific and technological complexity is easy enough to understand. In England and Wales, 15 percent of children aged 15 to 19 were attending school in the late 1950's, which compares with 62 percent of males in the United States and 59 percent of females.[17] In British institutions of higher education, 7.7 percent of the relevant age group were attending courses full time in 1958/59, whereas 30 percent were doing so in the United States.[18]

One must beware of the magic of mere numbers, and indeed the point is often made that in the United States many are poorly trained, in England a few truly educated. The habit, of course, is to compare loosely all of American and all of British higher education. Since Oxford, or Manchester, or London University are no doubt better than most American colleges and universities, the point may seem to be made. If, however, one compares the better fourth of American institutions with all the British institutions of higher education, which would seem to be fair, it is no longer so clear where the balance of excellence may lie. Indeed, it is now more frequently said that the margin of superiority is to be found on the western side of the Atlantic.[19] It should be borne in mind that one

[17]United Nations Economic and Social Council, *Basic Facts and Figures: International Statistics Relating to Education, Culture and Mass Communication* (Paris, 1959), pp. 24–27. In the 1961/62 school year, only 45 percent of all 15-year-olds in England and Wales were in full-time education. Central Advisory Council for Education, *Half Our Future* (London: HMSO, 1963), p. 7. This publication is commonly called the Newsom Report.

[18]Lord Robbins, *et al., Higher Education*, Cmnd. 2154 (London: HMSO, 1963), Table 17, p. 42. The Robbins Report gives higher percentages for Britain and lower ones for West European countries than had previously been customary. Cf., e.g., the UNESCO data in *Basic Facts and Figures*, pp. 24–27.

[19]Cf. C. P. Snow, "The Two Cultures: A Second Look," *Times Literary Supplement*, October 25, 1963, pp. 839 ff.

country has a system of mass education with large pockets of excellence and many areas of high competence; the other has an elitist system consisting of a few great, together with a number of adequate, institutions. In the word "elitist" is found one of the keys to understanding the difference. The Education Act of 1944 was less impressive as innovation than as continuation, and what it perpetuated, though admittedly in ever looser and broader ways, is the class system of England. At the age of 11 a few students are selected for the grammar schools of England; fewer still will ultimately enter a university. But the few are fairly well treated financially. They are set off from the many who leave school at 15 or stay on somewhat longer in "secondary modern" schools. This may not be merely a system of recruitment for the "Establishment," but indirectly it serves that purpose, as is often pointed out by the English themselves. In 1960, about one quarter of American students between the ages of 20 and 24 came from families with incomes under $5,000; another quarter came from families of $5,000 to $7,500 income, 21 percent from families whose incomes ranged from $7,500 to $10,000, and 29 percent from those over $10,000.[20] The education of the child is furthered by his family's higher income, but not decisively so. In Britain, while the data are not commensurate, the high correlation of children's education and their family backgrounds can be seen from Table 2.

Despite intensity of concern and consciousness of need, changes come slowly in England, and plans are hesitantly drawn. As long ago as 1938, the Spens Committee foresaw the inevitable raising of the school-leaving age to 16. The Education Act of 1944 provided for lifting the school-leaving age to 16 whenever a responsible minister should find doing so practicable. In 1959, the Crowther Report strongly urged that the task be accomplished between 1966 and 1969, when a temporary slump in the numbers of children in secondary schools was expected. The Robbins Report on Higher Education, coming four years later, was hailed by many for its bold look into the future. It offered proposals which if accepted should, in the words of the Report, make it "possible to maintain the present proportion of qualified school leavers who enter universities, but no more." [21] The Committee's calculations of future needs were conservatively made. From 1954 to 1961, for example, the proportion of the

[20]Herman P. Miller, *Rich Man, Poor Man* (New York: Crowell, 1964), p. 162. In 1959, the lowest 40 percent of families by yearly income received $4,800 or less, the next 40 percent received from $4,800 to $9,000, and the highest 20 percent received $9,000 or more (Table I-3, p. 7).

[21]Robbins, *et al., Higher Education*, p. 159; cf. p. 258.

33

TABLE 2 EDUCATIONAL LEVELS REACHED BY BRITISH CHILDREN BORN IN 1940/41—BY FATHERS' OCCUPATIONS

		CHILDREN'S EDUCATIONAL LEVEL		
		Percentage Reaching Full-time Higher Education		*Percentage Not Reaching Full-time Higher Education*
CHILDREN BORN IN 1940/41	FATHERS' OCCUPATIONS	*University Degree Level*	*Other*	
Boys and Girls	Non-manual Higher professional	33	12	55
	Managerial and other professional	11	8	81
	Clerical	6	4	90
	Manual Skilled	2	2	96
	Semi- and unskilled	1	1	98
Boys	Non-manual	15	4	81
	Manual	3	2	95
Girls	Non-manual	9	10	81
	Manual	1	2	97

Source: Robbins, *Higher Education*, Table 21, p. 50.

relevant age group attaining minimum university qualifications grew by an average of 0.37 percent yearly in England and Wales. In its projections, the Committee assumed that "the proportion of the age group obtaining these qualifications will continue to grow up to 1980 by annual increments nearly as large as the average since 1954."[22] The bold look into the future turns out upon examination to be more of a pained reaction to the recent past. Americans have been inclined to act on the assumption that if money is supplied, other educational resources will come forth in response to the increased demand. The English instead have accepted the thought that educational resources can only be gradually increased. Plans for expansion must then be painstakingly matched with these resources, and possibilities of dramatic growth are precluded. Even if the Committee's proposals for expansion are fully accomplished, recent rates of increase will lessen. In the nine years from 1954/55 to 1963/64, the number of home and overseas students in full-time higher education almost doubled. For the number to double again will require, if the recommendations of the Robbins Committee are followed, not nine but fourteen years.[23]

[22]*Ibid.*, p. 57.
[23]Put differently, the average rate of yearly increase will have dropped from 8 percent in the first period to about 5 percent in the second. Calculated from *ibid.*, Table 30, p. 69, which gives actual numbers for 1954/55 to 1962/63 and recommended numbers for 1963/64 to 1980/81.

Though there was almost no response at all to the crushing burdens of the depression decades, there is now at least a slow and timid reaction to the problems of education. Are the results in both cases merely the fruits of Conservative Party rule? It is difficult to know, for, between World War I and the general election of 1966, a government of the left commanded a secure majority of seats in the Commons for only five years. Insofar as political structure affects the behavior of both parties and the policies of all governments, the question is less troublesome. How political structure affects policy and helps to shape governmental decisions is the subject of the next chapter. In internal and external policy, the same qualities are wanted. Throughout this and remaining chapters, we shall be concerned with determining whether or not the respective political systems of Britain and America make it more or less likely that leaders will be sustained in office who will react quickly and firmly to problems at home or abroad; who will formulate sensible policies, whether domestic or foreign; who will be able to carry them through without debilitating amendments legislatively appended and without making concessions to so many clamant groups that the effectiveness of policy is dangerously reduced. We shall ask, in short, what different political systems lead us to expect by way of response to people (private interests, the opinions of the populace, the views and feelings of public officials) and to problems (the situations that call for attention whether or not the political system makes it easy to care for them).

Chapter 3

GOVERNMENTAL
STRUCTURE

In the informal evolution of British political arrangements, it is now often said that the Cabinet system is becoming a system of Presidential government.[1] The power of the Prime Minister over the Cabinet as well as over the House has increased. The Prime Minister, one may easily conclude, is no longer first among equals; he is simply first. It is difficult for even the most exalted Cabinet member to develop a base of power and influence comparable to that which the Prime Minister possesses by virtue of what amounts to his direct election by the people at large. Thus Harold Macmillan, with his party rocked by the Suez fiasco, sustained the resignation from his government of Salisbury in the Lords and Peter Thorneycroft, Enoch Powell, and Nigel Birch in the Commons shortly after he took office as Prime Minister. Publicly unshaken, he kept serenely on his course. Reasons abound for believing, as many people apparently do, that the ascendancy over the Commons of Prime Minister and Cabinet, or even of the Prime Minister alone, is all but assured.

But so it has seemed before. Eighty years ago, George Carslake Thompson, thinking of Palmerston and especially of Disraeli, identified "tendencies" that would cause the constitution "of its own accord to slide involuntarily, almost imperceptibly, towards a Caesarism." He drew attention to the "Presidential character" that he thought the Prime Minister's office had recently acquired. With the critical powers of the Commons dwindling and with the Prime Minister in fact holding office for a "fixed

[1] See, for example, Max Beloff, Letter to the *Daily Telegraph* (London), August 2, 1960; and R. H. S. Crossman's Introduction to Walter Bagehot, *The English Constitution* (London: Watts, 1964), pp. 1–57.

term," Thompson believed that the Prime Minister's tenure and power would more and more depend on the acclaim of the multitude.[2]

It is wise to be skeptical of such recurrent "discoveries."

Prime Ministers and Presidents

Is the Presidential hypothesis a passing fancy in the evaluation of British government, with such an interpretation periodically becoming popular as the power of the Commons happens to ebb and master politicians flow into the Prime Minister's office? Reconstruction of the hypothesis will help to reveal the strength of the Prime Minister's office and is a useful preliminary to systematic identification of the sources of the Prime Minister's and President's powers. Later we shall examine the British political system in order to uncover its checks and balances, which are less easily seen than those that operate in the United States.

Within their respective polities, the Prime Minister of England is generally thought to be more strongly placed than is the American President. The Prime Minister and Cabinet of course depend upon a continuing majority support in the House of Commons. The President, independently elected, does not depend for his tenure upon majority support for his program in the Congress. In practice, the Prime Minister is consistently supported by his party; the President is not. In England, if a party with a narrow majority were to split on an issue while the opposition stood firm, the government would come tumbling down. The narrower the majority, therefore, the more the governing party tends to stand firm. The parties can break ranks and the House can cashier a government, but since 1895 this has not happened to a governing party with a majority of seats. Questions of overall policy, and sometimes of all-important detail, of the direction of change and the meshing of programs, all seem to be left to the discretion of the government of the day, with the assembly chanting its ayes and nays in highly predictable fashion. Parliamentary government easily becomes Cabinet government, and Cabinet government in England has increasingly become Prime Ministerial government.

The majority party in the Commons cannot punish its Ministry without thereby punishing itself. Power and paralysis, control and submission,

---

[2]Thompson, *Public Opinion and Lord Beaconsfield: 1875–1880* (2 vols.; London: Macmillan, 1886), I, 18–19, II, 497–98.

are often not the contradictions one easily assumes them to be.[3] That the House of Commons is in low esteem is widely acknowledged in England. The confusion of parties in the 1920's, the weakness of the opposition in the 1930's and again in the 1950's are often, and with some reason, thought to be the cause. But the deeper causes are rooted in the system and will continue to work their effects.[4] Parliament advises and consents, and since consent is customarily granted, the assembly is reduced to a critical role. To criticize has long been a principal function of Parliament. What is new, developing in the later nineteenth century and becoming well established in the twentieth, is that the critical task has become almost the sole function.

Walter Bagehot subtly drew a distinction between fusion and absorption—legislature and executive being joined in the first sense but not in the second. The legislature, he wrote, is an electoral body, choosing, and, when it cares to, dismissing the Prime Minister. The Cabinet, a "creature" of the House, has "the power of destroying its creators."[5] Writing before the second great act of suffrage reform, Bagehot accurately reflected the practice of England. In the general election of 1857, the Liberals secured a clear majority; in 1858 the House dismissed the Liberal Government and without an intervening election brought the Conservative Government of Derby and Disraeli to power. The House was powerful not because the parties were disciplined but rather because they were not. Knowing that Members might cross party lines in numbers sufficient to upset a government, Ministers had to tread warily. Members, depending more than they now do on their constituents—local oligarchs, the interests of landed and commercial property—could often depart from their party's line with impunity. Elections in close constituencies could be and were bought.[6] Corruption, damnable though it may have been, gave to the Member an independence of party and to MP's of the governing party in the House of Commons a possibility of action aside from or against their Prime Minister. One could then speak of con-

---

[3]On this point and others, the work of Don K. Price is cogent and stimulating. See especially "The Parliamentary and Presidential Systems," *Public Administration Review*, III (Autumn, 1943), 317–34.

[4]Cf. the statements of Lloyd George on the ineffectiveness of the House of Commons in the period since the war and the possibilities, about which he was optimistic, of finding a remedy in a system of specialized committees. *Special Report from the Select Committee on Procedure on Public Business* (London: HMSO, 1931), pp. 41–60.

[5]Bagehot, *The English Constitution* (London: Oxford University Press, 1928), pp. 115–16, 13–14.

[6]Sir Ivor Jennings, *Party Politics: Appeal to the People* (2 vols.; Cambridge: Cambridge University Press, 1960), I, 104–7.

stituency interests and of assembly pressures upon the executive in England as one now talks of them in America.[7]

After the Reform Act of 1867 brought adult manhood suffrage to the boroughs and that of 1884 extended it to the countryside, Bagehot's distinction between fusion and absorption became increasingly difficult to maintain. Extension of the suffrage intensified the electoral scramble. Party organization, and with it party discipline, carried a larger premium The big battalions were marshaled. The Member of Parliament appeared increasingly as the obedient soldier.[8] One of the effects produced, gradually and without formal change in constitutional arrangements, was to make the election of the chief executive a matter of the voting public's determination rather than the assembly's. "The prize of power," Bagehot had written of America, "is not in the gift of the legislature, and no one cares for the legislature." [9] Having exaggerated the extent of Presidential dominance during the Civil War, he unreasonably assumed that the power of Congress would continue to ebb. He had failed to notice that the powers of the legislative assemblies are differently based in the American and British systems. Because the Congress can obstruct the President's program or force policies upon him, the President must listen to Congressmen's criticisms and adjust his policies to their preferences. Congress remains an object of considerable public interest.

The MP who would impress his views upon the government faces two important difficulties. First, it is hard for the back-bencher to come by the information he needs without research assistance, library facilities, or secretarial services. He is gravely handicapped in comparison with the Minister he may wish to question. Furthermore, committees that are *ad hoc* and without the power to "send for persons and papers" do not provide an opportunity for the private Member to become a specialist. It is difficult to know which questions to ask and harder still to follow through an important line of questioning. Second, if the piercing question should be raised, whether in Question Time or during debate, the government's hold on its majority means that it does not feel obliged to give a revealing answer. A critic without power ceases to command attention, and what Bagehot once wrote of America has become true of Eng-

---

[7]Cecil S. Emden, *The People and the Constitution* (Oxford: Clarendon Press, 1956), pp. 5–8.

[8]Cf. M. Ostrogorski, *Democracy and the Organization of Political Parties*, Frederick Clarke, trans. (2 vols.; London: Macmillan, 1902), II, 717. "The role of a 'private member' is reduced to a cipher; the greater part of his parliamentary activity consists in walking up and down the division lobbies; he is simply a voting machine."

[9]Bagehot, *The English Constitution*, p. 19.

land. What is impressive about Question Time, for example, is not so much the skill of the Minister in replying but rather his ability to avoid a substantial answer entirely. The more important the matter, the more noticeable the effect. In the 1930's the government simply evaded questions about defense and European affairs or gave answers that were grossly misleading. The government has long been able to get away with such practices in matters of foreign policy by pleading interest of state, the necessity of caution, and the importance of secrecy. In more recent years similar habits have grown in matters of domestic policy as well, as perusal of the Question Time pages in any volume of Hansard will reveal.

Proposals to strengthen the House in its relation to the government by compensating for the difficulty of obtaining information are confounded by the critics' lack of power. If specialized committees were established and their members became expert on one subject or another, might not, on occasion, the members of the committee who were of the government's party be persuaded to vote with the opposition? Foreseeing and fearing this development, would not the government be constrained to impose in committee the discipline it now exerts on the floor of the House? More frequently than at present, the Member would be put in the position of thinking one way and making known his thoughts, and then obediently voting in a contrary manner.[10] Bernard Crick has recently argued that staff, research facilities, and service on standing committees should be arranged for back-benchers so as to equip them to question Ministers with greater purpose and force. He wisely stopped short of recommending that committees be clothed with automatic powers to summon persons and papers or that they make motions and take votes. The alternative, other than doing nothing, is to recommend, as L. S. Amery once did and as Lord Boothby has done more recently, that functional committees be established that reproduce in miniature the Prime Minister's "basic relationship . . . to the Parliament as a whole."[11]

The strong discipline of the parties and the weakness of the Commons go hand in hand. Does the Prime Minister then, almost without restraint, set the direction of policy and give shape to the government's program? Is the contemporary Prime Minister truly master of all he surveys, as Sir Harold Macmillan once seemed to be? Is Britain rightly described as hav-

[10]Similar considerations are advanced by Herbert Morrison, *Government and Parliament: A Survey from the Inside* (London: Oxford University Press, 1954), p. 159.

[11]Crick, *Reform of the Commons* (Fabian Tract 319 [London: Fabian Society, 1959]), and *The Reform of Parliament* (London: Weidenfeld & Nicolson, 1964); Amery, *Thoughts on the Constitution* (London: Oxford University Press, 1947), p. 54; Boothby, Letter to the *Daily Telegraph* (London), August 5, 1960.

ing a Presidential government, though without the disabilities of the American system?

Sources of Executive Power

Because they are well appreciated, the sources of the Prime Minister's power can be briefly described. The Prime Minister is nationally elected; he is backed by a party that has won and would like to win again; he is reinforced by his function of distributing offices and the opportunity to dispense favors. Taken together, these factors secure the Prime Minister his tenure, support for his program, and a large measure of individual loyalty. Similarly the American President is the one person who can be described as nationally elected, but his policies are ordinarily opposed by important segments of his party and he himself is often pilloried by individual members of it.

A would-be MP wins his seat if sufficient numbers of voters wish the candidate's leader to become the next Prime Minister. Various studies have shown that who the candidate is and what he does, or even what the party organization does for him, make little difference in the voting of his constituency. Writing of the 1951 election, D. E. Butler expressed the opinion that in few constituencies did local efforts make a difference of more than 200 or 300 votes. Writing of the 1959 election, Butler and Richard Rose concluded that "the most brilliant of agents with the most perfect army of party workers could make no change in the representation of perhaps 550 of the 630 seats . . .; if all constituency electioneering were abandoned, the national outcome would probably be little altered." [12] If 550 seats are safe, one would like to know how much difference the identity of the candidate and the campaign he personally conducts will make in the other 80. Still, for the vast majority of MP's, one either has the appropriate party label or one does not become an MP. Once in Parliament, either the MP behaves in a way that enables him to retain the label or he faces a grave danger—indeed a near certainty—of being out the next time. Witness the fate of the five former Labour Members who ran in the 1950 general election without benefit of that party's label. All were defeated. The individual candidate receives most

[12]Butler, *The British General Election of 1951* (London: Macmillan, 1952), p. 243; Butler and Rose, *The British General Election of 1959* (London: Macmillan, 1960), pp. 119–20. Ostrogorski long ago noticed that elections had assumed the character of personal plebiscites, each constituency voting more for leader than for individual candidate. Ostrogorski, *Democracy and the Organization of Political Parties*, I, 608.

of his support because the voters want the leader of the candidate's party to become Prime Minister. The House of Commons functions not as a body that elects the Prime Minister but as a veritable electoral college in the American sense, which means in effect that the national and the individual constituencies have merged.

In the United States, while the President is elected by a national constituency, the Senatorial and House constituencies retain their distinct qualities. People can and do vote for a President of one party, a Congressman of another. In the three elections of 1948, 1952, and 1956, the Republican proportion of the Presidential vote varied by more than twelve percentage points. The Republican proportion of the Congressional vote did not vary by as much as four percentage points.[13] In present-day England, to discriminate in voting by office as well as by party is simply impossible. In the United States, where such a discrimination is possible, as it was in a special sense in nineteenth-century England, the representative enjoys a greater independence of leader and party. The strength of the member is the weakness of, or a limitation upon, the executive. The representative may be more responsive to the wishes of his particular constituency than he is to the arguments of a President of his own party. The latter can "only" argue that support for his program is what the national interest requires or the national constituency demands; the Congressman's particular constituency has the power to re-elect or depose him.

The position of the President as compared to that of the Prime Minister is made still more awkward by crucial differences in the power of patronage. Both executives have this power, though in somewhat different form; and more is written about it in the United States than in England.[14] In England it is more important, an assertion that can be explained in the following way: In America, it is possible to carve out a Congressional career, indeed a very satisfying one. The Congressman is decently paid; he has assistants and research facilities; he enjoys such perquisites as occasional trips to Europe or to more exotic parts; and, most important of all, he has influence and power. More tellingly put, these considerable gifts are within the provenance of the Congress itself. Gaining them does not depend upon the will or power of the President, and though the enjoyment of some of them is affected by the party leadership in the House and the Senate, the leaders may well act contrary to

[13]Angus Campbell, *et al., The American Voter* (New York: Wiley, 1960), pp. 11–12.
[14]See Peter G. Richards, *Patronage in British Government* (London: Allen & Unwin, 1963).

the interests of the President. Their actions are in any event limited by the general observance of seniority rules.

By contrast, the power of patronage in the hands of the Prime Minister is both an immensely strong and an infinitely subtle tool. For the MP there is scarcely the possibility of a Parliamentary career as such. Whether he is interested in emoluments or influence, in celebrity or service, his satisfaction depends largely and ultimately upon the disposition of the Prime Minister. It is the Prime Minister who elevates to office, ordinarily by a series of finely graded steps; and those he has raised he can also cast down, rudely or more gently, by dismissal from office or demotion, by having the sovereign effect a translation to the Lords, or by bestowing the appropriate one of a hierarchy of honors. He can attempt, often with success, to tame an unruly back-bencher by appointment to a Ministry or hope to remove him entirely by offer of a position outside of Parliament. Even the privilege of junketing, be it to Strasbourg or Turtle Bay, is his to grant or withhold.

Of three major sources of power—national election, party support, and the dispensing of patronage—the Prime Minister in the latter two is more favorably situated than the President. If the weakness of the President is the strength of the Congress, stalemate at worst and haphazard action at best may be the result. Still, one suspects that the Prime Minister is not as unrestricted as he appears to be and that the President is less tightly bound.

Electoral Restraints

One possibility, often mentioned, is that the Prime Minister and Cabinet, enjoying great power for the moment, are inclined to caution and made sober by the thought that the moment may not last. The alternation of prevailing parties, produced now by the voting public rather than by the Commons, limits the actions of government and renders fusion of power and the practice of democracy compatible. But the pendulum swings with notable infrequency. Rather than being a recent development, this is a pattern to which British, as well as American, governments have long conformed. As A. Lawrence Lowell pointed out nearly fifty years ago, long, slow fluctuations of parties have characterized English government since the death of Queen Anne in 1714. From that date, England was ruled by the Whigs for more than a generation; then, after a period of uncertainty, by the Tories from 1770 to 1830 with only short

43

intermissions; by the Whigs for a generation and a half, with only Peel's government as an exception; by Liberals and Tories alternately for about twelve years; thereafter largely by Tories from 1886 to 1906; and subsequently by Liberals from 1906 until after World War I had begun.[15] From the end of the wartime coalition to the autumn of 1964, the country knew only Conservative or Conservative-dominated Governments, except for brief periods of minority Labour Government in the 1920's and the six years following World War II. Lowell thought that frequent changes of party began with and were produced by the Reform Acts of 1867 and 1868. In the longer perspective now possible, the persistence of past patterns is more impressive than a new-found frequency of swings.

The government may nevertheless be constrained by the fear that high-handed action will set the pendulum swinging. The effectiveness of the cause may account for the invisibility of the result. This is the more likely given the narrow division of the popular vote between the two major parties since World War II. The Labour Government of 1950 to 1951, a minority in the country and with a margin of only five seats in the Commons, could nevertheless push through its bill for the nationalization of the iron and steel industry. But in response to criticism and no doubt with an eye on the main electoral chance, it delayed application of the policy. The succeeding Conservative Government, also a minority in the country but with more seats in the House, carried on most of Labour's policies and outdid them first in regulating and then in manipulating the economy. The behavior of the Conservative Party in office is sometimes attributed to electoral hopes—or fears—for the future.[16] Though the economic pressures of the Korean War provide an important part of the explanation, it is nonetheless widely and no doubt rightly believed that during thirteen years of Conservative rule Members and constituents of rightist persuasion were encouraged to silence their doubts about the pace with which controls were relaxed, taxation reduced, and marginal measures of nationalization undone—encouraged, that is, through leadership appeals to the desire to sink "socialism" once and for all by a dazzling succession of Conservative victories.[17]

So long as there is a second party in active and serious contention, the

---

[15]Lowell, *The Government of England* (New York: Macmillan, 1921), pp. 102–4.

[16]R. H. S. Crossman, *The Charm of Politics* (London: Hamish Hamilton, 1958), pp. 61–62.

[17]Cf. R. A. Butler, speaking at the 1963 Party Conference: "Let us, then, complete their [Labour's] education. Let us teach them a lesson. Let us beat them once again. For a fourth Conservative victory would mean the end for all time of the immature nonsense of Socialism." National Union of Conservative and Unionist Associations, *Report of the 82nd Annual Conference*, October 9 to October 12, 1963, Blackpool (London, 1963), p. 143.

possible swing of the pendulum is a constraint on the government in power, whether or not oscillation actually occurs. This restraint operates in both countries, but the extent of the limitation upon willful or capricious action is difficult to measure. One would expect it to be in some ways more and in other ways less of a constraint in England than it is in America.

Greater restraint may follow from the fact that the record of the government clearly appears as the record of one party, which can then be held accountable by the electorate. In addition, electoral pressures in Britain are more nearly unintermittent than they are even in America. It is true that in the United States a Presidential election has scarcely ended before preparations for off-year elections to the Senate and House begin, to be followed quite shortly by nomination and election of a President again. In Britain, however, there is an atmosphere of perpetual election, which comes in part from the government's power to dissolve Parliament at any time and which means that both parties must continually be ready to wage a campaign. Furthermore, because nearly always a governmental measure introduced in the House is as good as accepted, the drama of debate is replaced by journalistic speculation on how a given program will affect the public standing of parties and thus their electoral chances. Finally, because government is centralized, even local elections are significant largely as indicators of the rise and fall of the fortunes of parties.

In other respects, British governments have a greater latitude of decision. The electoral sanction circumscribes governmental undertakings less closely. In a general election the citizen votes for only one man. The voter must therefore accept or reject the party and its leader without qualification and leave aside any effort to discriminate by his vote according to men and to measures. In general, the electoral sanction in Britain is less of a constraint because the government in power can, if it wishes, have its way with unconcern for the election that may by its own choice lie some years in the future. The leader of a party may be sensitive to every nuance of opinion, as were Stanley Baldwin and Harold Macmillan. He may, however, be like Neville Chamberlain, arrogant in his sense of rectitude and convinced that, despite weighty objection within his party, his judgment will be borne out by the electorate's response. And indeed Chamberlain probably would have been voted in again if an election had taken place in the months after Munich.[18]

[18]In Lord Woolton's opinion, an unusual one, had there been an election in 1938 or 1939, Labour would have won. His view has the effect of lessening the blow of 1945. See the Earl

45

Given an inexhaustible supply of human frailty, is there not then a constant danger of Prime Ministerial dictatorship within the tenure of a given government and, depending on public mood, possibly extending beyond it? Even an overwhelmingly victorious President like Franklin Roosevelt or Dwight Eisenhower may quickly run into effective opposition in Congress. A corresponding statement cannot be applied to Britain's governors. If the limitations so far described should be insufficient, can other restraints be relied upon? We shall see the restraints more clearly if, in comparing the offices of the chief executives in the two countries, we look more closely at two of the sources of the Prime Minister's power: his election, in effect, by the nation at large and the discipline of the party of which he is the leader.

The Recruitment of Chief Executives

In both England and America, the substantial choice of the electorate lies between two men. A question as important as who will win the general election is how did these men become the alternatives from which a choice will be made. An MP becomes leader of his party or Prime Minister of England by long service in Parliament, by excelling in the qualities upon which that body places importance, and by proving his ability in successive steps up the Ministerial ladder. Along the way, he gains not only a variety of experience but a sense of responsibility, a knowledge both of the sometime desirability of action and of the ever-present difficulties thereof. What he may well lose is verve.

Since the Second Reform Act the average age of Prime Ministers, eighteen in all, upon first holding that office, has been just under sixty. The two youngest, and the only ones who scaled the heights before they were fifty, were the Earl of Rosebery and Harold Wilson. The oldest, at sixty-eight, was Neville Chamberlain. Their average service in Parliament has been twenty-seven years, during which time they had ordinarily served their apprenticeships in various high Cabinet posts. The exception, which does not disprove the rule, is Ramsay MacDonald, who, absent from the wartime coalition and with his party not previously in power, had never served in a Ministerial position. In the United States since the Civil War, there have been nineteen Presidents. Their average age upon

---

of Woolton, *Memoirs* (London: Cassell, 1959), p. 300. Cf. the more general comment of Schumpeter: "It is safe to say that even in the normal course of things—irrespective of the war, that is—the socialists would have again come into office before long. . . ." Joseph A. Schumpeter, *Capitalism, Socialism, and Democracy* (London: Allen & Unwin, 1943), p. 369.

accession to office was fifty-two years and eight months. Five were under fifty. The oldest, just over the English average, was Dwight Eisenhower at sixty-two. Since Congress is not a direct route to executive preferment, it is pointless to compare Congressional with Parliamentary service.[19] It is, however, safe and significant to say that the Presidency draws on a wider field of experience, occasionally—as with Grant and Eisenhower— on a field not political at all.

The English apprentice their rulers; the Americans do not. The conclusion can be drawn either way. What in America is lost in terms of safety may be made up for by boldness. What is gained in vigor may be lost through an incompetence untested by relevant experience and thus previously undiscovered. The difference is clear; its consequences must be carefully put. Let us consider the men who have held the chief executive position since the turn of the century. In Britain they are Balfour, Campbell-Bannerman, Asquith, Lloyd George, Bonar Law, Baldwin, MacDonald, Chamberlain, Churchill, Attlee, Eden, Macmillan, Home, and Wilson; in America, Theodore Roosevelt, Taft, Wilson, Harding, Coolidge, Hoover, Franklin Roosevelt, Truman, Eisenhower, Kennedy, and Johnson. Within both lists there are occasions for blushing and for rejoicing as well. One may say, without undue temerity, that both Roosevelts, Wilson, Truman, perhaps Kennedy, and surely Johnson[20] have displayed a personal vigor and boldness known among British heads of government only to Lloyd George and Churchill. Americans, like the British and most peoples around the world, have increasingly relied upon innovating and vigorous executive government. A Presidential government is better able to supply it than is a Parliamentary system. One may counter this statement, quite fairly, by saying the British Parliamentary system is less dependent on strong and forceful leadership than is the American government. In the United States, periods of governmental accomplishment correspond with the tenure of bold Presidents. In England, one would have to broaden the time boundaries, perhaps somewhat as follows: 1908 to 1922 and 1940 to 1950, to include Asquith's govern-

[19]Twenty-one of the thirty-five Presidents served in Congress, nine of nineteen since Lincoln. Even when a Congressman is nominated for the Presidency, he is seldom chosen from among the leading men of either House. Kennedy and Goldwater are recent cases in point. Neither of them made his reputation and gained his followers by excelling in the Congressional arts and achieving a position of leadership in the Senate.

[20]Three of these six succeeded to the office upon the death of a President, with, in the latter two cases, one strong personality following another. The high proportion of Vice Presidents on the list underscores the argument that follows by emphasizing the more varied processes by which the chief executive's office is attained.

ment as well as Lloyd George's, Attlee's first Ministry as well as Churchill's during the war.

The political importance of different ways of recruiting political leaders becomes clearer if we look briefly at some details of recent history. Macmillan was a party rebel in the middle and later 1930's in economic and international matters. As a Minister Resident in North Africa during the war, he combined dash and diplomacy. He was after the war a critic of Labour's policy toward Europe and long considered a "good European." What is most arresting is that he came to office after a career in important Cabinet offices, during which time it is difficult to say that he did much to distinguish himself other than to promote the building of 300,000 houses yearly from 1951 to 1954. With that exception, his performance was regarded as uninspiring even by the Conservative press. Nor was he the obvious candidate to succeed Eden. In the surveys of the British Institute of Public Opinion, among declared Conservative voters the preferences in the year preceding Macmillan's accession to the Prime Minister's office were as shown in Table 3:

TABLE 3 QUESTION: "IF SIR ANTHONY EDEN WERE TO RETIRE, WHO WOULD YOU LIKE TO SEE SUCCEED HIM AS LEADER OF THE CONSERVATIVE PARTY?"

	INTERVIEWS WITH CONSERVATIVE VOTERS			
	Jan. 14–26, 1956	Sept. 1956	Oct. 1956	Nov. 1–2, 1956
	(Preferences for candidates by percent)			
Butler	30	22	26	17
Macmillan	7	17	15	9
Other	13	24	21	19
Don't know	50	37	38	55

The pattern of preferences displayed in Table 3 prevailed among Labour, Liberal, and undecided voters as well, even to the point of putting Selwyn Lloyd third, often in a tie with Macmillan.

The MP who would be Prime Minister must satisfy his first constituents, the members of his party who sit in the Commons, that he would be competent and, according to the lights of his party, safe and reliable in office. The Members will also bear in mind that with him as their leader they will stand before the public and ask for its approval. These considerations require weighing votes as well as counting them. As a possible successor to Eden, Butler had more support in the country, and probably in Parliament as well, than did Macmillan. But apparently some important Members simply said: "No, under this man we cannot serve." They prevailed. There were various reasons, among them that Macmillan had been an enthusiastic supporter of the Suez venture from the outset. Butler had not been. The Suez supporters were alienated, which made it doubly difficult for Butler, who had long struck a fairly large number of Conservatives as unreliable. The Queen took advice, of course, from Eden, Churchill, and Lord Salisbury at least; and then the sovereign decided. The Party did not vote in or out of Parliament, for the leader of the Conservative Party was until 1965 not elected except by acclamation after he had become Prime Minister.[21]

The story was repeated, with variations, in the fall of 1963. Butler had again carried the day, but only with the people. Sir Alec Douglas-Home was hardly in sight. A *Daily Express* poll of October 16, four days before Home announced the formation of his Cabinet, produced the results shown in Table 4:

TABLE 4   BRITISH VOTER PREFERENCES IN OCTOBER, 1963[a]

	ALL PARTIES (percent)	TORIES ONLY (percent)
Butler	39.5	38.0
Hailsham	21.5	27.0
Maudling	11.0	10.5
Home	9.5	10.0
Others and undecided	18.5	14.5

[a]Reprinted in Iain Macleod, "The Tory Leadership," *Spectator*, No. 7073 (January 17, 1964), p. 67. In a poll taken by the British Institute of Public Opinion, also in October, 1963, favorites were ranked as follows: Butler (14 percent), Hailsham (10 percent), Maudling (10 percent), with many more respondents uncertain. Home was favored by only 2 percent of all voters.

Conservative MP's were reportedly asked for their first and second choices and, according to one of them, "whom they were 'dead against.'" In the opinion of the London *Times*, Butler would have been the better choice, in addition to having been publicly preferred and expected. Instead, the *Times* editorially concluded, it was "the blackball that counted in the end."[22] No outsider can really know, at least not officially, how the factors were weighed and the decisions made. The 1957 and 1963 successions are in this respect not very unusual. To recall an earlier instance, Ramsay MacDonald's selection as Prime Minister of the National Government in 1931 is still a matter of speculation and dispute.

[21]Bonar Law, in 1922, is the lone exception. See R. T. McKenzie, *British Political Parties* (London: Heinemann, 1955), pp. 35–36.
[22]*Times* (London), October 16, 1963, p. 12, and October 19, p. 9.

In the discussion so far, the Labour Party has been slighted. Its rules for choosing a leader are, within the electoral body of Labour MP's, entirely democratic. So also, in a complicated fashion, is the method adopted in 1965 by the Conservative Party. (To win on the first ballot requires a majority and at least 15 percent more votes than the nearest opponent. To win on the second round requires a majority, but not a 15 percent margin. If a third ballot is necessary, Members indicate their first and second choices; the votes received by the lowest-ranking candidate are redistributed to the second choices; the majority then prevails.) The democratic procedures now applied by both of the parties illustrate once more propositions made earlier. In both parties, the Members of the House of Commons, rather than the body of Labour or Conservative voters, choose the leader, who will become Prime Minister if his party is victorious. By some set of mechanisms, a party or some portion of it, must designate its leader, who will then be presented to the electorate as one of the two from which it must choose. Election by the Parliamentary parties is not a way of avoiding the difficulties of selection. There is no way of doing so. It is instead one way of meeting them. There is, as always there must be, a process of canvassing support and reducing to a small number the group of serious candidates. The MP, participating in the selection of a leader, has to bring into balance his personal preference and his sense of loyalty to individual candidates, his attachment to groups within the Parliamentary party, and his regard for the welfare of the party as a whole. He has to ask himself which candidate would best serve the party electorally and the nation as its Prime Minister. The democratic processes by which both parties now elect their leaders take place within comparatively small bodies. With MP's more dependent upon their national parties and less responsive to constituency wishes than once was the case, how well Parliamentary Members represent those who voted for them is often questioned.

Compared with British customs, the American method of producing Presidential candidates, although rowdier, is much less heavily veiled. In the summer of 1960, the *Economist* described the American system of nomination by primaries and conventions as simply an anachronism. It is amusing to find the British discovering that the institutions of another country are anachronistic, but many would agree with the *Economist's* later description of "the crazy-quilt procedure for nominating presidential candidates," which it believes to be "anything but rational." [23] The

[23]"Off the Goldwater Standard?" *Economist*, CCIX (December 21, 1963), 1261.

American way—of scattered primaries conducted by different rules in different states, of electioneering lasting months, if not years, of national conventions that look from a distance like three-ring circuses—impresses many Americans and most foreigners as supremely nonsensical.

Primaries are held in only seventeen of the fifty states and in the District of Columbia. Their importance varies from one state and from one pre-election period to another. Alfred M. Landon won the Republican nomination in 1936; Wendell Willkie did so in 1940. Neither had entered a single primary. Adlai Stevenson was chosen by the Democrats in 1952 without the test of a primary. Defeat in a single primary may be fatal to a candidate, as were the defeats of Willkie in Wisconsin in 1944 and of Harold E. Stassen in Oregon in 1948.[24] Some victories may be unimportant; others may go far to ensure to the victor his party's nomination. In 1960, Senators Hubert Humphrey and John F. Kennedy confronted each other in Wisconsin and West Virginia. Kennedy's victories, in the latter primary especially, gave some assurance that his Roman Catholicism would not be an insurmountable obstacle in November. In 1964, after Ambassador Henry Cabot Lodge won in New Hampshire and Governor Nelson Rockefeller in Oregon, the California primary became the one that Senator Barry Goldwater had to win in order to gain the nomination. Until the summer of 1964, no candidate in this century who had received more than 500 votes on the first ballot had failed to gain his party's nomination, nor had a convention failed in more than thirty years to nominate the man who led in the popularity polls.[25] Senator Goldwater, however, by concentrating upon lining up delegates, overcame his low popularity rating with the public at large. In doing so, he made dramatically clear a sometimes hidden dilemma. In order to gain the party's nomination, the candidate has to appeal to its regular members, which he may do by espousing policies ill-designed to impress a larger public.

Not by design but by accident, the American process of nominating candidates by primary and convention does assay their merits in a way as appropriate to American conditions as the different British processes of selection are to theirs. The extent of the differences between British and American selection processes, however, obscures the similarities that do exist. Without denying the differences, an examination of the similarities between the selections of Home and Goldwater by their respective parties can deepen comprehension of what goes on in both countries.

[24]Charles A. H. Thomson and Frances M. Shattuck, *The 1956 Presidential Campaign* (New York: Brookings, 1960), p. 40.
[25]James Reston, *New York Times*, May 13, 1964, p. 42.

51

Home was the least popular of the major contenders in his country. On the American side, Senator Goldwater was markedly less favored for his party's nomination than was Governor Scranton, who emerged in the weeks preceding the convention as his principal rival.[26] Both Home and Goldwater gained selection, in preference to their more popular opponents, by securing the support of some party stalwarts and leaders, much to the annoyance and dismay of others, who were persuaded in both cases that the man who had won would lead his party to defeat.[27] Neither method of selection ensures a wise choice or even one that is broadly acceptable. No system can. Both systems do permit the contenders for office to work and maneuver in order to advance their own fortunes and to avoid a choice they could least easily support. Butler and Maudling, Heath and Macleod, though they generally agreed on the policies the party should stand for and the type of man who should lead it, were also competing against each other for designation as Macmillan's successor. If they had supported one of their number and declared their unwillingness to serve under Home, their united wills would no doubt have prevailed. Similarly, had Lodge and Scranton entered the race earlier or even, acting later, had Lodge, Rockefeller, and Scranton agreed to back the candidacy of one from among them, Goldwater would probably have lost in California's June primary and thereby failed to achieve nomination in July.

In Britain, the one way of attaining the highest office is to climb the Ministerial ladder. In the United States, there are many routes to Presidential office and different ways of traveling along them. One politician may seek to demonstrate such popularity with the public that party leaders and convention delegates, wishing to nominate a man who can win the forthcoming election, will give him the nomination even though his views leave them uneasy. Another may secure the nomination without contest by virtue of the position he holds, as did Vice President Nixon in 1960 and as any President still eligible for office almost automatically does. Or, one may follow the route that Goldwater traveled. In each country, the process by which candidates are designated necessarily contains arbitrary and undemocratic aspects. It is not possible to make all

[26]"Suppose the choice for President in the Republican convention in 1964 narrows down to William Scranton and Barry Goldwater. Which one would you prefer to have the Republican convention select?" Answering this question in a Gallup poll taken in July, 1964, 60 percent of the Republican respondents named Scranton as compared to 34 percent for Goldwater; and 61 percent of the Independent respondents favored Scranton as compared to 26 percent for Goldwater. George Gallup, "Voters Prefer Scranton," *Boston Globe*, July 12, 1964, p. A3.
[27]Iain Macleod, "The Tory Leadership," *Spectator*, No. 7073 (January 17, 1964), pp. 65–67.

(Author)

decisions by the casting of votes, if only because at a preliminary stage the range of choice must be narrowed sufficiently to permit the public ultimately to announce its decision. American nominating practices achieve this, but only after permitting all men to contend for the highest office as long as they are formally qualified. In Britain, selection is made from a narrower field, and the final choice is less openly arrived at.

Where the Prime Minister comes out of and yet remains in Parliament, choice by the Parliamentary party, which knows its man, is nevertheless appropriate. And in the United States, the disordered primaries, the length of the pre-convention campaigns, and the bits of assorted nonsense, are not ill-suited to making a party choice in a system where the candidate may well come from outside of Congress, where the field of choice is much wider than it is in England, where the country is bigger and in some ways less closely knit. Both countries have developed methods of selection rather finely adjusted to bring forth the man who will suit the parties and also please the country. What sort of man will this be?

A part of the answer can be found in the characteristics already described. England's is an apprentice system, which is more likely than America's quite different system to produce not only an older man but also one who is safer and surer. We previously singled out the sources of the Prime Minister's power over members. This should not be done, however, without emphasizing the fact that the members collectively determine who will rise to the highest office. It is often remarked that Bagehot put last in a list of five the legislative functions of the House of Commons, but less often noted that in his estimate the function of electing a Prime Minister came first.[28] His ordering was perceptively accurate. With this substantial power now all but gone, the influence of Parliament has withered. But it has not died. The House no longer elects or dismisses; it does not obstruct the government's program. Each Parliamentary party does, however, select the man who will lead his party when it is out of power and become Prime Minister when it is triumphant. This process of selection creates a condition that serves as a gross restraint on executive power. It is usually not seen to be a limit at all, for the restraint is external to the process by which policy is formed rather than being, in the manner so familiar in America, a direct impediment to

---

[28] Bagehot, *The English Constitution*, chap. 5. The other three were to express the mind of the nation, to teach the people, and to inform them.

executive action.[29] The Prime Minister, insofar as he has great powers, is likely to be of an age and experience, a worldly wisdom if you like, that makes improbable his exercising them with full force and vigor. If it is true that England muddles through, here is part of the explanation, perhaps as important as the oft-cited national character to which ideological commitment and programmatic politics are supposedly alien.

In the face of long-enduring patterns, it can hardly be argued that the effects described are accidental. It can, however, be said that accidents may upset the pattern. Winston Churchill was such an accident. Member of Parliament since 1900 and the holder of more Ministerial posts than any politician in English history, he was richly qualified for the highest office. But he had been a maverick for most of his political life. A Conservative at the outset of his political career, he became a Liberal in 1906 and did not return to the Conservative Party until the mid-1920's. He was most often at odds with his party on great matters of state policy, first Indian and then European affairs. Nothing less than a crisis great enough to turn his party liabilities into national assets could have elevated him to the highest office. Writing in retrospect, Winston Churchill recalls that Baldwin, expecting a narrow victory, had hinted before the election of 1935 of appointment to high Cabinet office. The wide margin of victory made it possible to make no offer at all, and thus Churchill writes, "Over me beat the invisible wings." [30] Fortunately free of association with discredited governments, he could lead a national war effort. Uncontaminated by office, he was also untamed, indeed untamable. But the events required to raise him to the Prime Ministership, by virtue of their exceptional quality, cause the normal practice to stand out with greater clarity. Accidents do occur, but it takes great crises to produce them. To pull someone from outside the normal line of succession is not easily done.

When the Labour Party won the general election of October, 1964, Wilson became the youngest Prime Minister of England since the Earl of Rosebery took office in 1894. But in the British system of apprenticeship, even the Prime Minister who is unusually young approaches the average age of American Presidents. No matter how young they may be, those who are designated leaders of their party have had considerable Parliamentary experience. Wilson has sat in the Commons since 1945 and

---

[29]Restraints that arise from within the executive offices themselves are considered in Chapter 5, below.

[30]Winston S. Churchill, *The Gathering Storm* (Boston: Houghton Mifflin, 1948), p. 181.

when made leader of the party was one of only two men on Labour's front benches who had held Cabinet office.

That a pattern emerges from statistics on the age and Parliamentary service of England's Prime Ministers does not mean that behind the pattern lies an unbreakable rule. The fashion among chief executives may vary. John Fitzgerald Kennedy's becoming the American President was thought by some to mark the beginning of a youth movement among rulers. Age and experience, in the persons of Mao and Khrushchev, Adenauer, de Gaulle, Macmillan, and Eisenhower, had previously prevailed. It is, however, unlikely that the pattern will change very much. The United States is exceptional; most states of settled political institutions apprentice their rulers in one way or another. In governments with no limit upon length of service by one man in the highest office, young men of present political influence and with ambitions for themselves in the future are understandably reluctant to see a man in his forties become the country's chief executive; for he may block their own way for a quarter of a century. If comparative youth is a desirable quality in national leaders, one of the merits of limiting the American President to two terms, whether by tradition as before 1940 or by Constitutional stipulation as now, is to open the way to the selection of younger men for the office.

The Management of Parties

The limitations that work upon the Prime Ministers of England in the very process by which they are selected are as important as they are subtle, elusive, and generally overlooked. These qualities also characterize the limitations that derive from the Prime Minister's relation to his party and to Parliament, where his strength is often thought to be greatest. The situation in the two countries can be put as follows: the President can lead but has trouble getting his party to follow; the Prime Minister has the followers but on condition that he not be too far in front of, or to the side of, his party, which makes it difficult for him to lead. Party voting, it is often said, is so close to 100 percent that it is hardly worth mentioning.[31] This is misleading. There are a number of pressures upon the MP to vote with his party. Immediately there are the Whips. More

---

[31]See, for example, Samuel H. Beer, "New Structures of Democracy: Britain and America," in William N. Chambers and Robert H. Salisbury, eds., *Democracy in the Mid-Twentieth Century* (St. Louis, Mo.: Washington University Press, 1960), p. 40.

generally the conviction prevails that it is improper, except for the weightiest of reasons, to vote against the party that one has, after all, joined voluntarily and from whose label benefits have been derived, including of course election to Parliament. More often than not, the MP is at least roughly in agreement with his party's policy or position. Ultimately in the Labour Party, the Whip may be withdrawn, or, in extreme cases, the right to stand again as a member of the party may be denied. In the Conservative Party, where visible dissent is less common, such sanctions are seldom applied. In extreme cases the MP, by antagonizing his constituency, may fail of readoption. Finally, the Member who wishes to rise must ask himself how his behavior will impress the present and future leaders of his party.

The significance of the straying varies with the height of the fences, and these are high ones. When twenty-six Conservative MP's, including the tellers, voted in July of 1954 against their government on the question of removing British troops from the Suez Canal Zone; when eight who were present in the chamber refused in November of 1956 to endorse their government's intervention in Suez; when eight others refused the Whip in May of 1957 because the government had advised ship owners to resume using the Canal, they not only expressed their own deep disapproval of the government's policy but also indicated by their actions that many more were left feeling uneasy. The meaning and importance of abstention or voting with the opposition vary from one case to another and according to who the dissidents are. Voting is but one of many ways that back-benchers have of influencing their parties. All of them are used from time to time and watched with great care by Whips and by leaders.

It was previously mentioned that since 1895 the House has not voted a majority government out of office. Nor, one should add, does the Prime Minister any longer avail himself of the power of dissolution in order to discipline his possibly unruly party. No party with a comfortable majority of seats likes to fight an election, for there is always some risk of defeat. Ministers, enjoying the exercise of power, have more to lose than back-benchers. Anthony Trollope once had one of his Parliamentary characters remark of a rebellion against a Prime Minister of the 1840's: "There were fifty went against him then. . . . And what are fifty? A man doesn't like to be one of fifty. It's too many for glory, and not enough for strength." [32] Though discipline is much stricter now, large numbers of rebels cannot all be thrown out of the party. The requisite

[32]Trollope, *Phineas Redux* (2 vols.; Philadelphia: Gebbie, 1902), I, 55.

art for a Prime Minister is to manage the party in such a way as to avoid the defiance of the many or the rebellion of the few, if those few are important, rather than to levy penalties after rebellion has occurred. Most often the Prime Minister's worry is less that some Members will defy him than that his real and effective support will dwindle in the years between general elections, as happened to Churchill and to Macmillan in their last governments, and even more obviously to Eden. It is wrong to see the Parliamentary party as a brake on the government only when the party is split and the Prime Minister faces an unruly faction, for a party is never monolithic. A well-managed party will appear to be almost passively obedient, but the managerial arts are difficult to master. The effective Prime Minister or party leader moves in ways that avoid dissent, if possible by anticipating it. Concessions are made; issues are postponed and at times evaded entirely. If we think of the two parties as disciplined armies marching obediently at their leaders' commands, we not only ignore much important history but also overlook the infinite care and calculation that goes into getting groups, be they armies, symphony orchestras, football teams, or political parties, to act in unison. The functions of party managers are in these respects similar in America and in England, but in England the standards of conformity are higher, the lines between parties are clearer, and the means of ensuring party allegiance more fully developed. The Prime Minister can, with infrequent exceptions and those seldom fatal, count on his party to follow, but within limits that are set in part by the party members collectively.

Parliamentary debates no longer adequately educate and inform the people. It is difficult for the back-bencher to speak one way and vote another, though he occasionally does so. It is difficult, except in moments of crisis, to evoke the drama of debate when the result is a foregone conclusion. Don K. Price long ago noticed "that the Commons seem to be following the Lords into the status of one of the 'theatrical elements' of the British Constitution."[33] Bernard Levin, while a drama critic for the *Daily Express*, covered the Commons for *Spectator* as though it were theater and found it a wholly bad show. Two of Bagehot's five major tasks of Parliament are not well performed by it. These tasks, one might think, should become the Prime Minister's. The system makes it difficult for this to happen. The Prime Minister can only ask for what his party will give. He cannot say: the trade unions must be disciplined; or: the relations of labor and management must be recast, and industry must be

[33]Price, "The Parliamentary and Presidential Systems," p. 322.

rationalized; or: we must plunge into the waters of Europe that have looked icy to so many of us.[34] He cannot make such statements, even if he believes them, unless he is either sure that his party will come around without a major faction splitting off or willing to become a bold Prime Minister at the cost of being a bad party manager. "A Party has to be managed, and he who can manage it best, will probably be its best leader. The subordinate task of legislation and of executive government may well fall into the inferior hands of less astute practitioners." [35] Such were the reflections of Trollope upon the career of Sir Timothy Beeswax, a magical party manager whom Sir Harold Macmillan, a warm admirer of Trollope, must surely have found congenial. The roles of leader of the country and manager of a party easily come into conflict. The conflict is deepened by removal of the power of the House of Lords to obstruct. The one excuse for inaction that was built into the Parliamentary system is gone. The party that would act can do so. Because the party in power acts on the word of its leader, the leader must be cautious about the words he chooses to utter.

The leadership problem coupled with the apprenticeship factor goes far to describe the texture of British politics. The description is borne out by the operations of that consummate politician and reader of Trollope mentioned above. When Macmillan was at the height of his powers, the great game of British political analysis was to figure out what he was up to at any given moment. His tactic was not quite the one Roosevelt used in the late 1930's. Roosevelt first sent up trial balloons, notably in the quarantine-the-aggressors speech at Chicago in October of 1937, and in the Kingston, Ontario, speech ten months later. Finding them shot down, he waited to be pushed toward his preferred policy by domestic opinion and international events. Macmillan's tactic, a refinement of Roosevelt's and one that permits a greater initiative, was to equivocate and delay until the necessity for some decision or action became undeniable.

A minor but instructive example was provided by Macmillan's African trip early in 1960. From the center of British politics leftward, the fear freely expressed was that Macmillan would refrain from uttering a word in support of racial equality and independence for African colonial territories lest he antagonize and provoke the government of the country he would visit last, South Africa. Questioned in the House and pressed for

---

[34]For an examination of Britain's European policy, see Chapter 9, below.
[35]Trollope, *The Duke's Children* (3 vols.; Philadelphia: Gebbie, 1902), III, 169; cf. I, 216.

a promise that he would indicate support of African aspirations, he doggedly refused. With their worst fears confirmed, many were saying in effect: "Stop, Prime Minister! The course you are following may lead to chaos." When in his progress through Africa he did make mild-mannered comments in support of native populations, and when in South Africa he made an airy speech about the winds of change, all those who had trembled heaved great sighs of relief. It really seemed as though he had done something. If one goes back and reads the speech while forgetting the domestic political context, it is hard to see why. The explanation for such a tactic is clear. Neither the followers of Iain Macleod nor the devotees of Lord Hinchingbrooke were antagonized. The former could be pleased because something of the right sort was said, the latter because what was said had little meaning.

To erase a fear that you have first created is masterful politics. Was this uniquely a Macmillan manner or more generally a characteristic of Conservative leadership, or, more generally still, representative behavior of the Prime Minister in England? Recalling such Prime Ministers as Attlee, Baldwin, and Ramsay MacDonald, one can fairly describe the practice as an important part of the customary strategy of British political leadership. Seldom will a Prime Minister try to force a decision widely and genuinely unpopular in his party. The Prime Minister must preserve the unity of his party, for it is not possible for him to perpetuate his rule by constructing a series of majorities whose composition varies from issue to issue. He is therefore constrained to crawl along cautiously, to let situations develop until the near necessity of decision blunts inclinations to quarrel about just what the decision should be.

The leadership characteristics built into the system are reflected most clearly in questions of defense and foreign affairs. In these matters, decisions are sometimes forced, and temporizing is not always possible. The rending of parties and the open expression of dissent most often come with decisions taken on international issues, as we shall presently see.

The English system concentrates power in the hands of the Prime Minister but provides effective, though often informal, checks against its impetuous use. British government appears as a leadership system because British leaders are seldom effectively challenged. More accurately it should be said that in Britain the typical Prime Minister is a weak national leader but an expert party manager—characteristics that he ordinarily must have in order to gain office and retain it. Provision is then made for changing Prime Ministers suddenly in moments of national calamity. Because the British so often ride old horses, it is important that they be able to change them in midstream.[36]

Rather than argue that such remedies are developed so that systems can endure, it is more accurate to say that those systems do endure that have such elements of flexibility within them. In comparable fashion, it is important in the United States, with terms of Presidential office fixed, that the migration of power from one branch of government to another be possible. The weakness or immobility of the President may stir the Congress to action. A President who is too obviously strong may stimulate the Congress to a more united opposition. No President ordinarily likes to advocate policies or take positions that antagonize large and important segments of his party. He may seek, by persuasion and patronage, by postponing issues and trimming programs, to build a position that will gain widespread assent. He would ordinarily prefer to submit to Congress programs that his party will strongly support. In these respects the President behaves like a Prime Minister, but with differences in degree so great that they become differences in kind. The President, because his tenure does not depend on securing majority support in Congress, because he can be defeated on policies and still hold his office, because obstruction is an ordinary and accepted part of the system, is encouraged to ask for what at the moment may well not be granted, to educate and inform, to explain that the legislation Congress refuses to accept is actually what the interest of the country requires, to ask, indeed, for more than he wants, hoping that the half-loaf he may get will conform roughly to his private estimate of need. The gap between promise and performance, between Presidential request and Congressional acquiescence, is thus often illusory. The Prime Minister gets all that he asks, and yet major social and economic legislation is in England ordinarily a long time maturing. The President asks for much that he does not get, and yet the pace of reform is not slower, the flexibility and response of American government in practice are not less, than what is found in Great Britain.

The President is literally free to lead in a way that the Prime Minister is not. Congressmen, by the same token, are free to criticize the President regardless of their party affiliation. The MP who would get on with his political career is encouraged to conform, to express even deep-running

[36]One should add that the ease of doing so is usually exaggerated through overlooking the extent of political or personal difficulties that must occur or accumulate before the resignation of the Prime Minister is secured, as the fates of Chamberlain, Eden, and Macmillan all illustrate.

dissent from his party's program in modest and decorous terms; the Congressman is encouraged to dramatize minor disagreements even against an administration of his own party. Though exceptions abound, the tendencies clearly run this way and are directly a product of fusion in the one country, of checks and balances in the other. In the Labour movement, where power is checked and balanced, the practice of politics, especially when the party is out of power, is strikingly similar to the political conduct that prevails generally in the United States. In the face of conflict and open dissension, the leaders of the party are often constrained actually to lead, to explore the ground and try to work out compromises, to set a line of policy, to exhort and persuade, to threaten and cajole, to inform and educate, all with the hope that the party can be brought to follow the leaders.

In contrast to the mannerly and reasonable procedures of English government, American political procedures appear chaotic and disordered. The disorder is a condition that makes accomplishment possible. It has often been argued that the American government would be improved were the two parties disciplined somewhat on the English model.[37] But the President and the Congress have separate and enduring sources of power. Would a disciplined party in Congress support the program of its President? So long as a substantial separation of powers remains, the discipline of parties would almost surely create a situation in which Congress would become better able to oppose the President and follow a policy of its own. There would be deadlock. Or the Congress would capture the Presidency, and a Parliamentary system would be established in fact if not in form. A measure of incoherence in Congress and some fragmentation of parties are conditions of Presidential power.

Concluding Remarks

Conservatism is the English métier. England's talents have long been best expressed in perpetuating the old while making grudging and belated concessions to change, in maintaining a social system of wide inequalities of wealth while blunting the sharp edges of class conflict. Postponement of problems, evasion of issues, slow movement by minor adjustment: these have most often been characteristic of British politics since late

---

[37]See, for example, "Toward a More Responsible Two-Party System: A Report of the Committee on Political Parties," *American Political Science Review*, XLIV (September, 1950), Supplement.

Victorian days. It is perhaps impossible to say which is more important in accounting for the result, the traditions of society and the character of the people or political structures and forms. One can, however, say that political structure has accorded with the preferences of society's dominant parts. As Edmund Burke once said, a constitution is, or ought to be, a vestment fitted to a body; Britain's has been pleasingly snug. The interpretation of this chapter contradicts the more common appreciation of the British political system as one that encourages bold leadership and easily permits imagination, innovation, and coherence in policy.

Appearances are often deceptive. British Prime Ministers have been thought to be strong leaders because they are in public so ineffectively opposed. The fusion of powers, however, tempts the Prime Minister to place his concern for the unity of his party above his regard for the public interest and in rendering the party responsible in the eyes of the voter makes the government unresponsive to the needs of the nation. American Presidents have been thought to be politically weak and American government often in stalemate because powers rather than being fused are placed in opposition. The opposition of governmental powers, however, makes strong leadership without dominance possible and permits Congressional initiative and criticism without rendering policy incoherent. In the United States, problems are more directly confronted, alternatives more openly posed, leadership more firmly exerted, and policies more quickly geared to conditions than is true in England. In developing the thesis and applying it more specifically to foreign policy, we shall have to look closely at constituent elements of politics before proceeding to cases.

Chapter 4

ATTITUDES, PARTIES, AND BIPARTISAN POLICY

That politics should stop at the water's edge has long been a cry in both England and America.[1] The reasoning is clear. A people may disagree among themselves about the extent of governmental control of the economy, about the proper level and incidence of taxation, and about the distribution of wealth. When facing foreign countries, however, that same people, divided as they may be on domestic questions, should become a united body. Patriotic impulse, considerations of possible advantage in international negotiation, and the specter of military danger powerfully support the cry that unity is required. The tendency of politicians to draw foreign policy into the arena of party contention is thus widely deplored and feared.

The fear is produced by the mating of two worries. The first worry derives from a recognition that a country may at times improve its position in international relations by cooperating with others. If the foreign policy of a democracy is determined by competition among parties, an agreement made today may not be honored tomorrow when another party comes to power; and foreign nations will be reluctant to commit themselves. At the extreme, a picture is drawn of wild swings in policy: for example, a party whose leaders are bent upon appeasement may give

---

[1]Senator Vandenberg described bipartisan foreign policy as a mutual effort to "unite our official voice at the water's edge." Arthur H. Vandenberg, ed., *The Private Papers of Senator Vandenberg* (Boston: Houghton Mifflin, 1952), pp. 552–53. Cf. C. R. Attlee, speaking as leader of the opposition: "It is desirable, wherever possible, that, in foreign affairs particularly, Government policy should have the support of all. It strengthens us in giving what I believe is a necessary lead in international relations." House of Commons, *Parliamentary Debates*, Vol. 515 (May 12, 1953), col. 1062. Cited hereafter as *H.C. Deb.*

way to a party determined to stand firm, or isolation may suddenly be substituted for a policy of international involvement. But flexibility may be as desirable as continuity, and it is the need for flexibility that gives rise to the second major worry. Matching in importance the fear of erratic movements of policy is dismay born of the thought that once a party has committed itself in the eyes of the country at large to a foreign-policy position, the difficulty of shifting to meet a new situation in the world may be forbiddingly large. Out of these two worries, concern about partisan influence on foreign policy grows. If the vagaries of the public will are great and parties are their transmitters, it becomes important to insulate policy from the influence of parties. If elections are closely contested, the temptation of candidates to turn the country's difficulties abroad to electoral advantage at home may be irresistible. If politicians are to act in ways that serve the nation well, they may require the protection that would come with the removal of international issues from the realm of partisan debate.

From the fear of deep cleavages and wild swings, other anxieties arise. If parties are committed to conflicting policies, it may be difficult for either party when in power to carry out its policy effectively, and not only because other states would have little confidence in it. Seeking broader support in order to overcome a stalemate, the government may exaggerate some dangers while playing down others. In desperation, it may adopt some of the opposition party's policy in order to gain its support. A slipshod policy may result, one that in seeking a common denominator of support meets the foreign situation less well than the abilities and resources of the country would otherwise have permitted.[2]

Does the competition of parties actually interfere with the wise and orderly fashioning of foreign policy, as so many have feared? To answer this question it is less important to measure variations in opinion on international problems from one moment to the next than it is to examine commitments broadly accepted by the public at large.[3] Against this background, the effects on foreign policy of the contention of parties for political power can then be considered, along with the possible need of adopting political devices that would insulate policy from the disruptions of domestic political strife.

[2]H. Bradford Westerfield, *Foreign Policy and Party Politics: Pearl Harbor to Korea* (New Haven: Yale University Press, 1955), esp. p. 15.

[3]The relation of opinion to policy in the short term is the subject of Chapter 10, below.

Political Problems, Domestic and Foreign

Big changes in a people's politics occur infrequently; to work out their effects usually requires decades and perhaps generations. Arthur W. Macmahon, in a brilliant address, likened the alternation of political parties to the oscillation of a pendulum, which, while it swings back and forth, regulates the clock as it moves ever forward.[4] Occasionally, however, someone sets the clock noticeably forward or back. If the hands are moved too frequently, we never know what time it is. Politics gives way to revolution. If the hands are never set, the clock by losing a minute a day may become increasingly out of gear with the heavens. Differently put, one may look at politics as moving sometimes on a plateau with rivulets, gullies, and small hills upon it, which represent the comparatively minor challenges and adjustments of everyday affairs. Occasionally, the locus of politics moves from one plateau to another. Ascending or descending from one to the next is most often a costly, tricky, and perilous task. Viewed historically, the New Freedom of Woodrow Wilson and the New Deal of Franklin Roosevelt constitute attempts to scale new plateaus, as do the political, economic, and social reforms of a succession of Liberal Governments before World War I and of the Labour Government after World War II. Given a stable and democratic country, the often painful process of establishing policy requires building consensus, driving it home with a series of major actions, and then proceeding incrementally to perfect details and adjust policies to the interests of groups and the requirements of events.[5]

Is any part of this relevant to foreign policy? It may well seem that metaphors of pendulums and plateaus are inappropriate and incrementalism impossible to apply, whether one is worried about the making and conduct of foreign policy or the impingement of domestic politics upon it. Not so long ago the point was often made, and rightly so, that in the United States the winning or losing of elections, insofar as issues are decisive, depends on domestic policies and problems, not on distant and evanescent questions of foreign policy. Problems of foreign policy are now no longer distant; they are constantly present. Almost always since World War II, matters of foreign policy have ranked highest among the

[4]Macmahon, "Conflict, Consensus, Confirmed Trends, and Open Choices," *American Political Science Review*, XLII (February, 1948), 3.

[5]For the idea of incrementalism applied to domestic affairs, see Robert A. Dahl and Charles E. Lindblom, *Politics, Economics, and Welfare* (New York: Harper, 1953), pp. 82–85.

concerns of the public at large.[6] Indeed the old argument that foreign policy is electorally unimportant is revealed as a misleading truism merely by rephrasing it as follows: only those issues that people worry about will have electoral impact. Whether people care about foreign policy depends on time and circumstance. More often than not in the last quarter-century they have cared very much.

In terms of constancy of concern, international issues have been domesticated. Are there other similarities between domestic and international issues? Problems of governmental investment, the financing of research and development, urban renewal, highway building, programs for agriculture and for social welfare and education—all can be broken into pieces or parceled out to be handled at different governmental levels. Problems of foreign policy often appear to be different in type. They can be managed only by the national government, and it is often thought that they must be taken whole. When that great American experiment, Prohibition, clearly brought more bad effects than good, what had been done by altering the Constitution could be undone by repealing the earlier amendment. In international relations, however, an experiment tried and found wanting may bring changes in the world that no act of a single government can easily reverse. The United States fought World War II for military victory without giving much thought to the ways in which fighting the war would affect the subsequent peace. On the morrow of victory, it dismantled its military machine with breathtaking speed. The advance of the Soviet Union to the center of Europe was made easier by America's policies. No new policy, short of an aggressive war of liberation, could erase the effects that old policies had helped to produce. The effects of foreign policy are hard to predict and difficult to control, for the forces involved are subject to the manipulation of two or more countries. The irreversibility of the result joined with the greater unpredictability of events serves to establish an important difference between the problem of controlling or influencing the external as compared to the internal world. Nonetheless, as foreign affairs have increasingly commanded the attention of government, foreign and domestic problems have taken on a greater similarity. The more deeply the government is involved in the economy and society, the smaller is its opportunity to engage in whimsical legislative experiments. Because

[6]"With few exceptions, the international scene has dominated the thinking of the public over the years." Only occasionally has a matter of domestic concern crowded foreign policy out of first place, as did racial problems in April and October of 1963. Releases of the American Institute of Public Opinion, July 20 and October 1, 1963. Cited hereafter as AIPO releases.

governments have become more deeply involved, continuity from one government to the next has assumed some of the importance in domestic policy that it must always have in foreign policy. And as the government's responsibility for maintaining full employment has increased, the need of greater executive flexibility in financial and fiscal affairs has come to be widely accepted.

In these characteristics—the irreversibility of the act, the importance of continuity, and the need for flexibility—domestic governance of the present has come to resemble more closely the discharge of foreign-policy functions in the past. Completing the pattern of convergence from the other side, foreign policy has acquired the attributes of domestic policy. Having become expensive, foreign policy now involves the political problems of resource allocation and distribution that frequently plague domestic programs. American military spending, in and after the Korean War, has taken about 10 percent of the gross national product yearly and has accounted for 50 percent or more of the federal budget. Foreign aid, small when compared with military expenditures, is larger than most domestic programs. Not surprisingly, it has been subjected to the pulls, strains, and threats of disruption that beset controversial items of welfare spending at home.

That in many important ways the foreign and domestic problems of government have come to resemble each other does not necessarily lessen worry about the effect of opinion on policy. In democratic countries, opinion ought to have some effect on policy; one would expect parties both to help shape opinion and to transmit it. Whether or not the continuity of policy is thereby endangered and its content corrupted will depend on the nature of national opinion and the ways in which it changes.

The Plinth of Policy

Bryce, Friedrich, and Churchill, as mentioned in the first chapter, could see the continuity of American or British foreign policies because their vision stretched back so far. Current observers are more likely to see erratic behavior and uncertain response to shifting public moods because they naturally focus attention on the era of the two world wars. A moment's consideration, however, will show that the movement of foreign policy from one plateau to another is in England and in America much like the movement that takes place in matters of more purely domestic concern. In foreign policy, England's "splendid isolation" was at the turn of the century hesitantly replaced by a policy of alliance; her policy of isolation had outrun the means required to support it. In 1870, Britain produced more than half of the world's pig iron and one and a half times as much coal as Germany, France, Austria-Hungary, Russia, and the United States combined. By 1910 she found herself closely challenged for industrial supremacy by Germany and surpassed by the United States.[7] In response to changed circumstances, new policies were born: first a coming to terms with America in the 1890's, followed by alliance with Japan; then a system of alignments, formed with France in 1904 and with Russia in 1907. The alliance with Japan evoked protests. The arrangements with France and Russia took the form and name of Entente. Then, gradually and guardedly, arrangements were made that were kept secret not only from people and Parliament but until 1912 from the Cabinet itself.[8] The understandings with France and Russia were filled out until the substance of alliance was there, but not yet its name.

Unilateral action by England in great matters of policy had become impractical. To ally with others, however, was a break with long-standing habits; and such breaks are never complete. Long-term alliances formed and maintained in peacetime were, as new devices, uncongenial to England. By describing alliances as ententes and maintaining the fiction that Britain was not bound in case of war to come to the aid of her Continental partners, Ministers obscured the extent of Britain's changed circumstances and policies. Unfortunately, the disguise fooled governments as well as Parliament and people. Asquith and Grey, by leaving undefined the response that could be expected from Britain, permitted Bethmann-Hollweg to believe that Britain would not enter a war in which Germany and France were involved.

The smooth continuity and easy adjustment of British policy are symbolized by the acceptance of the Peace Treaty with Germany, including the Covenant of the League, after one day's debate in the Commons. The United States in contrast appears truly to be the erratic giant, which is so familiarly the image cast by the nation; its peculiar institutions caused the government to veer sharply from international collaboration to irresponsible isolationism. For a more sensitive interpretation, one must notice just what was erratic about American behavior. Championing the

[7]The data are conveniently summarized by A. J. P. Taylor, *The Struggle for Mastery in Europe, 1848–1918* (London: Oxford University Press, 1954), pp. xxix–xxx.
[8]Edward Grey, *Twenty-five Years* (2 vols.; New York: Frederick A. Stokes, 1925), I, 91–96.

League represented a radical departure in American policy; isolation was something to be returned to. Continuity was preserved; flexibility and responsiveness were lacking. The contrast in behavior between Britain and America, one may say, represents a slower adjustment by a more difficult political process in the latter country. More plausibly it can be argued that the British could move more quickly and easily because their inclination to isolation was embedded in a tradition of global involvement by unilateral action; their rule against binding military alliances in peacetime was tempered with the policy of taking *ad hoc* cooperative action at the moment of necessity. Such a tradition in England goes back to Elizabeth I; in America, to Presidents McKinley and Theodore Roosevelt. Americans were asked to make a more radical departure and to do so under circumstances that were less pressing. The two-ocean moat still afforded protection; time to mobilize would be available after a threat had appeared. The British were no longer so fortunately situated. America's power had increased relatively, and her position in the world had improved while Britain's declined.

Lord Phillimore's Report on the League of Nations evinced England's traditional thinking. The League would be a Concert of Europe, now given institutional form and modified to accommodate new powers in the world. In future crises, conferences would automatically be held, which would make unlikely the recurrence of such a war as the one just fought.[9] Britain was able to look upon the League as merely a projection of the past. For the United States to join the League could be seen only as a sharp break with tradition. Continuously from 1815 to World War I, the United States had followed a policy of isolation with occasional unilateral action mixed in. Many criticisms of American policy and much of the worry about its reliability derive from vivid memories of the difficulties intermittently experienced from the end of the nineteenth century through World War II as the practice of isolation became increasingly untenable and, in the end, unbearably dangerous. Any country, authoritarian or democratic in its organization, or, if democratic, Parliamentary or Presidential in type, would have trouble making the rapid adjustment from isolation to widespread involvement.

If circumstances change, policies can ordinarily be expected to change with them. But if a special explanation for America's long-standing pref-

[9]Cf. Lord Phillimore's brief suggestions appended to his survey of proposals for the peaceful settlement of disputes from Dante to World War I. *Schemes for Maintaining General Peace* (London: HMSO, 1920), pp. 65–67.

erence for isolationism can be found—in the national character, for example—then fears of reversion to it are heightened. The search for a special explanation, often undertaken, is seen to be illusory if the impulse to isolationism is viewed as a natural one for all nations, though few may have the chance to follow their inclinations. Isolation is a policy a country follows when it has no designs on the territory of other states and is not sufficiently threatened to cause it to combine with others for defensive purposes. A country proceeds unilaterally when its international ambitions can be accomplished unaided and without fear of harmful third-party interventions. Except when it needs help or protection, a state would prefer that in its policies and actions it not be entangled with others; for to be entangled means to be influenced, limited, compromised, and occasionally duped. The aspiration for self-dependence is as natural for the state as it is for the individual. Both the United States and England followed isolationist or unilateralist policies as long as they were able. For reasons that go beyond historical conditioning, important though that was, the movement out of isolation was then inevitably difficult.

The speed and sensitivity of the American adjustment in the years since World War II are as striking as the painful hesitations and protracted reluctance after World War I to forsake the comforts of the Western Hemisphere and leave aside the exhilaration of making occasional moral pronouncements to other nations without serious efforts to back them up. America's earlier diplomatic record nevertheless continues to color interpretations of her later accomplishments. Because the shift to a policy of involvement was reluctantly made and because in general the pleasures of acting alone are great, one may wonder if the new line of policy is firmly established. Having dramatically changed course in recent years, may not the direction of policy change as quickly again? The difficulties of international relations provide reason enough for disenchantment. Might there not be, out of frustration, a slow turning inward?[10] Or, balked and stopped short of the attainment of national goals, might the United States not succumb to false and dangerous promises of glorious victory cheaply won?

The foreign policy that Senator Strom Thurmond, Democrat, Dixiecrat, and now Republican of South Carolina, has described as "no win" is rejected as often by the left as by the right. With approximately equal

[10]Cf. Norman A. Graebner, *The New Isolationism: A Study in Politics and Foreign Policy Since 1950* (New York: Ronald Press, 1956).

ardor, those who reject it want to liberate men and to free the world from the threat of war. *The Peace Race* as an alternative to war or surrender, *The Limits of Defense*, with military means circumscribed because there are other ways to triumph, *Why Not Victory*, *Winning Without War*: left and right are sometimes so close in ultimate agreement that pairing titles and authors correctly becomes difficult. Each of the authors of the books whose titles have just been given—Seymour Melman, Arthur I. Waskow, Barry M. Goldwater, and Amitai Etzioni—reveals a wholly American spirit. Where Britons betray their "predilection for" or "spirit of" compromise, Americans reveal a passion for victory.[11] Goldwater, for example, has advocated "a strategy that *aims at victory*" without quite being able to describe it and has argued, like Representative Charles J. Kersten before him, that winning a political victory in the war against Communism is the only way to avoid a strictly military solution of the East-West crisis. Goldwater has proposed such measures as harnessing "world opinion quickly" and directing "it at an obviously power-mad nation or group of nations," as well as withdrawing recognition of the Soviet Union at the appropriate moment or at least breaking off diplomatic relations with her.[12] Though he notices risks, he takes comfort from the fact that "every time we have stood up to the Communists they have backed down." In quite the same manner, though by methods that differ, Melman, Waskow, and Etzioni urge their countrymen to get on with winning the Cold War. In a disarmed world, Waskow notes, the Americans and the Communists would both be trying to sell their "ideas and system of government. But democrats need not fear their own inabilities. We start ahead in this race. . . ."[13] Then why, one wonders, should the Communists run it? Seymour Melman nonetheless proposes "that a peace race be mounted to turn this difference in production capability [between the United States and the Soviet Union] into a major instrument for winning a world victory for freedom in society."[14]

Senators Thurmond and Goldwater, Messrs. Melman, Etzioni, and

[11]The "predilection" and "spirit" were ascribed to Britain by G. M. Gathorne-Hardy, *International Relations between the Wars* (4th ed.; London: Oxford University Press, 1950), pp. 400–401.

[12]Goldwater, *Why Not Victory? A Fresh Look at American Foreign Policy* (New York: McGraw-Hill, 1962), pp. 126, 154; and in his speech accepting the Republican Presidential nomination, San Francisco, July 16, 1964. For the views of Representative Kersten, who was one of the early and persistent advocates of an American policy of liberation, see Senate Hearings before the Committee on Foreign Relations, *Mutual Security Act of 1952* (82d Cong., 2d sess., 1952), pp. 508–10.

[13]Waskow, *The Limits of Defense* (New York: Doubleday, 1962), p. 88.

[14]Melman, *The Peace Race* (New York: Braziller, 1962), p. 133.

Waskow argue that, by adopting a simple and safe strategy that promises victory, America can avoid war and still be triumphant. General Mark Clark had argued some years earlier that we could not "drag the Soviets into a world war except at a time and place of their own choosing. They have been doing too well in the cold war." [15] The Russians, he implied, will not use military force because they have been doing so well without it; we will consequently devise a strategy by which the United States does well and they fare badly. The statement suggests a conclusion that none of the fierce warriors of the Cold War have drawn. In the optimistic argument of General Clark and the glittering promises of the peace-race strategists, it is overlooked that frequently the occasion for a state's resorting to military force has been the fear that it would lose in a peaceful competition. The fear has been present in the American mind so often since the war that to overlook the possibility of a similar Soviet worry is peculiar. So is the disproportion between the end in view and the means to be employed. Some military men have hoped to achieve total victory by employing limited military means. In a civilian version of the happy future, the triumph of the American system is to be secured without a destructive Soviet reaction being provoked.

In a nuclear world, it is almost as dangerous to seem to be winning as it would be to lose. One must worry, therefore, lest the ways that are promised to be easy and cheap should also prove to be popular. Are they, or might they become so? They are, of course, even now—with the followers of the right and the left. The worry is that they may become more popular still. From the time of Henry Wallace's Progressives to the National Committee for a Sane Nuclear Policy, however, the application of prescriptions from the left to international relations has been rejected. From preventive-war arguments and "go it alone" urgings in the latter portion of the 1940's and early 1950's to Goldwater's Presidential campaign in 1964, so have those of the right. Very likely the radical right and left will continue to be frustrated.

Through two difficult decades, those who have argued that the United States must bear costly international burdens with no end to the necessity of doing so in sight have consistently found ample support for their policies. This record is itself one reason for expecting that responsible voices will continue to prevail. It also helps to make clear a second reason for entertaining such an expectation. The stridency of critical voices,

[15]Senate Hearings before the Subcommittee of the Committee on the Judiciary, *Investigation of Interlocking Subversion in Government Departments* (83d Cong., 2d sess., 1954), p. 1696.

especially from the right, has misled many commentators on American policy. Richard Goold-Adams, intending a kindness to John Foster Dulles, argued that British observers underestimate the threat from the right that those who have fashioned American policy have had to contend with.[16] The threat was virulent in the heyday of Senator Joseph McCarthy, but it is more likely that the extent to which it placed foreign policy in jeopardy was overestimated at home as well as abroad than that it was too lightly considered. The very solidity of the foreign-policy consensus, the maintenance of international commitments, and persistence in pursuing responsible policies in the face of urgent counsels to follow different courses of action, helped to produce frustrations among dissenters such as were expressed in the bizarre activities of McCarthy and some of his followers. The structure of American politics brings minority views into exaggerated prominence. The ferocity of political contention easily gives a misleading impression by making it seem that the issue of arguments is more frequently in doubt than is actually the case. The advantage of such a political system is that it promotes the clarification of issues and the clear definition of policies. New plateaus are more quickly scaled, though in a way that constantly suggests that the mountaineers who lead the ascent are in peril. Because criticism can be directly and openly expressed by persons who have political power and influence, the President and those who support him are forced to marshal their arguments and mobilize their supporters.

The contrast with Britain is again a sharp one. Senator McCarthy and like-minded public figures forced a confrontation of issues and a clarification of America's international orientation at an early period of the Cold War. In Britain, the bold man of eccentric opinion becomes a figure of fun in the Commons or forsakes political life to employ his talents more actively elsewhere. If the Commons were a body in which dissent were politically more consequent, and if there were then, as no doubt there would be, a number of "Beaverbrooks" in it, Britain would long ago have come to a clearer and more durable definition of her position in the postwar world. Since policy is not decided by a public confrontation of parties or personalities, the facing of issues can more easily be avoided. Policies and problems may long remain unclarified.[17] The political tendency is reinforced by social conditions and customs. The defec-

---

[16]Goold-Adams, *John Foster Dulles: A Reappraisal* (New York: Appleton-Century-Crofts, 1962), p. 286.

[17]An extended illustration of the point is found in Chapter 9, below, devoted to Britain's European policy since the war.

tion to the Soviet Union in 1951 of Guy Burgess and Donald Maclean, both Foreign Service Officers, would have brought long and bitter recriminations had it occurred in the United States, but also investigations that might well have brought improvements in security arrangements. In Britain, there was scarcely a ripple. "If there's a debate," said one Labour MP at the time, "I shall point out that these two gentlemen belonged to the same class represented by the hon. members opposite."[18] Conservatives were not inclined to make political capital of the case, and of course neither was the Labour Government. Putting the point more generally, Austen Albu, Labour MP and Chairman of the Fabian Society, remarked, "We all feel guilty about the British class system; but have we considered how far McCarthyism may be a product of the lack of prestige accorded to an intellectual elite in the United States?"[19] Loyalty within classes and deference between them soften the hard edges of disagreements and conflicts. Many have worried that American foreign-policy reactions have depended on moods of the moment and the unpredictable outcome of political strife in a fragmented system. What has misled them, ironically, are the political structure and national style that in practice make for an early clarification of commitments.

One should not, however, slip into thinking that structure and style can ever guarantee clarity of policy, much less success in its execution. It is always wise to worry. The question is, how much should one do so? The magnitude of appropriate worry is further reduced by a third consideration: the extent to which American international involvement has been accepted by the public at large. Shortly before the Korean invasion, surveys made by Elmo Roper indicated that overwhelming majorities accepted the bipartisan foreign policies forged by Roosevelt and Truman, by Vandenberg, Dulles, and others. The public supported the use of American military force if the Communists struck first, but even in 1949 and 1950 when America enjoyed a monopoly of atomic weapons systems, only one of every one hundred who were interviewed wished to fight a preventive war against the Soviet Union.[20] In the summer of 1954, when Representative Pat Sutton called Senator Estes Kefauver of Tennessee a "left-wing internationalist," Kefauver accepted the label and won the Senatorial contest. A nationwide Gallup poll, taken at the time, found

---

[18]Political Diary, "Morrison and the Foreign Office," *Observer* (London), June 17, 1951, p. 5.
[19]Quoted from *Fabian News* of January, 1954, in Henry Pelling, *America and the British Left* (London: Adam & Charles Black, 1956), p. 154.
[20]Louis Harris, *Is There a Republican Majority? Political Trends, 1952–1956* (New York: Harper, 1954), p. 29.

that 61 percent of the people called themselves internationalist, with 17 percent preferring the isolationist label.[21] Walt W. Rostow, in a book published in 1960, concluded that "one can expect about 60 per cent of the American public to take what might be called an 'internationalist' position, about 25 per cent an 'isolationist' position, and about 15 per cent a 'don't know' position." [22]

It was not that the pattern of opinion had changed by 1964 but rather that Goldwater sought to change it. He did not seek to win by appealing to the bipartisan majorities, in and out of Congress, who have supported modest welfare legislation and a long series of difficult international measures. In 1963, as he worked to secure his party's nomination, he joined the bipartisan majority in support of foreign and domestic programs only 36 percent of the time, compared to 65 percent for the average Republican Senator.[23] Goldwater did not try to gather votes from the area of commitment where they existed in largest numbers; he tried instead to put together a coalition of the disgruntled. Playing upon dissatisfactions, which abound in a difficult world, he raised doubts about his abilities to continue a policy balanced between strength and forebearance—a policy that would preserve America's position in the world without running unnecessary military risks. Even the attack from the right, the most serious challenge since the war to the structure of American foreign policy, was conducted by maneuvering on the new plateau. So firmly has the bipartisan front on foreign policy been established that even Goldwater's challenge, launched from the periphery of American politics, was put forth almost entirely in terms of it: devotion to NATO and declarations that he would be able to strengthen the alliance; opposition to Communism and assertions that under his leadership the opposition would be more effectively conducted.

A fourth and final consideration makes for the stability of American, though not of British, attitudes. The solidity of the foreign-policy consensus and the depth of the acceptance of the fact that America must bear heavy burdens in the world are greatly increased by the pressures generated in a bipolar world. With a clarity and simplicity that are not present where many approximately equal powers contend, the responsibility of acting to block any attempt of the world's only other super-

[21]AIPO release, August 17, 1954.

[22]Rostow, *The United States in the World Arena: An Essay in Recent History* (New York: Harper, 1960), p. 511.

[23]Warren Weaver, "Goldwater Split His Senate Votes," *New York Times*, July 17, 1964, p. 12.

power to aggrandize itself obviously falls upon the United States. A disproportionate increase in the Soviet Union's strength would constitute in its mere existence a danger first and foremost to the United States. The risk involved in dropping one's guard has been clear both to the government and to the people. It has stimulated the one to call for sacrifices and the other to make them.

American Attitudes

The most ardent liberationists have been those who believe that masses of people enslaved by Communism can be set free while American federal expenditures are reduced. The Republican platform for the election of 1952 promised that a Republican victory would "mark the end of the negative, futile and immoral policy of 'containment' which abandons countless human beings to a despotism and Godless terrorism which in turn enables the rulers to forge the captives into a weapon for our destruction." Republican orators echoed the theme throughout a long summer. When President Roosevelt, in 1937, vaguely suggested that perhaps somebody should "quarantine the aggressor," there was a considerable outcry.[24] The different reaction in 1952 indicates that a dramatic change of American attitude had taken place within a period of fifteen years. One could scarcely say that the public at large was disturbed by the implication of the liberation policy that Republicans proclaimed. But in 1953 when East Germans rioted and in 1956 when Hungarians rose up in fury against their Communist masters, there was no politically important domestic protest against America's failure to come to their aid.

Before World War II, the question that constantly lay behind American decisions was: how can we avoid international involvement? Foreign policy is now made and conducted at an entirely different level. The question customarily asked has become: which involvements will best serve the nation's interests? Once the United States sought not to act at all or, on occasion, as in Latin America and the Far East, to act but always alone. The country now asks not whether to act but how; not are allies desirable, but where can they be found and how reliable will they be? The difficulties of American foreign policy must then be seen in a new light. It was difficult to define a sensible foreign policy in the 1920's and

---

[24]Franklin D. Roosevelt, "Speech at Chicago, October 5, 1937," in Stephen Heald, ed., *Documents on International Affairs: 1937* (London: Oxford University Press, 1939), pp. 582–87.

1930's and secure its acceptance. It is still difficult to do so. Questions of public support and Congressional acquiescence, of unity and coherence within the executive branch, run through both periods. But the difficulties now are over policies that are different in type from those of an earlier period. The line of foreign policy, the intentions pursued, the directions chosen are all new.

From 1778 to 1947, the United States did not commit herself in peacetime to a long-term political agreement with even a single nation. In ratifying the Rio Treaty and the Atlantic Defense Treaty, the United States took steps that were unprecedented in her history.[25] With the need for cooperation in security and other matters accepted, Americans have since argued politically about how many alliances are desirable, with whom, and on what terms, quite in the way they argue that the income tax is too progressive, or not progressive enough, or that rates are changed too slowly to be of help in combatting recessions or controlling inflation. They may worry that the new disease of "pactomania" has afflicted the Secretary of State, as some did worry about John Foster Dulles, or that neutrals are treated better than allies. But they have fully accepted a system of alliances, and criticism of some of the arrangements and additions to them or subtractions from them proceed roughly in the manner of revising the tax or labor laws.

Bipartisan Foreign Policy

Bipartisan measures achieved prominence in American politics first as a means of promoting unity in the face of grave danger and, after World War II, as part of a determined effort to avoid the errors made by Woodrow Wilson and the defeats his policy suffered. President Wilson had included among the American delegates to the Peace Conference at Paris only one Republican, Henry White, a career diplomat without political standing. President Roosevelt was careful to appoint Republicans in quantity and to choose only political leaders of prominence. Henry Stimson and Frank Knox were placed in 1940 at the head of the Army and the Navy. Studies of international organization were begun early on a nonpartisan basis, and when the time for implementation occurred, Republican leaders were appointed to positions of public importance. President Roosevelt described the American delegation to the meeting at

[25]Inter-American Treaty of Reciprocal Assistance, signed at Rio de Janeiro, September 2, 1947.

San Francisco that would establish the United Nations as, "in every sense of the word—bipartisan." [26] Harold Stassen, Senator Vandenberg, and Representative Eaton, the ranking Republican member of the House Foreign Affairs Committee, were Republicans appointed to the delegation; John Foster Dulles served as principal adviser.

Attempts to undo the errors of the past set precedents for the future. The bipartisan practices followed by executive and Congressional leaders who sought to mobilize support for the international undertakings that they had come to think of as unavoidable became common features of government. As Ernest A. Gross, then Assistant Secretary for Congressional Relations, expressed it in the fall of 1949, the aim of bipartisan foreign policy is to "make it virtually impossible for 'momentous divisions' to occur in our foreign affairs" and to provide a "continuity and consistency" in foreign policy that will survive the transfer of government from one party to another.[27]

H. Bradford Westerfield has identified the conditions upon which a truly bipartisan policy must depend. Those who are to collaborate with the administration on questions of foreign policy must be chosen by the opposition party; the administration must consult with them on all foreign policies that are jointly considered to be of major importance, and it must do so before final decisions are taken. Leaders of both parties must then bring Congressmen to support the policies that have been agreed upon.[28] None of the four requirements has been fully met in American bipartisan practices; some, given the political system, cannot be. Whatever the administration in power, a frequent complaint of the opposition has been that action is first taken by the President, and then, in the name of national unity, the opposition is asked to refrain from criticizing a policy that it has had no hand in fashioning. In February of 1963, for example, Senator Bourke B. Hickenlooper, ranking minority member of the Foreign Relations Committee, sharply questioned the practices of the Kennedy Administration. His statement, made at a press conference, was in reaction to Democratic protests that bipartisan foreign policy had been shattered by individual Republican criticisms of American actions in Cuba and by an earlier attack of House and Senate leaders

[26]"Report of President Roosevelt in Person to the Congress on the Crimea Conference," *New York Times*, March 2, 1945, p. 12.

[27]Gross, "What Is a Bipartisan Foreign Policy?" *Department of State Bulletin*, XXI (October 3, 1949), 504–5. The two most important studies of bipartisan foreign policy in and after World War II are Westerfield, *Foreign Policy and Party Politics*, and Cecil V. Crabb, Jr., *Bipartisan Foreign Policy: Myth or Reality?* (Evanston, Ill.: Row, Peterson, 1957).

[28]Westerfield, *Foreign Policy and Party Politics*, pp. 12–13.

on America's conduct of relations with Western allies. "Republicans have never been consulted in advance of decisions," Senator Hickenlooper said. "If you have no voice in or consultation about foreign policy you certainly are not bound to accept the Administration policy, particularly if you don't follow it." Only one instance could he recall, and that about a year and a half earlier, in which Republicans were consulted by the Kennedy Administration before a decision was made, and then "the decision was put out an hour after we left." [29]

Even where there is no quarrel about the adequacy of consultation and the extent to which opposition preferences have found a place in the administration's policy, there is, in the absence of party discipline, no way for Congressional leaders to assure that party members will support the President's policies with their votes. Westerfield was led by the absence of the conditions necessary for a bipartisan foreign policy to discard the adjective and substitute for it the term "extrapartisan." [30] It has aptly been said that the art of conducting such a foreign policy is to get the number of "Vandenbergs" to support the President that will permit him to say that the "Tafts" do not speak for their party.[31] If the President is to gain acceptance of his policy, foreign or domestic, he must make an appeal that extends beyond his own party. In domestic affairs, he will try to mobilize special interests and, at the same time, emphasize what the public interest requires. In foreign policy, he will seek to build cooperation between parties and to increase support for his measures by pointing to the dangers of disunity and dramatizing the national interest. Extrapartisan procedures must apply, with the American system of undisciplined parties, to domestic as well as to foreign policy. Westerfield is entirely right, so long as the focus is on Congress, to discard the term bipartisan.[32]

In the United States, where dissent is expressed by legislators who have the power to deny the President his program, a bipartisan policy is at once wanted and impossible to achieve fully. In Britain, where by virtue of party discipline a bipartisan policy is possible, the conditions that make it possible also mean that it is not needed. Either party in power can expect to carry its policy unaided by the other. A simple illustration

[29]"GOP Denies Any Role in U.S. Policy," *Washington Post*, February 27, 1963, p. 1.

[30]Westerfield, *Foreign Policy and Party Politics*, p. 16.

[31]Willmoore Kendall, "Bipartisanship and Majority-Rule Democracy," *American Perspective*, IV (Spring, 1950), 155.

[32]Bearing the necessary qualifications in mind, we have used the more familiar term, which is serviceable when discussing both the United States and England.

of the proposition is provided by the attack against Egypt launched by Eden's government in October and November of 1956. The government of any modern state is able to act on its own decision in a moment of crisis. The Suez adventure is, however, an instance of action being taken in the face of opposition expressed by the Labour Party over a period of weeks and despite deep doubts on the part of some Conservative Members. In a policy that unfolded still more slowly—Britain's negotiation for entry to Europe—the government of the day was able to pursue its policy despite the growing opposition of Labour and the skepticism of some of the government's own supporters. Under such circumstances, the hand of an American government would surely be stayed. Without the support of a fair number of Congressmen from the party out of power, many important measures of foreign policy would fail of acceptance.

Still, Britain is sometimes described as par excellence the country of bipartisan foreign policy, perhaps because of a failure to distinguish between bipartisanship as an aspiration to national unity and the use of the term to describe the political means of reaching the goal. Since British foreign policy does not depend on securing the support of opposition Members, bipartisan techniques need not be developed. In peacetime, they have not been widely and consistently used. On major matters of defense and foreign policy, the principal Ministers do frequently offer opposition leaders access to information that has not been made public. Leaders of the opposition, however, are wary of entering upon consultations lest their critical fangs be drawn by close association with the government's policy. Asking leading members of the minority party to undertake important foreign-policy tasks and appointing them to high public office, which in the United States are principal ways of securing support for policy from competing parties, are devices seldom employed in England.[33]

The absence of bipartisan practices has not produced a discontinuity of policy. In England as in America, most of the foreign-policy differences of the 1930's were submerged during the war. Ernest Bevin, in his first speech to the House as Foreign Secretary, was able to say that "the basis of our policy is in keeping with that worked out by the Coalition Government."[34] Much of the new-found unity has endured, buttressed by the pressures of electoral competition for office (soon to be discussed) and by other factors as well. One of them is the leaders' sense of responsibility, another their patriotism, still another the fact that the range of

[33]See Chapter 6, below.
[34]*H.C. Deb.*, Vol. 413 (August 20, 1945), col. 287.

choices likely to strike leaders of any party as being appropriate is limited. Near the end of his career as Foreign Minister, Bevin remarked almost with surprise that when dealing with other Western nations at an international conference "one almost forgets what party one belongs to." [35] World conditions, geographic situation, national traditions, economic and military capabilities: all of these have contributed to the similarity of positions taken by responsible political leaders on questions of foreign policy. More frequently than their followers, the official leaders of parties in Britain have been in basic agreement on foreign policy. To appear to be part of a bipartisan front has helped leaders of the opposition party to establish or maintain their national reputations for soundness, ability, and wisdom. When out of office after World War II, Winston Churchill adroitly gave the impression that his was still the guiding spirit of British policy. In presiding over a Primrose League demonstration at the Albert Hall, for example, he averred that Britain's socialist government had in the main adopted his ideas on European and international affairs, though so haltingly and clumsily that much of the advantage of doing so was lost.[36]

Whether in office or in opposition, Labour's leaders have frequently been unable to maintain a fully united front for a foreign policy that in general both parties subscribe to. On the Palestine question and on conscription in the later 1940's, on the question of Britain's proper attitude toward Communist states, on the matter of supporting German rearmament, on nuclear arms and participation in the North Atlantic Treaty Organization (NATO), large numbers, occasionally running in the seventies, have refrained from voting with their party in divisions on motions. While intraparty differences have flourished, cross-party agreement has more often remained firm. Still, important differences between parties have sometimes existed; and while policies can be carried without bipartisan procedures, one may still believe that steps to insure agreement between parties on the broad outlines of policy are required in order to decrease the chances that the policies of one government will be undone should the other party come to power.

The Distance between Parties

In the United States, it is important to maintain a bipartisan front on essential elements of the country's foreign policy in order to gather sup-

[35]*H.C. Deb.*, Vol. 475 (May 24, 1950), col. 2091.
[36]*Times* (London), April 29, 1950.

port for specific measures. In both countries, bipartisanship has been looked upon as a way of assuring the continuity of policies. How will the prospect of maintaining a bipartisan front be affected by the competition of parties?

One may imagine two parties, each with a real chance of gaining control of the government, standing for sharply different policies internally or externally. It is then difficult to identify domestic political forces that will cause them to come together on a broadly similar policy. Bipartisan procedures, which involve the conveying of information, the habit of consultation, and the attempt to associate the leaders of the opposition party with the government's policy, may well narrow an already small gap or hasten the closing of a slightly larger one. Can they do so if the opposition finds a large measure of support for a policy contrary to the government's? If that support approaches in size one half of the electorate, there is a limit to what technique can accomplish. In order to know whether or not a bipartisan policy can be maintained, one has to look outside of the legislative assembly in which parties confront each other and beyond the procedural requirements for conducting a bipartisan policy.

In the 1930's the Conservative and Labour Parties were worlds apart. A short list of differences might well read as follows, with the Conservative position put first in each entry: Empire and nation above international cooperation; British arms in preference to collective security; an economy based on individual incentive and private property rather than planning and nationalization. Such a drawing of contrasts is roughly accurate. If the differences indicated were real, they were clearly important. The gulf that opened between parties led some—not merely Harold Laski and Stafford Cripps but R. H. Tawney as well—to believe that the electoral success of Labour would provoke desperate resistance and perhaps bring violence in its wake.[37] Such fears resulted in part from contemplation of Fascist revolutions abroad. They also reflected a political perception at once keen and distorted. If parties differ widely and if a party newly come to power should move radically to tear up the fabric of society and sew it anew, violence is likely to appear as the partner of change. The measures of the Labour Governments of 1945 to 1951 did not produce the reaction that some had earlier expected. Many plausible explanations can be given: the sobering effects of office, to which Labour

[37] See Ralph Miliband, *Parliamentary Socialism: A Study in the Politics of Labour* (London: Allen & Unwin, 1961), pp. 197–99; Hugh Dalton, *The Fateful Years: Memoirs, 1931–1945* (London: Muller, 1957), pp. 41–43.

leaders who held positions in the wartime Coalition Government had already been subjected; the caution that comes from experiencing the difficulty of initiating change and attempting to control it in a complex society and economy; the impossibility of a single country shaping the world to its taste. Depression and war had increased the receptivity to change; changes came more slowly and were less far-reaching than some had expected. In consequence, major resistance did not develop.

Office may sober, and circumstances may impose some common qualities upon the reactions of different governments; but neither effect will permit us to say that methods and objectives will be continuous from one government to the next. Consensus is fragile if it rests on the sobering effects of office and the narrowness of the range of choice, for sober men may come to widely different conclusions, and choosing differently, even within a limited range, may be quite important.

One may then be led to wonder whether the differences between British parties were as large as they often seemed to be in the early 1930's. In an important political sense they were not. On the one hand, many of those who supported the Labour Party did believe that the Conservative Government was wholly bad, that a Labour Government would be clearly good, that much would be done by the latter in a radically new way. But the Labour Party of the early 1930's never came to power; the party that did come to power in 1945 was a noticeably different one. About two-thirds of the Labour Members elected in 1945 were new to the House. The party, supported by almost half of the voters of the United Kingdom, held 65 percent of the seats in Commons. No longer a splinter in the body politic, the party represented by the votes it received approximately half of a nation; by its policy, all of it. Having won for the first time the opportunity to form a majority government, party leaders in Parliament would want to win again. To do so, attention had to be paid to the sums that result from doing one's electoral arithmetic. Preferences for one set of policies over another mingled with different notions about the behavior that would bring electoral victories. In complex ways, which we shall now consider, the extent of differences or the degree of similarity between parties is thus decided.

Party Competition and the Similarity of Parties

More than a generation ago, Harold Hotelling demonstrated that the independent actions of two competing firms may produce a stable equilibrium. Hotelling's analysis accounted for the tendency of sellers to locate their businesses near to each other. He also suggested that it would explain the "homogeneous" quality of, among others, cider, furniture, churches, and political parties.[38] The theory is elegantly suggestive but necessarily elliptic. It is best to summarize it first in the beauty of its simplicity and then consider some countervailing complications. If two lemonade stands are located so close to each other that they compete for the same customers, one may wonder what kind of lemonade each of them will sell. We can assume that while each is free to vary the ingredients, which are equal in cost, both are limited to offering a single mixture. Will one offer a sickeningly sweet drink, the other a severely sour one? They will not if they wish to take in the maximum number of twenty-five-cent pieces. One seller can capture quarters from all the lovers of sour lemonade by increasing the proportion of lemon juice to sugar in his product. In doing so, he will permit the other to take over the larger portion of the market. Competition and the desire to increase profits push one purveyor to offer a lemonade that is much like that of the other.

The problems of parties striving to secure the election of their candidates are similar to those of firms seeking to increase their profits. The similarity has been impressively demonstrated by Frank H. Knight, Arthur Smithies, and Joseph A. Schumpeter, who have followed in Hotelling's footsteps. Anthony Downs has given the theory, applied to competing parties, its most complete development.[39] To turn the example from economics to politics, one simply reads votes for quarters and translates lemon juice and sugar as candidate's personality and party policy. Parties market a policy-personality commodity. They are paid for it in votes, which like pounds or dollars in the economy are the counters by which the score is kept and success accorded or failure meted out. The Detroit manufacturer who is asked, "What are you trying to make, automobiles?" might appropriately reply, "No, money." Manufacturing automobiles is merely the means to a profit. So the politician when asked, "What are you trying to do, get Social Security improved or NATO revamped?" might well reply, "No, I just want to get elected." Politicians

---

[38]Hotelling, "Stability in Competition," *Economic Journal*, XXXIX (March, 1929), 41–57.

[39]Knight, *The Ethics of Competition and Other Essays* (2d ed.; London: Allen & Unwin, 1936); Smithies, "Optimum Location in Spatial Competition," *Journal of Political Economy*, XLIX (1941), 423–39; Schumpeter, *Capitalism, Socialism, and Democracy* (3d ed.; New York: Harper, 1950), chaps. XXII, XXIII; Downs, *An Economic Theory of Democracy* (New York: Harper, 1957). Cf. E. E. Schattschneider — whose brilliant and incisive analysis, though different in method, is essentially the same as that of Anthony Downs — *Party Government* (New York: Farrar & Rinehart, 1942), pp. 85–93.

and parties seek office, and policies are a means to their goal.[40] Party leaders will, if they can, select the candidates and espouse the policies that promise to bring the largest return in votes. What could be more democratic? It would not behoove the Detroit or Luton industrialist to say, "I'll decrease my production and also encourage my competitors to do so, for automobiles are destroying our cities, and other modes of transportation should be more heavily used." We would not want to leave that decision to him and his friends even if we happen to agree with his conclusion. Of parties and politicians, one may say that they exist to offer a choice after first trying to figure out what the public will find congenial. In seeking the strategy that will bring victory, the politician acts in his own interest and also fills democracy's needs. "I would rather be right than be President" is a profoundly anti-democratic statement, betraying, as it does, enough hubris to have merited exile from any flourishing democracy of antique Greece.

If the preferences of voters cluster in the center with numbers dwindling as one moves toward either extreme, then the politics of a country will be stable and its policies moderate. If there are two parties in contention, they will be highly similar. Either that or one of them will have left the popular middle ground to its rival, while itself catering to small numbers of voters at one extreme or the other.[41] Illustration of the theory is provided in one way by Goldwater's decisive defeat in the 1964 Presidential election, an aberration in American politics, for not since 1900 had the major parties been so widely separated. Illustration is provided in another way by Wilson's and Home's snuggling together on policy preceding the general election of 1964. The fourteenth Earl suddenly emerged as a devotee of science and a warm admirer of modern technology. The Labour Party's leader, long regarded as leaning steeply leftward, carefully defined socialism out of existence and patriotically proclaimed the role that is Britain's "to play east of Suez."[42]

---

[40]Cf. Schumpeter, who records as follows a "saying attributed to one of the most successful politicians that ever lived: 'What businessmen do not understand is that exactly as they are dealing in oil so I am dealing in votes.' " *Capitalism, Socialism, and Democracy*, p. 285. For "oil," to be precise, one should read "pounds."

[41]Another possibility should be mentioned, though it is scarcely relevant to worries about continuity of policy. The vote in an area may traditionally go to one party, with the competing party standing for similar policies and yet receiving only a small percentage of the vote. See Samuel P. Huntington, "A Revised Theory of American Political Parties," *American Political Science Review*, XLIV (September, 1950), 675–76.

[42]"Socialism," according to Wilson, "means applying a sense of purpose to our national life: economic purpose, social purpose, moral purpose. Purpose means technical skill — be it the skill of a manager, a designer, a craftsman, an architect, an engineer, a nuclear physicist, or a doctor, a nurse, a social worker. But this is not to equate, as our opponents affect to do, Socialism

Where institutional arrangements tend to shape the electorate and then to divide it in two, there are pressures toward a corresponding distribution of opinion. If the political and electoral systems make it difficult for a third party to appear, or to survive, or to grow to a politically effective size, the two major parties are constrained to broaden their appeals and to attempt to cover between them most of the range of opinion held by important numbers of voters. Failure to do so will give a third party the chance to wedge itself in between its two larger competitors. The very success of the third party will almost surely stimulate either or both of the others to make more effective electoral appeals.

The policy positions of two competing parties begin to approach one another, and the candidates even begin to look and talk very much alike. Each party must, if it would win, combine in one package a selection of appealing issues and a description of policies bearing upon them: thus the emphasis on peace, prosperity, or whatever; the claims to greater effectiveness; the search for attractive candidates. Several dimensions are involved. Parties and politicians, in any given contest, must try to squeeze the many dimensions into one, especially so in England, where the voter chooses a single man and in doing so indirectly makes his contribution to the selecting of a governing party and a Prime Minister. In America, of course, different worries and desires can be expressed in voting for President and Congressmen.

The Condition of Parties and the Perceptions and Aims of Politicians

From the economic theory of democracy, it follows that, under the conditions specified, parties will tend to be similar, with a placid life for the nation assured by the resultant continuity of policy. But the predicted result is frequently not realized. Parties at times drift erratically apart, and some politicians deliberately or inadvertently act so as to widen the distance between themselves and their rivals. How do they happen to do so?

If most people want a government-owned steel industry, then both parties would be expected to offer it to them. In such a view, the problems of forming a party's policy are merely tactical. If politicians have

with technocracy. The essential leavening which Socialism brings to the industrial revolution of our age, is the leavening of humanity, which was so clearly absent from Britain's first industrial revolution." *Purpose in Politics* (Boston: Houghton Mifflin, 1964), p. vii. On Britain's role abroad, see *ibid.*, pp. xii, 215.

erred in making their calculations or have been slow to see what victory requires them to do, parties will display differences that the leaders of the losing party will regret. A party, moreover, cannot change policies as an actor changes costumes, without gaining thereby a damaging reputation for inconstancy. Adjustment of the policies of parties will always involve uncertainty and friction, yet the criteria by which adjustments of policy should be made are clear. Because of imperfect knowledge and skill and the frictions encountered, parties will be noticeably different, while each seeks to please the public. A sufficient choice is thus provided to fulfill the democratic requirement that alternatives be present, which the voters may weigh if they wish to.

Party competition leads to similarity of the policies for which parties stand, but factors internal to parties and characteristic of man's nature may as easily pull them apart. In the Labour Party in England and the Republican Party in the United States, politicians in abundance commit themselves to policies whether or not they seem to be popular, while in the Democratic and Conservative Parties greater numbers are impressed by electoral necessities. Political amateurs with conviction populate the Republican and Labour Parties; they are opposed in the Democratic and Conservative Parties by men skilled in the profession of politics. In part the difference is related to the electoral history of parties. Winning has not led to losing but to more winning for the Democratic and Conservative Parties. For the Republican and Labour Parties, the experience of losing has frequently been repeated.

Winning, which brings power, supposedly corrupts and, according to a common notion, saddles the governing party with embarrassing responsibility.[43] The opposition party, panting for power, stands ready to take over the governmental machinery after exposing the errors, follies, and chicanery of those who have been running it. Losing is a sobering experience, so the story goes, from which the party should learn its electoral lesson. Instead the loss of an election may engender feuds that sap the party's energy and by the spectacle presented to the public lessen its electoral appeal. Losing an election may indicate to political leaders how they should alter the party's appearance, but defeat may so weaken their hold on the party that it becomes difficult for them to follow the electoral imperative. Losing may then widen the distance between parties and lead to losing again.

[43]For a recent statement of this old thesis, see Angus Campbell, *et al., The American Voter* (New York: Wiley, 1960), p. 554.

The lemonade theory of politics explains electoral results, but it does not cover the full range of political motives. As the electoral lessons become clearer with successive defeats, they become more difficult to learn; for the attention of some of the "students" has drifted to other subjects. Unilateral disarmers and old-line socialists, for example, long pushed their programs at the price of debilitating party quarrels, for if their preferred policies did not prevail, the party's victory would in their eyes lack satisfying substance. Extremists of left or of right are not easily persuaded that party loyalty is a virtue; in their view, the loyalty of members to parties that are highly similar turns politics into a game whose outcome is a matter of indifference to society. Why should one behave in a way that increases the chances that the better party will win, when the policies of both parties are thought to be so unsatisfactory? Thus J. B. Priestley opposed the idea of the Labour Party being simply "an election-winning machine" and wished instead for a "radical Labour Party" that would refuse "any compromise with the Establishment." He added that if the party followed his advice, it "would undoubtedly lose the next election." Paul Johnson, who later became editor of the *New Statesman*, described the choice of the Labour Party as lying between "becoming a party of government, concerned primarily with administering a social structure to which it has become reconciled, or attempting to change the structure. I believe," he concluded, "it must and will choose the second, even though this involves a retreat into the political wilderness." Such statements provide clear illustrations of the politics of conviction or, one might say, the politics of the apolitical.[44]

The imperatives of political competition may conflict with the imperatives of party management. Without the prospect of victory, nobility of cause and purity of doctrine become the means by which followers are gained and kept steadfast. "The conviction of socialist righteousness in a decadent capitalist society" kept some Labour members loyal or at least held them within the party in long years of electoral adversity. The late Aneurin Bevan once wrote that so severe are the buffetings of politics and so many the disappointments the politician experiences that few, if any, can endure the political wars without the faith that in their ideology or in their most cherished proposals lie the answers to the country's ills.[45] It is

---

[44]Priestley, "Radical Temper," *New Statesman*, LVIII (August 29, 1959), 240–42; Johnson, "A Sense of Outrage," in Norman MacKenzie, ed., *Conviction* (London: MacGibbon & Kee, 1958), p. 217. Cf. R. H. S. Crossman, *Labour in the Affluent Society* (Fabian Tract 325 [London: Fabian Society, 1959]).

[45]Bevan, *In Place of Fear* (London: Heinemann, 1952), p. 96.

ironic that the most socialist of British democrats are the first to condemn the party or politician who supports a policy with the argument that this is what people actually want and are quickest to argue that some in the Labour Party know better than the voter what is best for him and the country. The Republican Party in like fashion has among its members an unreconstructed group that espoused such policies as the right-to-work laws in the elections of 1958, which they knew to be right while others knew them to be unpopular.

While losing is a punishment that in some ways encourages learning, it may also cause the party to become less competent and alert. A repetition of losses makes the party less attractive to those who would pursue a political career. Those who would act rather than merely orate, who would mold the best policy that men can agree upon rather than disdain any progress that falls short of ideal, are naturally drawn to the party that has formed the governments of their country during most of their lifetimes. Practice makes political professionals of those who have won for a long enough time. The party that repeatedly loses becomes heavily populated with passionate amateurs for whom ideological commitment ranks higher than ambition for office. More often than their rivals in the present generation, the Labour and Republican Parties have appeared as programmatic parties that would coincidentally like to win office. The Conservative and Democratic Parties, more deeply devoted to the project of perpetuating their control of government, have also responded more sensitively to popular opinion. Interparty and intraparty factors must often be represented by vectors of opposite tendency.

Those who perch at the extreme right or left of the political spectrum seek a change in the quality of response to domestic and international problems of which they have grown impatient. The distinction between the center and the extremes is found in the difference between reacting to a situation and wishing to act to change it. The extremes forget what is known at the center, that small changes may bring into being a noticeably different world with the passage of time, a thought clear in our minds now that exponential growth has been discovered to be so delightful, as applied to economic development in some parts of the world, and so distressing applied to population growth elsewhere. But, while the extremes forget what is known at the center, the center may know hardly anything at all. Those who represent the "vital center" of political life, searching for a common denominator, may be capable only of finding the one that is lowest and thus come to represent a deadly middle way. The policies of the stable American and British democracies may maintain an impressive continuity while immense changes take place in the world. That changes in policy gradually produced by domestic conflicts of interest and competition of political parties should carry the country at a speed that keeps pace with changing conditions is far from assured. One may do a little *better* each day until finally he does *well*, but it may be necessary in setting an appropriate direction of activity to have some notion of *best*.

A politician whose warmest desire is for his own and his party's advancement may be described as pandering to the people's whims and slavishly conforming to their greeds and lusts. It is more inspiring to think of political figures as seeking to lead their people to a greater accomplishment by showing them a grander vision. That such a motivation characterizes some politicians and is useful within a democratic polity makes it important in the theory and practice of democracy. Some politicians and pundits will always disdain victory if to achieve it they would have to modify or abandon the policies they cherish. By persevering propaganda or educational campaigns, they would bring the people to accept the truth that some political leaders think they already see. Still, it is difficult to provide leadership while losing elections. To win them, appeal should ordinarily be made to voters where they exist in the largest numbers. Thus Iain Macleod, expressing his dismay at Lord Home's being selected to become party leader and Prime Minister, dwelt upon the importance of a politician having "drawing power in the crucial central area of politics." [46] If there is a broad agreement on domestic and foreign policies and the national consensus promises to be stable, those who would compete by making their party different doom it to defeat and political impotence.

In Britain, views are formed and compressed to fit for the most part within the two parties; in the United States, policy views sprawl across them. The contrast between the two nations can be graphically represented by two pairs of intersecting curves as shown in the accompanying figure. (The curves give an impression of the distribution of opinion within parties; they do not depict the comparative political orientations of the two countries.)

The competition of two parties turns the more or less bell-shaped curve of national opinion into the curves for the parties that the drawings depict. The majority of the electorate, located in the middle, divides be-

---

[46]Macleod, "The Tory Leadership," *Spectator*, No. 7073 (January 17, 1964), p. 65.

FIGURE 1 DISTRIBUTION OF OPINION WITHIN THE LEGISLATIVE PARTIES

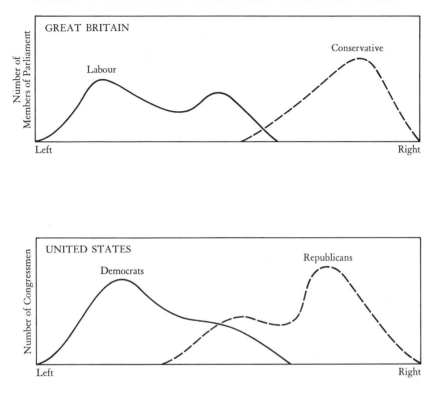

tween the two parties, each of which then finds its largest number of supporters a little to the left or the right.

In Britain, there is an overlap of views and commitments in the small
area where the two lines cross in the middle. In the United States, the
greater interpenetration of parties blurs the difference between them,
which is discovered only by finding their distinct centers of gravity.[47] In
Britain, while Labour Party members pull leftward or Conservative members gently tug in the opposite direction, leaders with an eye on the
voters mill around in the center. The journalist Henry Fairlie has cautioned Labour to guard against the tragic destiny of becoming a copy of
the American Democratic Party, which is reasonable advice from a man
who has supported their opponents.[48] The Democrats have won and won

[47]Cf. David B. Truman, *The Congressional Party: A Case Study* (New York: Wiley, 1959);
and David Butler, "The Paradox of Party Difference," *American Behavioral Scientist*, IV
(November, 1960), 4.

[48]Fairlie, "Inside Politics," *Daily Mail* (London), May 2, 1960, p. 6.

again and in doing so have had more of a hand in shaping American society than Labour has had in Britain's. But what impresses Fairlie and others is the supposed absence of difference between American parties, which denies the voters a choice. They have looked at American politics through British-made spectacles and then drawn comparisons with a British pattern that does not exist. As the term "Butskellism" suggests, it was in the later 1950's more difficult to find differences between, say, Macmillan, Butler, Macleod, and Maudling, on the one hand, and Gait-skell, Brown, Healey, and Callaghan, on the other, than between comparable sets of American leaders. If one goes to party conferences, reads the *Tribune*, the *New Statesman*, and the *New Left Review* or *Cross Bow*, the *Spectator*, and the *Daily* or *Sunday Telegraph*, he may conclude that British parties are more widely separated than their American counterparts. From looking at leaders in Parliament and at the policies they have followed, a different conclusion emerges. The content of bipartisanship in England can fairly be described as a sometimes uneasy yet ordinarily durable agreement among leaders of parties on the main lines and principal elements of Britain's foreign policy, with the rank and file of both parties most often pulling in opposite directions. Attlee's epistolary advice to the militant and left-leaning Harold Laski nicely illustrates the point. "Whether the postwar Government is Conservative or Labour," Attlee cautioned Laski in May of 1944, "it will inevitably have to work a mixed economy. If it is a Labour Government it will be a mixed economy developing towards Socialism. If a Conservative Government it will be an economy seeking to retain as much as possible of private enterprise. But both governments will have to work with the world and the country as it exists. There are limits to the extent to which the clock can be put forward or back." [49]

If one asks whether the differences between parties are greater in America or in Britain, no generally valid answer is possible. In most of the years since the war, American parties have looked more nearly alike than their British counterparts, but this is at least partly because in America the customary behavior of parties and the mixed pattern of Congressional voting obscure important differences while the discipline of parties in England causes even minor differences to stand out. In 1964, a year of national elections for both countries, the distance between parties was greater in the United States than in England. In the 1930's, the voters of

[49]Quoted in Kingsley Martin, *Harold Laski (1893–1950): A Biographical Memoir* (New York: Viking, 1953), p. 151.

both countries were confronted with a choice between parties standing for markedly different policies. In the years between national elections, the differences between parties are accentuated. In competing for votes in a national election, parties most often draw closely together. Even so, differences are always detectable. In Britain, the Labour Party is institutionally associated with the trade-union movement, and the majority of the poor have long noticed that Labour is more deeply committed to welfare programs than are the Conservatives. A Labour Government, more eagerly and gracefully than a Conservative Government would have done, began to divest the country of Empire; and Labourites embrace the United Nations with more warmth than Tories generally do. In the United States, lower-income groups and organized labor have noticed, and by quite consistent majorities have cast their votes accordingly, that a Democratic Administration will be more reluctant to regulate unions, will spend more money and spend it faster in order to get out of a depression, will run a deficit more cheerfully, will be quicker to support public health measures, to build houses, and to support other welfare programs than the Republican Party will be. In foreign affairs in this century, the Democrats have been the party of bold designs and have developed a deeper commitment to the multinational arrangements that the party's leaders have fashioned.

Reflections on Bipartisan Foreign Policy

Some of the worries about abrupt shifts in policy as parties change places can now be brought into perspective, and evaluations can be made of the importance or unimportance, the good or bad effects of bipartisan procedures and practices. Bradford Westerfield, in his work on American political parties and foreign policy, expressed the delicate hope for a little more party discipline in the future so that the behavior of the Congressional parties may more readily be controlled. He refrained from wishing for parties disciplined in the British manner, in the belief that such a solution would carry greater costs than benefits. He feared that with fully disciplined parties the national electorate would be offered a choice between "sharply contrasting partisan policies" and this "would seriously endanger the international position of the United States." [50] At this point, doubts arise and cast their shadows over much that has been written both

---

[50]Westerfield, *Foreign Policy and Party Politics*, pp. 6–7.

praising and condemning bipartisan practices in the realm of foreign policy.

If major parties in close contention for office can be expected to adopt similar policies, the bipartisan prescription has been written for a disease that the body politic is not afflicted with. In every election since the end of the war, each of the two major parties of Britain has commanded the vote of nearly one half of the nation. They cannot, as Winston Churchill urged members of the Conservative Party following the Conference of 1954, stand for drastically opposed policies or even be so very much different.[51] They cannot, he might have added, unless the country is to be poised always at the brink of civic violence. The appeals to Britons to respond as one nation, frequently made by Disraeli and Churchill himself, by Eden and Macmillan, are themselves evidence of awareness that two nations exist, that there is indeed a gulf to be bridged. The bridge has been provided by the habit of deference, lingering from an aristocratic past, which has been coupled with a sense of paternal duty. The gulf has been narrowed by the moderation that the political and party system has helped to produce.

The pressures of a bipolar party system encourage accommodation when party leaders seek to forge a majority coalition of voters. If national opinion is distributed according to the pattern of a bell-shaped curve, worries about the continuity of policy are small. Many forces combine to produce the result, though their efficacy is never assured. Among them, bipartisan practices have been of some importance, especially in the United States. Bipartisan procedures helped first to draw politicians of the minority party into association with the new foreign policy of the country and permitted them to support it without disloyalty to their own party. With a new line of foreign policy fully established, bipartisan practices have helped to make possible the continuation of party politics during an extended period of crisis. Willmoore Kendall and James Mac-Gregor Burns, devoted to the British political form, have deplored American bipartisan practices as blurring responsibility and deadening debate.[52] Parliamentary government supposedly sharpens the cleavage between the ins and the outs and focuses responsibility upon the majority party. Government by one party is thought of as being normal, yet in thirty-one of the years since 1895, Britain has at least technically been governed by a

---

[51]National Union of Conservative and Unionist Associations, *Report of the 74th Annual Conference*, October 7 to October 9, 1954, Blackpool (London, 1954), p. 114.

[52]Kendall, "Bipartisanship and Majority-Rule Democracy," pp. 146–56; Burns, "Bipartisanship and the Weakness of the Party System," *American Perspective*, IV (Spring, 1950), 169–74.

combination of parties.[53] Party responsibility is either completely realized or it is largely obscured, with the opposition function then being performed by a group within a party or a small party that stays out of the coalition. In America, with parties undisciplined, critics of the government abound. A constant problem of American politics is to tame the critics and pull them toward support of a program. Bipartisan procedures contribute to the result while allowing everyone to be critical and also permitting members of the party that has not won the Presidency to serve in executive positions.

When the distance between parties grows wider, concern for the continuity of policy abounds. Bipartisan procedures would then be welcome if only they could narrow the gap. But the gap exists because those in control of one party believe on intellectual grounds that an alternative policy is desirable and have persuaded themselves that with an alternative policy they can win. Asking for a united front in policy then amounts to saying to the leaders of one party, "Give up both the policies in which you believe and your chance for electoral victory." We come back to a statement made earlier: bipartisan procedures are useful only when they are not crucially needed, that is, when the leaders of parties are already in broad agreement on policy.

[53]Byrum E. Carter, *The Office of Prime Minister* (Princeton: Princeton University Press, 1956), p. 177.

Chapter 5

NATIONAL LEGISLATURES
AND
CHIEF EXECUTIVES

We can now trace some implications of the propositions made in Chapter 3. There, more emphasis was placed on Prime Minister and Parliament than on President and Congress. In considering the daily performance of governmental tasks, this emphasis will be reversed. Congress, more troublesome than Parliament, is also politically more important; and outwardly at least the political life of the President is more difficult than the Prime Minister's.

Congress and Foreign Policy

In the history of the United States, fewer than ten treaties have been defeated because of the rule requiring approval by two thirds of the Senators present. Other treaties that were lost were unaffected by the rule, for they received less than a simple majority anyway.[1] Since the narrow rejection of the Versailles Treaty that contained the League Covenant as an integral part, no major treaty has been lost in the Senate. But then, between the two wars, none came before it. The importance of the two-thirds rule as a barrier to international actions a President may wish to

[1]Dexter Perkins says that a total of four treaties have been lost because of the rule. *The American Approach to Foreign Policy* (Stockholm: Almqvist & Wiksells, 1951), pp. 155–56. Royden J. Dangerfield finds seven treaties defeated in this way up to 1928, to which must be added the defeat in 1935 of the Protocol by which the United States would have become a member of the Permanent Court of International Justice, which was defeated by 52 votes for and 36 against. *In Defense of the Senate: A Study in Treaty Making* (Norman: University of Oklahoma Press, 1933), pp. 311–12. For the period since World War II, see David Nelson Farnsworth, *The Senate Committee on Foreign Relations* (Urbana: University of Illinois Press, 1961), chap. 4.

take cannot be measured simply by the number of treaties that have failed. Some failures were spectacular and have been thought to be highly damaging to the United States and to the world. Because of the two-thirds rule, the President may refrain from negotiating treaties he would otherwise try to conclude, or he may attempt to tailor to the Senatorial temper those that he does submit for approval. At the turn of the century, Secretary of State John Hay, his difficulties over Senatorial passage of a peace treaty with Spain in mind, once exclaimed:

> A treaty of peace, in any normal state of things ought to be ratified with unanimity in twenty-four hours. They wasted six weeks in wrangling over this one, and ratified it with one vote to spare. We have five or six matters now demanding settlement. I can settle them all, honorably and advantageously to our own side; and I am assured by leading men in the Senate that not one of these treaties, if negotiated, will pass the Senate. I should have a majority in every case, but a malcontent third would certainly dish every one of them. To such monstrous shape has the original mistake of the Constitution grown in the evolution of our politics. You must understand, it is not merely *my* solution the Senate will reject. They will reject, for instance, any treaty, whatever, on any subject, with England. I doubt if they would accept any treaty of consequence with Russia or Germany. The recalcitrant third would be differently composed, but it would be on hand.[2]

Do such experiences, or the more memorable rejection of the League of Nations Covenant, demonstrate that the two-thirds rule is a bad one? Treaties become the supreme law of the land and, because they do so, require more than a simple majority of a single chamber. Yet treaties are made with other sovereign states and thus do not easily lend themselves to the devices appropriate to domestic legislation. Hamilton described the treaty provision as "one of the best digested and most unexceptionable parts" of the entire Constitution.[3] Nonetheless, it has from time to time been suggested that an ordinary majority of both Houses would be preferable to requiring two-thirds approval by the Senate. To change the rule by amending the Constitution would, however, be of little consequence; for by using executive agreements or concurrent resolutions and simple legislation, if Congress is willing, the President can accomplish most of his foreign-policy desires.

[2]Quoted in Henry Adams, *The Education of Henry Adams* (New York: Random House, 1931), p. 374.

[3]Alexander Hamilton, John Jay, and James Madison, "The Federalist No. 75," *The Federalist: A Commentary on the Constitution of the United States* (New York: Random House, 1937), p. 485.

The treaty rule is relevant then in two cases. The first of them causes no domestic trouble at all. It is the regulation of the routine relations between the United States and others, as is done by the many friendship, commerce, and navigation treaties, according to which international business is daily conducted. The other is the exceptional act of policy, which may be new, expensive, dangerous, or large in importance and which may have implications that extend over a number of years. In such matters, the President and State Department must consider the temper of the Senate and the mood of the country, prepare the way by exhortation and education, seek to change opinion if possible, and amend or add provisions to the clauses of treaties if necessary. It is sometimes said that only a few still worry about the restriction upon the power to conclude treaties, and that among those few are the President, officials of the State Department, and other executive officers concerned with foreign affairs. The habit of American government is first to exaggerate the obstacles to movement and then to work furiously to surmount them. This is known colloquially as "running scared," which is a healthfully invigorating exercise. It may well be that such measures as the Atlantic Defense Treaty and the Test Ban were won by such handsome margins (82 to 13 and 80 to 19) in part because Presidents Truman and Kennedy acted as though they might possibly not be approved at all. The wide margins by which they passed helped to establish the solidity of the American commitment.

The Atlantic Defense Treaty, for example, was made in accordance with the Vandenberg Resolution, which had been worked out in conferences among Marshall and Lovett of the State Department and Vandenberg and Connally of the Senate, with the occasional participation of John Foster Dulles. It was submitted to the Senate on April 12, 1949, debated on the floor on July 5, and finally passed on July 21. The delay was inconvenient; many of the statements made in the debate and during committee hearings were an embarrassment to American diplomacy. As one of many examples, consider the following discourse:

MR. CONNALLY. Regarding the inquiry propounded by the Senator from California [Knowland], of course we are interested in the peace of the world. But that does not mean that we shall blindfold ourselves and make a commitment now to enter every war that may occur in the next 10 years, and send our boys and resources to Europe to fight.

MR. DONNELL. I am glad to hear the Senator say that.

MR. CONNALLY. That is the view some people seem to take of the whole situation. The nations in Europe are not fighting now. All the outrages

98

which have been committed seem to be tolerated by the people of the countries involved. I do not approve of them, of course. But I do not believe in giving carte blanche assurance to these people, "Do everything you want to do, you need not worry, as soon as anything happens, we will come over and fight your quarrel for you. In the meantime you may have a good time, and bask in the sunshine of leadership which you do not deserve."[4]

Such statements must awaken some doubts abroad, even among those who know that they should be discounted. The words in themselves are harsh, and Connally was at the time the Chairman of the Senate Foreign Relations Committee. Because of the opposition of some Senators and the doubts entertained by Robert A. Taft, who in the end voted against the Treaty anyway, the language of the Treaty was weakened. An attack against one member was still defined as "an attack against them all," but now it was added: to be met by such action as each state "deems necessary."[5] The Treaty finally gained acceptance by a vote of 82 to 13. If the long process of examination and approval was a spectacle, it was at least an edifying one. Anyone who cared could learn much about the Treaty, the arguments for and against it, and the condition of the world that in the majority view made it desirable. The process was costly; it was also beneficial. Delay, embarrassment, and some obscuring of every state's commitment were the price paid; gaining wide support in the Senate and among the public was ample compensation. Some may cavil at the conclusion because it treats cavalierly a cardinal rule of the old diplomacy: that the language of all treaties be entirely precise. The rule is surely important in drawing a boundary, regulating trade, or setting the procedures of diplomatic intercourse. It is less so in such matters as we are discussing. The purpose of the Treaty was to get the states party to it to cooperate militarily, and possibly in other ways, over a period of at least twenty years. The accomplishment of such a purpose cannot be assured by the language of a treaty. The obligation to rally around at a moment of peril, because it may require the greatest of national sacrifices, will depend more on what happens after a treaty is made than on the words recorded in it. For these reasons, a hard-won but real national commitment is preferable to the gaining of an easy but nominal assent. If the treaty provision is not, as Hamilton thought, near to being the best part of the Constitution, it is far from being the terrible mistake that Secretary Hay understandably thought it to be. The requirement of a

---

[4]*Congressional Record*, XCV, Pt. 1 (81st Cong., 1st sess., 1949), 1165.
[5]The North Atlantic Treaty, Art. 5.

two-thirds vote remains, but it is no longer a major impediment to a foreign policy of action and involvement.

In a period when international involvements have been accepted as necessities even when they have been painful, the two-thirds rule has not kept the President or the State Department from fashioning suitable international arrangements. One must then wonder if the rule ever was a basic cause of American difficulties. It is not likely that the United States, even if she had joined the League of Nations, would have assumed greater international responsibilities in the years between the wars. If Woodrow Wilson had behaved more like a peacetime Prime Minister than like a President, by testing the ground carefully, avoiding a fight in the Senate, and forgoing a campaign in the country, the occasion for condemning the treaty rule would have been avoided entirely. But the United States would also have been less well educated and prepared for the international role that since 1941 has been hers to play.

Other types of Congressional obstruction have been more worrisome lately: among them, the constant disposition of Congress to pry into administrative details and to investigate officials and superintend their work. It is often feared that Congressmen acting as critics and investigators may harry the officials and the diplomats who need time to think, may frighten them into timidity where boldness is required, and may block their attempts to move with subtlety to meet complex and shifting situations whose implications most Congressmen are not equipped to comprehend.

Harold Nicolson, giving an Englishman's impression of American diplomats, wrote in the 1930's: "They enter a conference as Daniel entered the den of lions conscious that it is only their bright faith and innocence which will preserve them from the claws of the wild beasts by whom they are surrounded." He went on to describe the brash confidence of American businessmen negotiating with foreigners and marveled at the contrast between them and timid American ambassadors. Charles W. Thayer, himself a Foreign Service Officer for more than two decades, took notice of Nicolson's remark in order to point out that the cause of the diplomats' quavering was not, as Nicolson suggested, fear and suspicion of Continental diplomatists but rather their dread of the combined isolationist convictions and punitive powers of Congress.[6]

While the inclination to isolationism has waned, Congress has retained the power to tamper with policy and interfere with its conduct. Because

[6]Thayer, *Diplomat* (New York: Harper, 1959), p. 72.

the approval of appropriate Congressional committees is essential to the legislative success of a program, governmental officials are effectively constrained to submit themselves to Congressional scrutiny. John Foster Dulles estimated in November of 1955 that since becoming Secretary of State he had met "more than 100 times with bipartisan congressional groups."[7] Dean Acheson, reconstructing the period of his service in that office, complained that one-sixth of his working days in Washington were spent in preparing for and meeting with Congressional committees or less formal groups of Senators and Representatives; and he was able to point to the months of May and June of 1951 as a period when fully one half of his time was spent in these ways.[8] The Secretary, of course, is not the Congressman's sole source of information. Deputies, Assistant Secretaries, and assorted experts or interested parties inside and outside the government are also invited or required to appear before committees. They cannot be made to reveal all the executive branch may know or do, but they cannot avoid divulging a great deal. Congress, though it sometimes complains that it is kept in the dark, is clearly the best informed legislative body in the world.

Is the result worth the price paid to achieve it? Acheson and others have wondered if spending so much time informing and attempting to placate Congress represents the best use of the Secretary's talent and energy. Congress can be asked to exercise restraint and to remember that executive officers have other things to do, but major changes in practice are not likely to occur. Congressmen have the privilege of asking in committee; the Members of the Commons have the privilege of asking on the floor of the House. In the absence of effective ways of gaining information and pressing questions home, the House of Commons experiences increasingly the malaise that comes with performing an important task weakly.[9] The American Congress often appears tedious and presumptuous, willful and capricious, in the exercise of the powers of investigation and criticism with which it is plentifully endowed. But if an effective, partly independent critic is desired, it is difficult to say, and secure by appropriate institutional arrangements, "Thus far and no farther." With pleasing brevity, Max Beloff has set forth a standard account of America's internal difficulties in foreign policy, some of them generated by the separation of powers. At the Berlin Conference of 1954 he found that

[7]Dulles, "News Conference Statement," *Department of State Bulletin,* XXXIII, No. 859 (December 12, 1955), 965–66.
[8]Acheson, *A Citizen Looks at Congress* (New York: Harper, 1957), pp. 65–66.
[9]See Chapter 3, pp. 39–40.

Dulles was to some extent in the position of Molotov and somewhat in the position of Bidault and that Eden was differently placed from either of them. Like Molotov, Dulles was guided in his policy by ideological commitment. The question of America's recognizing Red China was conditioned partly by belief and thus became less a matter to be determined by international political calculation. Such decisions were also susceptible to the pressures of Congress and public opinion, however, and this fact established a similarity to Bidault. Both he and Dulles were without reliable majorities in their legislative assemblies. Congress could and did demand the right to control Dulles "in every detail," and in the power to ratify treaties and to appropriate money it possessed adequate means for the purpose. The President or the Secretary of State can, as Beloff put it, try "to muster a majority in the country which will bring pressure to bear upon a recalcitrant Congress. All the history of the last forty years goes to show how extremely difficult this is." The difficulty, he concluded, lies not merely in ideology but also in national institutions and long-standing habits: distrust of the executive, suspicion of the expert, great confidence in the right and the ability of the people to pronounce on complicated matters of policy.[10]

To take a final example of this viewpoint, George F. Kennan remarked, in an early expression of the theme he continues to hum, that history "does not forgive us our national mistakes [in foreign policy merely] because they are explicable in terms of our domestic politics. If you say that mistakes of the past were unavoidable because of our domestic predilections and habits of thought, you are saying that what stopped us from being more effective than we were was democracy, as practiced in this country. And, if that is true, let us recognize it and measure the full seriousness of it—and find something to do about it." The crucial words are "as practiced in this country." He is not saying that all democracies must be disadvantaged, but simply that the American democracy is. He doubts that the problem of making and conducting an adequate foreign policy "is soluble without constitutional reform—reform which would give us a parliamentary system more nearly like that which exists in Eng-

[10]From a paper given by Professor Beloff at the Conference on Teaching and Research in Comparative Government, held by the Italian Political Science Association in April, 1954. The paper is reproduced, in part, in Gunnar Heckscher, *The Study of Comparative Government and Politics* (London: Allen & Unwin, 1957), pp. 136–42. Beloff is obviously referring to the *1954* Berlin Conference, though *1947* is printed in the book. See also his National Summer School Lecture, "The American Role," in *World Perspectives* (London: Conservative Political Centre, 1955), pp. 52–61; and his book, *Foreign Policy and the Democratic Process* (Baltimore: Johns Hopkins Press, 1955).

land and most other parliamentary countries, a system in which a government falls if it loses the confidence of its parliament." [11] A Parliamentary government, Kennan believes, is able to frame and conduct its program without debilitating and disruptive interventions from the politicians. Either the government is able to carry out the policy that its wisdom dictates or, having lost support, it gives way to another that will in turn be able to act in accordance with its best judgment. His experience as Ambassador to Yugoslavia caused him to urge more strongly than ever that Congress should leave the executors of policy unmolested so that they may consistently apply their expert knowledge in ways they have learned to know are wise.[12] Arguing that Congress and the two great political parties must support what the international well-being of the country requires, he summons the ghost of Meinecke to assert the "priority of foreign policy"—that is, "the external problems of the country should be given precedence over the internal ones, and . . . foreign policy should not be permitted to become a function of domestic-political convenience." Few will quarrel with the need to put convenience aside. But the larger question raised by Kennan is whether or not the old institutions and ordinary procedures of American government serve sufficiently well, even with all of the adaptations that have resulted from the three great centralizing experiences of this century—world wars, extended depression, and protracted Cold War. Must we, as he urges, further "centralize and strengthen the conduct of foreign policy," which would require, among other things, a more forbearing Congress? Kennan has sharply pointed out that his activities as Ambassador were unfortunately circumscribed by the State Department and still more seriously limited whenever any question he raised had to be considered by two or more departments or agencies. The "main impediments" to his work, however, lay in "legislative action" restrictive of the Ambassador's activity and derived from "Congressional policy," which rigidly regulated American aid to Yugoslavia.[13] He concludes his comments on Congress by remarking that had he known how little value Congress would assign to his judgment, "in the light of an experience of nearly thirty years in the

[11]Kennan, *American Diplomacy, 1900–1950* (Chicago: University of Chicago Press, 1951), pp. 73, 94.

[12]Kennan, *On Dealing With the Communist World* (New York: Harper & Row for the Council on Foreign Relations, 1964), pp. 3–6, 20; J. Robert Moskin, "Our Foreign Policy Is Paralyzed," *Look*, XXVII (November 19, 1963), 25–27; "Impressions of a Recent Ambassadorial Experience," press release from the office of Senator Henry M. Jackson, November 3, 1963. The attributions that follow are from the latter source.

[13]On this question, see Chapter 8, p. 216.

affairs of the Eastern European area," he would not have accepted the appointment.

George Kennan is an exceptional person, who deserves well of the country he has served. In general, however, one must be skeptical in the face of the bureaucrat's claim to superiority in imagination, initiative, intelligence, or wisdom. Congress is not known for its readiness to defer to authority, which is both a source and a sign of its strength; and one cannot know how different, and possibly how much better, the bureaucracy itself is because of Congressional interference and meddling. Bureaucracies, unmolested, are not famed for their creativity. If they display the virtues of integrity and competence, little more can be asked. Congress, as a restraint upon the executive, displays a different set of virtues. Harshly critical attitudes and harassment that pries information loose are outstanding among them. Questioning by the Senate Foreign Relations Committee once revealed that the Ambassador designate to Ceylon did not know the name of that country's Prime Minister. Reflecting upon the ignorance and incompetence that Congressmen sometimes uncover, a veteran British civil servant in an erratically brilliant book found occasion to remark that some British envoys would display a similarly "abysmal ignorance" if only they were publicly examined.[14] Knowledge without imagination and competence within narrow limits would perhaps more often be discovered, but the important point remains: in Britain one has to guess; in the United States one can more easily know. It is well to have officials interrogated and their performance surveyed by a body whose approval or disapproval makes a difference. The harmful effects of the process are offset if the difficult and important task of checking and prodding a bureaucracy of immense size are accomplished.

The Separation of Powers and the Problems of Deadlock

The Report of the Plowden Committee on the *Control of Public Expenditure* states, with apparently no thought that the judgment is controversial, that "The Government could hardly make its own surveys fully available [to Parliament], since limits are quickly reached in the practicable disclosure of the Government's judgments of future uncertainties and intentions in detail for several years ahead in defence, major economic

[14]George K. Young, *Masters of Indecision: An Inquiry into the Political Process* (London: Methuen, 1962), p. 160.

policy, and of course in social policy and in legislation." [15] In the United States, executive privilege is a matter of recurrent controversy. Not all things are revealed by the President and other officials, nor can they be, but clearly Congress would not tolerate a situation remotely approaching the British condition, where general statements by Ministers replace detailed descriptions of programs and a careful account of how money requested will be spent. The fusion of executive and legislature, as in Britain, means that one must control the other. The separation of legislative and executive branches, as in America, places each in a position of strength.

Congress as an organization may be energetic, enterprising, and fearless, which does not in itself mean that Congress functions admirably as part of a political system. When strong powers contend, the outcome of the struggle must often be in doubt. Half a century ago, Max Weber argued that:

> It is impossible for either the internal or the foreign policy of great states to be strongly and consistently carried out on a collegial basis.
>
> . . . .
>
> Collegiality unavoidably obstructs the promptness of decision, the consistency of policy, the clear responsibility of the individual, and ruthlessness to outsiders in combination with the maintenance of discipline within the group. Hence for these and certain other economic and technical reasons in all large states which are involved in world politics, where collegiality has been retained at all, it has been weakened in favour of the prominent position of the political leader, such as the Prime Minister.[16]

Inertia in American foreign and domestic policy has disturbed many students of politics. Out of the wealth of his knowledge of American politics, V. O. Key, Jr., concluded that American political procedures notoriously encourage delay.[17] Stanley Hoffmann has drawn attention to the massive immobility of American policy.[18] Alastair Buchan has attributed the frustrations felt by Europeans in dealing with the United States in part to "a cumbrous process of internal debate," which makes American policy

[15]Lord Plowden, et al., Control of Public Expenditure, Cmnd. 1432 (London: HMSO, 1961), par. 74.

[16]Max Weber: The Theory of Social and Economic Organization, A. M. Henderson and Talcott Parsons, trans. (New York: Oxford University Press, 1947), pp. 399, 402.

[17]Key, Public Opinion and American Democracy (New York: Knopf, 1961), p. 45.

[18]Hoffmann, "Restraints and Choices in American Foreign Policy," Daedalus, XCI (Fall, 1962), 689–90.

"extremely hard to alter." [19] The critics are legion, and many of them carry great weight. Much of the criticism singles out Congress for special abuse. President John F. Kennedy, for example, in a press conference held shortly before his death, remarked with some feeling that while he remained responsible for protecting "the national interest," Congress threatened to deny him the means of doing so.[20] Some have seen a too massive continuity and, when alacrity of response is required, a tendency to react cumbrously to crises. Others have argued that the American democracy can act only in crises and that the separation of governmental powers divides political responsibility, renders policy discontinuous and incoherent, and makes the United States difficult for other nations to deal with.[21] These different judgments are not necessarily in contradiction. One vice may lead to another, and the American democracy may act the more impetuously in crises because it is unable to alter its courses of action in between them. Its policy may occasionally veer wildly from one line to another because every line is taken too late and clung to though the conditions that would once have made it appropriate have long since disappeared.

Max Weber's argument that collegiality "obstructs the promptness of decision" finds substantiation, it seems, in American institutions. Since the capacity to act with dispatch is essential to the proper conduct of foreign policy, it is well to consider his judgment carefully. The American government has been described as habitually deadlocked. The undisciplined parties permit the famous Midwestern Republican and Southern Democratic coalition to block the many programs of which its members disapprove and leave the President unable to move the recalcitrant Congress. James MacGregor Burns has argued the case at length. Despite the weight of opinion in their favor, Burns tells us, key domestic measures that were also of indirect importance to our foreign policy were blocked by the Congress in both the Eisenhower and Kennedy Administrations. "It is notable," he says, "that Kennedy's major foreign-policy proposal of 1961—long-term financing of foreign aid—failed at the very time that the nation was aroused over crises in Berlin and Southeast Asia. Perhaps the American people have become so benumbed by constant emergency that a crisis no longer serves the old function of providing broad support

[19]Buchan, "Partners and Allies," *Foreign Affairs,* XLI (July, 1963), 627.
[20]Kennedy, "News Conference on Foreign and Domestic Matters," *New York Times,* November 15, 1963, p. 18.
[21]Walt W. Rostow, *The United States in the World Arena* (New York: Harper, 1960), p. 509; and the letter from Earl Attlee, *Daily Telegraph* (London), August 9, 1960, p. 10.

for government action." [22] The effects of economic aid can be felt only over a period of years, which is presumably why Burns is so concerned about its long-term financing. It is difficult then to see what the crises he mentions may have to do with accepting a proposal affecting the process by which funds are allocated. It is easy to argue that long-term financing would be preferable but difficult to demonstrate what is usually assumed: that, given the continuity of the American aid program on the present bases, long-term financing would make truly important differences.[23]

Like many others, Burns wants the American government to break out of its immobility in foreign and military policy. He suggests not only that the disorder of parties and the chaos of Congress impede prompt and effective action but also that there are bold programs promising success, which a more sensible political system would put into effect.

> Vastly stepped up educational and cultural exchange, broadening of the powers of the United Nations, more sophisticated and longer range programs of economic aid to the new nations, the establishment of international universities and cultural centers, increased international collaboration in social and natural science and in space technology, follow-up action to the President's "declaration of interdependence" of the Western nations —the possibilities are almost limitless.[24]

The possibilities may be limitless, though from Burns's list this would never be guessed. The list is a mixture of items of controversial merit and of peripheral international political importance. The generally uninspiring quality of the items listed makes one wonder if there really has been such a discrepancy between what has been done and what might have been accomplished by a system of government in which the chief executive and other officials concerned with foreign policy were able to move more freely.

One who describes a nation's political system and practices as notoriously slow and frequently immobile may mean to say that other political systems are better suited to their tasks, or he may have in mind a vaguely imagined ideal system that would provide a better balance between leisured contemplation and the resolution of issues. Burns comments upon America's hesitation to adopt anti-depression measures in the 1930's but understandably fails to argue that other countries did any better. He regrets that the United States waited too long before beginning to aid the

---

[22]Burns, *The Deadlock of Democracy* (New York: Prentice-Hall, 1963), p. 4.
[23]For extended discussion of foreign aid, see Chapter 8, below.
[24]Burns, *Deadlock of Democracy*, p. 5.

underdeveloped countries but fails to remark that, belatedly or not, the United States did lead the way. Comparison with the performance of other political systems makes clear that over any period of, say, five or ten years much is done by the American government. Mere measures of quantity, however, will not suffice. One wants to know especially whether or not action is taken with the promptness required by international events and if the meshing of the many elements of foreign policy is decently accomplished.

One would expect that the United States, like any country that effectively lays claim to the allegiance of its citizens, would be able to act quickly and easily at moments of crisis, when patriotic impulses push the people together and time for the raising of dissentient voices is lacking.[25] One would then like to know if political leaders are sensitive and courageous in the identification of crises or are instead inclined to explain that all is well until everything goes wrong. The government's reaction defines as a crisis the situation that the actions of others have created. It is then almost a truism to say that new and costly policies are created only in reaction to crises. The American government since the war has been impressively ready to say that difficult situations abroad should be treated as though they were crises, which the United States should seek to meet or to mitigate. In no strict sense was it necessary to describe the plight of West European countries after the war as constituting a crisis for the United States. A similar statement can be made about the attack on South Korea, about Communist China's pressure upon the islands of the Formosa Strait, and about other cases.

In responding to crises, the United States has acted to retrieve immediate situations, but the actions have also occasioned broad innovations in policy and efforts on a grander scale. The boldness, coherence, and innovative skill of President Truman's foreign policy, built piecemeal in response to the appearance of dangers abroad, is surely impressive. The years since his Presidency have not been years of immobility in foreign policy but have instead been a time of calm persistence in the application and elaboration of a policy soundly conceived. Errors and occasional uncertainty are inevitable in any policy. Whether or not specific actions are to be applauded, however, America's policies in the Far East and elsewhere cannot be called irresponsible, unrestrained, or impetuous.

The President proposes; Congress disposes. But the President proposes many things, and Congress often disposes of them summarily. Because it

---

[25]For an examination of the problem, see Chapter 10, below.

frequently rejects proposed legislation, Congress has suffered a reputation for doing nothing. From the open manner in which agreement is sought and the periodic difficulty of securing it, the existence of stalemate is sometimes deduced. The process by which stalemate is avoided is taken as proof of its presence. In England, the political system discourages the open making of efforts to forge agreement on policies, lest dissension within parties be revealed. Under such circumstances, what Ministers ask for is nearly identical with what the legislature gives them, which is mistakenly taken as indication that leadership is strong, action is easy, and policies are properly coordinated.

But if the struggle over policy between the President and Congress is conducted as a competition in power, can one assume that the legislative product will often meet the needs of the day? Just as struggle is wrongly identified with stalemate, so competition is mistakenly associated with unpredictability. Of Fords and Plymouths one can say with near certainty that they will be very much like Chevrolets, and in most years the new models of all three manufacturers will look much like the old ones. So it has ordinarily been from one year to the next with foreign-aid bills, military budgets, and American policy toward particular countries and areas. Why this is so is made clear in part by identifying the aspects of policy that are argued about. Who "lost" China? Why was "victory" in Korea not gained or even sought? Will the foreign-aid program be adequate after Congress has gone over it? In such arguments over policy, the questions essentially at issue are not about whether in principle to accept a program costly in dollars and sometimes in lives. Rather, the participants ask how well a program has been carried out, just how far the country should commit itself, and whether or not the rewards will be proportionate to the costs. Majority opinion about America's role in the world is firmly established, which frustrates the excluded minority and leads them to noisy dissent. The range of opinion that has effectively set the terms of political competition is quite narrow, which helps to make policy stable. The continuity of policy is also promoted by the institutional relation of President to Congress and by the fluidity of the Congressional parties.

Executive Leadership

One of the errors commonly made in assessing the merit of American government is to assume that because a series of pitched battles are fought within Congress and between Congress and the President the policy that emerges must be as messy as the process by which it is made. Professor Herman Finer, for example, has rightly remarked that the American government at times speaks with many voices. As an instance, he cited Henry Wallace's effort, in 1946, to undercut the State Department's foreign policy and turn America toward conciliation of Russia. Finer failed, however, to notice that the incident provoked a quick clarification of America's direction and purpose. American policy toward Palestine, Finer added, was hopelessly muddled, "for so incoherent had the process of policy making been that the administration had never counted and accepted the cost" of its own recommendation. Palestine was thereby condemned to bloodshed.[26] The British politician L. S. Amery had already attributed that unhappy result to "the weak compromises, postponements, and fluctuations" of British policy, which is a sounder conclusion since Britain's responsibility had been paramount. Amery, indeed, offered Britain's policy on Palestine as a typical instance, one in which "the Foreign Office, anxious to avoid immediate trouble with the Arab States, has generally for many years now been at variance with such constructive policy as the Colonial Office has wished to carry out."[27] Turning back to Finer, we find that he offers finally, as an "incident full of instruction to the student of American government," the $1.5 billion reduction of funds for the European Recovery Program that Representative Taber led the Appropriations Committee and the House to make in June of 1948.[28] Finer told only a part of the story; much of the amount cut by the House was restored in the final appropriation. And he failed to see, in 1949, that ERP, generously supported despite Congressional trimming, was well on the way to its outstanding success. Finer has fallen into confusion by concentrating on process without paying attention to outcome. He also constantly implies and occasionally argues that a different process, one more like Britain's, would be much superior. If a policy made smoothly will surely be integrated, then the acceptance by Parliament of the Prime Minister's policies can be identified with the realization of coherence in the government's program.

It is at this point instructive to look at Amery's analysis more carefully. Having served in the Commons for thirty-four years (about half of them in office in a number of departments), he chose to repeat in the lectures

[26]Finer, *Theory and Practice of Modern Government* (rev. ed.; New York: Holt, Rinehart & Winston, 1949), p. 678.
[27]Amery, *Thoughts on the Constitution* (London: Oxford University Press, 1947), p. 94.
[28]Finer, *Theory and Practice of Modern Government*, pp. 678–79.

he published in 1947 words that he had written in the mid-1930's. They are worth repeating once more. There is, he asserted from his own experience,

> very little Cabinet policy, as such, on any subject. No one has time to think it out, to discuss it, to co-ordinate its various elements, or to see to its prompt and consistent enforcement. There are only departmental policies. The "normal" Cabinet is really little more than a standing conference of departmental chiefs where departmental policies come up, from time to time, to be submitted to a cursory criticism as a result of which they may be accepted, blocked, or in some measure adjusted to the competing policies of other departments. But to a very large extent each department goes its own way, following its own bent and its own tradition, fighting the "Whitehall War" to the best of its ability. . . .
>
> The whole system is one of mutual friction and delay with, at best, some partial measure of mutual adjustment between unrelated policies. It is quite incompatible with any coherent planning of policy as a whole, or with the effective execution of such a policy. It breaks down hopelessly in a serious crisis where clear thinking over difficult and complex situations, definite decisions (not formulae of agreement) and swift and resolute action are required.[29]

The fiction of Cabinet responsibility dissuades Parliament from trying to find out what has actually gone on and leads some political scientists to assume that the Cabinet's imprimatur on a policy is certification of its coherence. What has actually gone on for the most part is that the Prime Minister has presided, as a good chairman should, while each department has pursued its own policy. What Amery observed and deplored, Ivor Jennings made into a maxim of proper British governance. A Prime Minister in peacetime, he asserted, "ought not to have a policy. If he has able ministers, he ought to rely on them, and policies should come from Departmental ministers, assisted as they are by all the knowledge and experience that their Departments can offer." In Jennings's view, the good Prime Minister will offer his Ministers political advice, and in Cabinet he will conciliate and encourage them.[30]

In Britain, the government's program is normally a patchwork of the policies of different departments. In the United States, the government's program has come to be the President's, actually as well as formally hammered into shape by him and his immediate assistants. In comment-

[29]Amery, *Thoughts on the Constitution*, p. 87.
[30]Jennings, *The British Constitution* (3d ed.; Cambridge: Cambridge University Press, 1950), pp. 164–65.

ing upon the reaction of Congress to the legislative initiatives of Alexander Hamilton, Professor Lawrence H. Chamberlain remarked that despite "its growing reluctance, Congress could not resist the potent combination of information and concrete proposal which has ever been the special advantage of the executive." [31] Least well can Congress do so, it should be added, when the movement of events requires that response be rapidly made. With the growing importance of foreign affairs, the President's legislative star has further ascended. Until quite recently, the President's commanding presence has only sporadically been felt. The policies of the government have, through most of American history, depended on Congressmen's interests, public pressures, the force of events, and the fancies of Presidents. Radical changes in practice have recently been made. As Richard E. Neustadt points out, "In 1937, Mr. Roosevelt was bitterly attacked for sending prepared bills to Congress. In 1953, Mr. Eisenhower was attacked by his own partisans for failing to do so. In 1961, Mr. Kennedy not only recommended a complete roster of legislation but sent accompanying draft bills, over his own signature, to the two Houses of Congress." [32] Traditionally the strong President was the one who pressed his policies upon Congress. All Presidents now do so, including Eisenhower after his first year in office. The personal initiatives "of this century's 'strong' Presidents," guiding the economy, acting to prevent strikes or bring them to a conclusion, integrating foreign and military policies, "have now been set by statutes as requirements of office." [33] Thus Neustadt refers to the "routinized responsibility to take the policy lead" and to the "regular routines of office," which make Presidential leadership in legislation as commonplace as the veto power in Herbert Hoover's day.[34] Still, in leading the country, heading the administration, and shaping the legislative program, may it be, as Neustadt suggests, that the President's mode of action is "less creativity than crystallization"? While he "needs to be an actor" may he instead be "pre-eminently a reactor"? Does he typically "choose" rather than "originate"?[35]

---

[31]Chamberlain, *The President, Congress, and Legislation* (New York: Columbia University Press, 1946), p. 11.

[32]Neustadt, "Staffing the Presidency: The Role of White House Agencies," in Senate Subcommittee of the Committee on Government Operations, *Administration of National Security, Selected Papers* (87th Cong., 2d sess., 1962), p. 130.

[33]Neustadt, "The Presidency at Mid-Century," *Law and Contemporary Problems*, XXI (Autumn, 1956), 611.

[34]*Ibid.*, p. 623; Neustadt, "Presidency and Legislation: Planning the President's Program," *American Political Science Review*, XLIX (December, 1955), 1014.

[35]Neustadt, "Presidency and Legislation," p. 1015; "The Presidency at Mid-Century," p. 622; "Staffing the Presidency," p. 131.

To originate is scarcely an everyday task; most work must be less demanding than creation if the office of the President is to be endured by any man. Neustadt's evaluations are wholly perceptive, though he takes for granted a degree of initiative and an amount of originality in fashioning programs that, in order to draw a just comparison with England, should be more heavily emphasized. Whether or not it is adequate for Presidents to crystallize rather than to create depends on the quality of the original ideas and how easily they gain the President's attention. Whether or not reaction is a satisfactory substitute for action depends on how quickly issues are defined and problems thrown up to the highest levels of government. Whether or not a Presidency whose incumbents choose rather than originate can be safely sustained by the country depends on how soon the President is inclined to get into the line of departmental decisions and how varied are the perspectives, commitments, and talents of officials subordinate to him. The analysis in Chapter 3 and considerations that are presented in Chapter 6 support the conclusion that on all of these counts one can expect more sparkling performances from Presidents than from Prime Ministers.

Prejudice against a separation of political powers rests in important part on the notion that from the executive offices of government will emerge programs whose merit and coherence are assured if only the legislature refrains from tampering with them. Purely hierarchical arrangement, in which each office is subordinate to another until one reaches the head of government at the apex, is, however, a simple impossibility. Rule without what Weber called collegiality is inconceivable. The relevant question would then seem to be, which of the different types of collegial arrangement will encourage coherence of policy, persistence of action, the spirit of sacrifice where desirable, and ruthlessness to outsiders if that should be required.

The President, though he does not get all of his program approved and gets little in exactly the form he has asked for, chooses the terrain on which legislative controversy occurs. Congressional legislation of major public importance is rare. The position of the President as leader of the nation and chief artificer of its policy has been ground so deeply into the American system that even President Eisenhower could not consistently maintain his disinclination to play the foremost role. Crucial problems will be treated by the Congress largely in terms posed by the President. At the height of the Indochinese crisis in May of 1954, Representative Rayburn remarked that the Democrats were "ready to cooperate in a sound foreign policy" provided they knew "what that policy is." [36] That Rayburn, better than anyone else in the last fifty years, could have persuaded the House to follow his lead, makes his comment all the more significant. He was seeking a chance to back a policy, not to make one, well appreciating that Congressional government is inappropriate to conditions of complexity and crisis, which are the two outstanding characteristics of the day. Even those who wish to obstruct a particular program look to the President for a lead and bitterly complain if his requests are not fully and clearly set before the Congress. Just listen to the complaint that Senator Wayne Morse lodged against President Johnson: "He doesn't want to tell the country the form in which he, as Commander in Chief and President of the United States, thinks foreign aid legislation ought to be passed, which might I say is just elementary in this system of representative government. The country has the right to look to the President for recommendations as to the form it ought to take instead of passing the buck to the Congress." [37] The crucial problems will be treated in the President's terms, and the problems that Congress takes to be crucial will be the ones that the President describes as being so.

Still, losing legislation is a Presidential way of life. Why should anyone expect that the policies that clear the Congressional hurdle will represent just about all the legislation that the interests of the nation can be said to require? Losing is serious if the legislation is urgently needed. But if it is, the success of the President is likely. Presidents concentrate on gaining Congressional support for the policies they believe to be most important. No President will get *everything* he may wish for. Most Presidents, however, can get *any one thing*, if only they "wish" for it hard enough. This conclusion rests firmly on a tripod whose three legs are the institutionalized leadership of the Presidency, the nature of foreign-policy problems, and the fluidity of the parties in Congress. The first two have been discussed; the third we now turn to.

The Interrelation of Legislatures and Executives

In England, compromises are made within the parties, which try hard to maintain a publicly united front. Whether or not the distance between parties is wide, the choices of the voter are clearly distinguished. A major-

[36]*New York Times*, May 14, 1954, p. 1.
[37]Senate Hearings before the Committee on Foreign Relations, *Foreign Assistance, 1965* (89th Cong., 1st sess., 1965), p. 202.

ity gained in a national election is a majority for a party that will be able to carry out its advertised program. Majorities gained by American parties have, in contrast, been termed "Make-Believe Majorities." [38] It cannot be assumed that a victorious party will hold together sufficiently in Congress to put into effect any of the platform on which the party stood before the people. Those who highly value clarity of choice will prefer the system that forces firm compromises to be made within parties prior to the holding of elections. At what price, one may wonder, since benefits seldom come free, has clarity of choice been purchased? The British parties supposedly "give the national welfare right of way over minority interests." Although concessions are made to interests it is said that "those concessions are never so fundamental as to endanger seriously the party's loyalty to its national program." [39] But how was that program made up? The belief that the balance between sectional and national interests will always be justly struck is a baffling one. When parties are in close contention for office, the votes of small groups may be needed for victory. Leaders may then require their disciplined parties to accede to the demands of pressure groups in order to secure the votes of their members.[40] Some policies will be adopted in order to heighten the parties' appeal. Others will be forgone in order to avoid the disruption of parties. The better a party is disciplined, the more easily it obeys the electoral imperatives. Because both the perpetuation of a governmental party in power and the reputation of its opposition depend upon party unity, the temptation to avoid major issues while accommodating minor interests is great.

It is sometimes thought that majority governments are able to move easily, for with disciplined parties the government can act according to the will of what may be half of approximately one half of the nation. One should say instead that British majoritarian governments cannot often enough act boldly on matters that are at once important and controversial, for the half of the nation that the government happens to represent must be substantially agreed, in the person of its representatives, before policy will ordinarily be essayed. A Prime Minister refrains, if he can, from asking for policies that will split his party or spread discontent within it. The relation between the management of groups and

[38]James MacGregor Burns, *Congress on Trial* (New York: Harper, 1949), p. 39.
[39]*Ibid.*, pp. 38–39.
[40]The argument is beautifully developed by J. Roland Pennock, " 'Responsible Government,' Separated Powers, and Special Interests: Agricultural Subsidies in Britain and America," *American Political Science Review*, LVI (September, 1962), 621–33.

the content of policy is more clearly seen within the Labour Party than among the Conservatives. Hugh Gaitskell, having lost to the unilateral disarmers at the party's Scarborough Conference in October of 1960, continued to fight for his policy within the party. A year later, at Blackpool, he was vindicated. In his campaign to amend the public-ownership clause of the party's constitution, however, he had to give way. By a combination of victories and defeats, the party's policy was rendered less firm and less coherent, less appropriate to the country's needs and less attractive to the people than Gaitskell and one group of the party's leaders had thought it could be. The leader of the Labour Party has been comfortable in his office only when he has been able to maintain an effective alliance with a group of powerful trade unionists. In order to be able to do so his preference among policies must not be widely different from theirs.[41]

Leaders of parties in power have an easier time controlling their followers than do leaders of the opposition. Labour's leaders appear to have more trouble than their opposite numbers in the Conservative Party. This is partly because Labour is less often in power, partly because Labour settles its differences in public more often than do the Conservatives, and partly because Labour is a movement as well as a political party, and ideological commitment makes compromises difficult to fashion. The Conservative Party has been described as "a collection of evanescent pressure-groups"; Labour, as "a coalition of parties." The Conservative Party, more homogeneous than Labour, has no permanently alienated factions to deal with. The Conservative Party is made up of individuals whose views vary with issues; the Labour Party to a larger extent is composed of groups of some permanence, each with convictions about policy.[42]

If the government is to act, the party that has formed it must move nearly in unison. Whether the tendencies within parties are rooted more deeply in ideology or material interest, it is seldom easy for them to remain united in the face of great and new public issues. Important disagreements within the party are reason for postponing action until accommodations can be reached. The leader, whether of the government or of the opposition, becomes the target of contending individuals or groups and may preserve himself and strengthen his rule by long withholding his blessing from any of them. Reluctance to press for policies

[41]The six largest unions command a majority of all the votes at Labour Party Conferences. On the processes of union decision, see Alan Fox, "The Unions and Defence," *Socialist Commentary* (February, 1961), pp. 4–9. On the wider subject, see Martin Harrison, *Trade Unions and the Labour Party* (London: Allen & Unwin, 1960).

[42]S. E. Finer, H. B. Berrington, and D. J. Bartholomew, *Backbench Opinion in the House of Commons, 1955–59* (Oxford: Pergamon Press, 1961), pp. 112, 122–24.

116

that are controversial characterizes British government on both foreign and domestic fronts. In international situations that do not immediately and directly threaten the position of Britain, party unity may long be maintained, while decisions on policy are held in abeyance. More often than is the case with domestic problems, however, international events force the hands of Prime Ministers and deny them the luxury of time to work their political wiles on the party. At least since World War II, discipline has most often broken on questions of defense and foreign policy.[43]

The difficult processes of grouping and defining, of compromising and amending, must somewhere take place. The American system, unlike the British, throws questions unresolved by the parties or by the electoral process into the Congressional arena. Congress, openly wrestling with problems that have no solution and publicly pondering the imponderable, is in ill repute for the way it does its job. It is not incompetence and obstructionism that gain Congress its bad reputation but rather its visibility together with the difficulty of the tasks it undertakes. In the United States we know comparatively little, and in Britain nothing at all, of ignorant and silly suggestions that executive officials may have made and fought for within the bureaucracy. A Congressman of little knowledge and no influence may have his nostrum emblazoned in headlines. He may thereby do more to stimulate the wise to resist him than to endanger the country's policy. The Congressional visage is nevertheless disfigured.

Congress investigates the administration and superintends the bureaucracy. In Congress, legislative ideas and governmental programs germinate, the President's proposals are criticized, bills are amended in order to improve them and altered to bring them into accord with the national temper and sectional habits, some measures are hastened and others delayed, interests are mediated and the needs of the country debated. Congress legislatively imposes its views, or seeks to, upon programs and policies that are still controversial. It becomes involved in the processes of policy at the stage where final decisions have not yet been made, doubts still exist, and difficulties are unresolved. Parliament is informed of decisions only after they have been made and cannot know of the pressures and arguments that formed them. Congress acts and is criticized; the House of Commons does little and is assumed to be competent if only

---

[43]W. L. Guttsman, for example, counts twelve important cases of opposition from within the party to Labour's policy from 1945 to 1954. Nine were foreign-policy or military matters. "Changes in British Labour Leadership," in Dwaine Marvick, ed., *Political Decision-Makers* (Glencoe, Ill.: Free Press, 1961), p. 127.

someone would give it a job to do. Meanwhile committees and commissions are asked to do what representative assemblies ought to.[44]

Where government operates through a series of *ad hoc* majorities, the hand of the chief executive is strengthened. Since the late 1800's, the discipline of British parties has become increasingly firm. This means, as noted above, that decisions tend to be avoided or postponed for the sake of party unity. It is therefore odd that England has continued to be thought of as a country of strong executive leadership. The absence of party discipline in the United States means that the President seldom gets the support of all the members of his own party in Congress, but it also means that the opposition party will aid the President on all of the many occasions when its unity lapses. A system of casual majorities enhances the role of the person who can put them together. If there is to be persistently strong leadership, the President must supply it. The organization of Congress and the composition of the political parties give him numerous opportunities to do so. Groups are fluid, their members crisscross, interests and ideas conflict and overlap. Congeries of shifting interests and the comparatively even distribution of wealth permit one to say that the country, at least aside from the South, is homogeneous.[45] In a homogeneous country, groups can easily be shuffled. Though the point is not merely geographic, a look at electoral maps does confirm the proposition. In 1896, 1916, 1932, and 1948, the Democratic candidates were weak in the Northeast and strong in North Central and Western States. In 1904, 1920, and 1940, the pattern was reversed. Presidential candidates are better able than their opposite numbers in Britain to vary the image of their parties by putting together different electoral coalitions. It is at this point that the future President begins to emerge as a national leader. If his bid for office is successful, he then becomes the one who devises the legislative strategy by which Congressional groups are combined and recombined according to issue. Thus is his power in devising and securing a program completed. And if parts of his program are not passed, it is Congress, not the President, who is most often blamed. Thus is his power preserved.

The existence of broad national agreement on matters of foreign policy, the fluidity of parties, and the strong position of the President enable

[44]See the list of Committees of Inquiry into Social and Economic Matters appointed from 1958 to 1962, with an indication of subjects considered, in Bernard Crick, *The Reform of Parliament* (London: Weidenfeld & Nicolson, 1964), Appendix F.

[45]The many statements that England is a remarkably homogeneous island should be read as meaning that the crevice between classes runs throughout the land.

one to say that any crucial problem of foreign policy will be acted upon in terms that the President himself sets. The American variety of collegiality has not destroyed the coherence of foreign policy. In Lord Bryce's view, the reproach of democracy was its incompetence in foreign policy born of executive weakness. The virility of Congress has permitted the development of great strength in the Presidency without the risk of Presidential dictatorship.

Chapter 6

EXECUTIVE
ARRANGEMENTS

How executive offices are arranged and who fills them will determine much of the content of policy and the manner in which it is conducted. Fragmentation of the executive offices concerned with foreign affairs, inevitable in any state, offers ample opportunity for the Prime Minister or President to choose among contending ideas about policy, to encourage some lines of thought while discouraging others, to force decisions on some occasions and delay them on others. By whatever name, the foreign office, the treasury, and the military departments must be involved in all momentous questions of foreign policy. Not only between such different activities as defense and finance but also within any one realm divisions usually exist that offer the chief executive the opportunity to preserve his freedom of choice on matters of lesser moment. Foreign, Colonial, and Commonwealth Relations offices long overlapped in England; reorganization of the Defence Ministry, carried through in 1963 and 1964, leaves it still in a confederal condition roughly comparable to America's establishment in the later 1940's. In the United States, centralization of the Defense Department has proceeded rapidly, especially since the advent of Secretary McNamara. If a President were to disagree with a defense establishment able to speak with a single voice, he would be placed in a politically awkward position. The President's arena of routine choice shrinks as his opportunity to range some professional and departmental opinions against others declines. Fragmentation is wanted where the chief executive would preserve choice for himself while others bear most of the burdens. Where he would act directly, unity is desirable. The composition of the defense establishment and its conduct of military operations have become the direct concerns of the President, and the unity of the department an expression of his control. Elsewhere there is fragmentation enough. The Agency for International Development (AID), for example, remains only loosely related to the State Department, and what is most important, the President strengthens his own hand in foreign affairs by the assistants he brings directly into his Executive Office.

The administrative procedures and the appointment practices of the two countries are affected by the presence of disciplined parties in Britain and by their absence in the United States. Prime Ministers seek to manage their parties so as to maintain a united front. Individuals who can bring political support to difficult and controversial policies may be appointed to offices for which previous experience has in no obvious way prepared them. Ernest Bevin, a trade-union leader and Minister of Labour and National Service during the war, and Herbert Morrison, concerned entirely with home affairs during a long political career, were successively made Foreign Secretary by Prime Minister Attlee. To Edward Heath, Chief Whip and then Minister of Labour, Prime Minister Macmillan gave the task of negotiating Britain's entry to "Europe." Presidents similarly seek support for their policies from individuals and groups in both parties. Their choice of persons for high public offices is influenced by the necessity of winning Congressional votes. Replacement and transfer of departmental Secretaries and Under Secretaries, of Assistant Secretaries and their deputies, and even of officials below them, take place in large number when a new President comes to office. The extent to which the custom of making political appointments prevails gives rise to the fear that administration is rendered chaotic and the execution of policies impaired in the very process of seeking support for them.

Parties and Appointments

In focusing upon Congress, analyses of American efforts to contrive bipartisan support for foreign policy often come near to leaving the executive branch of government aside. The heart of bipartisan procedures, however, must lie in the executive branch, with their purpose being to bring Congressmen around.

John Fitzgerald Kennedy, elected President by less than half of the voters, developed bipartisan practices to their highest point. Robert A. Lovett, New York banker, Republican, and a high official in the War, State, and Defense Departments under Presidents Roosevelt and Truman, was reportedly offered by Kennedy his choice of being Secretary of State, Defense, or the Treasury. He served instead as Special Advisor to the President. C. Douglas Dillon, New York financier, Republican, and President Eisenhower's Ambassador to France before becoming Under Secretary of State for Economic Affairs in 1958, became Kennedy's Secretary of the Treasury. Robert McNamara, President of the Ford Motor Company and a registered Republican who had also contributed to the Democratic Party, was made Secretary of Defense. Dean Rusk, a Democrat from Georgia but no more apparently partisan than was McNamara, went to the State Department. The three most important Cabinet positions in any administration, all of which bear directly upon foreign policy, were filled by men who were politically almost colorless but collectively shaded toward Republicanism. The Cabinet as a whole was not highly political. Only three men, former Governors Ribicoff from the Northeast, Hodges from the South, and Freeman from the Midwest, could be described as Democratic political personalities. Even the Postmaster General, J. Edward Day, though he had once briefly been an assistant to Governor Adlai Stevenson, was appointed as an expert in management rather than as a politician. Going down the ladder from Secretary to Under Secretaries and Assistant Secretaries, and laterally to the heads of other agencies, the pattern was the same—an admixture of Democrats who had recently been politically active, men appointed for their experience and skills alone, and a number of Republicans.

The latter were placed with special care in positions of relevance to making foreign policy and carrying it out. John J. McCloy, banker, Republican, Assistant Secretary of War from 1941 to 1945, subsequently President of the World Bank, and then United States High Commissioner in Europe, became Kennedy's coordinator of United States disarmament activities. William C. Foster, corporation executive, Republican, Under Secretary of Commerce from 1946 to 1948, and thereafter head of the Economic Cooperation Administration (ECA) and Deputy Secretary of Defense under President Truman, returned to Washington in 1961 to become head of the new Arms Control and Disarmament Agency. John A. McCone, businessman and Republican, appointed to high defense positions by Truman and made Chairman of the Atomic Energy Commission by Eisenhower, became director of the Central Intelligence Agency (CIA) in 1961.

A number of others could be listed, but there is no need to multiply examples. It would be pointless, moreover, to draw up a statistical table, for the significance of the appointments lies less in their numbers than in the persons and positions involved.

President Eisenhower scarcely employed the executive bipartisan technique, which at first may seem surprising. After twenty years out of office and following the rapid development during and after the war of a group of people widely experienced in foreign and military affairs, one might have expected that a new Republican President would draw into his administration many of the people who had been brought to Washington by Presidents Roosevelt or Truman. But because the Republicans had emphasized during the campaign that a new broom would sweep aside inefficiency and corruption in Washington, it would have been difficult for the President to do so. Moreover, the balance of political forces made doing so unnecessary, or even unwise. Bipartisan procedures had been used to draw isolationists and those who would "go it alone" toward international cooperation. Democratic Administrations, in power during the three American wars of the twentieth century, had sponsored the League of Nations idea and the United Nations organization, authored the reciprocal trade program, inaugurated foreign-aid programs, and developed a world-girdling alliance system. They had driven home the commitment of the party to international involvement. To take hostages from the Democratic Party, when none was needed, would have made more difficult the main task of drawing into support of Eisenhower's policies those many influential Republicans who were inclined to oppose them. By 1956, only four Democrats had served Eisenhower in high positions related to foreign policy.[1] Nor were there many Republicans of the Eastern, internationalist sort who in the previous ten years had occupied so many important positions. Of them, Eisenhower employed mainly such men as John Foster Dulles, Lewis Strauss, and John A. McCone, whose Republican credentials had remained impeccable.

It is not the purpose of bipartisan procedures in the executive branch to give opportunity for service to persons from the minority party. Nevertheless, where they are used, one of the effects of the President's efforts to broaden support for his policies is to give individuals experience in high positions even while their party is out of power. In Britain the situation is markedly different. The sharp distinction between governing

---

[1] They were David K. E. Bruce, Walter S. Robertson, James F. Byrnes, and Gordon Gray. Byrnes and Gray had declared their support for Eisenhower in 1952. *Congressional Quarterly Weekly*, XIII[2] (July 29, 1955), 899–900.

and opposing denies to the party in power the opportunity to draw on the talents to be found in the opposition party. A centralized Parliamentary system funnels the able toward service in the national government and rigidly divides them into those who may serve now and those who must wait on the opposition benches until their own party triumphs. A large number are excluded and, while waiting, denied opportunity to develop their abilities by employing them constructively. Party government in a Parliamentary system is prodigal of politically skilled manpower. Forming a government in 1945, Attlee found Labour MP's available who had recently held political positions of prominence in the wartime coalition government; but when Harold Wilson formed his government in October of 1964, he was in a more difficult position. Out of office for thirteen years, Labour's front-benchers were at once old and inexperienced. Of the two MP's who were leader and deputy leader, in the previous Parliament, and the twelve who had been elected to Labour's Parliamentary Committee, only two had held Ministerial positions: Harold Wilson, as President of the Board of Trade, and Patrick Gordon Walker, as Secretary of State for Commonwealth Relations. The high average age of the fourteen elected members of the opposition front bench was also a reflection of the representational considerations that guide the voting of the Parliamentary Labour Party.[2] Ordinarily a place must be found for a woman, a Scot, and a number of trade-union members; considerations of balance between right and left necessarily affect the outcome. Of course it cannot be assumed that members of the Shadow Cabinet will receive important Ministerial appointments when their party comes into power. It was even thought that Wilson would look outside of Parliament for his Ministers to an extent previously unknown in the political practice of peacetime Britain, and this for three reasons: the shortage of experienced men on his side of the House, the desire of the Labour Party for economic and social change, and the importance of finding men of experience to help carry changes through. The expectation was strangely misplaced.

Students of British government have long said that one of the glories of the system is found in the opportunity to bring into Parliament men of special ability by finding safe seats for them, with the process made easier by the absence of residence requirements. But safe seats are prized, and the party leadership through its national machinery cannot often impose its will upon constituency selection committees. If it succeeds in doing so,

[2] Their average age in July, 1964, was fifty-six and a half years.

it may simply annoy the voters. Safe seats were found by the new Wilson government for Frank Cousins, a trade-union leader who was not previously a candidate for Parliament, and Patrick Gordon Walker, who, though defeated in the general election, was designated Secretary of State for Foreign Affairs. But the "safe" seat found for Gordon Walker was won by his Conservative opponent. It is simpler for the Prime Minister to have recourse to ennoblement, but to do so extensively would lessen still further the standing of Commons. The major offices of state must go to the MP's who have served their apprenticeships in Parliament over a period of years, and most of the minor offices must go to the younger or less important politicians on the back benches who will become impatient if more than a very few from outside of Parliament are favored with office. It is difficult for a Prime Minister to reach beyond the political profession to appoint men in large number to Ministerial office, and the difficulty of his doing so keeps wide the distance institutionally established between political and administrative positions. The Beaverbrooks, Bevins, and Wooltons stand out as wartime exceptions in Britain, whereas the easy transition from private to public employment is now a normal part of American political practice.

Of twenty-three Cabinet Ministers in Wilson's original government, all except Frank Cousins, the Minister of Technology, were old Parliamentarians. Of twenty-one Ministers not in the Cabinet, the only new face was that of Alun Gwynne-Jones, Minister of State for Foreign Affairs (Disarmament), who had been military correspondent of the *Times*. For compelling political reasons, Parliament is and must continue to be the route to executive preferment; and Members of Commons serve an apprenticeship that makes them eligible for office without giving them an opportunity to gain the experience that would fit them for it. Under such circumstances where will the Prime Minister find men experienced in administration rather than in public relations who have a zest for action rather than debate? Where will the Forrestals and McNamaras, the Lovetts and Goldbergs come from? Apprenticeship in Commons cannot be expected to produce many of them.

Political Appointments and the Problem of Turnover

Numerous critics have scored the American practice of leaving the President to fill by appointment administrative positions reaching quite far down into the bureaucracy. They have also been disturbed by the rapid turnover of officials. The two problems are closely related.

None of the Assistant or Under Secretaries of State, nor the Secretary himself, who were in office on June 30, 1948, had been in their offices two years earlier. Such facts are often recorded in order to indicate that instability of personnel is a serious defect of American government.[3] Senator Jackson's Subcommittee on National Policy Machinery, for example, heard from a number of witnesses that it takes a Secretary of Defense about two years to learn his job. By adding incumbents and dividing the sum into the years that had elapsed, the Senators were able to comment with alarm that the typical Secretary of Defense had left office just as he had begun to know what he was doing.[4] To complete the picture, Deputy and Assistant Secretaries of Defense had also served for an average of less than two years.[5]

This does seem rather bad. Fortunately, some of the statistics are misleading. When the Subcommittee drew its conclusions, seven men had served as Secretary of Defense in the brief history of the department. But counting the first and last in a short series distorts the answer that division then provides. It is more sensible to consider each Secretary's length of service (see Table 5).

TABLE 5   AMERICAN SECRETARIES OF DEFENSE

SECRETARIES	DATES OF SERVICE
James Forrestal	July, 1947, to March, 1949
Louis A. Johnson	March, 1949, to September, 1950
George C. Marshall	September, 1950, to September, 1951
Robert A. Lovett	September, 1951, to January, 1953
Charles E. Wilson	January, 1953, to October, 1957
Neil H. McElroy	October, 1957, to December, 1959
Thomas S. Gates	December, 1959, to January, 1961
Robert S. McNamara	January, 1961, to ——

Looking at the list of Secretaries may suggest some problems, but not the problem of gross inexperience. James Forrestal had been Secretary

[3] Cf., for a period a few months earlier, Kenneth W. Thompson, *Political Realism and the Crisis of World Politics: An American Approach to Foreign Policy* (Princeton: Princeton University Press, 1960), p. 157; and Joseph Frankel, *The Making of Foreign Policy* (London: Oxford University Press, 1963), p. 16. For the period 1921 to 1933, see Dexter Perkins, "The Department of State and American Public Opinion," in Gordon A. Craig and Felix Gilbert, eds., *The Diplomats: 1919–1939* (Princeton: Princeton University Press, 1953), p. 286, n. 2.

[4] Interim Report of the Committee on Government Operations made by its Senate Subcommittee on National Policy Machinery, *Organizing for National Security* (86th Cong., 2d sess., 1960), p. 17. Cf. the Subcommittee's Hearings during the same session of Congress: *Organizing for National Security*, Pt. III, pp. 509–10, 518–20; Pt. V, pp. 675–76, 742, 772.

[5] Paul Y. Hammond, *Organizing for Defense* (Princeton: Princeton University Press, 1961), p. 304.

of the Navy since May 19, 1944. By experience, intelligence, and administrative competence he was the best qualified man in the country to assume the newly created office of Secretary of Defense. Louis Johnson, though he had served as Assistant Secretary of War from June of 1937 to July of 1940, was appointed for reasons other than the experience he had had. The problem was not that his term was too short. General Marshall's appointment was made possible by an exception granted by Congress to the rule that military officers not be appointed to Secretaryships in the Department of Defense, and the exception was made precisely so that his long military service and considerable diplomatic experience could be made use of during the Korean War. Robert Lovett, who replaced him, was also, as indicated above, richly experienced and otherwise highly qualified for the office he assumed. Charles Wilson was Secretary of Defense for nearly five years. Neil H. McElroy, the man who replaced him and remained as Secretary for just over two years, had long been a business executive and was without any special qualifications for his new position. Thomas S. Gates took over from him in 1959 and served in the last year of Eisenhower's Administration. He was, in the opinion of many, a superb Secretary who might well have remained in the position had not the adequacy of American military dispositions become an issue in the campaign of 1960. In the Defense Department since the first days of Eisenhower's Presidency, Gates was Under Secretary of the Navy from 1953 to 1957, Secretary from 1957 to 1959, and Deputy Secretary of Defense in 1959.

Only two Secretaries have served for as much as four years, and five were in office for less than two years. Detailed description makes clear, however, that conclusions concerning rapidity of turnover have to be drawn with care. Four of the six short-term occupants of the office—Forrestal, Marshall, Lovett, and Gates—had long experience in defense and related matters and were appointed at least in part for that reason. If on occasion a man does not well fit the office, short terms are desirable; if on occasion others serve briefly, it is important to notice whether or not they are doing so as apprentices or were already well qualified by experience to meet the demands of the position.

The history of Defense Department Secretaries indicates that the pattern of recruitment and appointment is a mixture of tenure (Forrestal, Wilson, and McNamara) and turnover (the other five), of recruitment by lateral movement (Marshall from the recently held office of Secretary of State) and by climbing the highest rungs of bureaucracy's ladder

(Forrestal, Lovett, and Gates), of drawing upon experience (in the case of five of the eight) and of bringing in men from outside (Wilson, McElroy, and McNamara).

Rapid turnover may bring to office a succession of men with new ideas and perspectives. In a short term of office, however, there may be insufficient time to permit changes to take hold. New notions and methods will permeate the vast defense establishment only slowly unless there is a sufficient force available to give them great thrust. It is important in estimating the effects of personnel turnover to examine the relation between tenure of office and performance of function, including especially the effects of tenure upon innovation and continuity in matters of organization and policy.

Forrestal was the most influential of service Secretaries prior to his becoming Secretary of Defense. His tenure of office, ending in 1949, is a period in which there was a sufficient stability of personnel at the top to permit innovation, which was evident in legislation establishing the Department of Defense and in Forrestal's first efforts to manage the loosely united services. From 1953 to 1957 was another period of stability at the top, as have been the years beginning in 1961. In three periods since World War II, influence emanated from a man who remained in office for a number of years. The rapid shuffling of Secretaries has come in between those periods.

Throughout the years following military unification, a series of legislative measures and executive acts has established a trend toward unity in defense organization and has increased the powers of the Secretary of Defense. By the National Security Act of 1947, the Army Air Force was formally given the status of a separate service, which in fact it had already achieved. The Secretary of Defense at that time, granted few powers, was placed in the position of a committee chairman. Then, although initially skeptical of unification, Forrestal began within a year to ask Congress for greater powers. They were granted to the Department by the legislative amendments of 1949 and 1958. The powers of the civilian Secretaries in the Department of Defense were enhanced, and the degree of centralization was advanced.

By executive acts as well as by legislative amendment, the power of the Secretary of the Department over the separate services has increased in fairly steady progression. Disturbed by failures of the Joint Chiefs of Staff to achieve unanimity—failures which delayed or prevented action or led to vague and bland compromise reports—Secretary Gates began to sit regularly with them. His intervention served to break deadlocks and to hasten decisions.[6] Secretary McNamara continued the practice. During his brief period of office, Secretary Gates began to organize units at the Department of Defense level that would take over functions once performed separately by each service. Secretary Gates established the Defense Communications Agency and System. Secretary McNamara established the Defense Supply and Defense Intelligence Agencies and proposed to the President, over the opposition of the three separate Chiefs, that the intelligence officers of the services should no longer sit on the United States Intelligence Board.[7] The organization of unified and specified commands, responsible directly to the Secretary of Defense through the Joint Chiefs of Staff, has tended to reduce the separate services to the status of service agencies.[8] Though Secretary McNamara, like Gates before him, continued to say that he does not favor new unification measures but prefers to give the 1958 legislation a chance to take hold, the establishment of Department of Defense agencies furthered the process of centralization.[9]

Some time is required to carry changes through. Though innovation and continuity are closely related, they do not always depend on the long tenure of one man. Continuity is needed if innovation is to be possible, and innovation is necessary if the defense policy of the country is determined more by external dangers than by domestic political convenience. A succession of Secretaries, most notably Forrestal, Lovett, Gates, and McNamara, has furthered the process of unification. The persistence of organizational trends has been impressive.

In most of the agencies and departments concerned with foreign policy, recruitment and turnover at the level of Assistant Secretary and above follow roughly the pattern identified with the office of Secretary of Defense. Some individuals are appointed for political reasons, though seldom for political reasons alone—Adlai Stevenson at the United Nations; Chester Bowles, G. Mennen Williams, and George Ball at the Department of State; John Connally as Secretary of the Navy. Others are brought in as experts, and still others are kept on because of the knowl-

---

[6]Senate Subcommittee on National Policy Machinery, *Organizing for National Security*, Pt. V, pp. 729–39.

[7]Hanson W. Baldwin, "U.S. Intelligence May Alter Setup," *New York Times*, February 7, 1964, p. 9.

[8]Hammond, *Organizing for Defense*, chap. 13.

[9]For a statement by Gates to this effect, see Senate Subcommittee on National Policy Machinery, *Organizing for National Security*, Pt. V, p. 729. For McNamara, see the *New York Times*, December 28, 1960, I-59.

edge they have acquired. It is instructive in this connection to look in detail at the seemingly scandalous example previously cited: the complete turnover at the top three levels of the State Department in the years 1946 to 1948. Table 6 shows how long important officials in the State Department had held their posts as of June, 1948.

TABLE 6 LENGTH OF SERVICE IN TOP STATE DEPARTMENT POSITIONS, 1948

POSITIONS AS OF JUNE 30, 1948	OCCUPIED SINCE
Secretary, George A. Marshall	January, 1947
Under Secretary, Robert A. Lovett	July, 1947
Under Secretary for Economic Affairs, vacant	
Counselor, Charles E. Bohlen	July, 1947
Assistant Secretaries	
Political Affairs, Norman Armour	June, 1947
Occupied Areas, Charles E. Saltzmann	September, 1947
Public Affairs, George V. Allen	February, 1948
Economic Affairs, Willard L. Thorp	November, 1946
Transportation and Communications, Garrison Norton	March, 1947
Administration, John E. Peurifoy	March, 1947

The turnover in two years was complete, but was it disturbing? This was also, one may recall, the time that is occasionally described as a "golden age" of the State Department, a period of courage and creativity.[10] All the new men were qualified for their positions by the professions they had pursued (most of them in the Foreign Service) or had been recently engaged in matters directly related to the duties they had newly assumed. Some of them had simply moved up from the level directly below. Again in this case, a spectacular one, examination dulls the edge of critical comments about the rapidity of personnel turnover.

It is more useful to discuss *how* turnover takes place, and leave *how much* aside, for the filling and refilling of offices, if properly done, brings positive advantages in governance. The filling of offices is a means of building political support and broadening the base upon which policy rests. Even when office is a reward for political service rendered, the appropriate question to ask is not why is the appointee being rewarded but instead what will he do for the President and the country. Despite the low prestige of public service and the small monetary rewards it brings, no government approaches the American record, established in and after the New Deal, for drawing into its service so many men from the higher levels of business and the professions.

[10]Richard Neustadt, *Presidential Power: The Politics of Leadership* (New York: Wiley, 1960), p. 48.

The Coordination of Policy

Turnover of personnel refreshes the bureaucracy by bringing in people from outside of the government. From the shuffling of personnel a number of additional advantages can be gained, prominent among them coordination by movement of personnel from one office or department to another. It is appropriate to take some examples from among President Kennedy's appointees, for at the beginning of an administration enough new people are brought in to make many observers fear that policy will become erratic.

The technique of coordination by shuffling, which appears least usable in building a new administration, was nevertheless impressively employed by President Kennedy. C. Douglas Dillon, when he became President Kennedy's Secretary of the Treasury, brought with him John Leddy, a career official who had been one of his principal aides at the State Department, to supervise the Office of International Finance. Paul Nitze, formerly of Dillon, Read and Company, a Republican, and a member of the Policy Planning Staff under Truman and briefly under Eisenhower, became Assistant Secretary for International Security Affairs at the Department of Defense. Where once the State Department had looked to the Joint Chiefs of Staff for military information and advice, it now began to go directly to his office, which also became responsible for international negotiations insofar as they involved military matters. Nitze had as his principal assistant William P. Bundy, previously with the CIA. Bundy replaced Nitze in November, 1963, when Nitze became Secretary of the Navy. Roger Hilsman left his position as Chief of the Foreign Affairs Division at the Legislative Reference Service to become head of State Department Intelligence and then Assistant Secretary of State for Far Eastern Affairs until he resigned in February of 1964. Bundy was then moved into that office. James Webb, formerly Truman's head of the Bureau of the Budget and then Under Secretary of State, became Director of the National Aeronautics and Space Administration, with T. Keith Glennan, who had been its first Director, as a consultant. Thomas D. Morris, formerly Assistant Director for Management and Organization at the Bureau of the Budget, was made Assistant Secretary of Defense for Installations and Logistics. Eugene M. Zuckert, Assistant Secretary of the Air Force from 1947 to 1952 and then member of the Atomic Energy Commission until 1954, became Secretary of the Air Force.

131

The frequency with which persons are moved from one department to another means that a number of people in a given department are familiar at first hand with the people, policies, and procedures of other agencies. Understanding is gained, views are broadened, and the coordination of policy furthered.

With regard to Secretaries of Defense, periods of long tenure were found to be as significant as the arithmetical rate of turnover. Concern about the turnover of personnel within a department should lead one to ask whether enough positions have been occupied for a long enough time by a single person to give the department stability. The President and the Secretary of a department will have the same concern in mind. Thus Joseph Charyk, aeronautical engineer and missile expert, Assistant Air Force Secretary for Research and Development in 1959 and Under Secretary in 1960, was kept on in the latter position by President Kennedy. Lyle Garlock, a federal employee since 1934 and in the Department of Defense from 1948 to 1954, became Assistant Secretary of the Air Force for Financial Management in 1954 and was retained in that capacity by the new administration. James Wakelin, a physicist, became Assistant Secretary of the Navy for Research and Development in 1959 and remained so under Kennedy. To give an impressive final example, Wilfred McNeil, a fiscal officer of the United States Navy from 1941 to 1947, became in the latter year a Special Assistant to the Secretary of Defense and later served for a decade, ending in 1959, as Assistant Secretary of Defense and Comptroller.

The message to be formulated on the basis of the preceding analysis is not that there is no need to worry about transience of personnel and discontinuities in staffing. One part of the worry of Senator Jackson and other members of his Subcommittee is wholly well placed: namely, that good men have refused employment in Washington because the government has not been able to offer attractive salaries. Beyond that, one needs perspective, which has just been supplied and which suggests that the problem is not simply to reduce turnover but to strike the right combination of turnover for the sake of refreshment, shuffling of personnel from one agency to another to aid in the coordination of policy, and retention of some persons in a single office for a number of years in order to foster continuity of policy and procedure.

The right balance is not always struck. Foreign-aid agencies have been thought to exemplify the administrative chaos that the separation of powers produces. The case is instructive. From 1948 to 1966, AID and its predecessor agencies were directed by ten different persons. There is nothing spurious about this statistic. Until the time of David Bell, who was Administrator of AID for three-and-a-half years, no director had served for much more than two years. For the sake of innovation and stability of programs, the occasional service of a single director for a number of years is desirable. If long tenure is to be achieved, however, political support is required. An official of AID, upon his resignation from the agency, attributed the difficulties of carrying out foreign assistance programs to the rapid turnover of personnel.[11] The opposite statement can more appropriately be made. Shifts in organization and in directorship have occurred frequently because foreign aid has been controversial in purpose and because serviceable doctrines and effective techniques have proved hard to develop. New faces and new titles often appeared because the President hoped thereby to gain support for the agencies' programs. By this means among others, remarkable stability of expenditure for aid has been maintained during the past two decades, while programs have remained controversial and fairly unpopular.[12]

The conclusion to be drawn is then different from the one that is customary. It is political support for an activity and public belief in its usefulness that permits continuity. Such support and acceptance were evident, for example, in the cases of General Curtis LeMay, head of the Strategic Air Command for more than eight years, and of Admiral Hyman Rickover who long promoted the development of nuclear propulsion. Both of them had strong sources of support in Congress or within the executive branch, and the importance of their missions was widely acknowledged. For similar reasons, the heads of old or well-established departments—State, Defense, or Treasury, for example—roll somewhat less frequently than do the heads of new agencies that are not yet firmly established.

Ministers and Civil Servants

In Great Britain one can, with fair hope of success, play the game of guessing who the next Chancellor of the Exchequer, Foreign Secretary, or Defence Minister will be. They must come from Parliament, almost always from the Commons, and must be among the more prominent and experienced Members. In the United States, to bet on who will be ap-

[11]Felix Belair, Jr., "White House Accused of Retarding Foreign Aid Program by Interference," *New York Times*, November 18, 1962, 1-59.
[12]See Chapter 8, below.

pointed to comparable offices would usually be folly. President Kennedy chose as his Secretary of State and as his Director of the Bureau of the Budget men he had not met until he interviewed them for the jobs. Robert McNamara he scarcely knew before asking him to be Secretary of Defense.[13] Britons, marveling at the procedure, expected incoherence or worse.[14] Their worry was intensified by the apparent contrast with British and Western European practices. As in the Third and Fourth French Republics, so in Britain there is a considerable group of *ministrables*, men who by political affiliation and length of service constitute the pool of Parliamentarians from which the large majority of Ministers will be drawn.

Though in Great Britain problems of turnover are markedly different from those that prevail in America, they are perhaps as important. Most politicians spend years climbing to Cabinet rank. Once having attained it, they do not long endure. By the Prime Minister's decision, offices in general are rapidly exchanged; and over a period of years the body of men who have served becomes surprisingly large. After his party's victory in October of 1959, Macmillan formed a government of 81 members. Upon the adjournment for the summer recess in July of 1964, not quite five years later, 41 no longer held any office at all, and only 7 still occupied their original posts. In ten years of Tory rule, beginning in October of 1951, a total of 230 persons held office in successive Conservative Governments. Of 16 members of Sir Winston Churchill's peacetime Cabinet, 4 had survived—Macmillan, Butler, Thorneycroft, and Viscount Kilmuir. Of 18 non-Cabinet Ministers, 5 were still in office ten years later. Of more than 30 Parliamentary and Under-Secretaries, only 3 had lasted upon receiving promotion—John Boyd-Carpenter, Ernest Marples, and Dr. Charles Hill.[15]

Few Ministers serve long in any one position. There were 8 Secretaries of Defense in the United States from 1947 to the autumn of 1966; in Britain there were 12 during the same period or a total of 13 since the war. In the United States, years of stability have been interspersed with periods of rapid turnover. In Britain, only one Defence Minister has been in office

---

[13]Richard Rovere, "Letter from Washington," *New Yorker*, XXXVI (December 24, 1960), 52 ff.

[14]See M. J. C. Vile, "The Formation and Execution of Policy in the United States," *Political Quarterly*, XXXIII (April–June, 1962), 162–71.

[15]Gerald Kaufman, "Profile of a Parliament," *New Statesman*, LXVIII (July 31, 1964), 146; James Margach, "10-year Turnover at the Top," *Sunday Times* (London), October 29, 1961, p. 13.

for as much as three years, A. V. Alexander of Hillsborough from December of 1946 to February of 1950. Four have served for more than two years; five for less than one year. Three of the 13 moved up from the Admiralty or the War Office to become Ministers of Defence. Secretaries of State for War and for Air and First Lords of the Admiralty (to use their old and familiar titles) have been almost as numerous, with 12, 9, and 11 for those services, respectively, though a few individuals among them remained in their places for approximately five years. Defence Ministers have appeared and disappeared more frequently than most Ministers have, which, as with foreign-assistance agencies in the United States, is partly a reflection of British difficulties in defense policy, which we shall later examine. Nevertheless, in other Ministerial offices, except for Foreign Affairs and the Home Department, tenure for as long as four years is unusual. Two years is nearer the norm.

The MP out of office lacks the incentive to engage himself deeply in legislative affairs, for he is scarcely able to affect the conduct of administration or the writing of legislation. The MP in office, though a political specialist, remains a policy and administrative amateur confronting an entrenched bureaucracy. Where the American Secretary of a department or Assistant Secretary within it is expected to administer and manage, to draw up programs and put them into effect, a British Minister is more nearly in the position of a gentleman who presides, who explains to the civil servants what is politically supportable and to his fellow Parliamentarians what is practically possible. Ministers, who are the instruments the Prime Minister uses in dealing with the departments of government, come and go with a frequency that impedes the exercise of political control and increases the difficulty of carrying through changes in policy. Such habits were sensible when the society and economy were left to manage themselves, with the government intervening seldom and then only to make marginal adjustments. They still coincide with the requirements of any Conservative Government that is not intent upon legislating great changes and is therefore content to preside over affairs while making occasional modifications. Supposedly Ministers, supported by Parliament, frame overall policies, while civil servants contrive the necessary adjustments. The familiarity of the Crown's permanent servants with the arts of adjustment, the paucity of information available to the public and to Parliament, the short term that Ministers typically serve in any one position, the smallness of their number as compared to the mass of the bureaucracy, the demands made on their time by duties in Parliament and in their constituencies: all of these factors working together make it difficult for Ministers to take hold of their departments' affairs.

One might think that in these circumstances the Prime Minister would gather still more power unto his office by actively concerning himself with the affairs of the separate departments. On occasion he may do so, though he is not well equipped for the task. Two handicaps are especially detrimental. The first, generally overlooked, is the Prime Minister's customarily short term of office. Though the Prime Minister's ascendancy is based in part upon his outlasting his party associates, the Prime Ministerial office itself is not often long held. Since the Second Reform Act, Asquith holds the record, of nearly nine years, followed by Salisbury with intermittent terms of six and seven years, and then by Macmillan, Attlee, and Lloyd George, each of whom lasted about six years. In addition to the handicap of short and uncertain tenure that Prime Ministers frequently bear, the Prime Minister's staff is too small to elicit quantities of information and to uncover alternative viewpoints. There is for the Prime Minister no equivalent of the Executive Office of the President with Special Assistants who can reach for him into the affairs of the various departments. Prime Ministers since World War II have been inclined to play a personal role in foreign policy. It is striking that only seldom or belatedly have they done so in order to force decisions or hasten changes of direction in policy. They have instead specialized—as have leaders of the opposition—in making trips to Moscow and Washington in order to be able upon their return to instruct the Commons and impress the electorate.

In England as in America, some department heads will be men of great energy. If supported by the Prime Minister or President, they will impress their personalities and their policies upon their staffs. Also in both countries, some Ministers will be mere passengers, rewarded for past service, recognized for their political standing, and expected to make little present contribution. The executive arrangements that prevail in Great Britain, and this is the key point, make it more difficult than it is in the United States for the Minister who would effect changes to impress his will upon the bureaucracy. It is less a question, one must carefully note, of civil servants resisting the wills of their political masters than it is of Ministers not being in a position to behave masterfully. The stability of personnel just below the top heightens the effect of the rapid turnover that prevails among the Ministers who guide the policies of departments, which is compounded by the smallness of the number of the Prime Minister's appointees. The political appointees of the President occupy positions that reach down into the hierarchy of departmental offices. The Prime Minister's political appointees are a thin layer spread over a large bureaucracy.

"When a government changes in Britain," Anthony Sampson points out, "only seventy people change their desks in Whitehall, while in America hundreds of officials migrate." One should, of course, add that those seventy people change places frequently, with many disappearing as they do so. "Most civil servants," to cite Sampson again, "spend their whole lives in the same department, and only the most senior are switched around." [16] Senior civil servants in the military departments, for example, have spent on the average twenty-five years in government, with most of their time in a single department.[17] Permanent Secretaries in Britain have served on the average in 2.5 departments.[18] Other members of the administrative class who are of comparable age have ordinarily a still more limited experience.

Civil servants in Britain are divided into three classes, with movement between levels quite difficult.[19] Members of the top class especially are high in intelligence and competence and long on experience, but having their experience confined mostly to one realm of affairs, they may also be narrow in viewpoint. The American civil service, with its eighteen grades, permits a wider recruitment, a greater flexibility, and an easier movement both between grades and between departments. Government service in the United States has been a route to distinction easily open to those of middle-class origins. In England, men of high birth and expensive education have heavily populated the upper reaches of the bureaucracy, just as, outside of the trade unions and the Labour movement, they have occupied the "commanding heights" of the polity, economy, and society. A survey made several years ago by the Labour Party showed "that forty-four out of 148 directors of the joint stock banks, forty-six out of 149 directors of the large insurance companies and thirty-five out of 107 directors of big City firms were all old Etonians." The Financial Secretary to the Treasury reported to the Commons in June, 1963, that in the open competitions for appointments at the Assistant Principal level in the past

[16]Sampson, *Anatomy of Britain* (New York: Harper & Row, 1962), pp. 218, 230.

[17]William P. Snyder, *The Politics of British Defense Policy* (Columbus: Ohio State University Press, 1964), p. 119.

[18]Sampson, *Anatomy of Britain*, p. 238.

[19]R. K. Kelsall, *Higher Civil Servants in Britain: From 1870 to the Present Day* (London: Routledge & Kegan Paul, 1955), chap. 3.

ten years, 194 places went to Oxford men, 149 to Cambridge, 35 to London University, and 15 to "redbrick" universities.[20] In the United States, it is necessary to lump twenty-seven universities together in order to account for half of the degrees held by officials in foreign-affairs agencies.[21] In Britain the Foreign Office, more than the other departments of state, is populated by elegantly educated gentlemen of little experience outside their profession. Over 94 percent of foreign-service personnel have graduated from Oxford or Cambridge, and 70 percent went to British public rather than state-operated schools before attending university.[22]

Brian Chapman has pointed out that "apart from the occasional architect or surveyor recruited by the Ministry of Works, there are virtually no appointments made to senior posts from outside the ranks of the Civil Service itself." [23] Wider recruitment and provisions for bureaucracy's refreshment have long been called for. The Report of Lord Plowden's Committee, which gives some emphasis to these needs, finds its place in an honorable lineage. The government, reacting, now proposes to recruit yearly as many as three Assistant Secretaries (in the forty to forty-five age range) and as many as five Principals (from thirty to thirty-five years old), all of them to come from industry, commerce, and the universities.[24]

With departments displaying their competence in handling the affairs of each day, with most Ministers, including the Prime Minister, ill placed or badly equipped to wrench policy from its established direction, and with the legislature largely inactive, a situation has developed in which *ad hoc* bodies, committees or commissions, are appointed to study problems that cannot easily be ignored and to suggest courses of action. Educational problems at various age levels were in recent years examined by committees headed by John Newsom, Sir Geoffrey Crowther, and Lord Robbins. After Britain's economic growth had lagged badly behind that of her European competitors for more than a decade, the National Economic Development Committee was established, with "Neddy," as it is called, paired with "Nicky" (National Income Commission) to deal with the problem of keeping wages and prices in step with the economic growth rate. Between January of 1955 and March of 1961, social and

---

[20]Cited by Nicholas Davenport, *The Split Society* (London: Gollancz, 1964), p. 174n.

[21]James L. McCamy, *Conduct of the New Diplomacy* (New York: Harper & Row, 1964), p. 211.

[22]Lord Plowden, *Report of the Committee on Representational Services Overseas*, Cmnd. 2276 (London: HMSO, 1964), Annexes J and L. For a critical essay on personnel practices by an ex-Foreign Service Officer, see Geoffrey McDermott, "Reforming the Foreign Service," *New Statesman*, LXVI (August 16, 1963), 189–91.

[23]Chapman, *British Government Observed: Some European Reflections* (London: Allen & Unwin, 1963), p. 23.

[24]"Swing Doors in Whitehall," *Economist*, CCXI (June 13, 1964), 1220.

economic problems in Britain were investigated by four Royal Commissions and seventy-six committees. As is the case with the top levels of the civil service, recruitment of members to serve on committees is narrow. Many of the same names reappear on their rosters.[25]

C. H. Sisson, who is well satisfied with Britain's political institutions, has beautifully captured their spirit:

> Whatever politicians may make out of the electoral procedures which may result in their losing their jobs, an electorate which votes in such a way that an existing cabinet is overthrown is not saying that it will not continue to be governed substantially according to the same laws as before. It is in effect not objecting to the things that in general are done but in a greater or less measure to the way in which some of them are done. The Crown in short remains; the Constitution remains; the officials, who are ultimately the Queen's servants and not the politicians', raise their eyebrows and continue as before, only noting that certain emphases must be changed.[26]

In America it is still cause for dismay when a committee report calls for policies that then fail to materialize.[27] In Britain, the failure to produce a result or the inclination to edge slowly and cautiously toward one is by now an old story. Civil servants may "raise their eyebrows," and the government may bring in a modest program; but the committee is most often a device for exposing the complexity of problems and the perplexities of choice, for demonstrating a good intention while delaying action or postponing it indefinitely.[28] In the United States, while the expectation that the reports of committees will stimulate new actions or policies would seem to be misplaced, the intended effect of appointing a committee is often to gain support for a policy for which the President is already fighting or to increase support for an existing program.

Conclusion

With the prestige of the House of Commons at a low ebb and its ability to control the government waning, the civil service is often said to be the last and best check upon the Prime Minister. Though such a statement is

---

[25]See Peter G. Richards, *Patronage in British Government* (London: Allen & Unwin, 1963), p. 112.

[26]Sisson, *The Spirit of British Administration and Some European Comparisons* (London: Faber & Faber, 1959), p. 158.

[27]See Morton H. Halperin, "The Gaither Committee and the Policy Process," *World Politics*, XIII (April, 1961), 360–84.

[28]A. P. Herbert, "Anything But Action? A Study of the Uses and Abuses of Committees of Inquiry," in Ralph Harris, ed., *Radical Reaction: Essays in Competition and Influence* (2d ed.; London: Hutchinson for the Institute of Economic Affairs, 1961), pp. 249–302.

badly elliptic, the truth it contains is suggestive. In British government, there is an uneasy juxtaposition of career amateurs entrenched in the civil service and Ministers passing through at the top, an institutionalized habit of veiling information and playing down problems and of temporizing by adjustment rather than changing by decision. The arrangements that have evolved and now prevail are not bad in themselves. One must, however, ask whether they permit a reasonable combination of effective democratic control and administrative efficiency in an era of big government and during a period, which gives no promise of ending, of rapid change amidst the growing complexity of affairs. The circulation of officials becomes more important as governments come to impress themselves more widely and deeply upon the life of a nation. It was once the glory of Parliament and the pride of its Members that being an MP was but a part-time job, which, in permitting Members to remain gainfully employed, enabled them to bring to their legislative tasks the experience of their business or professional concerns. The broadening of governmental activity has long since created a situation in which political business, if it is to be done well, has to be done full time. Alternation of public with private engagements is more effective than the constant but part-time practice of politics. British governments shuffle their Ministers from one department to another in such a way as to lose the advantages of political control without gaining the benefits of different perspectives and varied individual experiences.

London and Paris are the foci of commercial, financial, cultural, and political activities; they are the hub cities about which the life of their countries revolves. Washington is a parochial city, the center of nothing but governmental activity. Politicians and officials in Washington have been compared to occupants of an army camp, with many of them waiting as though for a weekend pass that will permit them to visit the homes to which they will return when their tours of duty are over.[29] The figure is suggestive. A number of men move into government and out and then back in again. The process provides political control by placing the President's men in a number of key positions within each department. It provides refreshment of government, by recruiting men of varied experience, and renewal of men who alternate between Washington and the places of their private pursuits. As in Britain, there is an identifiable core, which maintains continuity; there is also a wider recruitment.

[29]Norton Long, "After the Voting Is Over," *Midwest Journal of Political Science*, VI (May, 1962), 183–200.

Chapter 7

THE POLITICS
OF
BRITISH MILITARY POLICY

In Chapters 2 through 6, the British and American political systems are examined together and with approximately equal care. A different procedure is followed in Chapters 7 through 10: each chapter is a case study for one country only. British military policy, to be considered in the present chapter, and American foreign-aid policy, to be taken up in the next one, do have this in common: in neither case can the policy in question be said to be necessary to the nation in an immediate or obvious sense. Britain would be as well or better off without a major-power defense policy, and the United States would perhaps not be worse off were it to reduce its aid to practically nothing. If these statements appear to be too strong, it will at least be agreed that Britain in its military policies and the United States in its aid policies have a wide range of choice. In the realms of policy indicated, both countries could do much less without jeopardizing important national interests; they would have to do much more in order to improve their international prospects to any important extent. For both countries, the constraints in the fields indicated are less close then is usual in questions of foreign policy. This is the point of essential similarity between policies that are substantively different. In examining them, attention is focused on one country at a time, with the other mentioned on occasion only to illumine the matter at hand.

How is policy affected by criticism, we ask in the present chapter. How closely is it constrained by public sentiment, and how responsive is it to the needs of the nation? Military policy, costly and continuous, yearly explained, amended, attacked, and defended, provides abundant material for anyone who would attempt to answer such questions. The adjustment of British military policy to international and technological changes has intermittently engaged the attention of the public. Occasionally it has become the subject of bitter Parliamentary debate. In 1955, a new rationale of policy was offered to Britain, and for a decade that rationale was insistently repeated. Policy itself remained nearly constant, but argument about it raged, and programs failed at huge cost and with alarming frequency. In 1965, a new Labour Government hesitantly began to emend the nation's objectives in order to check its military expenditure. It is worthwhile to describe this pattern of events before, at the appropriate moment, suggesting standards by which the performance is to be measured.

The Rhetoric of Influence and the Influence of Rhetoric

In 1953, the British *Statement on Defence* presented no military doctrine. The government was anxious to scale down and further stretch out the rearmament program undertaken in response to the war in Korea. The aim of policy was described simply as being to meet the commitments of the Cold War abroad and, in association with allies, to dissuade the Communist enemy from attack by maintaining defensive strength at home.[1] In the 1954 *Statement on Defence*, the building of "a force of modern bombers capable of using the atomic weapon" was announced. The "atomic bomb and the ability of the highly organised and trained United States strategic air power" would continue to provide the primary deterrent. To this deterrent, Britain would make a contribution. The army, though gradually reduced in size, would still bear for the British "the main burden in the cold war" and would stand ready to fight the "broken-backed" warfare that would take place should nuclear blows be first exchanged. The idea of making a nuclear contribution appeared for the first time; the independence and influence to be derived from a nuclear force were not yet described. The elements of strategy were laid out but not yet related to each other and emphasized. Doubt that Britain would "be able to afford both new weapons and conventional forces of the present size" did forecast a "gradual change" in the "direction and balance" of effort.[2]

Mindful of advances in science and enchanted with the possibilities of

---

[1] *Statement on Defence:1953*, Cmd. 8768 (London: HMSO, 1953), pp. 4, 3, pars. 5–7, 3.
[2] *Statement on Defence: 1954*, Cmd. 9075 (London: HMSO, 1954), pp. 4–6, pars. 11, 13–16.

their technological application, Sir Winston Churchill soon fashioned for Britain a military doctrine that has informed and infected her military and foreign policy ever since. For several reasons, the new doctrine bit deeply. It was adumbrated by Churchill in striking phrases that related military strategy immediately to everyone's life. Safety was described as "the sturdy child of terror," and survival was said to be "the twin brother of annihilation."[3] Such rhetoric implied a promise to preserve a leading role in the world for Britain. Finally, the new doctrine was compatible with old habits—to accord to one arm of the service a preponderant role, to operate globally on the basis of unbalanced forces, to rely in diplomatic and military crises on a division of labor among actual or potential allies.[4] Thus the 1955 *Statement on Defence* assigned an "even higher priority to the primary deterrent, that is to say to the production of nuclear weapons and the means of their delivery."[5] In Churchill's words, spoken in the House of Commons, the "grave decision" to make the hydrogen bomb formed the "core of the Defence Paper." Britain's nuclear efforts were again said to be a "contribution to the deterrent." They were now also described as a way of assuring that targets most important to Britain would be given high priority and more generally as a way of acquiring influence over American policy, which, it was indicated, Britain, dependent upon the American deterrent, did not at that time have.[6] The notion of the "broken-backed" war disappeared from the White Paper, but, lest nuclear weapons be the only recourse in even a minor European incident, it was argued that Britain would have to maintain conventional forces, which also would be needed to fulfill her "world-wide obligations."[7] Former Prime Minister Attlee, drawing attention to Britain's inability to afford atomic and hydrogen weapons along with "an immense mass of so-called conventional arms," rightly suggested that Churchill's policy had not been carried to its logical conclusion.[8] The elaboration of doctrine and its faithful translation into policy was to proceed under the aegis of Churchill's closest associates, first Anthony Eden and then Harold Macmillan aided by Duncan Sandys and a succession of Defence Ministers.

The program announced in 1955 was ambitious; when one got down

[3]House of Commons, *Parliamentary Debates*, Vol. 537 (March 1, 1955), col. 1899. Cited hereafter as *H.C. Deb.*
[4]See Chapter 1, above.
[5]*Statement on Defence: 1955*, Cmd. 9391 (London: HMSO, 1955), p. 9, par. 29.
[6]*H.C. Deb.*, Vol. 537 (March 1, 1955), cols. 1894–97, 1905.
[7]*Ibid.*, col. 1903; *Statement on Defence: 1955*, pp. 8, 10, pars. 26, 38.
[8]*H.C. Deb.*, Vol. 537 (March 2, 1955), cols. 2174, 2171.

to calculations, it appeared to be inordinately expensive. Expense and experience soon hastened the tempo of change in military policy. Whether fairly or not, the failure of the British expedition to Suez led some to conclude, as Christopher Hollis, formerly a Conservative MP, put it, "that without American support we could not sustain the most tin-pot of campaigns for more than three days." [9] Englishmen were naturally inclined to question the wisdom of spending large sums in order to maintain conventional forces that could not be used with success even against Egypt. In the months of disillusionment following Suez, some were able to console themselves with the notion that Britain could reestablish her great-power status by building her own nuclear deterrent. The trauma of Suez reinforced the conclusions of inquiries undertaken in 1955 and completed in 1956 at the direction of Sir Anthony Eden, who as Prime Minister was concerned with military costs that, projected from 1955's £1,527 million, threatened to reach £1,929 million in 1959. It was decided that what economic considerations required, military technology would permit. Through reliance upon nuclear retaliation, the number of men under arms could be further reduced.[10] The policy, charted in 1954, of gradually altering the balance of forces gave way in the Defence White Paper of 1957 to a program of revising "not merely the size, but the whole character of the defence plan." The program of Defence Minister Sandys, presented as a five-year plan, promised to eliminate waste by establishing "a broad framework within which long-term planning can proceed," to permit a reduction in strength of the British Army of the Rhine, to bring National Service to an end in the year 1960, and to discharge British "overseas responsibilities and make an effective contribution to the defence of the free world with Armed Forces much smaller than at present." It was estimated that defense spending would immediately fall by more than £100 million, with a further reduction promised for future years.[11]

The rhetoric of contribution and influence continued at full force; the contribution was to be made and the influence maintained by forces ever more widely unbalanced. Britain's "New Look" in military policy would supposedly permit the playing of her accustomed roles in the world at a cost the nation could reasonably be expected to bear. But a number of difficulties quickly became apparent.

[9]Hollis, "Ten Years of NATO," *Spectator*, No. 6862 (January 1, 1960), p. 8.
[10]Eden, *Full Circle* (London: Cassell, 1960), Bk. II, chap. 9.
[11]*Defence: Outline of Future Policy*, Cmnd. 124 (London: HMSO, 1957), pp. 1–10, pars. 3, 9, 22, 47, 40, 71, 72.

Dilemmas of Strategy

Britain was the first country to meet the problems posed for powers of the middle rank who decide to arm themselves with nuclear weapons. What is the military incentive for building a small nuclear force, such a country must ask, and what are the uses to which it may be put? Of the three major possibilities, only the first need be examined at length.

1. The late Hugh Gaitskell, exercising the opposition's privilege of speaking more plainly than the government can easily do, once said in the House of Commons: "I do not believe that when we speak of our having to have nuclear weapons of our own it is because we must make a contribution to the deterrent of the West." As he indicated, no contribution of consequence was made. Instead, he remarked, the desire for a nuclear force derives in large part "from doubts about the readiness of the United States Government and the American citizens to risk the destruction of their cities on behalf of Europe." [12] Many statements to the latter effect were made by Conservative Ministers, though never would they have admitted that Britain's nuclear effort made no noticeable contribution to the strength of the Alliance.

The nuclear superiority enjoyed by America in the early 1950's created in Europe a fear that the United States would too easily succumb to a temptation to retaliate massively. The arrival of strategic stability produced the opposite worry. In the words of a senior British general: "McNamara is practically telling the Soviets that the worst they need expect from an attack on West Germany is a conventional counterattack." [13] Behind the difference on strategy lies a divergence of interest. A policy of strategic nuclear threat makes the United States the primary target. A policy of controlled response shifts some of the danger as well as additional burdens to Europe. The countries of Europe, separate or united, have an incentive to adopt destabilizing military programs. Thus, in the 1964 *Statement on Defence*, the "unique contribution" of Britain's V-bombers and Polaris submarines was described as being to dissuade a potential enemy from attacking Europe "in the mistaken belief that the United States would not act unless America herself were attacked." [14] The

[12]*H.C. Deb.*, Vol. 618 (March 1, 1960), cols. 1136–38. Cf. Hugh Gaitskell, *The Challenge of Co-Existence* (London: Methuen, 1957), pp. 45–46.

[13]Quoted by Eldon Griffiths, "The Revolt of Europe," *Saturday Evening Post*, CCLXIII (March 9, 1963), 19.

[14]*Statement on Defence: 1964*, Cmnd. 2270 (London: HMSO, 1964), p. 6, par. 7.

145

contribution of Britain's nuclear force, it appears, has consisted of placing a British finger firmly on the American trigger. Where Britain led, France soon followed. The French Institute of Strategic Studies has justified nuclear diffusion in part with the argument that the uncertainty produced by a third power's nuclear force "considerably augments the opponent's belief in the possibility of a *first* strike" (italics added).[15] While it is understandable that lesser powers should, by mounting nuclear weapons, want to be able to decide when the United States should risk destruction, it is also easy to see that the United States will resist such an outcome. A force well protected will, for example, be less easily triggered, whether by allied or enemy action.

The military motives for nuclear independence arise from the doubtful durability of alliances in the nuclear age. The multiplication of nuclear establishments makes alliances less durable still. A third country, however, can neither trigger its ally's weapons nor deter an aggressor by its own threats to retaliate unless those threats are credible.

A British threat to use nuclear force in order to deter a conventional attack launched by a nuclear great power is a threat to do limited damage to the invading state at the risk of Britain's own annihilation. Is this credible? The Defence Statement of 1955 spoke of a policy that would "demonstrate that we have both the will to survive and the power to ensure victory." But the 1957 *Statement* said bluntly that "there is at present no means of providing adequate protection for the people of this country against the consequences of an attack with nuclear weapons."[16] The British, and the French as well, have too readily assumed that if the homeland is directly in danger, retaliation will be undertaken even at high risk of national suicide. What the Americans call finite deterrence (second strike, counter-city), the British call passive deterrence, a term which implies that nuclear response would be automatic. Though England may or may not choose suicide in the event, the defenders of the policy claim that even a slight possibility of British nuclear retaliation will deter an aggressor. The willingness of the Soviet Union to run the risk of seeing several of its cities destroyed will be proportionate, among other things, to the size of the prize. Notice, however, that the small nuclear power would be put in the position of initiating nuclear warfare;

---

[15]The conclusion is reported by André Beaufre, retired general and director of the Institute, in his essay on "Nuclear Deterrence and World Strategy," in Karl H. Cerny and Henry W. Briefs, eds., *NATO in Quest of Cohesion* (New York: Praeger, 1965), p. 221.

[16]*Statement on Defence: 1955*, p. 7, par. 21; *Defence: Outline of Future Policy* (1957), pp. 2–3, par. 12.

the superpower adversary, with a rich variety of military instruments at his command, could (if he wished) undertake actions none of which seemed to call for national suicide but all of which would be damaging. Retaliation by a small power, which is almost incredible, can be made entirely so by the would-be aggressor's own policy. One must then wonder what the deterrent value of an incredible threat will be. America's massive-retaliation doctrine, enunciated in 1954, was to make a "New Look" in military forces possible by permitting the substitution of nuclear for conventional forces; the difficulties that doctrine encountered now plague the builders of independent nuclear establishments.

If America's interest is closely tied to Western Europe's survival, then the American government is not free to withdraw the deterrent's protection from European states even should their behavior be displeasing. If American interests do permit disentanglement, then a considerable military capability, conventional and nuclear, is required in West European states lest all of their military threats be incredible. If a power of the middle rank can construct a nuclear force only by unbalancing its military establishment, a flexible military response, with the use of force adjusted to the magnitude of the threat, becomes impossible. A Western nation that equips itself with a small nuclear armory must continue to rely primarily on the American deterrent for its security, as both British and French officials have said on occasion. By threatening a nuclear response to a nuclear attack, however, such a nation may gain the leverage to save its cities by enabling it to opt out of a nuclear war between the great powers. The suicidal threat, if it is useful at all, is useful only in extremity. In building a nuclear force, a middle power assumes the military posture of Switzerland: to be (doubtfully) prepared to counter the ultimate threat to the nation at the expense of being unprepared for any other contingency. In strict military logic, such a country should be seen as bowing out of the great-power picture. So much for the first major possibility of making use of a small nuclear force.

2. If a middle power were engaged in a conventional action against a state of comparable or lesser size, the Soviet Union or the United States could threaten a nuclear strike in order to bring about a withdrawal. Would the possession of a small nuclear force by the middle power make such a threat ineffective? In the Suez adventure military action by Britain and France called forth Soviet rocket threats against them. It is sometimes thought that against states having no strategic nuclear forces such threats would be more readily credited and thus more likely to exert

pressure successfully against the conventional action itself. Other pressures against British and French action in Egypt were, however, more effective than the nuclear threats of the Russians.[17] A small military action is not worth and does not require nuclear interference by a great power, for it can be stopped in other ways. The situation is then reversed: the onus of threatening to use nuclear weapons first, in order to interdict conventional interference, is again placed upon the smaller power. Such a threat would not be credible.

3. As the United States and the Soviet Union have opened up a gap in military power between themselves and all others, so Britain, France, China, and states who may follow them can distinguish themselves from non-nuclear nations. Nuclear weapons do not raise Britain, France, or China to the level of the superpowers. Such weapons do set them apart from Germany, Italy, India, and others. Both the first and second uses presuppose the adequacy of the small country's nuclear threat when directed against the United States or the Soviet Union. A capability that is small compared to America's or Russia's may be adequate to its task; a certain minimum, doubtfully achievable in the foreseeable future, is nevertheless required. To counter a small nuclear force is not beyond the capabilities of the United States or the Soviet Union.[18] To employ a nuclear force requires complex and vulnerable systems of command and control; even to know when to use one against a superpower requires expensive early-warning systems, which a state of the middle rank can neither contrive nor afford. For the use of nuclear weapons against non-nuclear powers such requirements do not exist. A nuclear force, even if primitive and small, can be used against them with devastating effect. The results of nuclear diffusion are necessarily uncertain, but one point can sensibly be made: building a small nuclear force, though an unpromising way of seeking to maintain the integrity of one's state, may enable that state to act positively against equal or lesser powers.

Dependence and Influence

For more than a decade the primary international aim of Britain's military policy has been to enhance the influence of the nation. Among the

---

[17]See Eden, *Full Circle*, pp. 556–58.

[18]In February and March, 1965, at hearings before the House Armed Services Committee and Appropriations Committee, respectively, Secretary McNamara estimated that at a cost of eight to ten billion dollars the United States could develop an anti-ballistic-missile system to protect itself against a small nuclear attack such as China's primitive force might be capable of mounting in the 1970's. "McNamara Assays Peril from China," *New York Times*, May 15, 1965, p. 3.

many ways that influence can be generated, two are especially pertinent to Britain's efforts.

First, a state may gain influence by participating in an international division of labor. Interdependence describes a situation in which each party depends in part and for certain supplies and capabilities upon another. From a relation of genuine interdependence, influence develops. Without a nuclear establishment but with growing conventional forces, West Germany, for example, has secured a strong voice in America's European policy.

British Ministers have time and again indicated their acceptance of the duty to contribute to Western military strength. When the outbreak of war in Korea suggested a heightening of danger in Europe, Britain's response was firm and strong-willed. Indeed, the armaments program of the Labour Government exceeded the reasonable limits of the nation's capacities. By the London agreement of 1954, Britain accepted the duty of stationing four divisions and a tactical air force in West Germany. But the aspiration of the nation was for influence that would be global. Expensive though they were, such measures did not satisfy political formulations of national ambition. Obeisance continued to be paid to the concept of forces balanced within the Alliance. To secure them, the White Paper of 1957 reminded its readers, it was not necessarily "desirable that each should seek to contribute national forces which are by themselves self-sufficient and balanced in all respects." If each Ally were to specialize in the right way, all members of the Alliance would enjoy security at less cost. This seems perfectly sensible until one remembers that the same White Paper stated that "the free world" depends "for its protection upon the nuclear capacity of the United States," admitted that Britain could make no more "than a modest contribution" to the deterrent, *and yet* indicated that Britain would skew her forces in the same direction as America's.[19] If a sensible division of military labor is sought, a nation's contribution to the Alliance must consist of something that is needed. Whatever the amount of Britain's "modest contribution" in nuclear forces, it is a contribution in the realm of weaponry with which the Alliance is most abundantly supplied.

In a typical statement of the day, Harold Watkinson, then Minister of Defence, described the V-bomber force as making not a modest but "a powerful independent contribution to the deterrent power of the West."[20] At the same time, to the charge that Britain's nuclear force cost

---

[19]*Defence: Outline of Future Policy* (1957), pp. 2, 3, pars. 11, 15.
[20]*H.C. Deb.*, Vol. 618 (February 29, 1960), cols. 858–59.

more than it was worth, the reply customarily made was that it took only about 10 percent of the yearly defense budget. A real contribution could scarcely be made at a cost of 10 or even 20 percent of a £1.5 billion defense budget.[21] Contrary to his intention, Watkinson's response was another way of defining the tiny amount of Britain's contribution.

At this point in the rationale of British defense policy, the second principal way of generating national influence became important: the fiction of contributing to the balanced forces of the Alliance gave way to emphasis upon the independence of action that Britain's nuclear deterrent was supposed to make possible. One whose associates are unable to act apart from him enjoys the influence that derives from interdependence. One who is able to act apart from his associates exercises the influence that is gained from independence. To be able to act alone permits a wider choice and thus a greater influence at the moment when commitment to a joint endeavor is requested. An alliance partner, knowing this, is also more susceptible to influence in advance of the event. Great powers have influence. By their wealth and capabilities they affect the decisions and limit the actions of others, and only they are involved in events all over the world. The determination of British governments to play a global role required that Britain have her own nuclear weapons. Harold Macmillan, who was Minister of Defence in 1955 when the rationale of Britain's nuclear deterrent began to take form, became as Prime Minister the devoted exponent of British greatness and thus of the forces upon which he thought greatness must rest. He turned aside criticism of Britain's hydrogen-bomb tests in the spring of 1957, for example, with the statement that it was only "common sense to put ourselves in the position that we have been working for so long to attain, that we should not be in a weaker position than those other two great Powers."[22] A year later, he assured the nation that "the independent contribution" of a nuclear force "gives us a better position with respect to the United States. It puts us where we ought to be, in the position of a great power.

---

[21]Lt. Gen. Sir John G. Cowley, who had recently been Controller of Munitions in the Ministry of Supply, pointed out in a lecture given on November 4, 1959, that the British nuclear deterrent cost "something like 20 per cent of the total defence budget, or more than half as much as the whole Army Vote." "Future Trends in Warfare," *Journal of the Royal United Service Institution*, CV (February, 1960), 11. Lower estimates apparently reflect the cost of maintaining a force, rather than building one, and in recent years the saving gained by depending upon the United States for its modernization. On March 8, 1966, Michael Stewart, the Foreign Secretary, said that expenditure on the "nuclear element" would decline from a present 5½ percent to 2 percent of total British arms expenditure. *H.C. Deb.*, Vol. 725 (March 8, 1966), col. 1948.

[22]*H.C. Deb.*, Vol. 566 (March 5, 1957), col. 181.

The fact that we have it makes the United States pay a greater regard to our point of view, and that is of great importance." [23]

No single rationale for an independent deterrent would stand up to scrutiny. The strategy of its justification had to be a mixed one. To emphasize the contribution that Britain's nuclear force made to the strength of the Alliance was bound to call attention to its irrelevance. To dwell upon the question of the deterrent's possible military uses could only become embarrassing. In these trying circumstances, official statements ascended to a level of generality where the quest for disarmament and the maintenance of international influence replaced more concrete objectives of foreign and military policy. Rather than describe the power that nuclear weapons would generate, Ministers dwelt upon the status their possession would bring. Nuclear weapons were advertised as the means of gaining entry to the conference rooms in which international decisions are said to be made. Promoting meetings at the summit and pressing for an agreement to cease testing nuclear warheads became a part of Macmillan's stock in trade. Politically his most striking argument was the statement that he and his government, by promoting a Test Ban, had done more than the Campaign for Nuclear Disarmament to save the world's people from fallout; perhaps his nicest touch was to thank Presidents Eisenhower and Kennedy for their assistance in gaining this end.[24]

Britain produced by her own effort an impressive first-generation deterrent, the V-bomber force. She never succeeded in building a second generation of nuclear weapons. The attempt to move into the missile age by spending a small portion of a small defense budget on nuclear delivery systems was doomed to failure. Blue Streak, a liquid-fueled, fixed-site missile whose basic components were all of American design, was obsolete before it was ever produced. Its cancellation in 1960 should have made the emptiness of Britain's claim to nuclear independence plain for even the myopic to see.

Once the V-bombers became obsolete as a strategic force, Britain's nuclear weapons could only be symbolic. In claiming world influence, Macmillan sought to perform a conjuror's trick. With the added remark

---

[23]Quoted by R. H. S. Crossman from a television address. *H.C. Deb.*, Vol. 583 (February 27, 1958), col. 635.

[24]"Macmillan's Way," *Economist*, CCX (February 15, 1964), 577–78. Cf. Home's later statement in the Commons: "I was in the negotiations all through on the nuclear Test Ban Treaty. I have no doubt whatever that we would never have got that treaty unless the United Kingdom had been in a position to intervene from knowledge and had a status which could not be denied. We would not have got it if it had not been that we were a nuclear Power." *H.C. Deb.*, Vol. 704 (December 17, 1964), col. 588.

that since the policy had worked nicely for eighteen years after the war there was no reason for Britain's rulers to look for firmer footing, Coral Bell delightedly described the policy as one of managing "to walk upon the water." [25] It would have been wise to remember that for two thousand years no one had performed that particular trick without a puppeteer working the strings. The Nassau Agreement, by which Polaris was substituted for Skybolt as the future vehicle for Britain's nuclear warheads, gave the game away, if anyone had retained his illusions. "The case for British nuclear weapons," Bell nevertheless concluded, "has always been, essentially, that lack of them meant total diplomatic dependence on the U.S." [26] But trying to have them, without much pain or sacrifice, produced military as well as diplomatic dependence on America. A nuclear establishment maintained because of the desire to put "the 'great' back into Great Britain" turned England into a nuclear satellite of the United States.

The interests of intellectuals lead them to expose what politicians would like to conceal. Once the conjuror's trick is understood, it ceases to dazzle the audience. If a state's role in the world is based merely on the symbols of power, then the influence of that state will be merely symbolic.

Immaterialism is common in England. Having retired as Permanent Under-Secretary of State at the Foreign Office in 1953, Lord Strang, for example, carefully distinguished power from influence and argued that, given skill and finesse, possession of the former becomes with the passage of years less and less a necessary condition for the enjoyment of the latter.[27] That pretension to greatness is widely popular is illustrated by the vigorous nationalism that spreads across the political spectrum in England. Though illustrative statements from the extremes may strike one as being bizarre, their authors have simply taken seriously the pretensions common at the center of politics and expressed them with a naïveté that makes their emptiness apparent. Thus Field Marshal Montgomery, returning from talks with Mao Tse-tung and Chou En-lai, urged as a way to prevent war "a non-aggression pact between the leading land Powers in Europe and Asia. There would be the United Kingdom, France, Russia, and China. We would then have two groupings—N.A.T.O. with

[25]Bell, *The Debatable Alliance: An Essay in Anglo-American Relations* (London: Oxford University Press, 1964), p. 117.
[26]*Ibid.*, p. 125.
[27]Lord William Strang, *Britain in World Affairs: The Fluctuation in Power and Influence from Henry VIII to Elizabeth II* (New York: Praeger, 1961), pp. 13, 373.

the United States in the lead, and a Europe-Asian grouping with the United Kingdom in the lead. For obvious reasons the United States could not be a member of the Europe-Asian group, nor would she want to be. The United Kingdom and France would belong to both groupings—a hinge between the two, a solid hinge of pure gold holding fast to both groups." Mao, he reported, was enthusiastically in favor of the idea and willing to accept British leadership.[28] From the opposite political pole, John Rex and Peter Worsley, writing in the *New Left Review,* set out an elaborate argument for a new British foreign policy. "Unilateralism" they believe, "ought always to be seen and understood as the only strategic position which will permit Britain to act to prevent the general threat of nuclear war." The "powers," they argue, "will not, of their own accord, make peace: they will have to be led or shoved towards it." Britain can help to do this, but only if first she disentangles herself from commitment to one camp and adopts a policy of *"positive neutrality."* Believing disengagement in Europe desirable, they also believe that Britain, unhampered by allegiance to NATO, can use her "moral leadership" with the "firm aim of creating such neutral areas."[29] In the pages of the *New Left Review* and elsewhere the notion of Britain leading a positive neutral bloc, to include Yugoslavia, Egypt, India, and others, recurs. It is always assumed that such countries are anxious to be led and would be pleased to have England at their head.

Behind such thoughts lies the notion that the weaker a country becomes, the more influence it can have in the world. The most striking parody of widely prevalent attitudes came from an expected source. In the spring of 1965, Quintin Hogg told the Commons that though Britain once spoke to the world with the authority of power, "we speak with greater authority still today, when in place of our security we have vulnerability, when we have become one of the most precariously poised of all the societies of men on the face of this earth, almost the ideal targets for modern weapons of war." Asians, Africans, Americans, and Russians may survive a nuclear exchange; Britons would not. Therefore, Hogg reasoned, "when we speak about these matters we speak with all the moral authority of men and women who will be doomed unless we get the answer right, and unless we not only get the answer right but persuade our fellow men of the truth of what we are saying." The British, he added

---

[28]Field Marshal Viscount Montgomery, "China and 'The Ugly American,'" *Sunday Times* (London), June 19, 1960, p. 21.
[29]Rex and Worsley, "Campaign for a Foreign Policy," *New Left Review* (July–August, 1960), pp. 50–52.

in closing, "have not forgotten their precedence of teaching other nations how to live."[30]

Nineteenth-century British liberals, generalizing from the plentitude of England's power that made the use of force unnecessary, were inclined to think that right reason and a good intention could be substituted for the material bases of foreign policy. While the Liberal Party has dwindled to political insignificance, its idea has triumphed. The Conservative Party has in it more of aristocratic paternalism than of materialist free enterprise; the Labour Party, more of Methodism than of Marx. The Labour Party might have been saved from committing the immaterialist error in international relations by learning from socialist theory and the experience of domestic politics the importance of controlling the instruments of power. Some of course did, Ernest Bevin notable among them. But strangely enough those most deeply committed to old-fashioned socialism have been least inclined to realism in international relations. Those who call from the left for a socialist foreign policy reveal themselves as more British than socialist, for they combine a yen for recapturing past glory with a disregard for Britain's present weakness. The notion that Britain can and should "give a lead" is common to right and center and left.

Lionel Gelber, a Canadian and a veteran commentator on British-American affairs, believes that Britain has been able to maintain her special place in an era of American primacy by the multiplicity of attachments she has been able to maintain.[31] Gelber might better have concluded, and would have were he writing of any other country, that, given scanty power, to multiply interests is to compound weakness. The futility to which British pretensions to influence are reduced is illustrated by a statement of Sir William Hayter, a retired Ambassador and former Deputy Under-Secretary of State at the Foreign Office. "A country," he writes, "which aspires to exercise world-wide influence with as little material backing as Great Britain now possesses cannot afford to neglect the intangible advantages she can draw from the diffusion of her culture, which is widely respected, and in particular from the generalized use of her language which is now the nearest to a *lingua franca* that the world possesses." [32] The first clause in the statement ought to have prompted in

[30]*H.C. Deb.*, Vol. 707 (March 4, 1965), cols. 1649–50.
[31]Gelber, *America in Britain's Place* (New York: Praeger, 1961), p. 151.
[32]Hayter, *The Diplomacy of the Great Powers* (New York: Macmillan, 1961), p. 51. The great importance of the English language and culture in maintaining British influence in the world is frequently emphasized. See, *Planning* (No. 201 [London: Political and Economic

Hayter's mind the question "Should she?" rather than the implied, "How can she go about it?"

Such remarks reflect the policies and practices of British leaders. The furthest evolution and the clearest example of the influence game was provided by Harold Wilson shortly after he formed his first government. The American Ally, he solemnly informed the House, is little impressed with British claims to "a seat at the top table" if those claims are based on nuclear power. Instead, he reasoned, "when we argue about our right to a central place, whether in the Alliance, whether in the United Nations, whether in world affairs generally, about our influence, about our presence at the top table and all the rest of it, let us recognise that our rights depend on this world-wide rôle, that it is a distinctive rôle and that no one else can do it." [33] If the material bases for the global exercise of British influence are lacking, never mind. In the ultimate expression of immaterialism, the nation's influence is said to derive from her world-wide roles, whether or not she has the ability to play them!

The words and acts of Wilson's first government indicated that Britain would jockey for favorable position among the European states, while continuing to play at being a world power. The 1965 *Statement on Defence* drew attention to the Labour Government's proposal to form an Allied Nuclear Force (ANF), in which strategic nuclear weapons would be subject to "collective authority." [34] The contributors of nuclear weapons, Wilson explained to the Commons, would enjoy a privileged position in the management of the force. Put simply, West Germany, a new European state, or any other presently non-nuclear political entity would be prevented from acquiring control over the use of nuclear weapons, though arrangements for such states singly or collectively to exercise a veto could be envisioned.[35] At the same time, the V-bombers that Britain would retain "for commitments outside the N.A.T.O. area" would "help to provide some reassurance to non-nuclear powers." Commonwealth ties as well as nuclear weapons would enable Britain "to make a contribution towards peace-keeping in vast areas of the world." [36] As Healey had earlier declared, "there is at least agreement between the two sides of the

Planning, 1943]), in Harold and Margaret Sprout, eds., *Foundations of National Power* (Princeton: Princeton University Press, 1945), p. 210; C. M. Woodhouse, *British Foreign Policy Since the Second World War* (London: Hutchinson, 1961), p. 245.

[33]*H.C. Deb.*, Vol. 704 (December 16, 1964), col. 425.

[34]*Statement on the Defence Estimates: 1965*, Cmnd. 2592 (London: HMSO, 1965), p. 7, par. 14.

[35]*H.C. Deb.*, Vol. 704 (December 16, 1964), cols. 434–39.

[36]*Statement on the Defence Estimates: 1965*, pp. 8, 7, 9, pars. 15, 12, 20.

House that Britain's world-wide role is an essential role which Britain must perform and which, indeed, no other country is capable of performing if Britain does not." [37]

The White Paper of 1965 had restated Britain's three major military roles—to support a strategic nuclear force, to make a major contribution toward the defense of Western Europe inside NATO, and to assist in keeping the peace elsewhere overseas—and called for a review of the balance among them.[38] The 1966 *Defence Review* altered the balance of roles slightly without surrendering any one of them. First, the ANF was modestly described as "the best basis for discussion in this field" (though Healey, like his predecessors, immodestly claimed that Britain's nuclear force "will make a massive contribution to the deterrent power of our alliance" [39]). Second, support of the many alliances of which Britain is a member would continue. Finally, maintenance of peace around the world, it was said, "above all . . . justifies our military presence outside Europe." [40]

The military plans announced early in 1966 weakened Britain's military grasp without suggesting that her reach should be shortened. Plans to build an aircraft carrier were canceled, but the intent to buy 50 F-111A's from the United States was also revealed. The closing of the base at Aden was scheduled, but forces in the Persian Gulf, it was said, would be strengthened a bit. According to the government's statement, the number of troops serving abroad, outside of Europe, would be reduced by more than 30 percent; and yet it was promised that treaty and other responsibilities "east of Suez" would continue "for many years." [41] Commitments were to continue essentially intact, while defense spending dropped from 7 percent yearly to 6 percent of GNP. The "new" policy of the Labour Government amounted to keeping the roles, reducing the means, and changing the rationalizations.

An earlier "defence review," of which the results were announced in 1957, was prompted by burgeoning costs and a desire to perpetuate the

---

[37]*H.C. Deb.*, Vol. 704 (December 17, 1964), col. 612.
[38]*Statement on the Defence Estimates: 1965*, p. 6, par. 7.
[39]*H.C. Deb.*, Vol. 725 (March 7, 1966), col. 1795.
[40]*The Defence Review*, Cmnd. 2901 (*Statement on the Defence Estimates: 1966*, Pt. I [London: HMSO, 1966]), pp. 5–7, pars. 11, 16.
[41]See the statement of Healey, in *H.C. Deb.*, Vol. 725 (March 7, 1966), cols. 1778–79. As of January 1, 1966, Britain had 1,475 troops in the Caribbean, 64,797 in West Germany and Berlin, 22,150 in the Mediterranean, 26,850 in the Middle East, and 54,050 in the Far East. The figures include all services but not men on the ships at sea. *Defence Estimates: 1966–67*, Cmnd. 2902 (*Statement on the Defence Estimates: 1966*, Pt. II [London: HMSO, 1966]), Annex G.

nation's influence at a price Englishmen would be willing and able to pay. The review that was completed in 1966 originated in the same concerns and reached, in one respect, an identical conclusion: the perpetuation of world influence could be managed at a more reasonable price. In another respect, 1966 was reminiscent of the period prior to 1955. In British policy now as then, "contribution" is emphasized to the exclusion of the ability to act alone. Before Suez it was clear, despite statements that implied the contrary, that Britain would not use nuclear weapons on her own. After Suez it was widely believed that even limited military interventions would be undertaken only with American approval and support. In the White Paper of 1966 and the debates that accompanied it that belief was officially affirmed. The promise was made that Britain "will not undertake major operations of war except in co-operation with allies." The vain quest for world influence has inevitably led to dependence.[42]

Policy Empirically Designed

It is not unusual in complicated affairs of state to aim for a certain result and produce an entirely different one. The American Constitution, to cite one example, was designed to be proof against parties. To cite another, the Act of Settlement, which conferred the reversion of the crown upon the House of Hanover, carefully separated the functions and powers of government in Britain. In each case, results confounded the designers' expectations. It is nevertheless extraordinary to find, as in British military policy, such a series of unfortunate effects produced by a policy that the country persists in.

Why has policy gone awry? The ingrained British habit of proceeding empirically, of eschewing scientific analysis and criticism on intellectual or theoretical grounds, of preferring common sense to abstract reasoning provides an important part of the answer. The empiric leans on precedent, carefully digests past experience, and cautiously takes one step at a time. This may or may not be a good way of proceeding; it is surely a conservative way. How serviceable it is will depend on the problem at hand and the conditions that prevail.

The difficulties of proceeding empirically are sharply illustrated by the timing of British decisions. As the policy of Duncan Sandys was insti-

---

[42]For the promise, see *The Defence Review* (1966), p. 7, par. 19. On dependence, cf. the speech by Christopher Mayhew upon his resignation as Minister of Defence for the Royal Navy. *H.C. Deb.*, Vol. 725 (February 22, 1966), cols. 254–65.

tuted, Russia lofted its first Sputnik. The building of the Blue Streak missile was announced in 1958; the project was abandoned two years later. So long as Blue Streak was being defended, Polaris was described as "extremely costly" and "unlikely to remain undetectable." Its movements, according to Defence Minister Watkinson, "could be closely watched by an enemy."[43] Just before the Nassau conference in December of 1962, Ministers proclaimed and the press reported that Britain required Skybolt in order to survive as a nuclear power. The view was attributed to Peter Thorneycroft, who had become Minister of Defence, though American officials had warned from the outset that Polaris would be a safer and surer bet. With Skybolt canceled and Polaris missiles substituted for it, Thorneycroft returned to London eagerly supporting the new arrangement. It was, he said, "an imaginative advance in the field of cooperation in the Western alliance" that would provide "features of an independent British deterrent which is essential for our sovereign rights to defend ourselves."[44] Britain might hope to build and maintain submarines to carry sixty or seventy missiles; the United States would have about two thousand missiles by 1968. The huge cost of a small force was suggested in headlines and borne home in the articles that followed. Britain's dependence upon America was made clearer than ever before. George Brown's charge that Nassau demonstrated the bankruptcy of the government's defense policy carried more conviction than Macmillan's and Thorneycroft's defensive statements. The story was an old one. The government's policy had collapsed once more, and the policy to replace it was made in Washington.

England in early 1960 urged a reduction in NATO requirements for materiel kept on hand from a three- to a one-month supply. A military action in Europe would either be small and abortive or would escalate to the nuclear level. In either event, few ground troops would be needed. American strategists in the late 1950's and the Kennedy Administration from the outset questioned these assumptions. To escape from the alternatives of suicide or surrender, the United States urged the importance of building a conventional defense capability in Europe. The British Army of the Rhine, with manpower diminished, remained unable to fight without quickly reaching for nuclear weapons. From observing the military exercise "Spearpoint" conducted by British and American troops in Ger-

[43]*Times* (London), February 11, 1959, p. 10.
[44]*Philadelphia Bulletin*, December 22, 1962, p. 2. Cf. his statement, reported in the *Times* (London), December 24, 1962, p. 4: "This horse is in the stable. It is sound. You can take it out and run it tomorrow. Skybolt is not in the stable and is thought to be lame."

many in October of 1961, Anthony Verrier concluded that "most of the theories about containing aggression, which are believed and practised in BAOR (if nowhere else)" were exploded and that the "unnecessary and dubious dependence on nuclear weapons causes so many strains within the alliance, and produces doubts as to whether BAOR, as it is today, can be said to perform any useful role at all." [45]

British policy on military posts abroad is another striking example of policy empirically made.[46] With a far-flung network of bases, expensive to maintain and becoming in series politically untenable, the makers of military policy apparently did not ask themselves what British bases are for in a bipolar, nuclear-armed world but instead made decisions base by base whenever political pressures in host territories grew. When the price of hanging on becomes forbidding, the discovery of good reasons for leaving is remarkably facilitated. The base at Suez was described by Churchill and others as essential to the military and economic interests of Great Britain in the Middle East—until Churchill himself announced that in the atomic age Suez was no longer tenable and, fortunately, Britain could get along without it anyway. The fashion then came to be to describe Cyprus in terms used earlier to adorn the British presence in Suez, until the Cyprus base became unusable, which made it necessary to transfer such adjectives as essential and vital to Aden. The effect of proceeding empirically is to suppress assumptions without eliminating them and to focus upon means without relating them adequately to military and political conditions, economic capability, and changes in technology.

Year after year governments get the policies they ask for, yet military policy has been a mixture of fiasco and folly—military arrangements ill accord with the international aims of the nation; some military policies are inconsistent with others; heavy spending produces little benefit. Brigadier Fernyhough, Director of Ammunitions and Stores, was quoted on the floor of the House of Commons in February, 1960, as estimating that: "In relation to its small size and large commitments, the British Army must be one of the worst equipped in the world." [47] In December of

---

[45]Verrier, "Strategic Thinking in Europe: Reflections on 'Spearpoint' and 'Bootjack,' " *Journal of the Royal United Service Institution*, CVII (May, 1962), 125, 129. Cf. the comment of the Defence Correspondent of the *Times* ("The British Army in Germany," *Times* [London], October 17, 1963, reprinted in *Survival*, VI [January–February, 1964], 37–38): "It is not necessary to go deeply into the mysteries of nuclear strategy and tactics to be convinced that an army that can offer a defence in Europe only by using nuclear weapons may in the event be unable to offer any defence at all."

[46]Cf. Lt. Col. DeWitt L. Armstrong, "The British Re-value Their Strategic Bases," *Journal of the Royal United Service Institution*, CIV (November, 1959), 428.

[47]*H.C. Deb.*, Vol. 618 (February 29, 1960), cols. 916–17.

1961, Sir William Hayter expressed dismay over the decision to abolish National Service and to rely more heavily on nuclear weapons. He described British forces as puny in size, her divisions in Europe as able to fight only with nuclear weapons, her forces in general as wrongly located (with too many in Asia and too few in Europe). In numbers of men mobilized, he found Britain "the fifth Power in Nato, after the United States, France, Turkey and Italy." And, he added, "In the proportion of mobilised manpower to the total national labour force we come eleventh. . . ."[48] In July, 1963, Alastair Buchan found Britain to be the seventh power in the world in terms of mobilized manpower.[49] Britain spends a higher proportion of her national product on defense than any other country of comparable size.[50] The result of such heavy expenditure was no more apparent in armaments than in manpower, in the navy and air force than in the army, in the new field of rocketry than in the old field of conventional weapons. By 1963, except for the 105 mm. gun and the Thunderbird missile, all of the army's major modern weapons were foreign. In the same year, the main strength of the navy consisted of nine ships that had been built or laid down during World War II. Only 25,000 men were absorbed by the element that constituted the "teeth" of the navy. The air force, which had concentrated single-mindedly on heavy bombers, was left by the cancellation of the American Skybolt with a force that was obsolescent, even with the development of the Blue Steel stand-off missile.[51] The TSR.2 plane was not yet available; its production was in fact to be canceled two years later. Planes suitable for support of the army had almost disappeared. The history of British missile development has been one of false starts, unproductive duplication, unimaginative competition among services, sluggish development, and cancellation of most projects after the expenditure of large sums of money. As one defense correspondent has said of missile development in England: "No pattern emerges at any stage of its proceedings. Neither control nor continuity of thought can be discerned" in the programs.[52]

It is easier to redefine capabilities as requirements change than it is to recast objectives or reconstruct military forces. With alarming frequency, Britain has followed the easier course. As the warning time for England, should Soviet missiles be directed against her, shrank to four minutes, it

[48]Hayter, "Forces Too Few and Far Away," *Observer*, December 10, 1961, p. 10.
[49]Buchan, "Manning Britain's Defences," *Observer*, July 21, 1963.
[50]See Healey, *H.C. Deb.*, Vol. 707 (March 3, 1965), col. 1341.
[51]David Divine, *The Blunted Sword* (London: Hutchinson, 1964), pp. 16–17.
[52]*Ibid.*, p. 214.

was declared that four minutes was time enough to enable V-bombers to get off the ground, another claim that met with skepticism.[53] With the canceling in 1960 of the British Blue Streak and in 1962 of the American Skybolt it became clear that a weapons system to replace the V-bombers would be a long time in coming. It was thereupon declared, despite improvements in Soviet air defense, that the useful life of V-bombers would last until 1970; and TSR.2, originally intended as a tactical aircraft, was modified to permit it to make long-range nuclear strikes. The plane came to be described by spokesmen for the Conservative Government as capable of performing conventional and nuclear, tactical and strategic missions. As always, descriptions glowed more brightly as the moment for scrapping the weapon approached.

Parliamentary debates are littered with Ministerial descriptions of weapons coming along—tanks, antitank weapons, ground-to-ground missiles, air-to-ground missiles. "We cannot," the Defence Minister once explained to the House, "put our money on all the horses, like the Americans can, and we therefore have to back our fancy." [54] Many of the horses that Ministers have picked have failed to stay the course. Defense debates have been described by some Members of Parliament as miracles to behold. Ministers summon whole weapons systems into existence in the heat of debate on the floor of the House of Commons. Impressed with their own sleight of hand, Ministers and Members easily slip into talking as though an intention to develop a weapon brings an immediate accretion of strength.[55] The effect is demonstrated more significantly in acts than in words. The plan to end National Service was announced, and the final decision to do so taken, on the basis of nuclear substitutes, many of which are still not available, and in accordance with a military concept now rejected by both the United States and the Soviet Union. Almost all informed commentators, Ministers aside, express dismay at the condition of military equipment and skepticism about the implementation of stated future intentions. England is the only major NATO country without some form of compulsory service. The question of whether or not sufficient volunteers would come forth was answered by engaging in a num-

[53]See the Strachey-Watkinson exchange, *H.C. Deb.*, Vol. 618 (March 1, 1960), cols. 1035–36.
[54]*H.C. Deb.*, Vol. 600 (February 25, 1959), col. 1139.
[55]George Brown, formerly the spokesman of the Labour opposition on matters of defense, frequently berated them for doing so. See *H.C. Deb.*, Vol. 549 (February 29, 1956), cols. 1203–9; *ibid.*, Vol. 564 (February 13, 1957), cols. 1290–91; *ibid.*, Vol. 600 (February 25, 1959), col. 1158; *ibid.*, Vol. 618 (February 29, 1960), cols. 867–69.

bers game with statements so hedged and confused that the number obtained could be described as just what was wanted.[56]

In 1965 the Labour Government, consciously imitating the American Department of Defense under McNamara, instituted operational analysis and adopted functional costings. The decisions announced as a result of the *Defence Review* were, however, strikingly like those of Conservative Governments—dropping one base at a time, canceling the latest crop of weapons under development, and creating some new ones on the floor of the House, which can at the moment be said to assure the future strength of the country and later on can be courageously canceled by the government of the day.[57] It is true that criteria for maintaining a base or deciding to close one were more clearly defined. The Labour Government has now stated that countries will not receive military aid unless they are willing to provide the needed facilities.[58] But such criteria themselves indicate the surrender of policy to events.

It was long a maxim of military strategy that weapons may change but principles do not. The maxim set forth an important truth so long as military means changed slowly. Given the long period of Britain's hegemony in the world, pursuing a policy of cautious adjustment was both effective and wise. To proceed empirically is inappropriate where changes come rapidly and the source of change lies outside of the nation's arena of control and influence. An empirical policy in a period of great change quickly gets out of gear with events. To move empirically means to evade basic decisions. British aspirations have remained constant and military roles have accrued, while the nation's tautly stretched resources have become inadequate to the accumulated tasks of her foreign policy. Instead of some obligations giving way to others, all have been borne, and each has been progressively less well fulfilled. An empirical government considers each problem as it becomes pressing and carefully makes one decision at a time. In her military policy, Britain has made a number of decisions each of which might be said to be sensible. Taken together they have formed a peculiar policy.

---

[56]The point was tellingly made on a number of occasions by George Wigg. See, for example, *H.C. Deb.*, Vol. 618 (February 29, 1960), cols. 909–12.

[57]To cite a recent example: the future development of "a small surface-to-surface guided weapon for use against missile-firing ships" will, according to Healey, make possible the protection of British ships in the absence of carriers. *H.C. Deb.*, Vol. 725 (March 7, 1966), col. 1793.

[58]*The Defence Review* (1966), p. 7, par. 19.

The Effects of Organization

The empirical cast of mind facilitates compromise and encourages political leaders to coast with events. The British political system itself has similar effects. Leopold Amery was cited in Chapter 5 as saying that a Cabinet policy, as such, scarcely ever exists, that "to a very large extent each department goes its own way," that the political system "is quite incompatible with any coherent planning of policy as a whole, or with the effective execution of such a policy," that attempts to reconcile conflicting departmental views ordinarily produce "weak compromises, postponements and fluctuations." [59]

Seen in this light, the Ministry of Defence takes on the appearance of a little cabinet, with the Defence Minister presiding over the three service Ministers and the Minister of Aviation. The reorganization of the Ministry of Defence in 1963/64, a move toward unification, left the services intact and incorporated their rivalry at the highest organizational level. [60] The Defence White Paper of 1957 had seemed to prefigure a wildly skewed military establishment. Nuclear weapons would strengthen the nation; reduced expenditure on military manpower would save money for the country. The "New Look" of Duncan Sandys appeared to embody a governmental decision. But the attempt to maintain sizable forces east of the Rhine and east of Suez made it impossible to achieve the promised imbalance. Instead of one arm being favored to the neglect of other forces, equally small sums of money were doled out to each of the services. With the Prime Minister and the Treasury setting the ceiling on military expenditure, the services have bargained fiercely over the division of funds. Policy continued to be the product of compromise among services, and none of them fared markedly worse than the others. Despite the stated intention, Britain became a nuclear power without unbalancing her forces, as Table 7 indicates. It is the weakness in conventional troops that has given the impression, a false one, that some other part of the military establishment must have been favored. The army was not very large, but with conscription abolished, it was large enough to be costly. The abolition of conscription was another decision of political

---

[59] Amery, *Thoughts on the Constitution* (London: Oxford University Press, 1947), pp. 87, 94.

[60] Cf. William P. Snyder, *The Politics of British Defense Policy, 1945–1962* (Columbus: Ohio State University Press, 1964), chap. 8; Divine, *The Blunted Sword*, pp. 237–39; Philip Abrams, "The Late Profession of Arms: Ambiguous Goals and Deteriorating Means in Britain," *European Journal of Sociology*, VI (1965), 255–57.

convenience, extravagant in relation to the country's resources and out of line with her foreign policy.

George Brown, when he was Labour's spokesman on questions of defense, correctly described the period from 1957 to 1959 (and he might have included earlier years as well) as one in which

> the individual Services fought like mad to protect their own forces and their own projects. By so doing, they prevented the savings which at that time the right hon. Gentleman thought he could make and sought to make.
>
> . . . .
>
> In fact, I believe that we are back to the old 1957 position and that this year there has been no central defence policy, which is why the Minister makes no mention of doctrine. We are back to the old days of a straight bargain between the three Services, in which they have each got as much of the money as they could and are putting it to the best use they can for their own purposes.[61]

Decision by bargaining and compromise has prevailed, especially on the Chiefs of Staff Committee and the Defence Research Policy Committee. Representatives of all three services sit on these two committees, which consider policies that are important to the separate services. William P. Snyder, who has published a thorough and perceptive study of the making of British defense policy, points out that the composition of these committees and the nature of their tasks result in familiar practices: "decisions can be postponed or, as often happens, the problem may be referred for additional study even though the important elements have already been thoroughly canvassed; decisions can be stated in vague and general terms with limited operational significance; and finally, the affected departments can agree by log-rolling, that is, by supporting the proposals of another service in return for its support on a different issue." [62] Similar practices prevailed in America, at least until McNamara became Secretary of Defense. They may do so again. Snyder reports a senior British officer as saying: "A quite accurate description of the operations of the Chiefs of Staff Committee has been written by General Maxwell Taylor, and appears in his book, *The Uncertain Trumpet.*" [63]

Similarities abound between the United States and Great Britain, but differences remain important. In England, the struggle that takes place among the services is largely invisible to the public, the press, and Parlia-

---

[61]*H.C. Deb.*, Vol. 600 (February 27, 1959), cols. 1155, 1160–61.
[62]Snyder, *The Politics of British Defense Policy, 1945–1962*, pp. 164–65.
[63]*Ibid.*, p. 165.

TABLE 7 Allocation of British Defense Budget, 1949-66

	NAVY	ARMY	AIR	DEFENCE (CENTRAL) AND AVIATION
1949/50	25.2%	39.2%	27.2%	8.4%
1950/51	24.4	39.8	28.9	6.9
1951/52	24.4	38.0	29.0	8.6
1952/53	23.8	37.0	30.0	9.2
1953/54	23.8	35.7	30.5	10.0
1954/55	24.1	33.2	32.3	10.4
1955/56	24.0	33.0	30.7	12.3
1956/57	22.5	32.7	30.9	13.9
1957/58	24.7	27.1	33.0	15.2
1958/59	25.4	29.6	30.7	14.3
1959/60	24.6	29.0	32.8	13.6
1960/61	24.4	30.3	33.4	11.9
1961/62	24.5	30.1	32.4	13.0
1962/63	24.8	29.9	32.3	13.0
1963/64	26.3	29.6	30.3	13.8
1964/65	27.1	28.9	28.1	15.9
1965/66	27.0	29.2	28.1	15.7

Source: Computed from Central Statistical Office, *Annual Abstract of Statistics* (London: HMSO, 1959, 1961, 1966), pp. 253, 259, 269. Expenditures by the separate services for military public works are not given for the years 1963/64 onward; they are in those years excluded from the computations.

ment. Even those important interests that feel grievously put upon by a Minister have little incentive to appeal to the Commons. The executive offices are the only arena of governmental decision. In the United States, Congressmen are appealed to because they exercise influence. They enjoy power because in the absence of discipline the administration needs their votes and cannot count on getting them. In Britain, where the decisions of Ministers determine the way in which MP's will vote, the struggle over policy remains locked in the Ministry of Defence or the Cabinet.

Organization and procedures accord with England's empirical habits. All interests are regarded as legitimate: the problem of policymakers is to arrive at a compromise among them, to find an accommodation that all will accept. Since the aim of the government is less to control than to accommodate, it is unfashionable, or bad form, to set interests in opposition publicly so that, by a dialectical process, a resolution can be achieved. The objective instead is to strike a compromise that all of the important interests in conflict can live with. Thus each program is at the moment acceptable, but the result taken in summation over a period of years is chaotic.

The Impact of Criticism

Two features of the British political system, subtly interdependent and almost contradictory, define the relation that ordinarily prevails between criticism, needs, and opinions, on the one hand, and the actions of the government, on the other. First, the critics are weak and the British system is impervious to the points they may make. Second, the government is sensitive to public sentiments vaguely felt and broadly expressed.

The customary behavior of British governments is more clearly seen if comparisons are made with the United States. Changes of policy and adjustments of governmental action in the United States are hastened by recurring criticisms publicly and impressively made. Until sometime in the early 1950's, it was widely believed that military affairs were the exclusive province of the professional. The economist outside of government could know what he needed to about fiscal questions and from his knowledge and professional standing comment with effect upon the government's policy. The layman who was concerned about military affairs did not have the experience and supposedly could not get the information necessary to make authoritative criticisms of military policy or constructive suggestions about it. The paucity of expert knowledge outside of the services, it turns out, was a product of indifference rather than disability and denial of access. As the critical importance of military affairs came to be recognized, experts came forth. Their doing so was facilitated by a looseness of governmental structure that encourages military men, differing among themselves, to carry their cases to Congressional committees in search of wider support. A large quantity of information, as compared to what is available in England, thus becomes publicly known. This has in itself eased the would-be private expert's path to greater knowledge and higher status. In the role here described, Congressional committees are, however, primarily *consumers* of information and ideas. Their primary contribution is to pry departments open, to render the processes of policy visible, to make the conflicts of interest and contrasts of ideas apparent to the concerned public. Thus experts and interests from outside the services get a chance to affect military policy.

That the layman can be recognized as expert is also made possible by national attitudes and the educational system of the country. The practice of consultancy has come to prevail in military as in other departments of government. Executive departments, like Congressional committees, are consumers of information and ideas generated by quasi-public and private institutions. "Thus, we find," Colonel Robert Ginsburgh has noted, "the RAND Corporation working primarily with the Air Force, the Research Analysis Corporation with the Army, the Operations Evaluation Group at M.I.T. with the Navy, and the Institute for Defense Analyses with the Joint Chiefs of Staff and Defense Department. In addition, there are some 350 other nonprofit corporations, some 300 college research centers, and 1400 industrial companies, as well as various private foundations and scientific advisory committees—all involved in some degree in the business of thinking about military problems." [64] The suppliers have multiplied in number, thus assuring that a variety of views will be offered. The status of the experts is supported by their institutional affiliations, and their authority is enhanced by the fact that their criticisms and analyses can sometimes at least be seen to make a difference in the policies and practices of government. The institutes and experts, which multiplied in the 1950's, came to exercise an influence on military policy that now makes some of the career soldiers and sailors feel like outsiders. [65]

Dissatisfaction must be reckoned with where there is a chance to make criticisms that will tell and to make suggestions that will be listened to. In England dissatisfaction finds a different expression. It is difficult for the few specialists in military affairs to carry their criticisms home. Factors that make in America for the spreading of expert knowledge and the establishment of sources of authority outside of the civil government and the professional military ranks are largely lacking in England. With bases of power independent of the President, Congressmen are fearsome critics of the government, whether or not it is of their own party. Because the reactions of Congressmen matter, outside interests appeal to them, and the administration pays heed to their views. The irresponsibility of parties makes the government highly responsive. MP's, in contrast, are weakly placed to criticize, dissent, or press alternative policies on the government. The disciplined Members of responsible parties have no effective way of interposing their wills or bringing pressure directly to bear. The discipline of parties which renders government responsible thereby makes it less responsive to criticism and less receptive to outside advice. The numerous foreign-policy research institutes in America have as coun-

[64]Ginsburgh, "The Challenge to Military Professionalism," *Foreign Affairs*, XLII (January, 1964), 260.

[65]See the sharp statements by General Thomas D. White, formerly Air Force Chief of Staff, "Strategy and the Defense Intellectuals," *Saturday Evening Post*, CCXXXVI (May 4, 1963), 10; and Admiral George W. Anderson, formerly Chief of Naval Operations and then Ambassador to Portugal, *New York Times*, September 5, 1963, p. 19.

terparts in England only the Institute of Strategic Studies, the Royal United Service Institution, and the Royal Institute of International Affairs. They have not been equipped or inclined to undertake operational research or quantitative analysis.[66] While a flood of official and semiofficial information and analyses pours forth in America, only a trickle appears in England. Seldom is a dissident voice from the military heard in public. The mildly critical lecture of General Cowley, delivered in early 1960, caused a flurry in Parliament and the press precisely because it was so much an exception.[67]

One may well argue that enough is known, partly from American sources, partly because what is at issue are the major lines of military policy rather than detailed questions of equipment and tactics, to permit incisively critical evaluations to be made. What is more important is that ways of establishing the authority of the critics—by permittng them access to departmental sources—are lacking. Furthermore, the evolutionary movement of policy and the invisibility of the processes by which it is formed obscure influence even where it may be present. These two characteristics compound the difficulty of any lay critic who would establish the authority to speak on questions of military policy, for nothing adds so much to the prestige of the expert as the impression that his advice makes a difference.

At first glance, it is puzzling that with many politically alert persons upset by British military policy, successive Conservative and Labour Governments have been able to maintain their course—or rather, to continue to drift. Some explanation of the slow response of British policy to criticisms and conditions has been given in preceding chapters. In military policy the difficulties are acute. Former service Ministers may occasionally adopt a critical view and speak with a voice that Ministers must hear because back-benchers are listening and may be impressed. The number of retired regular army officers serving in Commons is surprisingly large when compared with their total number in British society.[68] In a rapidly changing military environment, however, the knowledge and the authority of former Ministers and soldiers quickly erode. Most former officers and almost all the recent Ministers are in the Conservative Party, where personal inclinations and party mores tend to still their voices. With oc-

[66]"The American Strategic Revolution—V: Realistic Tactics for Britain," *Times* (London), August 2, 1963, p. 13.
[67]Cowley, "Future Trends in Warfare."
[68]Philip Abrams, "Democracy, Technology and the Retired British Officer," in Samuel P. Huntington, ed., *Changing Patterns of Military Politics* (New York: Free Press, 1962), pp. 166, 170.

casional exceptions, Conservative back-benchers become less willing to criticize their government the more vulnerable its policies become, lest the political standing of the party as a whole be weakened. The Labour Party, even during the governments of Macmillan and Home, when British defense policy was obviously a shambles, was unable to launch an effective assault. It has at best been difficult for Labour to convey the impression that in this field its competence may be greater than that of the Conservatives. During more than a decade of Conservative rule, Labour was at its worst on questions of defense, torn by problems first of German rearmament and then of nuclear weapons. Inside and outside of Parliament the Labour Party alternated between open splits and uneasy compromises.

The problem is not peculiar to Labour. On questions of defense and foreign policy, divisions appear within parties more frequently than is the case with domestic problems. Since World War II, conscription, German rearmament, Suez on three important occasions, and nuclear weapons recurringly have provoked serious internal discord in one or the other of the two major parties. Sometimes at least, events in the world set the pace to which parties are constrained to adapt. Where decisions are less easily postponed, the importance of the arts of party management is dramatized. The government will of course try to find the policy that at once serves the country and satisfies the party. Both the party's and the nation's interests are embodied in foreign policy. If the interest of the former should dominate, will not the opposition be quick to attack? The matter is not so simple. If the opposition should attack in other than platitudes and on more than peripheral matters, it may itself fall apart. Labour's official leaders defended Blue Streak as long as the government continued to do so. Wilson in March of 1964 held confidential talks with Home on defense and had earlier suggested forming a bipartisan front on defense policy.[69] Skeptical of the so-called independent deterrent, Harold Wilson dropped the notion of independence but kept the deterrent. Spokesmen of the Labour Party when it was out of power were unwilling to say simply that the British deterrent made no useful military contribution and should be disposed of; instead, they suggested that British weapons should be merged somehow with NATO forces or simply permitted to run down. This may have satisfied nobody fully, but it had the considerable merit of provoking few to adamant dissent. Like governing

[69]Anthony Howard, "Leftist Legacy," New Statesman, LXVII (March 27, 1964), 482–84; James Feron, "British to Debate Defense Problem," New York Times, January 10, 1964, p. 7.

169

parties, opposition parties try to mute those members who have ideas on policy that are out of the ordinary. At the Conservative Party Conference in October of 1965, Enoch Powell spoke like a little Englander and a good European. Put up by the Party to lead off the debate on defense in March of 1966, he sounded as though he were devoted to the perpetuation of Britain's global role and persuaded that the Labour Government was doing too little to sustain it. Different wings of the party could find some crumbs of comfort in the performance: for some he said the right things; others could solace themselves with the thought that he did not really mean them.

The management of the opposition party is a difficult task; challenges to the government will in many cases hazard the opposition's appearance of unity. It is safe and often politically wise to confine criticism to routine questions of cost and administrative efficiency and to peripheral matters of policy—in short, to concentrate on scoring points in the debate. Since the opposition party as well as the governing party is a responsible body —constantly and collectively presenting itself to the electorate for approval—the bold attack inevitably implies that in office it will adopt a bold and controversial policy. For this reason, the tiresome game is played in the Commons of Ministers, when they are attacked, demanding that the opposition either say what it would do if it were in power or assent to the government's policy. Thus Conservative Governments responded to criticism by twitting Labour spokesmen on their own party's difficulties. Prime Minister Macmillan's reply to a critical Labour motion was typical. Leaving pacifists aside and concentrating upon those within the Labour Party who agreed that England should have a nuclear deterrent, he said in the defense debate of April, 1957:

> I am not sure whether this is still the official view of the Opposition Front Bench. . . . We have what seems to be a compromise. . . . We are to rely on the nuclear deterrent—but not unduly. We are to postpone our bomb tests—but not for very long. We are to ask other Powers to agree to abolish all bomb tests, and if by any chance they should agree, then presumably they would be left with the fully tested bomb and we should be left with a bomb which had not been tested at all. So, of course, we should have to rely on American nuclear power for our defence. In the same breath the same hon. Members tell us that it is humiliating to obtain, whether by gift or purchase, an American rocket because the warhead is under American control until we can make our own. Then, to crown it all, the House is asked to withhold its approval from a policy which lacks firm decisions.[70]

[70]*H.C. Deb.*, Vol. 568 (April 17, 1957), cols. 2044–45.

On a later occasion, Thorneycroft defended the independent deterrent by first questioning the Labour Party's attitude toward the Polaris missile base, which the government had granted to the United States, and then challenging Labour to give "absolute assurance," if indeed it did wish to rely on America's nuclear deterrent, that it supported the American base. To the delight of his own supporters, Thorneycroft asked the opposition, "Can we have that assurance?" He concluded, since Labour's leaders remained silent, that "the whole of this argument, which has gone on for two days, is rendered absolutely meaningless by the Opposition's failure to answer this question." [71]

In England, debates are held to defend or attack a policy that has already been made. In America, deliberation takes place as part of the effort to find a policy or to form one. Individually or in committee, Congressmen probe, investigate, register information, criticize policy and performance, and suggest amendments and alternatives. All of these operations they perform before, during, and after policy is set by the administration's acts or by national legislation. In Britain, the House of Commons cannot be involved in the earlier stages of legislation or executive decision. The constitutional principle requiring that Parliament be the first to be publicly informed precludes early investigation and discussion, for Parliament cannot be informed until the government is ready to press its proposals into legislation. At that point, the government cannot politically afford to lose a debate. Parliament is presented with a finished program that will ordinarily be changed by no more than some alteration of detail. If the government is challenged, it must protect itself by defending its policy. Vigorous debate then makes changes in policy less likely. And the opposition, if it boldly attacks, must be prepared to accept publicly the reputation of standing for a policy contrary to the government's. Debate then inhibits deliberation. The orderly confrontation of two parties, each publicly responsible for the positions it takes, reduces their flexibility, puts a premium on playing it safe, and turns both of them to the steadfast pursuit of popularity. In England, policy is constantly debated, but the aim of the argument is to make a favorable impression on the voter. In the United States, elections can be perpetually prepared for without seriously damaging the government's performance, and the prospects of candidates can be constantly canvassed, because the electoral game is less closely joined to the process of justifying policy.

American observers of the English political scene sometimes interpret

[71] *H.C. Deb.*, Vol. 690 (February 27, 1964), col. 759.

vociferous support for positions widely separated from the government's as an example of dissent that somehow increases the possibilities of change. David Riesman and Michael Maccoby, for example, tell us that "Americans concerned not only with disarmament but with opening up the political climate to debate on the issue have looked at Britain as a country where issues confined to the margins of discourse in the United States are openly debated."[72] Discontent coupled with impotence easily produces feelings of alienation, which more often find expression in emotional spasms than in careful analyses and in reasoned discussion. That in England one can take a peripheral position and find a public response should be interpreted as an effect of the closed quality of governmental arrangements and the slow responsiveness of the political system in a society in which class divisions remain important. In a class society, feelings of antagonism against the strata from which governors are most frequently recruited encourage attempts to mobilize minorities against the policy of the day by playing upon vague desires for radical change. Thus the Campaign for Nuclear Disarmament has made gestures of rejection rather than sustained efforts to find a workable policy in a difficult world. Focusing attention on grandiose desires diverts attention from reforms that might actually be achieved. Rather than to increase the prospect of change, the effect of the CND was, from the founding of the movement in 1958 and for several years thereafter, to drive the political middle together in defense of an unsatisfactory policy that continued to look better than its wildly stated alternative.

The Influence of Opinion

Britain, then, has perfected a politics of gradual adjustment, with leaders more alert to public attitudes and opinions than they are to needs and opportunities, to criticisms and counsel. Such a judgment is controversial, for England has long been thought of as a country in which Prime Minister and Cabinet are much less closely constrained by public opinion than is the American government. Sir Ivone Kirkpatrick, Permanent Under-Secretary at the Foreign Office when Bevin was Foreign Secretary, reports that his chief was impervious to warnings that his policy might be unpopular in Parliament, press, or trade unions.[73] Kenneth Younger, reflecting on twenty months of service as a Minister in the Foreign Office,

[72]Riesman and Maccoby, "The American Crisis," in James Roosevelt, ed., *The Liberal Papers* (New York: Doubleday, 1962), p. 23.
[73]Kirkpatrick, *The Inner Circle* (London: Macmillan, 1959), p. 202.

was surprised to find that he could remember no occasion on which he or his superiors had been greatly affected in important decisions by public opinion.[74] At the same time, Younger avers, "the government tends to identify itself almost unconsciously with a vaguely sensed general will." [75] Lord Strang, who was Kirkpatrick's successor, fully agrees. Arrangements for the control of foreign policy he finds adequate to their purpose, which is "to ensure that foreign policy conforms to the general will or, in other words, that foreign policy is of a piece with the characteristic behaviour of the community." [76] The result is achieved, Younger and Strang both believe, through MP's asking questions and Ministers listening to the murmurs of approval and disapproval evoked by their answers. The description is accurate enough. Limits on the Prime Minister's and the government's power are gross and external. Kirkpatrick, Younger, and Strang have said something important, though it may not be quite what they intended. There are no immediately effective impediments to the government's actions. Freedom of governmental action, however, must mean ineffectiveness of Parliamentary control even in a slowly developing crisis, as Labour and Conservative MP's who opposed the Suez adventure, Younger among them, ruefully noticed.

The Prime Minister has the ability and sometimes the will to act aside from the opinion of the moment. This does not mean that British governments will pay no attention to domestic political costs. It means instead that how necessities are defined, costs estimated, and political courage summoned are questions for the government itself to decide. "In fact," an American student of British defense policy has recently written, "public opinion places few limitations on policy choices." [77] If one is concerned about direct obstacles to policy in a short period of time, then it is fair to say that opinion in Britain does not prevent a government from following a line. It is, however, important to distinguish, on the one hand, opinion pressing immediately upon government from, on the other hand, the government's reaction to public attitudes and inclinations over the years. How is a government restrained? The answer to this question varies from one country to the other. British governments, broadly in accord with party and public desires, may be immovable on measures. What major policies will the public be willing to sustain over a period

[74]Younger, "Public Opinion and Foreign Policy," *British Journal of Sociology*, VI (June, 1955), 169.
[75]*Ibid.*, p. 171.
[76]Strang, "The Formation and Control of Foreign Policy," *Durham University Journal*, XLIX (June, 1957), 108.
[77]Snyder, *The Politics of British Defense Policy*, p. 54.

of years? Answers to this question may be as restrictive of governmental action in England as in America. Public opinion, which is not an obstacle to immediate acts and specific programs, nevertheless exerts a gentle pressure that over a period of years encourages tendencies and tends to shape policies.

In the making of defense policy, pressures and stringencies at home must be coped with while policy is constantly adjusted to technological developments and changing conditions abroad. Because military policy is prey to the actions of other peoples, a good defense policy becomes difficult to make and maintain. But Britain's troubles cannot be excused by reference to outside events. Given the odd structure of the British military establishment, it is difficult to think of important types of crisis that the country could meet by employing its military forces—or any that it would actually need to.

Labour leaders in opposition frequently charged Conservative Governments with failing to align military and foreign policy: the country's military forces could serve no useful purpose abroad. The criticism was at once just and beside the point. Military policy *and* foreign policy have been only distantly related to the country's situation because governments, attuned to the mood of the nation, have used their international policies to serve their domestic political purposes. Macmillan well knew that the people found the assertion of influence exhilarating, and Home in one general election featured the theme that a Conservative Government equipped with H-bombs would perpetuate the global influence of the nation. In writing of British and American discussions about the cancellation of Skybolt, Henry Brandon reported that "whenever the British political argument cropped up about the need to maintain an independent deterrent Washington suggested earnestly and with raised eyebrows that defence was a serious business—not merely symbolic." [78] For Britain, however, it *has* been merely symbolic. Britain's military policy has been devised for the sake of prestige, and her strategy has been designed for the home front. In view of the easy choices that international conditions have afforded to powers of the second rank, British policy has been unnecessarily expensive and surprisingly unsuccessful. Britain could have freely chosen her objective. Having picked one, she could have let it be the placebo of the government's pride and the cynosure of her people. A succession of governments throughout the 1950's and into the

[78]Brandon, "Skybolt: The Full Inside Story of How a Missile Nearly Split the West," *Sunday Times* (London), December 8, 1963, p. 29.

1960's nevertheless failed to describe a feasible objective of policy and stick to it.

Opinion and policy are related in complex and subtle ways. The public acquiesced in expensive and onerous programs, including conscription, as long as the government and leaders of the opposition espoused them. As the direction of policy wavered, the malaise of the public grew. For the past decade, the pattern of opinion has been one of discontent without focus. The public has weakly supported or mildly dissented from the bewildering policy of a succession of governments.[79] At the same time, the leaders of parties have been mindful of opinion. They have been unwilling to support the reintroduction of conscription even though they have complained of high defense costs and have underscored the nation's weakness in conventional forces. Policy has not been responsive to party and public criticisms.

Partly because governments have been intent on making themselves popular, they have failed to gain firm public approval of Britain's military policy. Policies obviously pursued for the sake of popularity finally begin to cloy. If governments pursue the appearance of power and entertain their people with the illusion of influence, the public's awakening, for being long postponed, is all the ruder when finally it comes.

If the government is free to do what it thinks necessary in its foreign and military policy, it is also free to pursue its fancy abroad and to contrive foreign and military policies to serve its domestic political interests. To the French Foreign Minister's urgings to action at the time of the Rhineland crisis, Stanley Baldwin replied that he did not understand international relations but knew that the British people wanted peace.[80] Both parts of his reply were true. For the next several years, British governments were unmindful both of dangers abroad and of criticisms at home. When finally it could no longer be denied, England responded magnificently to Hitler's challenge. For several years after the war, the

---

[79]Three examples give a fair impression of the condition of public opinion. In the fall of 1955, 32 percent of respondents in a poll cited defense as the item of expenditure that should be cut first if the government should decide to reduce its spending. Food subsidies and atomic power development followed at 21 and 17 percent, respectively, with no other item receiving as much as a two-digit response. Early in 1960, when asked for an opinion on the government's intention to increase spending on specified items, approval and disapproval were expressed as follows: Roads, 75 and 13 percent; Education, 68 and 19 percent; the National Health Service, 67 and 19 percent; Armaments and Defense, 27 and 54 percent. From March of 1960 to May of 1963, anywhere from 19 to 33 percent of those asked for their opinions favored Britain's withdrawing from the circle of nuclear powers. In fifteen polls, on the average 24.2 percent favored that option. In the same period, from 24 to 41 percent, or an average of 33.8 percent of all respondents, preferred that Britain continue to make her own nuclear weapons.

[80]Winston S. Churchill, *The Gathering Storm* (Boston: Houghton Mifflin, 1948), p. 197.

British government moved firmly if not boldly to redress the imbalances and remove the social and economic deficits that three decades of wars and depression had left. Churchill's and Attlee's first governments suggest that the force of the greatest circumstances is needed to move England to vigorous activity at home and abroad. In the history of the past half-century, these years appear as an interlude. Governments in the 1920's and 1930's lived with the illusion of safety; in the 1950's and 1960's they have deluded themselves with the appearance of power. The government of any state may be tempted to follow the course that seems easy, to continue a line of policy that has proved tolerable abroad and is tolerated at home. Some of the reasons for British governors persistently inclining toward political comfort and safety were adumbrated in Chapter 3. The operation of opinion within the political system adds to the effect, as consideration of British military policy helps to make clear.

Conclusion

As well as anyone in the postwar world, Macmillan expressed the aspirations of England or at least struck the pose that the country's politicians have found comfortable. The leaders of both parties have played the "influence game" with enthusiasm. They would rather ask Macmillan's question—how does Britain compare with the United States and the Soviet Union?—than worry about more relevant comparisons with France, West Germany, Italy, and Japan. For a decade, talk of Britain's military and policing responsibilities in the colonial and formerly colonial areas bravely continued, while the substitution of firepower for men proceeded apace. If the talk was seriously meant, a conventional establishment, useful in Europe and elsewhere as well, would have been appropriate. Instead, nuclear weapons, more to cover Britain's weakness than to interdict third-party intervention, were dispersed to the Middle and Far East.

With carriers disappearing from her forces, with air cover to be available only from island-based airplanes, with a small army ill-equipped and spread thinly from West Germany to Singapore, Britain is able to do little more than make a threat, a military gesture that may sober the erratic chief of an unstable state. "Often a rifle or even a stave and wicker shield will be enough," Healey has said.[81] But what if firing blanks at the natives fails to pacify them, and what happens if a small military action gets out of hand? "When our tasks are reduced," Healey later declared,

[81]*H.C. Deb.*, Vol. 704 (December 17, 1964), col. 612.

our forces "will be able to do all the jobs that we shall retain, without the overstretch from which our forces have been suffering in recent years." His account of future tasks left little room for reduction. He described the reduced role of Britain as follows: "we shall be able to carry out all our treaty commitments, particularly those for N.A.T.O., CENTO and S.E.A.T.O. . . . we shall be able to carry out a large range of peace-keeping tasks like that in East Africa two years ago, entirely on our own, while maintaining a powerful deterrent against intervention by others . . . and we shall also be able to make a powerful contribution to allied operations if we so decide." [82]

In the early 1960's the rhetoric of contribution and influence became more and more bewildering: to derive influence from a nuclear force while depending for component parts upon another country; to pose as a first-class power by maintaining a third-rate military establishment; to play a global role with the world's seventh-ranking army. The first Wilson government reacted not so much by making a decision as by uttering a confession. Britain will continue to seek a measure of control over the resources of others, especially those of the United States, and this will presumably continue to be advertised as exercising influence or more generally as "giving a lead." Britain's independent deterrent had been maintained in large part in order to be able to place a finger on the American nuclear trigger. Other detonators, it seems, are again important. Making more than a tiny conventional effort exhausts Britain's available military resources. Britain can initiate small military actions only to draw others in if they are not quickly ended. She wishes, in other words, to place her finger on the American conventional trigger. For this purpose, even her residual nuclear power may be of some use. The intention of quickly raising the level of violence, of responding with nuclear weapons to a conventional challenge, can make sense only against non-nuclear nations. The third use of a small nuclear force, described above, is the only one that remains important. Let us suppose Indonesia were to move against Malaysia. A British threat to use nuclear weapons could conceivably follow, which might cause Indonesia to stop short or might persuade the United States to offer the support of the Seventh Fleet and American Marines in order to avoid the use of nuclear weapons. Britain's military specialty will be to threaten actions that others may wish to finish.

Loyalty to the Atlantic Alliance, maintenance of a special relation with

[82]*H.C. Deb.*, Vol. 725 (March 8, 1966), cols. 2044–45.

the United States, and, from 1955 for a decade, military independence: these have been the three principal elements of British policy. Each combines oddly if at all with the others. Preserving an independent military status in order to enjoy, if need be, the influence of the recalcitrant has not been possible for England. She has remained in international finance and in military materiel too closely dependent on America. At the same time, Britain has failed to turn British dependence into Anglo-American interdependence. Entranced with the nuclear symbols of power, she has been unable to participate effectively in a military division of labor. Profession of loyalty to the principal ally and the aspiration to independence have not been reconciled; they have continued to conflict, and the conflict has weakened her policy.

Britain has played the "game of influence" while wishing to enjoy a reputation for being loyal and cooperative; has aspired to independence while relying on American technology and military force; has sought economy in defense while claiming a world role; has planned to skew her military establishment in order to become a nuclear power while making military policy by a series of compromises among services. Labour leaders when out of power promised to stop wasting "the country's resources on endless duplication of strategic nuclear weapons" and to strengthen "conventional regular forces." [83] In office, they have retained nuclear forces and have forecast a cut in the regular army. Unable to combine programs so as to form a sensible policy, Britain has been unable to quit doing the same ineffective things over again. Following her empirical bent, the country has failed to establish a sensible relation between interests, commitments, and capabilities. Policy has instead been sacrificed to habit, tradition, and political popularity.

The contrast provided by Gaullist France illuminates the oddities of British policy. In finally extricating herself from her imperial possessions, France also shed her overseas military burdens. In building a nuclear establishment, she forsook most of her conventional commitments. From the nation's military condition, President de Gaulle has apparently drawn the appropriate political conclusion and now aspires to the position of potential negotiator from a position of neutrality in Asia while maintaining the least involvement compatible with the nation's defense in Europe. A state of the middle rank can become a nuclear power only by ceasing to be a global one. Under de Gaulle, France

---

[83]"The New Britain," Labour's Manifesto for the 1964 election, in *The Times House of Commons: 1964* (London: The Times Office, n.d.), p. 281.

has scaled down her commitments with the sensible hope that she will thereby increase her independence and in some ways enhance her influence. De Gaulle has been able to decide to stop doing some things and to refrain from doing others. He has known how to retreat and, above all, how to say "no," as the leader of a relatively weak state should. A quiet dignity for the nation and a serene life for its people have resulted.

A lesser state cannot play a world role without depending on others; to pursue independence requires reducing the nation's ambitions. A political decision is needed, lest all things be tried and all be done badly. It has been argued at times that if Britain were to surrender her nuclear deterrent, she would in doing so "opt out of the mainstream of power." [84] The argument embodies a wistful estimate of her recent power and position. At the Labour Party Conference of 1957, the late Aneurin Bevan made a powerful speech in which he emphasized the importance of England's maintaining a moderating influence in the world. If a proposed resolution against the testing, manufacturing, and use of nuclear weapons were carried, he asserted, "you will send a British Foreign Secretary, whoever he may be, naked into the conference chamber." [85] England, however, can no longer afford her Foreign Secretary a complete wardrobe. The choice is not between being naked or fully clad, but rather requires deciding which garments can be omitted with the least danger to the nation and embarrassment to its diplomacy. At the same Conference, the late John Strachey, a former Secretary of State for War, argued that the effect of unilateral renunciation of nuclear weapons "would be to make Britain the wholly dependent satellite of the United States." [86] It has instead been Britain's desire to do everything at once, her attempt to play a world military role for less than two billion pounds yearly, that has caused the country to become a dependent power.

Two billion pounds is no trifling sum to spend annually. As mentioned earlier, Britain spends proportionately more on defense than any state of comparable size. Seeking influence abroad and popularity at home, British governments have not tried to get something for nothing; they have, by not regulating their ambitions and ordering their policies, succeeded in getting very little at quite a high price. Several factors have combined to produce the result: the private nature of the argument over policy, the interest of the government in maintaining the appearance of unity, the

[84]Bell, *The Debatable Alliance*, p. 107.
[85]Labour Party, *Report of the 56th Annual Conference*, September 30 to October 4, Brighton (London, 1957), p. 181.
[86]*Ibid.*, p. 177.

empirical cast of the nation's mind, the unresponsiveness of the political system to criticisms and conditions (combined anomalously with its sensitivity to opinion). If defense organization and policy are to depart from past patterns, forceful Defence Ministers strongly backed by their Prime Ministers will be required. It is doubtful that a parliamentary-apprentice system can consistently provide Ministers with enough strength to force coherence of policy and a sufficiently long tenure of office to permit the enforcement of unpopular decisions upon the recalcitrant services.

Chapter 8

FOREIGN AID
AND
AMERICAN POLITICS

Having concentrated in the previous chapter upon the vexatious problem of military policy in Britain, we now examine at length the similarly bothersome problem of foreign-aid programs as they have been politically fashioned by the American government. A number of questions come to mind: Have foreign-aid programs been imaginatively conceived and responsive to the needs of American foreign policy? Have programs been stable or prey to the vagaries of Congress, as the customary "cliff-hanger" atmosphere of the President's yearly struggles with Congress would seem to indicate? How in general is the responsibility for the defects and merits of programs to be apportioned among Congress, the President, and the people at large? Ambivalence about foreign-aid policy has often pervaded the government and produced uncertainties about programs in the legislative and executive branches alike. Ambivalence is rooted in the difficulties abroad that American aid programs try to cope with and gives rise at home to acute political and administrative problems, which are inevitable where the attempt must be made to serve two attitudes at once. The argument of this chapter will be that the rapid emergence of new policies, reasonably aligned with the needs of foreign policy, and the maintenance of controversial programs over a period of two decades has on the whole been impressive. The argument cannot be made without consideration of the difficulties inherent in the aid business. They will be examined under three headings: the novelty of foreign aid as an instrument of policy, the question of America's advantages or disadvantages as compared with the Soviet Union in dealing with the underdeveloped countries, the problem of discerning ends and apportioning means.

181

The Precedents of Foreign-Aid Programs

The policies of aid-granting countries have conformed to one of four principal patterns. States at times follow a money-rather-than-blood policy, as Britain long did in her relations with Europe. Supporting the military activities of a Continental country was often found preferable to sending English soldiers abroad to fight.[1] A second pattern is one of money-now-less-blood-later. Foreseeing the possibility of a war against Germany, France, for example, loaned Russia over $4 billion in a period of some twenty years preceding World War I. Though the money was on loan, an element of aid was present, for Russia could not have hired the money as easily or as cheaply elsewhere. It was the policy of France to encourage the use of her money in ways that would directly increase Russia's military capabilities against Germany. Thus France urged the construction of railways pointing at Germany whether or not such lines would have an important commercial use and despite the fact that Russia would have preferred to prepare for a war against Austria-Hungary, whom she could actually hope to defeat. The intention of France was not that Russia should one day fight for her; rather the fear or the hope was that they might someday be fighting together. It was desirable to build up the military capacity of the country that might one day be a partner in war. A third pattern, too familiar to require elaboration, is one that combines money and blood, with the richer country in a wartime alliance providing material support while at the same time committing its own troops to battle. Finally, aid is sometimes granted on humanitarian grounds: to give relief to victims of flood and famine or to ease the recuperation and recovery of peoples who have suffered in war.

The American states received the first and second types of aid, which are often combined, from France, Spain, and Holland during the Revolutionary War. The United States has been the grantor of all four types, most notably during and after both world wars. Following World War II, the United Nations Relief and Rehabilitation Administration was backed largely by American resources. It was based on the assumption that guided American military and foreign-economic policies—that with the war ended the world would rapidly find security in a system of cooperating states. Help was needed in repairing the ravages of war so that each

[1] E.g., British subsidies to Prussia in the eighteenth century. Cf. subsidies to Britain and Russia provided by the United States prior to her entering World War II.

country could once again stand on its own feet. As Secretary of State, Cordell Hull revived the old diagnosis and dream of American liberals. Economic dissatisfactions cause war; free trade brings peace.[2] In messages delivered in 1945 and 1946, President Truman described America's goal as that of promoting her own prosperity by first helping other nations to become self-supporting and then trading with them on a larger scale. On such assumptions and with such hopes America granted $6 billion and loaned another $8.5 billion between August, 1945, and April, 1948.[3]

The threat of crisis in Greece along with England's withdrawal of her financial support (necessary in view of other claims on her resources) produced in the spring of 1947 the rapidly improvised response embodied in the Truman Doctrine. Whereas aid to relieve and to help reconstruct was, as the terms imply, a temporary measure, the Truman Doctrine, designed to cope with emergency, bespoke an awareness that emergencies were here to stay. In universalist language, President Truman, addressing a joint session of Congress, proclaimed his belief "that it must be the policy of the United States to support free peoples who are resisting attempted subjugation by armed minorities or by outside pressures."[4]

The severe winter of 1946/47, with its accompanying shortage of fuel for home heating and industry, compounded Europe's economic difficulties. Again the response of the United States was dramatic and swift. At Cleveland, Mississippi, on May 8, 1947, Under Secretary of State Dean Acheson advanced the idea that aid longer in term and larger in quantity was needed. Secretary Marshall, with the greater authority of his office, repeated the proposal at the Harvard Commencement in June of 1947. The statement of Marshall, vague but suggestive, met prompt response from Ernest Bevin, the British Foreign Minister. Truman put the power of the Presidency behind the complex and expensive program that began to take shape. The Herter Committee reported on Europe's need for emergency aid; the Krug Committee surveyed American natural resources; the Harriman Committee examined the noneconomic factors that bore upon the proposed recovery program; the Council of Economic Advisers concluded that America could afford to spend 2 to 3 percent of her gross national product yearly in aid of other countries. In the largest informa-

[2]Hull, *The Memoirs of Cordell Hull* (2 vols.; New York: Macmillan, 1948), I, 81.
[3]William Adams Brown, Jr., and Redvers Opie, *American Foreign Assistance* (Washington, D.C.: Brookings Institution, 1953), p. 115.
[4]"Address by the President (Truman) to a Joint Session of the Congress, March 12, 1947," *Documents on American Foreign Relations: January 1–December 31, 1947* (Boston: World Peace Foundation, 1949), IX, 7.

tion campaign in its history, the State Department undertook to inform and persuade the public of the program's importance.

In August of 1947, the Committee for European Economic Cooperation called for the expenditure of $29 billion for European recovery during the next four years. Alerted in December of 1947 by Secretary Marshall's report of the failure of still another Council of Foreign Ministers' meeting, sobered by his warning that no settlement in Europe was possible until Western Europe had shown whether or not it could recover its vitality, and stimulated by the coup in Czechoslovakia in February of 1948, the United States planned to contribute to the recovery of Europe $17 billion by June of 1952. An Interim Aid Bill for Europe had been passed in December. President Truman asked Congress to approve the European Recovery Program by the first of April, 1948, so that American action might influence the elections to be held in Italy on the 18th of that month. Congressional response was rapid; in March, the program gained the approval of both houses by overwhelming majorities.

Aid of types one, two, and four was present, but more was involved as well. Aid was given not merely to counter an immediate danger but to bring countries to a point where they could meet any crisis and even help others to do so. Not loans but grants were the major form in which aid was given; regional rather than national planning was the intended objective, though it was not always achieved. Aid would continue until the job was done. It was completed by January of 1952, instead of by June as had been forecast, and at a cost to the United States of some $12 billion instead of the expected $17 billion. By the end of 1951, industrial production for all fourteen recipient countries had exceeded the goal originally set and reached 135 percent of their 1938 level.[5] Billions had been expended efficiently and without corruption, without great restiveness on the part of the European countries playing the unaccustomed role of recipients of gifts and without a flagging of will on the part of the donor. As part of a foreign policy becoming more coherent with the passage of time, a system of military protection was thrown about the European economies, which, having become richer than they had ever been before, were now a prize that might more sorely tempt an aggressor.

Aid on a long-term basis, first given in response to crisis or near-crisis conditions in Southeastern and Western Europe, moved outward to Asia after the communization of China and the onset of the Korean War and

[5]See the country-by-country chart given in Brown and Opie, *American Foreign Assistance*, p. 249. If West Germany is excluded from the calculation, the average level attained was 145 percent.

was concentrated more heavily in Latin America after Castro came to power in Cuba. The merits of the Marshall Plan are hardly ever denied. As aid came to be extended ever more widely and in a greater variety of ways, uncertainty grew, difficulties mounted, and criticism attended all of the programs. Difficulties in part are rooted in the novelty of programs. Foreign-aid policy, as conceived and initiated by the United States, is something new under the sun. While the policy is not without precedents, it goes beyond all of them. Since the war as never before, aid policies have been designed to deal with entire regions, indeed with major portions of the globe, without the expectation of direct returns to the donor, either military or economic, but with the much grander hope of changing national capabilities permanently and transforming whole societies and political systems. The novelty of programs heightens the uncertainties of policy. Strategies become difficult to determine, results are not clearly demonstrable, and expectations are hard to define with sufficient precision to provide guidelines for policy.

The Comparative Disadvantages of the Soviet Union and the United States

A favorite thesis applied to international relations by students and commentators during the interwar period held that the peoples of backward countries, the "have-nots" in the terminology then fashionable, would wage war to gain access to a larger and fairer share of the world's resources if the "have" countries did not voluntarily grant them their due. In the event, the threat to the Western democracies came from Japan, Italy, and Germany, countries whose people were better off than most, though not as wealthy as the richest. That an axis of major enmity would run between the "haves and have-nots" and become the locus of violence in the world proved to be a wholly erroneous notion. Fears comparable to those of the 1920's and 1930's have reappeared. In one form, more commonly encountered in England than in America, the new fear is a simple, unselfconscious revival of "have versus have-not" worries. When Sir Alec Douglas-Home was Prime Minister of England, he told the Commons that the rich–poor, white–colored, North–South, or horizontal division of the globe, which he thought was in danger of forming, would be "a horror worse than anything the world has seen." [6] A struggle be-

---

[6]House of Commons, *Parliamentary Debates*, Vol. 688 (February 6, 1964), col. 1356. Cited hereafter as *H.C. Deb.*

tween the advanced and the backward countries, Home and others have thought, would inordinately complicate the Cold War or even replace it. It is difficult to see how this could be. In an impoverished country, much of the population hovers between malnutrition and death. The people who are worst off are weakest and thus least of all a threat to others.

If the underdeveloped countries are not very potent, control of them would not be of much positive value to one great power or another. Gains made among the poor would have to be immense in scope to alter the balance between any or all of the Communist states on the one hand and America on the other. Some people have experienced an apocalyptic vision of which the substance is suggested by the following questions: "What if all of Africa, or Latin America, or Asia should fall under Communism's sway? How then would the United States and other Western democracies survive?" [7] If this were the worry, investing in a foreign-aid program would be like taking out an insurance policy against being struck dead by a horse and buggy on the streets of New York City. Behind the worry must lie some such reasoning as this: setbacks will occasionally occur; if a defensive position is long enough maintained, defeat becomes inevitable. In such reasoning, two points are overlooked. First, triumphs breed their own resistance. Hypnotized by the domino theory whereby one country's falling under Communist control supposedly causes neighboring states successively to put their necks under the yoke, the United States has been inclined to overlook the opposite effect, which is as likely to occur. A country that becomes Communist thereby alerts its neighbors and elicits the attention of the United States, as the case of Cuba indicates. Second, the "loss" of a state to Communism cannot be assumed to redound to the advantage of a single world movement. In terms of a global competition for power, American "losses" may be nobody's gain; and if Communist China should somewhere extend its control, the Soviet Union may have more reason to worry than the United States.

It may be that the United States is at some small disadvantage in the "third world" as compared to the Soviet Union. The question will be considered in a moment. What should be immediately clear, however, is that a country seeking to add to its strength by influencing or controlling underdeveloped countries faces such great difficulties that small advantages are of little consequence. Since the underdeveloped countries can only with difficulty manage and administer their own affairs and feed

[7] In accordance with the present convention, the term "Western" is meant to include Japan.

their own people, a state to add appreciably to its strength by extending its control would first have to develop the capabilities of the area it came to dominate. This multiplies the already considerable difficulties of establishing control in the first place. Aid given to a backward country cannot have much effect, at least not in the short run, and is therefore a weak instrument of policy. But since the vaunted advantages of Communism have not been evident anyway, no very effective instrument is needed by the United States. The Soviet Union has succeeded in imposing its control only where its armies were present; neither by guerrilla warfare nor by subversion have the Chinese Communists "liberated" anyone. Except for the Cubans, the most bothersome insurgents of Communist coloration—the Hukbalahaps, Malays, and Indochinese—organized and began to operate before Communist China was founded. Both in terms of the benefits to be won and the ability to win them, the fear that Communist states will overwhelm the world with strength gained in the underdeveloped countries disappears once it is examined. The concern that remains is not so much that control of the underdeveloped countries would benefit Communist states materially as it is that the extension of such control would damage the West psychologically. The inarticulate worry that forms the premise of American aid policy is that the communization of successive portions of the underdeveloped world would corrode the will of the West. Seen in terms of national interest, the granting of aid is a preventive policy directed against that kind of demoralization.

In pursuing such a policy, what disadvantages if any does the United States suffer as compared to the Soviet Union? In the world since World War II as before it, the underdeveloped countries, including China, have not constituted in themselves a direct danger to the peace and security of the more advanced nations. The fear that has recently seized many is rather a modulation of the worries of the 1930's—that the poverty and suffering of economically backward peoples give a conclusive advantage to those Communist states that seek to enlarge their influence. At least since the French Revolution, it has been noticed that a little improvement whets the appetite of the people and increases their impatience for further betterment. Moderate rates of improvement destroy customary arrangements without establishing the basis on which new ones can be founded. Where poverty and illiteracy grip the people and political experience is confined to a small elite, the onset of social and economic change renders the situation unstable. Under such conditions, only an

187

authoritarian government is able to maintain order. Communism, with its Russian record of turning a peasant economy into an industrial behemoth, with a creed that justifies human sacrifice now in exchange for a promised future good, with its experience in bending masses ruthlessly to the will of their masters, offers, it is said, a recipe that the economically under-developed countries will be inclined to follow.[8]

The leaders of backward countries, with their anti-colonial programs fulfilled, have self-consciously groped for an ideology. Communism, if it appeals to them, lies ready to use. Some aspects of Communism may well serve their purposes, especially in building a movement and organizing a party that will help to support the new institutions of the state. But the interests of the Soviet Union, or of Communist China, would not thereby be served. The question of benefits to present Communist states is seldom distinguished, as it should be, from the question of Communism's appeal. The Soviet Union has not been able to fasten its control upon under-developed countries that once seemed to be within its grip. In 1958, it was thought that Kassem's taking power in Iraq would open the way to Communist domination of the country. It did not. By 1963 the Soviet Union found that Iraqi Communists were being persecuted despite a sizable Soviet aid program worked out with the government at Baghdad. Quantities of aid extended to Egypt have scarcely produced a better re-sult. The Soviet Union has been rebuffed in the Congo and in Guinea. It has encountered more criticism of the quality of goods delivered as a part of its loan programs and more blame for the failure to supply spare parts than gratitude and a resultant inclination to welcome Soviet influ-ence. Soviet leaders may well wonder where their advantages, of which they may read in American newspapers and journals, can be found.

If the Soviet Union does somehow gain from the appeal of Communist ideology, it loses by the rigidity added by ideology to its own foreign policy. By its own standards, the Soviet Union cannot say that it has suc-ceeded unless other countries are brought into close ideological and polit-ical alignment with it. The United States need ask only that her benefici-aries remain concerned to maintain their integrity and that they develop a modest ability to do so. These requirements coincide with their inclina-

---

[8]See, for example, Zbigniew K. Brzezinski, "The Politics of Underdevelopment," *World Politics*, IX (October, 1956); Adam Ulam, "The Historical Role of Marxism and the Soviet System," *World Politics*, VIII (October, 1955); Reinhold Niebuhr, *The Structure of Nations and Empires* (New York: Scribner, 1959), pp. 27–28; Mancur Olson, Jr., "Rapid Growth as a Destabilizing Force," *Journal of Economic History*, XXVII (December, 1963), 529–52. Olson's article is an especially useful summary and analysis of the relations between economic growth and political stability.

tions. One must suspect that America's often deplored inability to spell out an ideology suitable to those of grossly different experience and condition is more a strength than a weakness. With no ideology to export, the United States has none to impose. Nor does America's defensive interest require one. The Soviet Union has been more inclined than the United States to extract economic and political payment for its aid. The self-avowed objectives of its aid policy are to win friends, influence nations, and secure a larger measure of conformity between the recipients' policies and its own.[9] America's ends are served if the separate states are made politically more viable by the aid they receive. The thought is reflected in words used by Secretary Rusk when speaking of the newly independent states: "They will take points of view on particular questions which differ from ours. They will criticize us specifically on certain points, sometimes in the most vigorous terms. But the test is whether they are determined to be independent, whether they are trying to live out their own lives in the way in which their own people would like to have them shape it."[10] Aid to independent states given by other non-Communist countries, and possibly even aid granted by the Soviet Union, may then also serve American interests.

America, it is true, does not know the recipe for success in the underdeveloped countries, whether success is to be measured in terms of their economic advancement, their political stability, or their willingness to cooperate with the United States. But if America does not, neither does Russia. A country such as India, with four-fifths or more of its population engaged in growing, processing, transporting, and marketing food, cannot by its own efforts maintain adequate standards of nutrition. It is surely important to notice that Communism's greatest failures have come in the agricultural sector. Despite the supposed advantages of Communists operating in the third world, the fruit has not ripened and dropped into their laps. The United States, one may think, is doubly well off. Economically capable of doing much more for the underdeveloped countries than is the Soviet Union, the United States, to fulfill the requirements of her foreign policy, need ask less of them.

In one way, however, the United States faces a more difficult problem than does the Soviet Union. The United States is impelled to defend non-

[9]Cf. Lucian W. Pye, "The Foreign Aid Instrument: Search for Reality," in Roger Hilsman and Robert C. Good, eds., *Foreign Policy in the Sixties* (Baltimore: Johns Hopkins Press, 1965), p. 109.
[10]"Secretary Rusk's News Conference of November 17," *Department of State Bulletin*, XLV (December 4, 1961), 925.

Communist states all over the world; the Soviet Union, as the state that would move forward, has been able to pick the places on which pressure could most easily be exerted. The difference of situation and intention has been reflected in patterns of alliance. The Soviet Union has tried to weld together and lead a small band of states pure in their Communism according to the Soviet model. The United States, as the defensive power, has been inclined to guarantee the security of almost any state that has been or might possibly be threatened. The pattern is evident in national aid programs as well. From January of 1954, the year in which the Soviet aid program began, to June of 1962, 7 countries received 79.4 percent of economic aid granted by the Soviet Union. In the same period, commitments were made to 24 countries.[11] In striking contrast, the United States extended economic aid in some form to 104 countries in the period covered by fiscal years 1946 to 1962 and in the latter year was still aiding a total of 90 countries. An effort to concentrate assistance in order to achieve greater impact had, by fiscal year 1964, brought the United States to the point of committing 70.9 percent of AID (Agency for International Development) assistance to 30 countries.[12]

By the requirements that derive from a defensive stance, the United States has been led to disperse its effort. The Soviet Union by its narrow standards of conduct, ideologically derived, has sacrificed breadth of political influence. In partial compensation, the Soviet Union has presumably made some gains in effectiveness by taking advantage of the offensive state's opportunity to pick its spots and concentrate its efforts.

The Soviet Union and the United States have neither found it easy to control states that are ill-equipped to control themselves nor been able to gain much advantage from those that are impoverished. Imperialism in its heyday was little enough rewarding to the master countries of empire.[13]

---

[11]Recipient countries in descending order of amount committed were India, United Arab Republic, Afghanistan, Indonesia, Cuba, Iraq, and Syria. The total amount of economic aid commitments was $3.56 billion. The Soviet Union granted in addition about $2 billion in military aid. Of total economic and military aid commitments by the Bloc ($6.93 billion), the Soviet Union accounted for 80.8 percent, East European countries for 13.3 percent, and Communist China for 5.9 percent. Calculations made from George S. Carnett and Morris H. Crawford, "The Scope and Distribution of Soviet Economic Aid," in *Dimensions of Soviet Economic Power*, studies prepared for the Joint Economic Committee of the U.S. Congress (Washington, D.C.: GPO, 1962), pp. 474, 462.

[12]Senate Hearings before the Committee on Foreign Relations, *Foreign Assistance, 1963* (88th Cong., 1st sess., 1963), pp. 100, 89, and 18.

[13]J. A. Hobson estimated at the turn of the century that while individuals might gain from imperialist policies, the mother countries of empire did not. John Strachey has more recently calculated that while Great Britain as a whole enjoyed some economic advantages from her imperial holdings, those advantages were not very large. See Hobson, *Imperialism: A Study* (London: Allen & Unwin, 1902); and Strachey, *The End of Empire* (London: Gollancz, 1959), chap. 4.

The technology of exploitation may have improved in the interim, but so have the possibilities of enriching one's country by developing its internal resources. Given the international political environment, the means of resisting the will of a single more powerful state may also be more readily available. Each would-be master can, as ever, be played off against another. Both the Soviet Union and the United States have found it difficult to gain effective and useful influence over any sizable portion of the third world. The opposition of each to the efforts of the other makes probable failure more nearly a certainty. Instead of saying that in the third world the Soviet Union will win, which no experience bears out, one might better say that neither the Soviet Union nor the United States is likely to gain much more than heartache.

Conflicting Ends and Uncertain Means

The aims of American foreign policy, broader than Russia's, are sometimes vague and often in conflict. The United States has sought to promote in other countries attitudes of friendly cooperation, along with self-dependence and integrity; political moderation and stability, along with reform and economic advancement. Will the ends of the aid-granting and receiving countries coincide, and when they do, will the coincidence last? In an underdeveloped country, the regime that is provident for the sake of its citizens may by its frugality be punishing itself. In March of 1962, the government of Argentina fell partly because its head, Arturo Frondizi, had pursued economic policies of austerity, which American officials believe to be essential if the Alliance for Progress is to benefit the people of Latin America.

Underdeveloped countries may be too unstable to follow their own interests steadily, let alone bring their interests consistently into harmony with those of another country. Beyond this consideration, a state, whether politically stable or not, may disagree with the donor about some policies of mutual concern or diverge gradually from him, especially if the aid received helps to build up a self-reliant state. France holds the record as the largest recipient of American economic and military aid, and yet de Gaulle's government has been opposed to America's preferred European policy, disruptive of NATO's logistics, militarily uncooperative with members of the Alliance, unresponsive to pleas that the Peoples' Republic of China not be recognized, and highly critical of America's efforts in

191

Southeast Asia.[14] In 1963's foreign-aid hearings, Senator Fulbright drew attention to the amount of American largesse as a preliminary to asking Mr. Bell, the Administrator of AID, the following question: "Won't you agree that our experience with France is somewhat disillusioning since the 14th of January [1963]?" Assenting in part, Mr. Bell hastened to remind the Committee that "the basic purpose for an assistance program has been and is to assist other countries to establish themselves as independent and self-supporting nations." [15] That purpose had certainly been accomplished. A country that has the political, economic, and military strength to maintain its integrity thereby has the ability to follow policies that will at times collide with those of the United States. Fulbright's frustrations are easily understood. Yet who would argue that the purposes of America's foreign policy would be better served by a France that in its weakness would be a prey to internal subversion and external threat and thus still a candidate for American assistance? The hope that the recipient state will become self-dependent naturally conflicts with the hope that in its foreign policy it will be easily amenable to the wishes of the donor.

In the most rudimentary sense, the ends of aid programs cannot be constant and clear, for the aims of foreign policy are necessarily changeable and sometimes cloudy and blurred. The stability of some countries is wanted—namely, of those that are friendly or at least quiescent. The political instability of the troublesome will at the same time be wished for. Where the promotion of someone else's stability is an objective of the donor, difficult and ambiguous choices may have to be made between seeking to induce slow economic growth, which leaves the state too weak to defend its existence, and trying to encourage rapid economic growth (i.e., economic *instability*), which is likely to disrupt the country politically. Slow change may permit social tranquillity by requiring that few adjustments be made. The association of political disorder with economic change has led one writer to suggest that the United States concentrate more on aiding countries that are at an earlier stage of development and less on those that seem to be ready to move into a stage of fairly rapid economic growth.[16] Such concentration would surely be cheaper. One may

---

[14]Net obligations and loan authorizations for France in the years 1946–62 were $9.414 billion. The United Kingdom came next with $8.705 billion. Data from Statistics and Reports Division, AID, *U.S. Foreign Assistance and Assistance from International Organizations: July 1, 1945–June 30, 1962* (Revised; Washington, D.C., 1963).

[15]Senate Hearings, *Foreign Assistance, 1963*, p. 84.

[16]Olson, "Rapid Growth as a Destabilizing Force," esp. p. 548; cf. Brzezinski, "The Politics of Underdevelopment."

also believe, however, that thresholds are present. Very slow or very fast growth may be more easily compatible with political stability than a growth rate that falls in between. Rapid growth may bring a better balance between the creation of expectations and their fulfillment. Accomplishments may become tangible and visible; revolutionary yearnings may in part be satisfied by revolutionary economic accomplishments and thus deny to political agitators many of their natural followers.

Max Millikan, W. W. Rostow, and George Liska, among others, have proposed that aid be given according to a banker's concept: advertise the availability of funds and the conditions that the would-be recipients must meet; then serve all customers who conform to the standard established.[17] It is sometimes said of bankers and their clients that anyone can get a loan at reasonable interest provided only that he does not need it. The owner of property can post it as collateral; those who are indigent, unable to offer security for the loans they seek, will be unable to borrow the funds they may desperately need. In like fashion, countries that cannot demonstrate the administrative and organizational ability to carry a good intention through, countries that are incapable of maintaining monetary stability and fiscal order, are the very ones that desperately need help. Thus, on economic grounds, P. N. Rosenstein-Rodan has rejected the gradual and orderly procedures associated with the banker's concept and argued that only massive injections of capital can give to an underdeveloped economy the impetus that will carry it forward at a pace noticeably faster than the rate at which population is growing.[18]

In running a bank, the banker's concept is appropriate; it can be applied while the government or charitably inclined individuals look after the public interest by aiding the needy. In the granting of aid, the wider interests of the nation are involved. Political criteria must be applied, which may require denying aid to those who are economically worthy and granting it to those who are reckless and improvident. Because the problem of relating means to ends is inordinately difficult, a mechanical solution is sorely wanted and surely unavailable.

Uncertain of the relation of means to ill-defined ends, those who make aid policy or seek influence over it are further bedeviled by the smallness of means in relation to the objectives in view. In all but a few cases,

[17]Max F. Millikan and W. W. Rostow, *A Proposal: Key to an Effective Foreign Policy* (New York: Harper, 1957), chap. 7; George Liska, *The New Statecraft: Foreign Aid in American Foreign Policy* (Chicago: University of Chicago Press, 1960), pp. 197–202.
[18]Rosenstein-Rodan, "Notes on the Theory of the 'Big Push,'" in Howard S. Ellis and Henry C. Wallich, eds., *Economic Development for Latin America* (London: Macmillan, 1962), pp. 57–66.

the amount of economic aid given has been small in relation to the recipient country's gross national product. Of all countries, India in recent years has been by far the largest recipient of American economic assistance. In 1961, American aid received was 1.9 percent of India's GNP; for such other large recipients as Pakistan and, in proportion to her size, Colombia, it was 2.5 and 2.3 percent respectively.[19] Amounts that are small in relation to a country's economy may nevertheless be crucial. They may be large in absolute terms and, should they be stopped, may not be easily replaced from other sources, which are often already drawn upon heavily. Some leverage is gained, and if the American interest and that of the recipients is in economic growth, not much may be needed. It is, nevertheless, foolhardy to think that all good things—efforts toward efficiency, a modicum of equity in the distribution of the domestic product, the formulation of friendly foreign policies—will gracefully come forth from the recipients.

For some other countries American aid has been a substantial proportion of domestic production: countries such as Israel, which has been the special object of American favor, or countries such as South Korea and South Vietnam, where the United States has thought that her security interests demand an extraordinary effort. In 1961, American economic assistance was 16.8 percent of Korea's GNP and 12.3 percent of South Vietnam's.[20] Over such countries, may the United States not expect to exercise a decisive control? Hardly. The granting of extraordinary sums to a country indicates, more clearly than mere words can do, that the United States believes her interest to be entwined with the continued existence of the recipient country. If American interest makes it difficult to quit giving aid to a country, its government need not respond smartly to advice it receives. Those lavishly aided have been no more amenable to American influence than others have been, as experience with Chiang Kai-shek, Syngman Rhee, and Ngo Dinh Diem has abundantly demonstrated.

America's interest is served if other states are able to maintain their independence. Since even those who are wretched pull toward independence, small amounts of aid as tokens of America's good wishes may some-

---

[19]"Relation of U.S. Economic Assistance to GNP of Recipient Countries," a memorandum submitted by Secretary Rusk to the Senate Hearings, *Foreign Assistance, 1963*, p. 18.

[20]*Ibid.*, Food for Peace as well as AID assistance is included. The value of shipments under Titles I and IV of PL 480 is figured at export market value; for other shipments of agricultural products, value is calculated according to the cost to the Commodity Credit Corporation. To adjust American figures overall to world prices, some downward revision is required. The percentages given in the text, however, would not be greatly affected.

times suffice. Political aid would be cheap; development aid is expensive. But the United States is also concerned that independent states be stable and steadfast, that they be able and willing to withstand Communist encroachment. The economic well-being of countries has been thought necessary to the establishment and maintenance of their political integrity. To promote such a condition no reliable strategy, which would accord means and ends and discriminate among potential recipients, has been available. Not knowing whether it is possible to achieve goals that are themselves imprecisely defined makes it both risky to concentrate funds on a small number of countries and hard to justify spending large sums of money.

In justifying its defense budget, the American government does not promise that $50 billion spent yearly will bring the millennium. Of a sum one-tenth as large in foreign aid, glorious claims are made. The very difficulty of discerning goals that can reasonably be expected to materialize invites exaggeration. Other states, Britain and France for example, can ask: do we gain in prestige from expenditures on aid and perhaps preserve a commercial advantage? If the answers are affirmative, their governments can be well satisfied. The United States would also be pleased by such answers, but more important questions would remain. How does economic condition affect political stability? What is the relation between internal political form and the behavior of an underdeveloped country in international relations? How can aid from outside promote a desired domestic situation? Questions of ends and means are so difficult that discussion of them often trails off into vacuous statements about creating "a new world order" wherein all peoples can find appropriate places and live harmoniously together.[21] The route from the present to the future world is unfortunately not discernible in useful detail, and the notion that expenditures on aid, necessarily modest in relation to the immensity of problems, can establish the United States in the role of history's midwife is disturbingly utopian.

Domestic pressures encourage political leaders to exaggerate their hopes for the future. "The fundamental task of our foreign aid program in the 1960's," President Kennedy once told Congress, "is not negatively to fight Communism: Its fundamental task is to help make a historical demonstration that in the twentieth century, as in the nineteenth—in the southern half of the globe as in the north—economic growth and politi-

---

[21]For a recent example, see Pye, "The Foreign Aid Instrument: Search for Reality," pp. 109–112.

cal democracy can develop hand in hand." [22] By 1961, when the statement was made, such rhetoric had begun to pall, for it had been heard so often. The majesty with which the aims of the program are described is a part of the yearly attempt to persuade Congress to accept the administration's program. All arguments—from humanitarian appeal and Christian duty to the invoking of American security interests narrowly defined —are used and must lead whoever is listening either to suspect the President and other responsible officials of knowing exaggeration or to expect too much from the program. Years of describing the program in unduly glowing terms help to explain Congressmen's disillusion with the results that have been achieved.

Congressional Interference and the Integrity of Policy

It is the executive's prerogative to formulate and carry out foreign policy. So from the days of John Locke onward most political commentators, whether liberal or conservative, have thought. To the extent that foreign policy is an executive job, uncontrolled and perhaps uncontrollable, the frustrations felt by Congressmen are easily understood. The importance of foreign policy must be measured primarily by the dangers involved. Its domestic political impact is dramatically brought home by counting the dollars expended. In terms of dollars spent as well as the dangers involved, foreign policy overshadows all the other concerns of government combined. The debt of the United States is largely attributable to the wars she has fought. On a per capita basis, the national debt stood at $28.77 in 1917 and at $242.54 in 1919; at $325.59 in 1940, after years of deficits during the Depression, and at $1907.62 in 1946. Foreign affairs since the fiscal year 1941 have taken three-fifths or more of each year's federal budget.[23]

If Congress is to establish financial control over matters of foreign policy, it must do so where dollars are spent in quantity. The cost of maintaining the Department of State and its missions abroad has amounted to less than one-half of 1 percent of the federal budget. On military spending, the public follows the chief executive's lead.[24] So

[22]"Special Message to the Congress on Foreign Aid, March 22, 1961," in *John F. Kennedy, 1961 (Public Papers of the Presidents of the United States* [Washington, D.C.: GPO, 1962]), p. 205.

[23]James L. McCamy, *The Administration of American Foreign Affairs* (New York: Knopf, 1952), pp. 7, 5.

[24]See below, p. 273.

does Congress. From 1946 to the present, only once, in 1952, has Congress cut the President's request for military appropriations by as much as 8 percent, and in that instance $38 billion of unobligated funds were carried over from the preceding year.[25] Because of the special position constitutionally occupied by the Senate, the House is excluded from direct participation in many matters of foreign policy. Aid bills represent most of the few chances it has to affect directly the making and conduct of policy. With spending on most foreign programs either very small or almost inviolable, it is natural that the Senate as well should concentrate much of its attention upon aid. Since military spending has become less controversial, the aid program is the one item on the legislative agenda where questions of money, administration, and the content of policy all come together in a way that permits Congress to get at them. In authorization and appropriation stages together, foreign aid occupies the attention of Congressional leaders yearly for as long as does any other single issue, domestic or foreign.[26]

In the decade and a half during which America has extended aid to underdeveloped countries, Congress has proved itself to be niggardly and erratic—at least that is the charge that was customarily made until the Presidency of Lyndon B. Johnson. Each spring as the authorization and appropriation process has begun and each summer as it has wound to its dreary conclusion, the American press has given the impression that whether or not there would be an aid program at all was seriously in question and that whatever survived of the program would be much less than the President wanted and the nation's interest required. Fans of foreign aid pillory Congressmen, who, it is said, appropriate insufficient funds and do so for only a year at a time, which leaves the fate of long-term programs in doubt. President Kennedy, in his message to Congress of March 22, 1961, sweepingly declared that existing foreign-aid programs and concepts "are largely unsatisfactory and unsuited for our needs and for the needs of the underdeveloped world as it enters the Sixties." "Short-term financing," he said, "has weakened the incentive for the long-term planning and self-help by the recipient nations which are essential to serious economic development. The lack of stability and continuity in the program—the necessity to accommodate all planning to a yearly deadline—when combined with a confusing multiplicity of Ameri-

[25]Samuel P. Huntington, *The Common Defense: Strategic Programs in National Politics* (New York: Columbia University Press, 1961), p. 63.
[26]James A. Robinson, *Congress and Foreign Policy-Making: A Study in Legislative Influence and Initiative* (Homewood, Ill.: Dorsey Press, 1962), p. 56.

can aid agencies within a single nation abroad—have reduced the effectiveness of our own assistance and made more difficult the task of setting realistic targets and sound standards." The plea was for "continuity and flexibility" in the program and the "only way" to get it, Congress was told, was by instituting a program of long-term planning and financing.[27] Presidents Truman and Eisenhower had made similar requests. Congress has refused to be persuaded by the appeals of three Presidents.[28]

The adequacy and continuity of programs as they are affected by domestic political processes are considered in later sections of this chapter. The question to be taken up now is this: with policies prey to Congressional interference, does the substance of policy become disjointed?

Critics with various ideas about policy have united in condemning Congress for expressing in authorization and appropriation acts its prejudices against some countries and in favor of others. Congress has smiled upon Spain and Taiwan while limiting or even eliminating particular programs for Poland and Yugoslavia. It may be difficult to understand that aiding a Communist country, if it is in conflict with other Communist states, can be in the American interest and, at the same time, easy to think that fervently anti-Communist countries alone deserve assistance. Senator Knowland, leader of President Eisenhower's party in the Senate though often opposed to his foreign policies, continuously argued that Yugoslavia's declared devotion to Communism should be weighed more heavily than her independence of the Soviet Union. Tito, and Nehru as well, he thought, were bent upon persuading other countries to forsake the Western alliance and adopt neutralist policies. The prejudices of unsophisticated Congressmen, it is feared, are collectively expressed in programs that withhold from some countries the amount or type of aid that would best serve the American interest and lavishly reward others where the American interest is seemingly more obvious but actually less pressing.

President Eisenhower, like Truman before him and Kennedy and Johnson later, argued that the neutrality of other states is not necessarily against the American interest, that the decision of how much aid to give whom should be made pragmatically.[29] Despite widespread agreement among officials and experts on how American interests in neutralist states

---

[27]Kennedy, "Special Message to the Congress on Foreign Aid, March 22, 1961," pp. 203, 204, 209, 206.

[28]The appeals were not always unequivocal. See below, p. 202.

[29]Sherman Adams, *Firsthand Report: The Story of the Eisenhower Administration* (New York: Harper, 1961), pp. 374–76.

or independent Communist countries should be viewed, Congress has time and again proved recalcitrant. Dean Acheson once cited legislation in regulation of aid to Yugoslavia as a horrible example of what happens when Congress takes upon itself the direction of foreign policy. By Public Law 726, passed in the summer of 1956, Congress forbade the giving of aid to Yugoslavia beyond ninety days from the date of the Act, unless the President should find and report to the Congress that Yugoslavia remained independent of Soviet control and had not changed those of her policies upon which the decision possibly to give American assistance was based, that Yugoslavia was not participating in any program for Communist world conquest, and that to assist her continued to be in the interest of American security. In October of 1956, Eisenhower, finding the Congressional conditions fulfilled, declared that Yugoslavia was reliable enough to deserve economic aid but not yet aircraft and heavy equipment. The Congressionally prescribed procedure placed Yugoslavia in a position of dependence upon an uncertain benefactor in a fashion that she found insulting.[30]

Such legislation restricts the President and may annoy Communist countries that are inclined to edge away from the Soviet Union. The more direct effect is to put the President in a difficult political position by requiring that he make public his judgment of Communist governments. Other restrictions imposed by Congress have been less harmful than had been feared and have sometimes been helpful. The Hickenlooper amendment to the aid bill for fiscal year 1963, which enjoined the granting of aid to states that expropriate American-owned property without compensation, also lessened Presidential discretion. While the provision did not dissuade Ceylon from nationalizing American holdings, it did encourage Brazil to compensate American power companies for property that had been taken. On balance, according to Secretary Rusk, the amendment "worked out pretty well in a number of situations."[31] The stipulation that aid not be given to a country that attacks an American ally does not seem unreasonable. The requirement that all projects costing $100 million or more be approved by Congress is comparable to what is required in matters of domestic financing.[32] In 1963, Congressional distaste

---

[30]Acheson, *A Citizen Looks at Congress* (New York: Harper, 1956), p. 108, n. 9.

[31]Senate Hearings, *Foreign Assistance, 1963*, pp. 29–30.

[32]Sec. 620(k) in the Foreign Assistance Act of 1961, as amended, which was added by Sec. 301(e)(3) of the Foreign Assistance Act of 1963, and amended by Sec. 301(f) of the Foreign Assistance Act of 1964.

for American financing of India's Bokaro Steel Mill made this provision famous, or infamous. Those who viewed Congressional obstruction as being merely willful overlooked in customary fashion the fact that Congressmen had a good point. Indian experience with large-scale steel mills financed with German capital had been a mixture of success and failure. An adequate supply of raw materials was not assured. The production of steel in the previous year had fallen 20 percent short of rated capacity.[33] It was not clear that to commit over $500 million to the first stage of the Bokaro project would be a wise expenditure of funds. Those who are unhappy with the exercise of Congressional control might find themselves equally unhappy without it.

Critics of Congress have focused on Congressionally imposed restrictions, and Presidents have understandably opposed legislative action in order to keep a free hand even though the restrictions themselves were sometimes useful as warnings to foreign countries and sometimes acceptable in substance to the administration. Those who blame Congress for the ills of the program merely assume that refusal to appropriate what the President has requested impairs programs and renders policy discontinuous. (The assumption is examined below.) They overlook the remarkable absence of corruption in the spending since the war of well over $100 billion in aid of foreigners, a record that should be credited in part to the persistent carping of Congress. They pay more attention to restrictions imposed than to useful innovations developed and supported by Congress. Congress has often seemed to slash away at the program with glee. It has also, as John Montgomery points out, "introduced positive innovations in foreign aid practice. The use of agricultural surpluses as a means of augmenting aid was conceived jointly by Congress and the Department of Agriculture; Congressional initiative lay behind the transition from a 'balance-of-payments' to a 'project' basis in the determination of aid levels; and finally, Congress provided the initial impetus for establishing the Development Loan Fund, the International Development Association of the World Bank, and the Office of the Inspector General and Comptroller of Mutual Security." [34] Blame for the defects of aid policy and credit for its merits should be more evenly shared than is customary between the executive branch and Congress.

---

[33]With capacity rated at 6.0 million tons, 4.8 million had been produced. See the statements of David E. Bell in Senate Hearings, *Foreign Assistance, 1963*, pp. 122, 324.

[34]Montgomery, *The Politics of Foreign Aid: American Experience in Southeast Asia* (New York: Praeger for the Council on Foreign Relations, 1962), pp. 220–21.

Foreign Aid and the Executive Branch

In the executive branch as in Congress, foreign aid has often been thought of as a temporary program that could be gradually abandoned as its objectives were achieved. In 1954, putting down such hopes as being illusory, the Eisenhower Administration recommended that the Mutual Security Act be extended for a four-year term in order to avoid the effort and uncertainty of securing yearly appropriations. Congress refused. While the President continued to ask for fairly large sums and to speak strongly of the program's importance, it became clear that his administration was not united. In 1955 and 1956 George Humphrey as Secretary of the Treasury, Rowland Hughes as Director of the Bureau of the Budget, Herbert Hoover, Jr., as Under Secretary of State, and John B. Hollister as Director of the International Cooperation Administration (ICA) were said to be members of a "4-H Club." Smitten with the truism that a sound economy is essential to America's strength in the world and wedded to a conservative definition of the federal spending that could be afforded without endangering the economy, each of them was inclined to rate frugality in government higher in importance than assistance to foreigners.[35] In 1957, Eisenhower's own Secretary of the Treasury suggested that the President's budget could be cut and, replying to a question from the press, counseled that unless governmental spending were reduced "you will have a depression that will curl your hair."[36] The President was pulled in two directions, between sympathy for the economizers and commitment to the costly programs to which the Eisenhower platform and campaign had pledged the party. The effect of administrative dissension and executive uncertainty was to weaken the strong appeal the President made to the nation in support of security expenditures, including foreign aid, on May 21 of that year.[37]

In the same year, President Eisenhower sought to establish the practice of financing the Development Loan Fund by borrowing from the Treasury, which would provide, as yearly appropriations supposedly could not, the continuity essential to the purposes of the Fund. Though the finan-

[35]Hollister is an interesting example of a man appointed by President Eisenhower to administer a program that the administrator did not really believe in. Cf. Eisenhower's first Commissioner of Internal Revenue, T. Coleman Andrews, who opposed the progressive income tax while running in 1956 as a third-party candidate for the Presidency.

[36]Richard E. Neustadt, *Presidential Power: The Politics of Leadership* (New York: Wiley, 1960), p. 66.

[37]*Ibid.*, p. 72.

cial basis proposed by the President was rejected by Congressmen who feared they would lose control of the program, the Senate Foreign Relations Committee was prepared two years later to accept it. It was now Eisenhower's turn to oppose, through the Republican leadership in Congress, the shift to long-term financing that he had earlier sought. The President asked for the measure and emphasized its importance, "yet when the issue is drawn," Senator Fulbright bitterly remarked, "he gives his support to those who deny the means by which to accomplish the objective." The Secretary of the Treasury, who was now Robert B. Anderson, had met difficulty in selling the long-term bonds of the government. He insisted upon further economies, and his concerns took precedence over the country's foreign policy.

> This is an illustration [Fulbright remarked] of the lack of coordination and the apparent inability to bring together in any reasonable manner the administration policies in the foreign field. They all go off in different directions. As I said yesterday, I think what has happened is that the administration has permitted the Secretary of the Treasury to override the Secretary of State and the whole Department of State on the determination of foreign policy.[38]

In the Eisenhower years, as the above instances suggest, foreign-assistance programs encountered as much trouble in the executive branch as ever they experienced in Congress.

Organizational disarray has increased Congressional doubts about the sensibility of plans and the effectiveness of operations. From 1948 to 1966, six successive agencies and ten different directors were responsible for drawing up programs and dispensing aid abroad. The relation of aid agencies to the State Department and to other governmental agencies responsible for assistance has usually been uncertain and has often been changed. "No objective supporter of foreign aid," President Kennedy told the Congress, "can be satisfied with the existing program—actually a multiplicity of programs. Bureaucratically fragmented, awkward and slow, its administration is diffused over a haphazard and irrational structure covering at least four departments and several other agencies." [39]

The disorganization, constant reorganization, caution, timidity, and uncertain purpose of the assistance program has been caused in part by the yearly experience of Congressional harassment. It used to be said that personnel of ICA, whether serving in Washington or overseas, custo-

---

[38]*Congressional Record*, CV, Pt. 10 (86th Cong., 1st sess., 1959), 12424, 12563.
[39]"Special Message to the Congress on Foreign Aid, March 22, 1961," p. 203.

marily spent one-third of their time preparing materials for presentation to Congress.[40] The fear that their activities would draw Congressional ire must have made bold and imaginative action seem forbiddingly dangerous. On the one hand, just as an actual or threatened attack may occasion a new sense of unity and purpose in a country previously divided, so in the process of Congressional criticism and competition the strength and esprit of an agency may be forged. On the other hand, a sense of obloquy may develop that induces an attitude of quiescence and gradually renders the agency immobile. With AID and its predecessor agencies neither extreme has been reached. Presidents have usually stood firm. From 1948 to 1964, all Presidents and Vice Presidents and all nominees for those offices went out of their way to support the program. Presidents have repeatedly asked Congress for what was previously denied. Nor has the aid agency, by whatever name, often bowed its bloody head. One must add, however, that in all of the years since the European Recovery Program, neither Presidents nor the departments and agencies involved have been able to work out a rationale for foreign assistance that would convince others of its worth because the responsible officials had first convinced themselves.

The difficulties posed by Congress, the shortcomings found within the executive branch, and the immensity of problems in the countries succored by assistance programs may lead one to marvel that foreign aid has survived at all. A large part of the reason for its survival is found in the merits of both Congress and the Presidency, which the many criticisms, of the former especially, serve to obscure.

Domestic Politics and the Survival of Foreign-Aid Programs

The impression is sometimes given that Congress has opposed policies that the people in general would favor, that far from reflecting popular inclinations, Congress has acted contrary to them.[41] Actually public opinion has been closely balanced between approval and disapproval of foreign aid and has often shaded toward a negative view. In the era of the Marshall Plan and in the years following, favorable responses have ordinarily been given when poll-takers first specified that "Congress has

---

[40]Montgomery, *The Politics of Foreign Aid*, pp. 218–19.
[41]Cf. Edward S. Mason, *Foreign Aid and Foreign Policy* (New York: Harper & Row for the Council on Foreign Relations, 1964), p. 9.

voted to spend less money," or "the President has proposed that we cut down the amount of aid we send our allies," or some relatively small figure—$3 or $4 billion—was mentioned. Confronted with such information, respondents have inclined, by from 36 to 56 percent, to adjudge the program about right in amount, with 36 to 20 percent still preferring to spend lesser sums, and only 4 to 9 percent wishing that the government would spend more.[42] Whatever the percentage favoring or opposing economic aid, opponents of the program have held their views with higher intensity than have those who support it.[43] Aid generally is given a low priority. Samuel Lubell, in one of his surveys, asked what the government should do if it were to have an extra billion dollars to spend. Defense, education, and medical care were most heavily favored; space shelters and more liberal pensions ranked somewhat lower; foreign aid placed at the very bottom.[44] Technical assistance, the provision of foodstuffs, and the Peace Corps have been popular. Economic aid in moderate quantities has been publicly preferred to military assistance. West European and Latin American countries have been favored over African and Asian recipients; allies have been preferred to neutrals and neutrals to Communist countries.[45]

The aid program, especially if it is quite small in amount or has already been cut, draws tepid applause. Larger programs and aid for Communist or neutral countries meet a cooler response. Given the interests, habits, and traditional associations of the nation, such patterns of preference are hardly surprising. They are, however, politically important. Since the middle 1950's, less assistance has been given to European allies as aid programs have been concentrated more strongly upon expensive efforts to stimulate and sustain economic development; Asian and African countries have become increasingly the targets of foreign-aid policy, and neutralist India has become the most favored of all the recipients.[46]

[42]Based on five polls by the National Opinion Research Center (NORC)—August, 1949 (90/168); March, 1950 (96/276); May, 1953 (130/340); April, 1954 (137/355); April, 1957 (156/404)—and on one by the American Institute of Public Opinion (AIPO)—March, 1958 (No. 596).

[43]AIPO has at times asked the very general question: "How do you feel about foreign aid—are you for it, or against it?" The percentages of respondents for and against have been as follows: 1958, 51 and 33 percent; 1963, 58 and 30 percent; 1965, 57 and 33 percent; 1966, 53 and 35 percent. "The Gallup Poll," *Philadelphia Bulletin*, March 13, 1966, Sec. I, p. 26. On the problem of the intensity of opinion, see V. O. Key, Jr., *Public Opinion and American Democracy* (New York: Knopf, 1961), pp. 212–14; Alfred O. Hero, Jr., *The Southerner and World Affairs* (Baton Rouge: Louisiana State University Press, 1965), p. 206.

[44]Samuel Lubell, "Public Is Concerned over Spending," *Philadelphia Bulletin*, July 10, 1961, p. 10.

[45]Alfred O. Hero, Jr., "Foreign Aid and the American Public," *Public Policy*, XIV (1965), 81–84, 88–94.

[46]See below, pp. 213, 217–19.

Preceding paragraphs present a summary of tendencies. One must add that opinions about foreign aid rest on a slender base of information and that, in comparison to opinions on prominent domestic issues, attitudes may be unstable in any short period and inconsistent from one issue to another.[47] As well as examining the direction of opinions, one also must look at their sources. Increasingly in the years of the Cold War, a high degree of national homogeneity has been displayed on issues of foreign policy. Regional differences have declined, and broad agreement in accepting foreign involvement and military commitments has ordinarily bound supporters of the two different parties together. In part, opinion on foreign aid conforms to the pattern. Differences in attitude between urban and rural residents are minor, though with the latter less well informed and somewhat more skeptical. Cross-party cohesion is high, with Republicans slightly more disposed to favor the program.[48] As with other indicators of internationalism, those who have gone to school for a larger number of years are more inclined to approve of foreign aid. With regionalism taken as a variable, the homogeneity of attitudes toward aid significantly decreases, as it does on other international questions. The people of the Southern and Border states have less knowledge about foreign problems and find internationalist measures less attractive.[49] Specifically, Southerners favor economic aid less than do persons elsewhere in the country whether aid is to be unilaterally given or multilaterally distributed; and they more heavily endorse reductions in the amount to be granted.[50]

Southern Congressmen, accentuating the disapproval of their constituents, have more consistently opposed internationalist measures than have other groups, whether separated by region or by party. The point is easily exaggerated. The internationalism of Southern Congressmen was such a marked feature of their behavior before World War II that it now becomes easy to slip into calling them isolationist. Southern internationalism has waned, and yet in recent years about 40 percent of Democratic Representatives from the South have supported the aid program.[51] From

[47]Cf. Hero, "Foreign Aid and the American Public," pp. 72–78.

[48]As Hero points out (*ibid.*, pp. 110–11), the edge disappears if the income factor is controlled.

[49]Ithiel de Sola Pool, Robert P. Abelson, and Samuel L. Popkin, *Candidates, Issues, and Strategies* (Cambridge, Mass.: M.I.T. Press, 1964), p. 93, Table 2.5.

[50]Hero, *The Southerner and World Affairs*, pp. 205–16.

[51]See below, Table 8, p. 208, which gives a breakdown of votes on final authorization of yearly assistance bills for the years 1951 to 1966. A few words of explanation are required. Votes on appropriations are crucial, but in such votes the mixture of motives is confusing. Some will vote for the final appropriation because they are pleased that so many dollars have been cut; others may support a truncated bill only to foreclose still further reductions. On

the outset, Southern Democrats were less strong in their support of aid programs than were Democrats from other parts of the country. Since the early Eisenhower years, the Democratic Party has been badly split on the issue. Fiscal conservatism is strong among Southerners. The civil rights issue may have increased their oppositional tendencies. The industrialization of the South has eroded the basis of free-trade sentiments and helped to turn Southerners inward. The geographic shift of foreign-aid programs from European to underdeveloped countries has apparently also lessened Southern support. Senator Walter F. George, when he was Chairman of the Senate Foreign Relations Committee, remarked that Egypt's planned dam at Aswan, by irrigating an additional two million acres of land, would injure American cotton exports. He declared his adamant opposition to America's offering assistance.[52] Many Southerners are reluctant to aid their colored competitors.

While the Democratic Party is split on the issue, the Republicans are far from united. Republican Congressmen have been skeptical of aid programs throughout the period. Skepticism has been especially marked among those from the Midwest who, like Southern Congressmen, have diverged more sharply from their colleagues than regional patterns of public opinion would have led one to expect. The inclination of Congressmen to support a President of their own party moderated the pattern during the Eisenhower years without changing it basically.

Foreign aid is not opposed by the public, nor is it firmly supported. The people will not press Congressmen to improve or enlarge the program. They will not punish those who cut or oppose it. Still, in repeatedly granting less than the President has requested, Congressmen have reflected the public's uncertain and skeptical attitudes. As it enters the Congressional arena, the fate of the aid program has in most years been in doubt. The pattern of opposition and support by party and region has long remained constant. Overall, opposition has gradually increased, from about one-third of House votes in the 1950's to about two-fifths in

---

balance, it appears most useful to take votes in the House rather than in the Senate, where the numbers are so small that accidental and personal factors easily distort the pattern; to take authorization rather than appropriation bills, for the reasons just mentioned; and to take always the final authorization vote, even though preceding votes on amendments have sometimes been more significant, in order to permit comparisons to be made over a number of years.

[52]*New York Times*, April 28, 1956, p. 1. On this and preceding points, see Malcolm E. Jewell, "Evaluating the Decline of Southern Internationalism through Senatorial Roll Call Votes," *Journal of Politics*, XXI (November, 1959); Paul Seabury, *The Waning of Southern Internationalism* (Princeton: Princeton University Center of International Studies, 1957); Charles O. Lerche, Jr., "Southern Congressmen and the 'New Isolationism,'" *Political Science Quarterly*, LXXV (September, 1960); Hero, *The Southerner and World Affairs*, chap. 5.

the 1960's.[53] Why this has happened can now be simply said. The aid program, increasingly non-Western in emphasis since about 1953, has evolved in the direction of least popularity; and as it has done so the area of the country most inclined to internationalist views has become, in its opinions and in the votes of its representatives, less internationalist than any other region. The difficulties of foreign aid have been compounded by growing disenchantment on the part of liberal Congressmen who were once its most faithful supporters. The disaffection of the faithful is an indication that neither they nor other political leaders have been able to find a satisfying rationale for the program.

Under the circumstances, problems of foreign aid are ever more frequently taken to illustrate the shortcomings of the American political system. "American inventiveness in conceiving foreign aid has not been matched," according to Lucian Pye, "by an American political process capable of giving its creation positive and sustained support. Indeed foreign aid seems uniquely able to expose our most vulnerable weakness in conducting foreign affairs, our inability at times to coordinate our division of powers. Annually the foreign aid program triggers such a clash between Congress and the administration that at times Washington seems to forget who our real enemies are." [54] In the heat of legislative struggles, perspective may indeed be lost; students of politics should try to regain it. In order to do so, two points must be seen clearly.

The first requires paying attention to what the struggle between Congress and the President has been about. There has been no important Congressional argument in favor of abolishing the program. Even Representative Passman, who for a decade served as hatchet-man to the program by virtue of his tactically powerful position as Chairman of the Subcommittee on Foreign Operations Appropriations, publicly expressed his reluctant acceptance of foreign aid as the basis of America's foreign policy.

> I am opposed to foreign aid; it has been, in my opinion, one of the greatest foreign-policy failures in history. But, as a realist, I recognize that it is, however distasteful, a political "fact of life" today.
>
> Our foreign aid is the basis of such foreign policy as we have. Over the past 16 years, Washington administrations have made long-term "moral" commitments that involve our country's good faith and that must, as a matter of course, be fulfilled.[55]

[53]See below, Table 8, p. 208.
[54]Pye, "The Foreign Aid Instrument: Search for Reality," p. 94.
[55]Otto E. Passman, "Why I Am Opposed to Foreign Aid," *New York Times Magazine,* July 7, 1963, p. 16.

TABLE 8 Votes on Foreign-Aid Authorization Bills in the House of Representatives, Calendar Years 1951–65

	1951	1952	1953	1954	1955	1956	1957	1958	1959	1960	1961	1962	1963	1964	1965
Number of affirmative votes	260	246	280	260	273	275	254	259	271	243	287	250	224	230	249
Number of negative votes	101	109	108	126	128	122	154	134	142	131	140	164	186	175	148
Percentage of total House votes that were negative	28	31	28	33	32	31	38	35	34	35	33	40	45	43	37
Percentage of Republicans voting negative[a]	50	53	41	40	41	38	39	41	40	39	45	57	70	67	66
Percentage of Southern Democrats voting negative[a]	22	22	28	51	51	50	70	58	66	66	55	63	65	59	60
Percentage of other Democrats voting negative[a]	2	1	2	4	3	4	11	8	14	16	6	8	7	7	7

Source: Figures are compiled from *Congressional Quarterly Almanac*. The Southern states are the eleven states of the Confederacy.

[a]Figures indicate the percentage of total votes cast by those in a given category.

While he grudgingly granted the necessity of continuing the program, Passman, backed by his subcommittee, steadily pressed for large reductions of the amount to be spent. The Appropriations Committee, in its financial conservatism, supported its subcommittee. The Foreign Affairs Committee, which may at times have wished to press for larger appropriations, would only have exposed its weakness by doing so. Though Congressional auguries have long remained unfavorable, the survival of the program has not been at issue.[56]

To say that survival has not been at issue is no assurance of the program's future, nor is survival of the program necessarily the symbol of its success. The second point, to be borne in mind in order to achieve a proper perspective, requires matching opposition to programs with their content. To take an example from the best essay written on the politics of foreign aid, David Truman has recently made the following statement: "The record, using 1953, 1959, and 1961 as reference points, will indicate that opposition to foreign aid in the House is strong, persistent, and growing." [57] Legislative history, thus typically summarized, gives the impression of a fixed program yearly clearing the Congressional hurdle by ever-narrowing margins. If the content of programs as well as the strength of opposition to them is considered, a different impression emerges. The growth of opposition to aid programs overall has run parallel to changes in the direction of programs. It has also corresponded to increases in the number of dollars supplied.[58] As Congressional opposition to foreign aid has increased, so has the overall size of programs! This surely makes the performance of the American government appear in a light different from that cast by the analyses previously cited. Most students of the politics of foreign aid have reacted to the virulence with which opposition has been expressed and have not paid sufficient attention to the aid programs that the government has fashioned.[59]

With opinion on questions of foreign aid evenly balanced, the President has been able to secure the essential elements of the policies he has fashioned. Even were opinion skewed in one direction or the other, the

[56]In 1965, with members reshuffled by the new Chairman of Appropriations, Passman's subcommittee was no longer inclined to heed its leader's calls for reductions in spending.

[57]Truman, "The Domestic Politics of Foreign Aid," *Proceedings of the Academy of Political Science*, XXVII (January, 1962), 150.

[58]See below, Figure 2, p. 212, which gives figures for aid over the years. For a consideration of continuity, country by country, see pp. 215–17.

[59]Cf. the bewilderment expressed by those who have noticed that economic aid is both more popular with the public and more sharply cut by Congress than is military assistance. The seeming anomaly of Congressional behavior is removed by remembering that military aid since the middle 1950's has declined in absolute amount as well as in proportion to the total aid bill, while economic aid has steadily increased.

low correlation between the votes of Congressmen and the views of their constituents on foreign-policy measures would leave the President in a strong position.[60] Though usually some distance behind and always uttering cries of anguish, Congress has followed its Presidential leader. Publicly the impression given has been of a program slashed in amount and hammered into mush, and the conclusion most frequently drawn is that here at least the governmental division of functions has rendered programs puny and incoherent. The examination of programs will belie the conclusion.

The Stability and Adequacy of Foreign-Aid Programs

One has so often heard that the effectiveness of the assistance program depends upon its being financed on a long-term basis that he may easily conclude that the failure of foreign aid to bring impressive improvements abroad can be explained by Congress's failure to authorize and appropriate funds for more than one year at a time. One has so often heard that a given amount was essential, only to see a much smaller amount appropriated, that he may easily think that hardly ever has enough money been made available.

Seldom are impressions widely current further removed from reality than is the case with the foreign-aid program. Much of the impression of discontinuity in aid programs derives from the statements of administration spokesmen who use every rhetorical device to awaken the people to the importance of the program and to prod Congress into supporting it. Salesmen for the program may come to believe their own rhetoric, as much of the press seems to have done. Statistics, partially examined, appear to confirm the impression that words of cajolery have given.

Victory and defeat for the program are often defined in psychological and domestic political terms, and a shift in the President's legislative strategy may call forth a diametrically different description of results that are nearly identical. Fiscal 1964, for example, was one of the most difficult years for the program. The friends of foreign aid were dismayed; doubts about the survival of the program were widely expressed. In sharp contrast, fiscal 1965 was described as a year of victory for foreign aid.

---

[60]On the question of correlations between public opinion and Congressional votes on foreign as compared to domestic policies, see Warren E. Miller and Donald E. Stokes, "Constituency Influence in Congress," *American Political Science Review*, LVII (March, 1963), esp. 51–52. Cf. Pool, *et al., Candidates, Issues, and Strategies*, p. 35n.; and Hero, "Foreign Aid and the American Public," pp. 72–78, 80n., 112–13.

The continuity and adequacy of the program, insofar as they are affected by Congressional action, should be measured in terms of the net obligational authority granted by Congress over a period of years. In terms of dollars made available, 1965's "success" is approximately equal to 1964's "failure." More attention should be paid to the net result of the process and less to the percentage by which Congress cuts the President's budgetary request. (See Table 9.) In addition, the misleading practice has prevailed of considering the military- and economic-assistance programs separate from the other flows of capital and goods that fall within the American assistance program. The data most often set forth, and the part of the program that made Representative Passman famous, combine the appropriation for AID with the yearly appropriation for military assistance. Expenditures for shipping agricultural goods abroad and the loans of the Export-Import Bank are major items that should also be included.

How to add up the amount of aid given is a troublesome problem. The OECD (Organization for Economic Cooperation and Development) countries that have combined with Japan to form the Development Assistance Committee have agreed upon counting as foreign aid all long-term governmental capital flows, including loans made for a period of

TABLE 9   CONGRESSIONAL RESPONSES TO PRESIDENTIAL FOREIGN-AID REQUESTS

FISCAL YEAR	REQUEST	AUTHORIZATION	APPROPRIATION OF NEW FUNDS	PERCENTAGE CUT
		(in billions of dollars)		
1948/49	7.37	6.91	6.45	12.5
1950	5.68	5.59	5.04	11.3
1951	8.17	7.98	7.48	8.4
1952	8.50	7.58	7.28	14.4
1953	7.90	6.49	6.00	24.0
1954	5.47	5.16	4.53	17.2
1955	3.45	3.02	2.78	19.4
1956	3.53	3.42	2.70	23.5
1957	4.86	4.12	3.77	22.4
1958	3.86	3.39	2.77	28.2
1959	3.94	3.68	3.45	12.4
1960	3.93	3.58	3.22	18.1
1961	4.88	4.79	4.43	9.2
1962	4.77	4.26	3.91	18.0
1963	4.78	4.57	3.90	18.4
1964	4.53	3.60	3.00	33.8
1965	3.52	3.51	3.25	7.7

Source: AID, "Comparative History of Authorizations and Appropriations for Budgeted Programs" (mimeo.). The figures include, for the appropriate years, funds for ERP, China Aid, Point 4, Mutual Security, Mutual Defense, and Foreign Assistance.

FIGURE 2 U.S. Economicᵃ and Militaryᵇ Assistance to Foreign-Assistance Act Countries

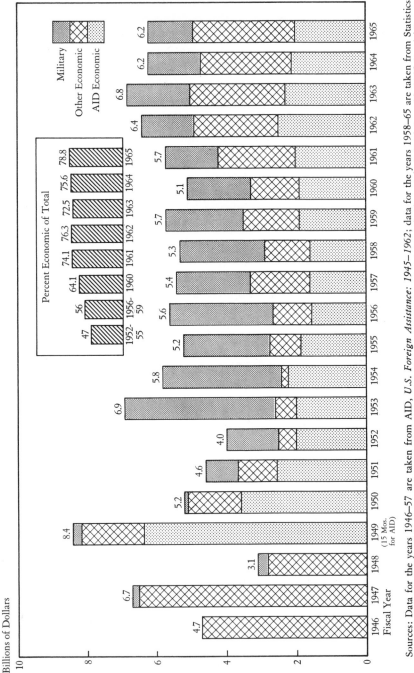

Sources: Data for the years 1946–57 are taken from AID, *U.S. Foreign Assistance: 1945–1962*; data for the years 1958–65 are taken from Statistics and Reports Division, AID, *U.S. Overseas Loans and Grants and Assistance from International Organizations: July 1, 1945–June 30, 1965*, Special Report Prepared for the House Foreign Affairs Committee (Washington, D.C., 1966).

ᵃNet obligations and loan authorizations.

ᵇValue of goods delivered.

five years or more. Accepting the definition makes international comparisons possible. The receiving country, if it borrows money rather than accepting so much as gifts, may feel that its *amour propre* is saved. What is saved now may be lost later. It is estimated that the return flow of interest payments amounted in the year 1964 to about 40 percent of the $9.5 billion that the richer countries had in that year given, loaned, or invested.[61] As demands for repayment multiply with the passing years, terms will almost surely be renegotiated to the borrowers' benefit, which will increase the element of aid that is already involved in making loans at less than commercial rates. In the short-term, what matters is the quantity of goods made available for which payment need not be made now. In the long-term, even loans may turn out to be gifts, with the fiction of lending used to obscure the dependence of the recipient upon the supplier.

With these considerations in mind, aid figures will be looked at in several different ways so that some conclusions can be drawn. Toward that end, Figure 2 presents total yearly net obligations for economic and military assistance from fiscal year 1946 through 1965.

Contrary to common belief, appropriations for foreign aid fluctuated widely from the end of the war to the early 1950's and since then have displayed a remarkably steady progression. Fiscal years 1946 through 1952 are the years of greatest instability in the amounts of aid provided. This was also the period during which the United States came to realize that rehabilitation assistance given for a few years would not be sufficient to create European economies of vitality and that America's economic relations with her wartime allies could not yet be put on a commercial basis as was attempted in the lending of $3.75 billion to Great Britain in 1946. The experience of these years underscores what should already be obvious: that stability has to be thought of in terms of conditions and the objectives of policy as well as the number of dollars appropriated. The rapid decline of appropriations from fiscal year 1949 through 1952 reflects the success of a program. The sharp increase in fiscal year 1953 reflects the shifting of attention to new areas of difficulty and danger, of which the United States was especially made aware by the war in Korea. Aid to Near Eastern, Far Eastern, and South Asian countries rose dramatically. Military assistance became more important and in fiscal years 1953, 1954, and 1956 accounted for more than one-half of the total.

[61] Bernard D. Rossiter, "World Bank Reports Slowdown in Money Flow to Poor Nations," *Washington Post*, September 27, 1965, p. A 11; based on the *Annual Report* of the Bank for International Reconstruction and Development.

FIGURE 3 U.S. Economic Assistance,[a] by Major Program

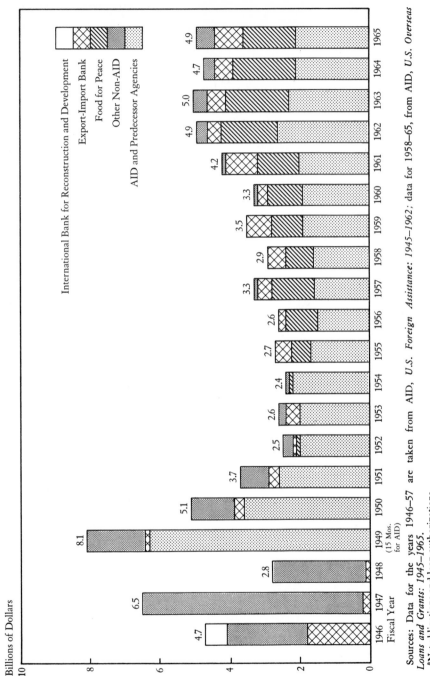

Sources: Data for the years 1946–57 are taken from AID, *U.S. Foreign Assistance: 1945–1962*; data for 1958–65, from AID, *U.S. Overseas Loans and Grants: 1945–1965*.
[a]Net obligations and loan authorizations.

Leaving military assistance aside for the moment, economic aid of all types fluctuated by fiscal yearly net obligations between $2.4 billion and $2.7 billion in the years 1952–56, between $2.9 billion and $3.5 billion in the years 1957–60, and between $4.2 billion and $5.0 billion in the years 1961–65, as shown in Figure 3. Fiscal year 1958 represented a low point, for its period, of $2.9 billion. One may say that a decrease in net obligations of more than 10 percent from the preceding year (to be followed by an increase of more than 20 percent in the year following) represents a possibly bothersome discontinuity. Part of the decline is accounted for by a temporary drop in the then fairly new agricultural program.[62] From fiscal year 1958 onward, net obligations incurred for the ICA or AID portions of the total assistance program have been: $1.620 billion (1958), $1.916 (1959), $1.866 (1960), $2.012 (1961), $2.508 (1962), $2.297 (1963), $2.136 (1964), and $2.026 (1965).

Taking military and economic assistance together, variations are in proportionate terms still less marked. In regular progression, aid became increasingly economic, with military assistance declining from 53 percent in fiscal years 1952–55, to 44 percent from 1956 to 1959, and to approximately 25 percent in the early 1960's.[63]

The picture is not one of perfect continuity with all movements upward or downward accomplished in finely modulated progression. Nor is the foreign-aid story one of sharp jumps explicable in terms of domestic political considerations that should have been kept separate from the content of foreign policies. Examination of aid allocations bears out the statement made in the preceding section: for a decade beginning in the middle 1950's, just in the years when critics of Congress were loudest, obligations undertaken moved quite steadily upward.

The variation in funds available has roughly accorded with the play of fortune in the politics of the world, yet statistics for economic and military programs as a whole may conceal fluctuations experienced by individual countries. Undoubtedly they do. Looking at the record country by country, one may nevertheless be surprised by the ease with which changes in amount from one year to another can be explained in a sensi-

---

[62]Products and funds were available. The problem was to send agricultural surpluses where they were needed without disrupting international trade relations. See Senate Hearings before the Committee on Foreign Relations, *Mutual Security, 1957* (85th Cong., 1st sess., 1956), pp. 520–28.

[63]Here and elsewhere, one must remember that the amounts of military aid given are in some instances kept secret and are thus excluded from the calculations.

ble way.[64] We shall look at the two countries about which Congressmen and the public have consistently been skeptical: Yugoslavia and India.

Yugoslavia has been granted $2.7333 billion in military and economic aid from the United States since World War II, $2.4352 billion since fiscal year 1949. Of the total amount, 25 percent has been military. From a level of absolute zero in fiscal year 1949, American aid was extended in steadily increasing amounts in the critical years following Yugoslavia's break with the Soviet Union. The figures for economic and military assistance combined are, by fiscal years: $40.0 million (1950), $95.5 (1951), $166.8 (1952), $283.2 (1953), $298.3 (1954), $279.1 (1955).[65] Since fiscal year 1955, there has been, appropriately enough, decline over-all with occasional fluctuation, as follows: $153.3 million (1956), $139.2 (1957), $139.8 (1958), $180.7 (1959), $77.1 (1960), $148.4 (1961), $119.7 (1962), $112.4 (1963), $75.2 (1964), and $97.6 (1965). Assistance to Yugoslavia, directed to the political objective of enabling the country to stand apart from the Soviet Union, has not been intended primarily to assist in the development of the country. In such circumstances, the amount given should vary with immediate needs, and wider fluctuations may well be appropriate. However one may view it, the steadiness of American aid in Yugoslavia's critical years is impressive.

India falls squarely in the developmental category. It was often said in the middle 1950's that peripheral countries in Asia were favored to the relative neglect of India. In fiscal year 1956, Taiwan received $430.7 million, South Korea $610.1 million, South Vietnam $363.6 million, for a total among them of $1,404.4 million. India was granted only $92.8 million. The population of the first three together was 32 million; India's alone, 387 million.[66] Aid to India was indeed sporadic and relatively small until fiscal year 1957. In the eleven years from 1946 through 1956, only $624.3 million were provided. But in the following nine years $5,258.1 million were allocated to India. In fiscal 1956, $92.8 million were set aside for India; in fiscal 1957, $364.8 million. This sudden increase is less an indication of discontinuity than a clear demonstration of the effect of a decision to invest American hopes heavily in the future of India. Was the decision delayed and the program subsequently truncated

[64]The AID booklets on which Figures 2 and 3 are based also provide a record of the amount and type of aid available for each recipient country yearly.

[65]For 1950–52, figures show total rather than net obligations and are from Office of Statistics and Reports, ICA, *U.S. Foreign Assistance and Assistance from International Organizations: July 1, 1945–June 30, 1960* (Washington, D.C., 1961); AID, *U.S. Foreign Assistance: 1945–1962*; AID, *U.S. Overseas Loans and Grants: 1945–1965.*

[66]Population figures are based on data given in S. H. Steinburg, ed., *The Statesman's Year-book* (London: Macmillan, 1959 and 1963), and are for the years 1955 and 1956.

by public and Congressional distaste for neutralist India? Whatever one's answers may be, it should be remembered that from the American perspective Western Europe necessarily came first, and next came those countries of Asia immediately threatened by Communist encroachment. Whether truncated or not, American assistance programs have now made India the most favored of countries; and the progression to higher levels of commitment has been fairly steady: $364.8 million (1957), $305.5 (1958), $366.7 (1959), $733.5 (1960), $596.4 (1961), $766.8 (1962), $714.6 (1963), $691.6 (1964), and $718.2 (1965).[67]

Whether in terms of aid policy in general or of aid programs country by country, continuity has been impressive. The conclusion conflicts with common impressions, which are rooted in two errors. Congressional opposition to some projects, controversial usually for good reason, is thought to indicate that Congress has interfered with the executive's proper prerogatives and destroyed the symmetry of programs. Moreover, fluctuation of amounts is too easily equated with instability. International political conditions are not fixed, and many of the recipient countries are themselves inconstant.

Matching the record of American aid against conditions in the world, one is tempted to suggest that aid has more often been too stable rather than too unsteady. The common argument for sustaining a project is that it is already begun; the countries most likely to get aid next year are the ones that now receive it; the sum given in recent years is the surest clue to future amounts. Those who worry about discontinuity have overlooked the force of inertia and failed to examine the record.

The overall pattern of aid distribution by country and area bears out the conclusion suggested by the case of India: if the imposition of Congressional preferences has distorted the pattern, the distortions have been smaller than has generally been thought. China, Spain, and Israel may have received additional sums of money because they have been favored by politically powerful Congressmen. Such an explanation is not appropriate for other countries that have been major recipients. In the fiscal years from 1946 through 1964, eighteen of the world's poorer countries have received more than $1 billion in military and economic assistance, and a total of twenty-six have received more than $500 million, as shown in Table 10.

[67] AID, *U.S. Foreign Assistance: 1945–1962*; and AID, *U.S. Overseas Loans and Grants: 1945–1965*. Before 1962, India received only economic aid; since then, the data on military aid have been kept secret.

TABLE 10   RECIPIENTS OF SUBSTANTIAL U.S. AID, POORER COUNTRIES

COUNTRY	AMOUNT IN MILLIONS OF DOLLARS	MILITARY AID AS PERCENTAGE OF TOTAL
Over $1 billion		
Korea	6301.9	36.3
India	5882.4	n.a.[a]
China, Republic of	4755.5	53.2
Turkey	4755.2	55.4
Japan	3934.1	27.3
Greece	3669.9	48.5
Pakistan	2937.3	n.a.[a]
Brazil	2788.3	9.7
Yugoslavia	2733.3	25.4
South Vietnam	2377.5	n.a.[a]
Philippines	1888.9	24.8
Spain	1863.9	31.3
Iran	1549.5	46.0
Indochina[b]	1535.2	46.2
Chile	1125.0	9.9
UAR	1080.9	0.0
Israel	1073.4	2.6
Mexico	1029.9	1.1
Under $1 billion		
Indonesia	868.2	7.9
Colombia	724.8	10.8
Argentina	707.5	9.7
Peru	630.8	19.9
Poland	548.2	0.0
Portugal	516.7	64.6
Morocco	516.1	6.2
Jordan	510.6	7.2

Source: AID, *U.S. Overseas Loans and Grants: 1945–1965.*
[a]Military data classified secret.
[b]Undistributed.

Successes and failures in some areas and worrisome situations developing in others largely account for the shifting of American concern from one part of the world to another. In simple fashion, Table 11 shows the changes that have recently occurred. The reasons for Latin America's ascending in the hierarchy of recipients are as obvious as the reasons for Europe's decline. The greater concentration of American efforts upon the Near East and South Asia, upon countries running from Greece and the United Arab Republic to India and Nepal, has gone parallel with America's increasing attention to India. The small decline in expenditure on Far Eastern countries, from Korea and the Philippines to Indonesia and Burma, is explained by a mixed pattern of partial successes and failures. Burma and Cambodia have been unwilling or reluctant to draw on American resources. Indonesia, at times inclined to make military threats against her neighbors while flirting with Communist China, became a less attractive candidate for large sums of aid. The Philippines, Japan, and Taiwan are now self-dependent or nearly so, in large part because of American help in the past. Korea received less as she began to recover from war and as the active threat from China shifted to the south; South Vietnam received more.

TABLE 11 TOTAL U.S. ASSISTANCE, BY REGION

REGION	1958	1959	1960	1961	1962	1963	1964	1965
				(in millions of dollars)				
Near East and South Asia	1598.1	1613.5	1925.2	1747.2	2227.2	2189.6	1948.3	2044.6
Latin America	424.4	630.3	396.9	969.6	1218.4	1090.6	1324.2	1349.1
Far East	1613.2	1659.5	1316.6	1335.0	1302.9	1592.6	1276.6	1402.5
Africa	109.6	191.9	224.0	471.2	518.4	516.4	406.5	364.4
Europe	1387.9	1249.1	1154.0	877.4	704.5	764.3	709.9	706.0

Source: AID, *U.S. Overseas Loans and Grants: 1945–1965.*

Though the general pattern of distribution may be sensible, has not Congress by its interference kept expenditures always a little below what the fulfillment of programs and the achievement of the objectives of policies would have required? In unguarded moments, Presidents, State Department officials, and even personnel of AID and its predecessor agencies will say that so far funds sufficient to meet American commitments and to cover the important programs have been available.[68] Though Congress may not have rendered existing programs ineffective, has it not impeded the hatching of new and bold ones? The regional approach of the Marshall Plan is inappropriate elsewhere in the world, for Asia, Africa, the Near East, and Latin America do not have Western Europe's unity. One may, however, wonder what the results would be if massive resources, well beyond the present level, were poured into India. India is large enough to be treated as a region and, many have thought, important

[68]Often overlooked is the contingency fund that Congress places at the President's disposal. During fiscal years 1959–65, it varied from $50 to $275 million and averaged $176.3 million yearly.

219

enough to merit assistance on the ERP scale. When it has so often been inordinately difficult to get an aid program through the Congress, is it reasonable to expect the President to have the courage to suggest, unprompted by an international crisis, that expensive departures should be made? In broader and more important senses than those so far examined, is aid policy not disrupted and made inadequate by the interaction of executive indecision and Congressional recalcitrance, which are both products of the political structure?

It can be argued that any strategy of foreign aid would be preferable to the eclectic policies that the United States has pursued. It was remarked in an earlier chapter that American foreign policy, having become expensive, has taken on some of the qualities and acquired some of the liabilities of domestic welfare programs. Whether at home or abroad, it may be desirable to concentrate public resources on one problem or one region at a time, with the hope that the aided sector, made healthy and vigorous, will carry others along. Instead, because of the pressures of opinion and the temptations of politics, it is the squeaky wheel that gets a squirt of oil whether or not the general welfare is thereby best served. At home, if a few are favored as part of a strategy thought to be ultimately in the interest of all, others will often complain. In foreign policy, if aid is given to some countries, domestic politics may require that others also be assisted. Congressmen have themselves criticized the wide dispersal of dollars, and officials of AID have taken pride in marginally narrowing the program. The wide dispersal of aid may nevertheless be furthered by the executive's fear that concentration on a few bold programs would make the administration exceedingly vulnerable should those programs fail.

The external policy of a country is in part determined by its internal constitution. In the American system, conflicts are heightened by institutional frictions that are a part of the structure of government. Ideas and interests, opinions and policies are easily drawn into the political competition, both between parties and between different branches of government. The collisions that occur clarify purposes and establish the ground upon which policy can be based. On questions of foreign aid, there have been collisions enough, and yet a strong consensus has failed to emerge. The diffusion of aid as a form of compromise may have been prompted by the structure of the American government.

Criticism, however, can easily overshoot the mark. Compromise may be desirable if controversial programs are to find support over a period of time. That the problems of the underdeveloped countries have proved intractable is not the fault of any government. In the face of an intractable problem and amidst the ambiguities of international relations, the American government has been able to introduce new programs and sustain old ones while nearly all programs have remained controversial.

A country with a large foreign-aid program is bound to encounter difficulties and suffer disappointments. Political considerations inevitably affect the content of programs. Recipients of aid readily develop the suspicion that they are being subjected to a new imperialism and easily develop a defensiveness born of a sense of dependence. From the standpoint of backward countries and donors alike, would it not be desirable to establish an international agency for the collection of funds and the distribution of aid? Could not such an agency plan programs objectively, maintain them steadily, lay down conditions for recipients to meet without incurring their resentment, and insulate donors and recipients from each other's politics? It is sometimes said that the International Bank for Reconstruction and Development accomplishes these admirable objectives, a statement that is at once misleading and irrelevant. The modest aim of the Bank is not to develop national economies but to help in the financing of useful and profitable projects. Even so, the decisions of the Bank are inescapably political as well as economic. The establishment of an international agency to take over national programs of assistance would not remove the need for executive discretion but would entrust discretionary powers to a committee. It would not eliminate domestic political considerations for the donors but would confront them with a different question: how much money should each of them contribute to the international agency? It would not eliminate political considerations from the allocation of aid but would turn the political process of allocation into one that took place among donors, each trying to serve the interests of its foreign policy; among recipients, each seeking favor; and between recipients on the one hand and donors on the other. The new system, if it can be imagined, would be interesting without being very constructive.

Conclusion

Impediments to the success of national aid programs are numerous; methods are uncertain, and benefits problematic. Under the circumstances, one should be skeptical of the claim that the ills of American policy can be attributed to the division of governmental powers. A summary of points made earlier in the chapter will help to show why.

Students of economic and political development, in and out of government, differ widely on such vital matters as the ability of an economically underdeveloped country to absorb large amounts of capital suddenly and use them effectively. Nor would the political and social effects of aid programs more massive than the present ones be predictable. In any event, America's defensive position in the world makes it appropriate for her to distribute aid more widely than does the Soviet Union. New crises have shifted the focus of the American foreign-aid program, but so have criticisms of old programs and the introduction of new concepts. ERP represented a new concept in international relations as well as a departure in American foreign policy. Granting substantial sums in aid of countries that seek to make themselves over, in polity, society, and economy, is something new under the sun. The pressures of the Cold War have encouraged innovations in policy and prompted a burgeoning of the literature on economic growth and political change. In the shifting patterns of aid are embodied both long-term and short-term considerations, response to the crisis of the moment and farsighted concern for a country such as India, who was heavily aided long before she skirmished with China in 1962.

Reflection on the American program's changing pattern leads one to say that the concentration of aid has depended in large part upon recent experience and the presence of crises. The long neglect of Latin American countries, resented by their leaders and deplored by many in the United States, is often cited as an instance of inexcusable lack of foresight. Power has to be guarded most carefully, however, where it exists in greatest magnitude. By this standard, Latin America was not of first importance. Countries in an area are not helped, it is said, until one of their number is threatened or taken over by Communists. Sometimes this is so. It is even understandable. Threats have to be met where they occur. Among the economically underdeveloped countries, they occurred first in Southeastern Europe and in Asia, not in Latin America. There is little evidence that Congress would resist new programs at once boldly and carefully constructed even if they promised to be expensive. ERP, of course, was overwhelmingly accepted by Congress. Members of Congress were prominent among those who were dissatisfied in the middle and later 1950's with the military emphasis upon peripheral countries in Asia.[69] While aid to Latin America prior to 1961 was small and erratic, this was hardly the fault of the Congress. It is unlikely that a bigger program for Latin America coming earlier than the Alliance for Progress would have been rejected by Congress or cut by anything more than the customary percentage.

Budgetary decisions necessarily entail a conflict of priorities, in this case the priorities of one claimant of aid over another, of economic aid programs as compared to military expenditures, and of foreign programs of all types set against domestic demands for governmental expenditure. At times, heads of departments and agencies have been as intent as Congress has been to hold aid spending down. There is little indication that in the absence of expected Congressional opposition grand new aid programs would emerge from the executive branch. It is more likely that quarrels about dollars and programs would shift to the executive branch, there to be waged between foreign-aid economizers and would-be bold innovators. Doubts and differences within the government would be less visible, and it would seem to the interested public that aid policies were more "rational" and the allocations of money more reliably made. The difficulty, one must suspect, is more with the world than with Congress. Where is the bold program promising success with a high enough probability to merit large-scale financing by taking resources away from their present public and private uses? Congressmen in increasing numbers have been dissatisfied, as President Kennedy was, with the organization of assistance and have felt deeply the need to depart from a program that has in most of the underdeveloped countries contributed mainly to keeping economic pace with the increase in population and thus to perpetuating misery, which is deemed preferable to death. Congressional criticism of assistance programs and the inclination to cut funds is, in one part, the result of enthusiasm for economy where the interests of constituents will not be directly damaged and, in another part, the result of impatience at spending large sums where little progress is made because conditions are so difficult. Impatience is understandable; the frustrating situations that give rise to it are amenable to no easy solution and probably not to any solution at all that is within America's power to effect. Aid programs, to hazard a judgment, will be sustained at a higher level either if international crises force the United States to step up the effort or if new and promising programs can be developed. At that imaginary new

[69]See, for example, Representative Henry S. Reuss, "Foreign Aid: Misspent, Mislabeled, and Misunderstood," *Reporter*, XX (February 6, 1958).

level, Congressmen would continue to criticize loudly and, depending on the President's legislative strategy, make reductions of varying size in the program. The United States would be on a new plateau of policy, and all of the old political analysis would apply. Meanwhile, aid programs have been maintained with striking consistency at a substantial level of spending.

Chapter 9

BRITAIN
AND
EUROPE

According to the conventional assessment of British government, the Prime Minister and Cabinet, or perhaps the Prime Minister alone, once decided upon a new course of action, can move swiftly; for strong measures can be taken to hold back-benchers of the government's party in line. Macmillan was able to decide quietly and announce suddenly that the United Kingdom would negotiate for membership in the Common Market, a decision controversial in the country and in his own party as well. Superficially viewed, Macmillan's European decision is an excellent example of the British government's ability to rise above private and public doubts and make a firm decision on a difficult matter of policy. The decision to "pool sovereignty," as Edward Heath, who was to be the principal British negotiator, described it, is as momentous as any decision a government is ever called upon to make.[1] British traditions and interests, and the attitudes long clustered around them, guaranteed that the decision would be an unusually difficult one. Macmillan nevertheless acted firmly and did so in the face of an uncertain public opinion, a skeptical attitude on the part of the Labour Party, and uneasiness running to hostility and open resistance from within the ranks of his own party. The decision to seek entry, one may easily think, was a bold move by a British Prime Minister radically different from any action an American President under similar circumstances would have been able to take. Surely an American President, though he may have wished to act and

[1]House of Commons, *Parliamentary Debates*, Vol. 645 (August 3, 1961), cols. 1670–89. Cited hereafter as *H.C. Deb.*

might have tried to do so, would not have been able under such conditions to carry his policy within his own country.

It is the conventional assessment of British government, supposedly validated by Macmillan's European policy, that is examined in the present chapter. Whether it was wise or foolish for Macmillan's government to wish to carry the United Kingdom into Europe is not the concern here. Judgments of the case for Britain's entry vary with national perspective, depend upon one's views of the desirable relation of international political forces, and are affected by guesses about what Britain's political orientation as a member of the Common Market would have become had she been able to join it. To cast light on such factors would require an analysis much different from the one that follows. The chapter instead examines the impediments to Macmillan's policy and his efforts to overcome them. Its objective is not to evaluate the government's aims, but to understand the manner in which policy was formed and to estimate its adequacy as measured against those aims.

From the End of the War to the Summer of 1961

Beyond Britain's major political and economic interests lay great political traditions that run contrary to a commitment to Europe. British feelings were reflected when, according to de Gaulle, Churchill during the war years told him bluntly: "This is something you ought to know; each time we must choose between Europe and the open sea, we shall always choose the open sea. Each time I must choose between you and Roosevelt, I shall always choose Roosevelt!" [2] While Churchill after the war gained a world reputation as a champion of European unity, he continued to cherish England's "special relationship" to the United States and her role as mother country of Empire and Commonwealth. "As I look upon the future of our country in the changing scene of human destiny I feel the existence of three great circles among the free nations and democracies." So Winston Churchill described the world for members assembled at the Conservative Party Conference of 1948.

> The first circle [he continued] for us is naturally the British Commonwealth and Empire, with all that that comprises. Then there is also the English-speaking world in which we, Canada, and the other British Dominions play so important a part. And finally there is United Europe. These three majestic

[2]Charles de Gaulle, *Unity: 1942–1944*, Richard Howard, trans. (New York: Simon & Schuster, 1959), p. 253.

circles are co-existent and if they are linked together there is no force or combination which could overthrow them or ever challenge them. Now if you think of the three interlinked circles you will see that we are the only country which has a great part in every one of them. We stand, in fact, at the very point of junction, and here in this Island at the centre of the seaways and perhaps of the airways also we have the opportunity of joining them all together.[3]

Such metaphors have laid hold of the British imagination. Sometimes one finds Britain pictured as a connecting link, at other times as a linchpin, and again as a bridge between the old world and the new, or between the Europe of the Six and the wider Organization for European Economic Cooperation (OEEC).

Though many looked upon Churchill as the champion of European unity, it is clear at least in retrospect that in his calls for European political unity he always carefully qualified the position that Britain would take. In his famous speech at Zurich University in September of 1946, he urged the importance of creating anew "the European family in a regional structure called, it may be, the United States of Europe." He added, however, that France and Germany must take the lead. "Great Britain, the British Commonwealth of Nations, mighty America, and I trust Soviet Russia—for then indeed all would be well—must be the friends and sponsors of the new Europe and must champion its right to live and shine."[4] If Europe were truly to unite, England, standing aside, would extend her good wishes. In statements that allowed for British participation, on the other hand, Churchill was careful to limit political association to the form of a grand alliance. International cooperation, rather than supranational integration, and, moreover, a cooperation with Europe that would leave England free to tend to her other world interests, was always the keynote.

Churchill's call for a European army, made in August of 1950 when fighting in Korea had heightened Europe's sense of danger, is the one instance in which Churchill seemed to imply that England would go further in her commitments to the Continent. Introducing his motion to the Assembly at Strasbourg, he called upon his fellow members to "make a

[3]National Union of Conservative and Unionist Associations, *Report of the 69th Annual Conference*, October 6–9, 1948, Llandudno (London, 1948), p. 153. Alternately he described the "world temple of peace" as resting upon "four main pillars": the United States, hopefully the Soviet Union, the British Empire and Commonwealth, and a Europe "with which Great Britain is profoundly blended." *Times* (London), October 12, 1950, p. 4.

[4]Randolph S. Churchill, ed., *The Sinews of Peace: Post-War Speeches by Winston S. Churchill* (Boston: Houghton Mifflin, 1949), p. 202.

gesture of practical and constructive guidance by declaring ourselves in favour of the immediate creation of a European Army under unified command, and in which we should all bear a worthy and honorable part." [5] One is reminded of the ringing Declaration of Anglo-French Union made in the dark days of June, 1940, which Churchill later described as "an immense design whose implications and consequences were not in any way thought out" but which he nevertheless accepted as a dramatic move "clearly necessary to keep the French going." [6] Was this new effort an attempt to rally support for a tightly organized army in which England would participate, or was this a dramatic effort to give heart to a young alliance in its first time of trouble?

It was a French amendment to Churchill's motion that called for putting the unified army "under the authority of a European minister of defense." As a member of the British party in opposition, Churchill personally accepted the addition. In the following November, Ernest Bevin, Foreign Secretary in the Labour Government, declared that Western Europe was "not able to stand by itself" and described the proposed European Defense Community (EDC) as being too limited. He dwelt instead upon the importance of building an Atlantic Community and drawing Western Europe into it.[7] Though Labour was reluctant, many Europeans, impressed with Churchill's informal role as leader of the unity movement, hoped that a future Conservative Government would carry Britain more deeply into Europe. To dedicated Europeans, Churchill's reactions, when once again he became Prime Minister, were painfully cautious. "There is the N.A.T.O. Army," he told the House of Commons at the end of 1951. "Inside the N.A.T.O. Army there is the European Army, and inside the European Army there is the German Army. The European Army should be formed by all the European parties to N.A.T.O. dedicating from their own national armies their quota of divisions to the Army or Armies now under General Eisenhower's command." Clearly Churchill did not mean to include Britain when he described the European army as being formed by all the European parties to NATO. Thus, he added: "As far as Britain is concerned, we do not propose to merge in the European Army but we are already joined to it." [8] Churchill had provided inspiration, his government now accorded its blessing, and like a

[5]Council of Europe, Consultative Assembly, *Reports* (Strasbourg, 1950), Pt. I, p. 228.
[6]Winston S. Churchill, *Their Finest Hour* (Boston: Houghton Mifflin, 1949), pp. 205, 208.
[7]*H.C. Deb.*, Vol. 481 (November 29, 1950), cols. 1172–74. Cf. the statements of Bevin and Attlee, *H.C. Deb.*, Vol. 446 (January 22–23, 1948), cols. 409, 615.
[8]*H.C. Deb.*, Vol. 494 (December 6, 1951), col. 2596.

flying buttress Britain would support a European military structure from outside. As Churchill later put it, Britain is "with" but not "of" Europe. Britain would not "be merged in a Federal European system" but would always seek to associate "Western Europe with the North Atlantic Alliance." [9]

Churchill's policy was identical with Bevin's. The OEEC had been fathered by Bevin in quick and imaginative response to Secretary of State Marshall's suggestion of American willingness to aid European states economically. It was essential to the operation of the European Recovery Program. The Brussels Treaty of March, 1948, establishing a Western Union of Britain, France, and the Benelux countries, had been a means of attracting American political and military support to Europe.[10] It was the precursor of NATO and has been recurringly refurbished as a means of associating Britain with Europe and Europe with a wider world. Britain, with her parties in agreement, was unwilling to participate directly in the EDC, but the failure of EDC prompted her to sponsor the Western European Union (WEU), an enlargement upon the Brussels Treaty and a means of bringing German military strength into NATO. Whether a Labour or a Conservative Government were in power, Britain remained skeptical of all arrangements merely internal to Europe and held herself carefully aloof from them. She eagerly sponsored proposals and helped to fashion institutions that would draw American power into Europe and bring Europe and America together in an Atlantic Community.

By scholars and politicians alike, it has often been said that in the years after the war the leadership of Europe was Britain's for the taking, that Europeans were eagerly awaiting her lead. It is hard to know what such statements mean. Britain did try to lead Europe, in the only direction Britain thought desirable and in the only way she found congenial. The depth and persistence of her convictions in these matters is overwhelmingly impressive. To do more in Europe, Britain would have had to do less elsewhere. She was persistently unwilling to give up her world roles as leader of Commonwealth and Empire, political counselor to the American government, and mediator between East and West. To lead Europe, from her reduced position of power, Britain would have had to

[9]*H.C. Deb.*, Vol. 515 (May 11, 1953), cols. 891, 893.
[10]*Treaty Series No. 1*, Cmd. 7599 (London: HMSO, 1949); and *Final Act of the Nine-Power Conference Held in London, September 28–October 3, 1954*, Cmd. 9289 (London: HMSO, 1954).

abandon British ideas and alter British commitments in order to become herself more European. No longer the strongest of West European countries, her leadership would have come first to be resented and then to be challenged.

The attitude of Britain to the European Coal and Steel Community (ECSC), like her reaction to the EDC, extended across parties. Conservatives were wary of French *dirigisme*, Labour of the *dirigistes*. The leadership and most of the rank and file of both parties were unwilling to surrender Britain's freedom of action. In Parliamentary debate, the proposed supranational authority was described by members of the Labour Party as an anti-democratic agency responsible to no electorate.[11] The earlier glimmering of Labour Party interest in the movement for European unity had disappeared with the postwar failure of European socialists to maintain or to gain power in their separate countries. Sir Stafford Cripps, when Chancellor of the Exchequer, had argued that the government could not let decisions affecting coal and steel pass out of its hands and still be responsible for the economy. He implied that those Conservatives who were urging the importance of British participation in negotiations for the establishment of ECSC would run the risk of surrendering Britain's control over her own economy. Prime Minister Attlee cited the supranational "principles underlying the French proposal" as the reason for his government's refusal even to participate in negotiations.[12] Conservative leaders, who also rejected the principle, urged that Britain negotiate in order to limit its operation. Explaining his party's position, Churchill made it clear that the difference between the two major parties turned on a question of tactics. "I would add, to make my answer quite clear to the right hon. and learned Gentleman, that if he asked me, 'Would you agree to a supra-national authority which has the power to tell Great Britain not to cut any more coal or make any more steel, but to grow tomatoes instead?' I should say, without hesitation, the answer is 'No.' But why not be there to give the answer?"[13]

Conservative leaders did not object to the Labour Government's decision not to join a supranational organization, but they did deplore

[11]*H.C. Deb.*, Vol. 476 (June 26, 1950), Anthony Greenwood, cols. 1957–58; John Hynd, cols. 1978–87; Geoffrey Bing, cols. 2002–10.

[12]*H.C. Deb.*, Vol. 476 (June 13, 1950), cols. 35–37.

[13]*H.C. Deb.*, Vol. 476 (June 27, 1950), cols. 2147–48. Cf. Harold Macmillan at Strasbourg, August 15, 1950: "Our people will not hand over to any supra-national Authority the right to close down our pits or our steel works. We will not allow any supra-national Authority to put large numbers of our people out of work in Durham, in the Midlands, in South Wales or in Scotland." Council of Europe, Consultative Assembly, *Reports* (Strasbourg, 1950), Pt. II, p. 434.

Labour's lack of diplomatic finesse and did blame the government for missing the opportunity to negotiate a different type of arrangement. The Conservative Party, returned to power, did not alter Labour's policy of aloofness, although it did put forth vague proposals for a loose association with Europe.[14] In the words of Anthony Nutting, where "Bevin would declaim 'I won't have it'; Eden would say, 'Let us try to find another way.'"[15] One of the other ways, now known as the Eden Plan, was authored by Nutting and offered to Europe in the early months of 1952. The Plan was designed to placate Europe while preserving British sovereignty. It provided for institutional rearrangements that would permit British representatives to sit as observers and on occasion participate in debate and discussion. "In this way Great Britain could," according to Nutting, "play a part without being committed to the obligations of membership of any supranational agencies. In this way too we could preserve the organic links between the Six and the rest of Western Europe at ministerial and parliamentary levels. We could, in short, obtain a form of associate membership of the developing community of Europe."[16]

Vague proposals are of less consequence than decisions to act. The response of the Conservative Government to the Messina Meeting in June, 1955, from which the European Economic Community (EEC) and the European Atomic Energy Community (EURATOM) emerged, was much the same as Labour's reaction to the ECSC: Britain did not participate in the negotiations. This time politicians and the press united in almost ignoring the meeting. The collapse of the EDC and the seeming inability of the European movement to develop enough momentum to project the ECSC type of arrangement into broader economic and political realms had confirmed Britain's belief that without her participation Europeans would accomplish little. Only when the Common Market began to take form and to threaten a damaging discrimination against British trade with Europe did the government react.[17]

The form of the reaction is significant, for it illustrates fully the continuity of political attitudes and the durability of national objectives. At-

[14]In the June 27, 1950, debate just cited, Churchill, for example, raised "the question of whether there could be two grades of members of such a body—full members and associate members."

[15]Anthony Nutting, *Europe Will Not Wait: A Warning and a Way Out* (London: Hollis & Carter, 1960), p. 41.

[16]*Ibid.*, p. 42.

[17]Cf. Mark Bonham-Carter's retrospective assessment: "We did not believe that the Common Market would come to anything, and at the same time we overrated our own importance." This appeared in his article: "Yes, because the UK Is a Part of Europe!" *Western World*, II (August, 1959), 29.

titudes are nicely reflected in the tripartisan agreement that prevailed in the House of Commons debate of November 26, 1956, on the British proposal to negotiate a free-trade arrangement between the six countries of the EEC and the other nine members of the OEEC. All who spoke in the debate agreed upon essentials except Arthur Holt, a Liberal Member, and Martin Maddan, a Conservative, who would have gone further than the government in coming to terms with the EEC, and Gerald Nabarro, also a Conservative, who would not go at all.

Harold Macmillan, Chancellor of the Exchequer, opened the debate for the government by making the customary reference to the three worlds of which Britain is conceived to be a part—Commonwealth and Empire, the English-speaking world, and Europe. As Macmillan emphasized later in the debate, he, "for one, would be no party to any arrangements which drew us away from the Commonwealth." [18] Harold Wilson sought to outdo him by identifying Labour as "the Commonwealth party." [19] These were intended not as expressions of idle sentiment but as statements from which conclusions about policy derived. Wilson urged that specific, effective measures be taken for increasing Commonwealth trade.[20] Macmillan insisted upon one series of exceptions from free-trade arrangements: drink, tobacco, and foodstuffs for man or beast, whether raw or manufactured. "We must," he said, "remain free to continue to grant to this great volume of imports the preferential arrangements we have built up over the last twenty-five years." [21]

As second and third points, Macmillan drew attention to Britain's role within the Atlantic Alliance, while noting that by geography and by culture Britain is European. As such, she is "moved by the continued efforts of the post-war world to strengthen the unity and cohesion of the old world." [22] The trick to be accomplished was to preserve England's role in the two circles of longer radii without being excluded from the developing European market. England's free-trade proposals were so attractive to her because they promised large gains with almost no costs to offset them. Macmillan dwelt on the desirability of forming a single market of 250 million people and described in some detail the advantages "for which we might hope from a free trade area of this kind for manufactured goods—that really is what it is." [23] In addition to those already

[18]*H.C. Deb.*, Vol. 561 (November 26, 1956), col. 49.
[19]*Ibid.*, cols. 59–60.
[20]*Ibid.*, cols. 61–62.
[21]*Ibid.*, col. 41.
[22]*Ibid.*, col. 35.
[23]*Ibid.*, cols. 36, 37, 43.

mentioned, major themes reflected in almost all speeches were that Britain would not and could not join a customs union, nor under any circumstances would she subscribe to a supranational authority. Finally, because the plan if accepted would take from twelve to fifteen years to implement, it was not, according to Macmillan, "a course . . . upon which we feel we could launch as a purely party matter." Since it would take such a long time, it would not be proper to start unless all parties and all sections of industry and labor were by and large agreed.[24] By the testimony of a number of speakers, they were. In closing the debate for the government, Peter Thorneycroft, then President of the Board of Trade, aptly summed up the many speeches made in the following way: "First, that we cannot enter into a Customs union, and, secondly, that we cannot have free trade in agriculture." [25]

In the free-trade-area negotiations, Britain attempted to gain full access to the Common Market in fields where the British economy was strongest without being willing to contribute to the EEC by liberalizing her immigration laws, providing grants for capital development, adjusting her internal economic policy, or accepting obligations that rest upon entrepreneurs in matters of external tariffs and social charges. Anthony Eden's government continued to act on the familiar assumption that Europe without England would never find unity, stability, and economic well-being. In addition to the unfortunate choice of a "free trade" label, which was sure to offend France, Reginald Maudling, who as Paymaster-General negotiated for England, made the British attitude clear by postponing all controversial matters and then presenting the English package at the end, to be accepted or rejected.[26] If Europe needed England, he must have been thinking, European countries would have to accept her conditions. Instead, de Gaulle gained experience in the casting of vetoes. His spokesman, Jacques Soustelle, announced on November 14, 1958, that "it is not possible to create the Free Trade Area as wished by the British, that is with free trade between the Common Market and the rest of the OEEC but without a single external tariff barrier round the seventeen countries, and without harmonisation in the economic and social spheres." [27] Britain had underestimated the will of France as expressed by

[24]*Ibid.*, col. 53.

[25]*Ibid.*, col. 155.

[26]T. Balogh, "Unequal Partners," in G. D. N. Worswick, ed., *The Free Trade Proposals* (Oxford: Blackwell, 1960), pp. 126–27.

[27]*Financial Times* (London), November 15, 1958. Quoted in Miriam Camps, *The Free Trade Area Negotiations* (Policy Memorandum No. 18 [Princeton: Princeton University Center of International Studies, 1959]), p. 20.

de Gaulle and had overestimated the pressure that her Continental partners would be able to put upon the French.

Toward a New European Policy

The hesitations of Britain's European policy over more than a decade reflected an unwillingness to place Europe above her other interests or even on the same level with them. Reluctance had given way to tepid flirtations in the late 1950's and, finally, to a restrained courtship beginning in July of 1961 when Macmillan announced that his government was ready to negotiate for admission to the EEC. Reasons for the gradual change in direction over a period of years are easy to detect. They can be summarized under three headings—governmental debacles, Britain's relative decline, and the success of European organizations. Suez had demonstrated the inability of two of the strongest middle powers, acting in concert, to carry out their policy. The canceling in 1960 of the Blue Streak missile had cast doubt on Britain's ability to convince anyone of her nuclear independence. The collapse of the Summit Meeting in May of 1960 was disillusioning to Britons, for many had enjoyed and some had taken seriously Britain's role as broker between East and West. There were severe limits to what Britain alone could do. There was also growing doubt about the meaning of describing the Commonwealth as the greatest multiracial grouping in the world, as its best hope for peace, and as a great market of 600 million people. European trade was increasing faster than Britain's and faster than that of the European Free Trade Association (EFTA).[28] Britain's economic growth rate was persistently low as compared to her European competitors. There was no crisis to react to, but problems and pressures had accrued over a period of years to the point where a considered British response was called for.

Where could she turn? EFTA, or the Outer Seven as it is sometimes called, would do little for Britain's trade. Chancellor of the Exchequer Heathcoat Amory bluntly described its economic inadequacy before the agreement was signed. "We do not," he said, "look for any dramatic increase in exports, because many of the tariffs are low and the process of their elimination will be gradual."[29] EFTA's "prime purpose," as Edward Heath frankly said, "was to enable us to reach agreement with the other

[28]EFTA was formed in 1960 by the U.K., Norway, Sweden, Denmark, Austria, Switzerland, and Portugal.
[29]H.C. Deb., Vol. 615 (December 14, 1959), col. 1065.

countries of Europe." [30] EFTA, it was hoped, would increase the bargaining power of the Seven in future negotiations with Europe. "We in the Stockholm group are determined to use the convention," said Macmillan, "as a starting point to an agreement between all OEEC countries." [31] At least since 1957, British Ministers had drawn attention to the dangers that would follow from a permanent division in Europe. The fear of a split, it was hoped, would encourage European countries to do business. Once the division had taken the form of two separate institutions, it was played upon more fully. Heath, for example, in explaining the decision to apply for membership in the Common Market, gave emphasis to the government's fear that economic separation "would lead to a political division which would weaken Europe." [32]

Britain had aligned herself with six other countries, all of them small, some of them not very wealthy, many of them with low tariffs anyway, and some of them neutral. A trade war between the Six and the Seven would damage the latter more heavily, for it was the smaller, the weaker, and was unable by its intent and by its constitution to bring the separate tariffs of its members into line. Since the countries of EFTA traded less among themselves than with the Common Market, it might seem that by giving preference to each other they could hope to divert trade from the Common Market and that Britain would benefit by displacing Germany, especially in the Scandinavian market. In 1958, Germany sent 27.5 percent of her exports to the countries of EFTA, which was more than twice the proportion of any other EEC member and approximately equal to her export trade with the Common Market. Nine-tenths of her exports to EFTA consisted of manufactured goods, and nearly two-thirds of them went to Switzerland and the Scandinavian members. Because they were countries with low tariffs, however, the preference they gave to Britain would not greatly impede Germany's trade. France, against whom leverage was most needed, did relatively little business with the members of EFTA. Finally the losses of trade for the countries of the Common Market that the forming of EFTA might threaten were overbalanced by a decision to step up the EEC's schedule for reducing internal tariffs.[33] With the economic threat of little meaning, the thinly veiled warnings of

[30]*H.C. Deb.*, Vol. 640 (May 18, 1961), col. 1669.

[31]*H.C. Deb.*, Vol. 612 (October 27, 1959), col. 77. Cf. Maudling, *H.C. Deb.*, Vol. 606 (June 9, 1959), col. 801; and Amory, *H.C. Deb.*, Vol. 609 (July 23, 1959), col. 1540.

[32]*H.C. Deb.*, Vol. 645 (August 3, 1961), col. 1680.

[33]Emile Benoit, *Europe at Sixes and Sevens* (New York: Columbia University Press, 1961), pp. 86–91. Trade data are conveniently given in "At Sixes and Sevens," *Economist*, CXCI (May 30, 1959), 867.

Macmillan, Heath, and others would seem to take on a greater political importance.

On closer inspection, however, it is difficult to see just what their political importance might be. In discussing the "so-called division of Europe," Walter Hallstein, President of the Commission of the European Economic Community, once said: " 'Political divisions' are not automatic chemical reactions. They can only occur if politicians want them—and I can't imagine any statesman being willing to take on such a responsibility." [34] Macmillan and other British Ministers did not want a division in Western Europe; they did think they could improve Britain's bargaining position by taking advantage of the widespread distaste for such an outcome. But would the failure of EEC and EFTA to come together mean the perpetuation of a divided Europe or merely the isolation of Britain? Seeking an all-OEEC arrangement became irrelevant as the establishment of the Organization for Economic Cooperation and Development (OECD), agreed upon in January of 1960, brought the United States and Canada directly into economic relation with Europe. EFTA was bypassed, and the special relation of Britain to America was reduced in importance. Britain's playing the part of America's economic spokesman in Europe was no longer possible, for the role had been removed from the script. Macmillan hastened to Washington in search of support for a wider and looser organization of Europe. The United States, however, preferred a Western world resting upon two pillars rather than three. If Britain would not come to terms with the EEC, she would, it appeared, be isolated from the Continent and estranged from America. In May, the Seven, meeting in Lisbon, announced their readiness to negotiate with the Six. Less than a month later, the Six, adopting the position previously taken by France, flatly turned them down. EFTA had failed to accomplish what Heath had described as its "prime purpose." The government's European policy was in ruins.

In the Commons debate of August 3, 1961, Heath drew attention to the belief widespread in Europe that "we want all the advantages of the developments in Europe without undertaking any of the obligations of the other members of the Community. It is that belief which has caused considerable difficulty in our relations with Europe." [35] With Britain's intentions suspect, her economy sagging, and her international position

[34]"An Exclusive Interview with President Hallstein," *Bulletin from the European Community*, No. 39 (January, 1960), p. 2.
[35]*H.C. Deb.*, Vol. 645 (August 3, 1961), col. 1683.

weakened, an unequivocal statement of intentions and an elaboration of the full extent of commitments to be undertaken were required if Britain was to seek entry with reasonable hope of success. Several factors combined to make a firm decision more easily possible. In 1958 and before, the Foreign Office and the Treasury had felt that Europe was politically and economically of little importance to Britain, whose links with the United States and the Commonwealth were paramount. With shifts in personnel occupying important positions in both departments, attitudes toward Europe and estimates of what Britain's interests required had by 1961 changed almost completely.[36] Skepticism and distaste for Europe were replaced by admiration for what the EEC had accomplished and enthusiasm for England's participation. De Gaulle had meanwhile demonstrated by his policy that membership in the EEC need not noticeably impair a nation's ability to play international politics on the grand scale and that, in economic matters, supranationalism did not leave the state unable to protect its interests. The way was prepared for a bold decision by England. The problem politically was to make it and carry it through.

The Prime Minister's Decision

In the negotiations of 1957 and 1958 Maudling had attempted to draw the six countries of Western Europe into a wider free-trade grouping, different in its nature from the Continent's Customs Union. Macmillan on July 31, 1961, announced Britain's willingness to accept European institutions, to which Britain would in some measure adapt. The important questions were then: to what extent was England willing to abandon positions previously taken, and how far were the Six ready to go in order to meet her? We shall concentrate upon the first of these questions.

Linked with Macmillan's statement of Britain's wish to join the EEC and his expressions of optimism over the success of the negotiations to be undertaken were indications of the British interests that would have to be accommodated. We will not, it was said in a variety of ways, neglect the interest of British agriculture, let the Commonwealth down, leave our EFTA parters in the lurch, share nuclear secrets with France, or sever close ties with our American cousins. Nor would there be any derogation of Britain's sovereignty beyond the economic and social spheres. Reservations on the first three points were a part of the statement that Parliament was asked to endorse: the government sought authority to negoti-

---

[36]Nora Beloff, *The General Says No* (Baltimore: Penguin, 1963), p. 86.

ate in order "to see if satisfactory arrangements can be made to meet the special interests of the United Kingdom, of the Commonwealth and of the European Free Trade Association." [37]

Ministers, judged by their statements, had not really revised their definition of British interests. They had merely changed their estimates of what the situation would permit. Where once it had been said with stultifying frequency that joining the Six would mean choosing Europe in preference to the Commonwealth, which could never be done, it was now said that no choice need be made.[38] Where earlier and often it had been argued that a trading arrangement with Continental Europe that included agricultural as well as manufactured goods would leave Britain's internal interests unprotected, it was now thought that arrangements could be found that would protect British agriculture while satisfying European desires.[39] The third of the interests singled out in the motion was of more recent origin. EFTA had begun to operate in May of 1960. Selwyn Lloyd, in his last days as Foreign Secretary, described Britain's obligations to her new partners in the following way: "In loyalty to them we must ensure that any plan to secure political and economic unity in Europe takes care of their interests and their preoccupations and is formulated after full discussion with them." [40]

Did the government believe what it said or merely say what it believed to be politic? Did it speak truths bluntly, even if the truth proved unpleasant, or was its policy to turn on the nuance of words whose meaning would only later be revealed? In the debate of November 26, 1956, Macmillan had emphasized that Britain would ever insist upon its freedom to grant preference to Commonwealth imports.[41] Now he spoke more loosely of maintaining "the true interest of the Commonwealth." [42] It is often tempting in foreign policy to speak with two voices. If one line is taken at home and another abroad, puzzlement will grow as to which audience the government is trying to fool. Were the difficulties of speaking at home while foreigners were listening fairly well managed? How,

[37]*H.C. Deb.*, Vol. 645 (August 2, 1961), col. 1480.

[38]Cf. Duncan Sandys, who as Secretary of State for Commonwealth Relations closed the debate for the government: "I believe that my European friends will not misunderstand me if I say that if I were forced to make this cruel choice I would unquestionably choose the Commonwealth. Happily, we are not confronted with this dilemma." *H.C. Deb.*, Vol. 645 (August 3, 1961), col. 1775.

[39]Cf. Macmillan, *H.C. Deb.*, Vol. 645 (August 2, 1961), cols. 1486–88; and Sandys, *H.C. Deb.*, Vol. 645 (August 3, 1961), cols. 1771–72.

[40]*H.C. Deb.*, Vol. 627 (July 25, 1960), col. 1103. Cf. Macmillan, *H.C. Deb.*, Vol. 645 (August 2, 1961), col. 1486; Sandys, *H.C. Deb.*, Vol. 645 (August 3, 1961), col. 1773.

[41]Cited above, p. 232.

[42]*H.C. Deb.*, Vol. 645 (August 2, 1961), cols. 1493–94.

we shall want to know, did the political customs and conditions of Britain shape the government's decision and affect its execution? Were issues aired or obscured? Had the situation of the country and its relations with Europe become the subject of open and serious discussion among interested groups early enough to permit difficulties to be understood, problems to be identified, and possibilities to be seen from widely different perspectives before the government's policy had hardened and become identified with its prestige? Because of the weakness of Britain's international position, the firmness of her new purpose would have to be demonstrated. Because she had waited until European economic integration was nicely in process, important concessions would have to be made. Was the government able to take a strong European line in spite of internal impediments, or was Britain's negotiating position further weakened by the pressure of national attitudes and forces?

The Commonwealth Ideology

So often are we reminded that British policy proceeds empirically that we easily overlook her ideological commitments. Devotion to Commonwealth is one of them. It is supported by deeply ingrained national attitudes. Important among them are strains of national glory from the past that echo in the present.

The tradition of Commonwealth rhetoric in Britain is a long one. Gladstone, speaking to the Mechanics Institute at Chester in 1855, repudiated all crass and material reasons for Britain's having acquired an Empire: whether to enhance her reputation, increase her revenues, establish a monopoly of trade, secure a larger field for the operation of patronage, or extend her territory. Why then did England support the expenses of empire? Quite simply, in order that it might be said that she had done her duty. "We think," Gladstone noted, "that our country is a country blessed with laws and a constitution that are eminently beneficial to mankind, and if so, what can be more to be desired than that we should have the means of reproducing in different portions of the globe something as like as may be to that country which we honour and revere?" The "object of colonisation," in words Gladstone borrowed from the Radical Mr. Roebuck, "is the creation of so many happy Englands." [43]

Victorian England, possessed of vast power, found maintaining an Em-

[43]Paul Knaplund, *Gladstone and Britain's Imperial Policy* (London: Allen & Unwin, 1927), pp. 198–203.

pire more attractive than the prospect of imperial devolution, but as England's power declined, Gladstone's Commonwealth idea came to be more widely embraced. The *Empire* was founded, formed, and maintained by Great Britain. The greatest naval power in the world also offered the largest market. She could supply and protect her far-flung associates and also absorb their produce. The *Commonwealth* is shaped by forces pressing upon it from outside. As England's trade declines as a proportion of total world trade, the countries of the Commonwealth must increasingly look elsewhere. They must also find others to defend them. In 1940, New Zealand asked Britain for naval protection against the threat posed by Japan. Britain replied that none was available. After Pearl Harbor, American military power in Asia gradually replaced Britain's. ANZUS, a defense arrangement formed by Australia, New Zealand, and the United States and from which Great Britain is excluded, marked the culmination of this process.[44]

With the material bases of Empire gone, Commonwealth ties have come to depend on sentiment and tradition, which the mother country feels more deeply than most of her children. Though the ties of sentiment and tradition are stronger than "realists" in politics will often admit, they do not endure forever. Tradition embodies the past, but tomorrow the past is what was done today.

Statements that dwell upon the majesty and importance of Commonwealth must, as political rhetoric does, bear a considerable discount. There is, nevertheless, a danger that slogans may come to be believed by those who so often repeat them. "The British Commonwealth," one learns from a Conservative Party pamphlet, "has greater resources of political experience than any other nation [*sic*]. Moral leadership in the 'cold war' against the new barbarism must, therefore, devolve largely upon its shoulders. To those who believe that the days of world leadership for the British Empire and Commonwealth are over, we reply 'British leadership is more vital to the future of civilization now than at any time in history.' " [45] The conviction was more simply stated by Anthony Eden: "The British Commonwealth and Empire is the greatest force for peace and progress in the world today." [46] More recently and from the other

---

[44]Cf. Denis Warner, an Australian journalist: "Naturally, the ties of Commonwealth, heritage, and tradition remain strong in Australia. But when it comes to foreign affairs and defense, Australia looks to and confides in the United States: Canberra has secrets that it shares with Washington but not, to the unconcealed irritation of the British, with London." "The Shadow and Substance of the ANZUS Pact," *Reporter*, XXX (June 4, 1964), 21.

[45]*Conservatism 1945–1950* (Conservative Political Centre, No. 90 [London, 1950]), p. 151.

[46]*United for Peace and Progress: The Conservative and Unionist Party's Policy, General Election 1955* (London, 1955), p. 12.

major party, one finds Denis Healey saying: "We have to restore the faith of our friends in Asia, Africa, Australia and New Zealand in our ability in this country to make the Commonwealth the nervous system, the spinal column, of a new world order." [47] Finally, Harold Wilson, before he became Prime Minister, asked by way of warning what damage rushing headlong into Europe would do to "the Commonwealth as a whole, this unique multi-racial community of 700 millions, the greatest guarantee of peace and security in this divided world?" [48]

As even its stoutest defenders must know, the Commonwealth is not going to be the "spinal column" of a new order, nor has it been the greatest force for peace, progress, and security in a divided world. Commonwealth countries lack geographical coherence and political compatibility. Within the Commonwealth, the numbers of those stricken by poverty exceed the capability of the wealthy to render them assistance. Britain supplies only one-third of the aid funds received by Commonwealth countries and but 10 percent of total economic assistance to India.[49] Though such facts are well known, they have not caused a lessening of confidence. Prime Minister Alec Douglas-Home, speaking to the House of Commons, asserted that the Commonwealth could still bridge the racial gulf and added that "if people are searching for a new role for Britain, this is it." [50] Such views of the Commonwealth provide another example of the immaterialist attitude that was described in Chapter 7. Rather than awakening doubts of Britain's ability to play a world role, material weakness has led to an emphasis upon nonmaterial forces. It is a natural inclination of the weak to define influence in terms of moral force, for they have little of any other kind. The force required is proportionate to the end in view. Britain, stronger than most, has been inclined to play down the importance of material strength, for the ends she has entertained have outrun her means.

As Britain has declined in the world, Englishmen have devoted more and more attention to defining her role. The more definitions one reads, the harder it becomes to understand just what the role is supposed to be. The Commonwealth is offered to the world as an object of emulation.

---

[47] Labour Party, *Report of the 61st Annual Conference*, October 1–5, 1962, Brighton (London, 1962), p. 175.
[48] Wilson, *Purpose in Politics* (Boston: Houghton Mifflin, 1964), p. 113.
[49] Overseas Development Institute, *British Aid—1: Survey and Comment* (London, 1963), p. 7.
[50] *H.C. Deb.*, Vol. 696 (June 17, 1964), col. 1322.

Yet those who offer the model will often admit that the Commonwealth relation itself cannot be precisely defined. Thus C. M. Woodhouse, formerly Director-General of the Royal Institute of International Affairs and a Conservative MP since 1959, writing of the Commonwealth, notices that "all the formal links dissolve under close inspection." [51]

The contradiction between Britain's global pretensions and her material insufficiency often leads that practical nation to retreat into mysticism. The Commonwealth endures, it is sometimes said, precisely because it permits almost anything: policies of neutralism or of alliance, contrary votes in the United Nations, bitter quarrels as between India and Pakistan, outright opposition to the actions of England as in Egypt in 1956, the organization by Ghana of anti-Europe campaigns in Africa, and the admixture of such fictions as the one that the exclusion from the United Kingdom of Pakistani and Indian textiles is voluntary. All differences, save the anomaly of a racialist South Africa in a multiracial Commonwealth, can be encompassed, for, it is said, differences unite. Of United Nations debates the *Economist* remarked that "Commonwealth countries sometimes lead both the left and the right wing" and added that "they also often appear, very helpfully, in the centre." But according to that journal, "this is precisely the special value of their Commonwealth association. Not like-minded, not linked by blood, often opposed in their economic interests, sometimes in direct dispute with one another (as over Kashmir or Rhodesia), they form the only group that straddles at least some of the major divides in a split world." [52] Disputes set the scene for reconciliation, and setbacks stimulate growth, for "in an ever changing Commonwealth, it is precisely those changes that are seen as fatally damaging it that may prove, in the light of history, to have enabled it to survive." [53] To decline gracefully and to lose an Empire without great bloodshed are difficult tasks rarely accomplished. It was an immense contribution of the Commonwealth mentality to ease the adjustment. The magnificence of the contribution should not lead us to overlook that by the same notion other adjustments were made more difficult. It is hard for Britons to say that they are part of a growing Commonwealth that really means something in the world and then set out on a policy of mixing and losing their identity in Europe.

---

[51] C. M. Woodhouse, *British Foreign Policy since the Second World War* (London: Hutchinson, 1961), p. 232.

[52] "Commonwealth End," *Economist*, CCXI (June 6, 1964), 1075.

[53] *Ibid.*

The Interests and Policies of Britain and Europe

The Commonwealth represents the fulcrum of feeling at which the problem of Britain in Europe becomes wholly confused. In the miasma of Commonwealth myths, the influence and excellence of Britain are often exaggerated and the virtues of West European states and the institutions they have contrived lose their luster. Hugh Gaitskell, a man of integrity and logic, of passion and political commitment, summed up in his person and expressed in his harsh and eloquent speech at the Labour Party Conference in October of 1962 the contradictory ideas and aspirations of many Englishmen. Each logical statement hid an emotion; every datum concealed an attitude. The arguments for and against Britain's entry were, he noted, closely balanced; yet in tone more clearly than in content he came out firmly against it.[54]

If Britain stayed out, she would face a Common Market tariff of 10 to 15 percent.[55] This, Gaitskell implied, is no great impediment to Britain's trade with Europe. One may easily agree. If so, it becomes hard to see how a dismantling of preference within the Commonwealth can be so very important to England or to any of its other members. Gaitskell put the preference Australia gives to Britain at an average of 10 percent on 85 percent of Britain's exports to her.[56] Preference to Britain on all of her trade with Commonwealth countries, a figure Gaitskell did not give, is estimated as being presently less than 5 percent and gradually decreasing. If a 10 to 15 percent tariff is not an important factor in Britain's trade with Europe, it is hard to see how a lesser preference within the Commonwealth can matter very much. If the virtue of maintaining a system of preferences within the Commonwealth is nevertheless dwelt upon, it becomes unnerving to find that in the view of many Britons the preference the Six give to each other makes them a discriminatory trading bloc. If Europe is such, then so is the Commonwealth. Europe's vice is, however, Britain's virtue in the eyes of those who prize the association, for a part of the system of preference is freedom for Commonwealth products to enter the British market, and many of the Commonwealth countries are economically underdeveloped. Britain looks outward and

---

[54] *61st Annual Conference of the Labour Party*, pp. 154–65.
[55] *Ibid.*, p. 155.
[56] *Ibid.*, p. 156.

offers a helping hand. "We are . . . the one great multi-racial bridge in the world, bridging all peoples, all views, and indeed almost all ideologies," George Brown told the Conference that Gaitskell had earlier addressed. "We care for the poorer nations of the world, and the multi-racial Commonwealth of nations is a grouping in which trying to help the poor from the resources of the rich is one of the great principles." [57]

In contrast the Six countries of Europe, according to the view common in England, are building a tight little, discriminatory, inward-looking, Cold War oriented bloc.[58] Is Europe, Gaitskell asked, "inward-looking or is it internationally minded?" He could not say, for Europe has "two faces and we do not know as yet which is the one which will dominate." [59] Britain should be prepared to enter Europe, according to Gaitskell, only if Europe were to experience "a change of heart." [60] The change required, according to the statement laid down by the Labour Party's National Executive Committee, would be "a conscious decision to liberalise their commercial policy and to become an outward-looking rather than an inward-looking community." [61]

Gaitskell's speech was a powerful political appeal on a question that divided Labour's political leaders. It was also in many ways typical of political thinking and feeling in Britain. On May 7, 1963, in the first major statement of British policy to a representative European audience after the breakdown of the Brussels negotiations, Heath contrasted Britain's and most of Europe's "wish to see the larger Community and the outward-looking Europe which I have described rather than the smaller and more limited approach," which he obviously meant to attribute to France.[62]

Such statements are made often and repeated with obvious sincerity. They illustrate the importance of attitude and the political unimportance of fact. The Ottawa Agreements of 1932 recognized and buttressed by preference a situation in which the overseas dominions supplied primary

---

[57]*Ibid.*, p. 193.

[58]See *ibid.*, Gaitskell, p. 165, and George Brown, pp. 190–92. And cf. Douglas Jay, Labour MP and long-time opponent of Britain's entering Europe, "Time to Think Again," *New Statesman*, LXIV (December 7, 1962), 816: "Month by month the Six, and the Commission in particular, have shown themselves more narrowly protectionist, inward-looking and inspired by bigoted French selfishness."

[59]*61st Annual Conference of the Labour Party*, p. 158.

[60]*Ibid.*, p. 165. Cf. Frank Cousins, *ibid.*, pp. 181–82; and Kenneth Younger, *Changing Perspectives in British Foreign Policy* (London: Oxford University Press, 1964), p. 123.

[61]*61st Annual Conference of the Labour Party*, p. 246.

[62]Council of Europe, Consultative Assembly, *Official Report of Debates* (Strasbourg, 1963), I, 59.

materials and especially foodstuffs to Britain in exchange for capital and manufactured goods. It would be rather surprising if an arrangement made thirty-odd years ago by a small number of countries should be just what is needed now when many more countries are included.[63] Devotees of the Commonwealth maintain that it is. The myth of the Commonwealth must be placed against its reality if one is to understand Britain's position in the world, the concern of Commonwealth countries, and the interests of underdeveloped countries generally.

British exports have declined, as a proportion of world trade, from 10.0 percent in 1953 to 8.4 percent in 1964, a fall by one-sixth in little more than a decade.[64] The markets of the primary producing countries have meanwhile grown less rapidly than those of other countries. The Commonwealth, having wed weakness to weakness, has understandably failed to breed strength. Under the circumstances, the direction of British trade has changed considerably, as shown in Table 12.

TABLE 12   DISTRIBUTION OF U.K. EXPORTS BY TRADE AREA

EXPORTS TO	1953	1959	1963	1964
Sterling Area	47.0%	40.3%	35.6%	34.8%
Western Europe	27.4	27.6	37.3	37.8
of which EEC	13.1	14.0	20.3	20.4
of which EFTA	11.9	11.5	13.6	14.1
North America	12.4	17.2	12.6	13.5
Rest of world	13.2	15.0	14.5	13.9

Source: EFTA, *EFTA Trade: 1959–1964* (Geneva, 1966), p. 104, Table C.8 (iv).

Much of Britain's Commonwealth and Sterling Area business, one must add, is done with countries that are hardly impoverished. The interests of the underdeveloped countries, as distinct from England's, are most clearly revealed if we look at the amount of their exports to the United Kingdom and to the countries of the EEC and notice how they have changed over a period of years, as shown in Table 13.

[63]Cf. the harshly critical article, one of a series of three, written by Enoch Powell under the label of "A Conservative." "Patriotism Based on Reality, Not on Dreams," *Times* (London), April 2, 1964, p. 13. Cf. also Macmillan, *H.C. Deb.*, Vol. 645 (August 2, 1961), col. 1485.

[64]Sino-Soviet area countries, Cuba, and for the later year, Indonesia, are excluded from the calculation. Based on Statistics Bureau, International Monetary Fund, *International Financial Statistics: Supplement to 1964/65 Issues* (Washington, D.C., n.d.), p. xiv; and *International Financial Statistics*, XIX (May, 1966), 34.

TABLE 13   IMPORTS FROM DEVELOPING COUNTRIES

IMPORTS OF	1953	1959	1960	1961	1962	1963	1964
			in millions of dollars (c.i.f.)				
U.K.	3442.7	3929.4	4117.2	4079.1	4005.5	4327.0	4413.3
EEC	——	6768.5	7576.3	7612.9	8189.4	8904.2	9945.1

Source: EFTA, *EFTA Trade: 1959–1964*, Statistical Appendix, Table 90.

In proportion to population, the United Kingdom provides a large market for the exports of the primary producers. Yet the EEC, though said by the British to be inward-looking, offers a larger market and one that is growing more rapidly. Between 1959 and 1964, British imports from the developing countries increased by just over 2 percent yearly. The EEC's imports from the same countries grew about four times as fast.[65]

Problems of trade, had Britain entered Europe, were of concern to Commonwealth members, but mainly to those already highly developed —that is, to Australia and even more so to New Zealand. New Zealand, the Commonwealth country most dependent upon Britain as a market, sends to the United Kingdom yearly about two-thirds of her total exports, almost all of which originate in the farm sector, and which in turn contribute about 30 percent of New Zealand's national income.[66] In 1957 and 1958, however, Australia and New Zealand had gained from the United Kingdom the right to reduce the preference they gave her. Already pressing against the limits of Britain's ability to absorb their primary products, they wished to be able to bargain for tariff concessions elsewhere in order to enlarge their markets.[67]

[65]So also did those of EFTA if the U.K. is omitted. EFTA, *EFTA Trade: 1959–1964* (Geneva, 1966), p. 45.

[66]James P. O'Hagan, "Australia and New Zealand in the Export Recession," *Monthly Bulletin of Agricultural Economics and Statistics*, VIII (June, 1959), 1, 4.

[67]Except for the bumper year 1953, Australia's exports to the U.K. steadily declined in absolute amount from 1952 to 1963; and despite a considerable increase in 1964, the amount exported to the U.K. in that year was still below the 1952 level. New Zealand's exports to the U.K. declined in absolute amount from 1952 to 1963. Though in 1964, after a sharp upturn, they were above the 1952 level by 19 percent, her exports to the rest of the world had increased in the meanwhile by 234 percent. The calculations are based on two of the joint publications of the U.N. Statistical Office, the International Monetary Fund, and the International Bank for Reconstruction and Development, *Direction of International Trade, Annual Issue: Annual Data for the Years 1938, 1948, and 1952–1955*, Statistical Papers, Series T, Vol. VII, No. 6 (no place, n.d.), pp. 265, 268; and *Direction of International Trade, Annual Issue: Annual Data for the Years 1948 and 1956–1959*, Statistical Papers, Series T, Vol. XI, No. 9 (New York, 1960), pp. 363, 366. Also International Monetary Fund and International Bank for Reconstruction and Development, *Direction of Trade, A Supplement to International Financial Statistics: Annual, 1960–64* (Washington, D.C., n.d.), pp. 132, 297.

In seeking to join the EEC, Britain faced agricultural problems at home as well as trade problems within the Commonwealth. Britain's agricultural policy was incompatible with European arrangements. Adjustment would have been difficult. British farmers receive two-thirds of their net yearly income as subsidies from their government.[68] British agriculture, fostered by governmental subsidy at tremendous cost to the public, produces two-thirds of the temperate foodstuffs consumed in Great Britain. The subsidies producers receive amount to a substantial protection, estimated for the year 1954–55 to be the equivalent of a 30 percent tariff.[69] The policy can be described as one of growing at home a great deal more than one should for the sake of economic efficiency and importing the rest at the lowest prices ordinarily obtainable. The policy of fostering high-cost farming in Britain may have made sense when the prevailing style of warfare meant that a siege economy might have to be maintained. It hardly makes sense now. Britain has not adjusted her agricultural policy either according to her own interest or in order to give additional meaning and effect to her outward-looking pose. The United Kingdom, followed closely by the United States, is noticeably more protectionist than is the EEC. "Ninety-six per cent of the common external tariff duties," according to a recent study, "are at 20 per cent or less, as against 72 per cent for the United States tariff and 69 per cent for the United Kingdom tariff. Only an infinitesimal proportion (0.3 per cent) of the common external tariff duties is above 25 per cent whereas the proportion is 21 per cent for the United States and 25 per cent for the United Kingdom. Thirteen per cent of United States duties and 21 per cent of United Kingdom duties are even above 30 per cent."[70] To say that Britain looks outward means, so far as Commonwealth members are concerned, agricultural free trade in what is left of the British market after political pressures have been first exaggerated and then accommodated. Seldom has the verbal art raised a residue of self-interest to a higher level of humanitarian idealism.

[68]J. Roland Pennock, " 'Responsible Government,' Separated Powers, and Special Interests: Agricultural Subsidies in Britain and America," *American Political Science Review*, LVI (September, 1962), 622; Peter Self and Herbert J. Storing, *The State and the Farmer: British Agricultural Policies and Politics* (Berkeley: University of California Press, 1963), p. 221.
[69]Production figures from Macmillan, *H.C. Deb.*, Vol. 645 (August 2, 1961), col. 1485; Self and Storing, *The State and the Farmer*, p. 223. Tariff equivalent estimated by E. F. Nash, "The Competitive Position of British Agriculture," *Journal of Agricultural Economics* (June, 1955), reported in Self and Storing, *The State and the Farmer*, p. 221.
[70]"Tariff Study Shows Community Less Protected Than U.S.," *European Community*, No. 70 (April, 1964), p. 3. The data in this article are from Political and Economic Planning Organisation (PEP), *Atlantic Tariffs and Trade* (London, 1962).

Such a harsh judgment cannot be justified without considering policies other than those that apply to trade in agricultural produce.

Taking at their face value statements previously cited, one would expect to turn to the record of expenditures on foreign aid and find Britain giving generously of her substance to help those in greatest need. Since France is accused by the British of running an imperial operation in the guise of an aid program, one might also expect that in Britain's case there would be little relation between past political association and present recipients of British aid. Such thoughts are not borne out by the record.

If the EEC is an inward-looking bloc, it is so despite the great aid expense born by France, its second wealthiest member. If French aid can be written off as evidence of "an outward-looking" attitude because it goes mostly to her former colonies, then so can British aid. The direction of aid given by European countries, whether by Britain or France, Belgium, Portugal, or Holland, is historically conditioned.[71] Where French aid is concentrated upon countries of the French franc area, British aid goes almost entirely to areas still politically dependent upon her or formerly so. In the period 1954/55 to 1961/62, Britain dispensed £743.5 million in economic aid. Some 63 percent went to colonial territories, 22.5 percent to independent Commonwealth countries, and 14.5 percent to others. A large part of the small amount that found its way outside the Commonwealth and Colonial circle went to a few other countries—Libya and Jordan prominent among them—where special military and economic ties exist.[72] Multilateral aid is an insignificant portion of the British program, as has been true for all aid-granting countries other than the United States and West Germany.

Within the British program, grants in the same period prevailed over loans by more than two to one for countries still politically dependent. For all others, in or out of the Commonwealth, loans have predominated in approximately the inverse ratio. Britain, along with West Germany, has objected on principle to loans being made at interest below the commercial level lest distortion of the money market occur. Until recently, the

[71]Chairman, Development Assistance Committee, *Development Assistance Efforts and Policies in 1961 of the Members of the Development Assistance Committee* (Paris: OECD, 1962), p. 26; cited hereafter as *Development Assistance in 1961*. Net aid contributions, official and private, in 1963 were larger per capita from the EEC countries than from EFTA, and much larger still from the U.S. To wit: EFTA, $12.27; EEC, $13.85; U.S., $23.98; all OECD countries, $13.22; U.K., $14.70. Estimates of the OECD, in *EFTA Reporter*, No. 117 (April 5, 1965), p. 1.

[72]*Aid to Developing Countries*, Cmnd. 2147 (London: HMSO, 1963), pp. 15, 42–47.

British government has loaned money to underdeveloped countries at the rate at which it can borrow plus a small charge for administration, though long repayment periods have been granted.[73] France has extended most of its aid in the form of grants, to the extent of 90 percent of total bilateral aid in 1961. What lending she does is on very liberal terms both in rate of interest and repayment period.[74]

Within their aid programs the French have been more liberal than the British. The French program overall has by far been the larger.[75] The data in Table 14 indicate this and permit a comparison with other countries.

Western Europe has, as Gaitskell said, "two faces." So has every country or area: one looking outward, the other inward. Building from states that have long been sovereign an association that will hang together, whether as federation or confederation, is the most difficult of political tasks. Any organization by including some must exclude others, which introduces an element of discrimination.[76] That an organization exists first for the benefit of its members strikes British critics as obvious and good when it is a question of the Commonwealth but as somehow deceitful and malicious when the EEC is at issue.

British Attitudes

Who looks inward, who looks outward? By convictions born of experience, Britons are conditioned to say, "We do, and Europe does not." In many other ways, less concrete but not less important, Britain's approach to the Continent was impeded by national habits and beliefs that could not easily be overcome. The late John Strachey characterized the evolution of British rule in India as being from "pillage and intimacy" to "decency and distance." He added, with illustrations: "Especially after the Mutiny, the fatal doctrine of racial superiority came more and more

[73]*Ibid.*, p. 15. In June of 1965, Barbara Castle, Minister of Overseas Development, announced that loans to the poorer countries would be made free of interest or management charges.

[74]Senate Hearings before the Committee on Foreign Relations, *Foreign Assistance Act of 1963* (88th Cong., 1st sess., 1963), p. 19. Very soft loans are a significant amount of the aid program only for the United States, France, and Portugal (OECD, *Development Assistance in 1961*, p. 22).

[75]It has been argued that France gains from the favored position her manufactured goods enjoy in the countries of the Franc Zone and that the industrial development of the member countries is thereby retarded. At the same time, France takes primary products from them at prices well above the level of the world market. See, e.g., United Nations Economic Commission for Africa, *Economic Bulletin for Africa*, I (June, 1961), 10; and Food and Agriculture Organization, "Commodity Stabilization Funds in the French Franc Area" (mimeo., 1962), pp. 23–24.

[76]Fritz Erler, "The Basis of Partnership," *Foreign Affairs*, XLI (October, 1963), 87.

TABLE 14 VOLUME OF U.K. FOREIGN AID COMPARED WITH THAT OF FOUR OTHER COUNTRIES

(in millions of dollars)

DONOR COUNTRIES	GRANTS AND GRANT-LIKE CONTRIBUTIONS[a]			TOTAL OFFICIAL FLOW[b]			TOTAL OFFICIAL AND PRIVATE FLOW[b]		
	1962	1963	1964	1962	1963	1964	1962	1963	1964
United Kingdom	252.3	253.8	279.7	417.7	414.2	490.5	630.7	627.4	(799.2)
France	871.9	708.8	684.3	977.0	843.0	841.4	1,286.6	1,178.7	1,288.6
West Germany	214.4	171.7	173.4	427.0	421.5	459.5	681.5	557.6	743.6
Japan	83.3	86.1	78.3	165.2	171.5	178.4	(302.0)	(285.4)	(277.5)
United States	2,970	2,866	2,711	3,713	3,842	3,534	4,517	(4,579)	(4,849)

Source: OECD, *Development Assistance Efforts and Policies: 1965 Review* (Paris, 1965), Table 1, pp. 124–25.
[a]Including grants, net loans repayable in recipients' currencies, net transfers of resources through sales for recipients' currencies, and grants and capital subscriptions to multilateral agencies.
[b]Excluding credits of five years and less. Parentheses indicate official estimates.

to dominate the imaginations of the British in India.[77] Native peoples, whether they were to be plundered, ruled, or uplifted, were not to be turned into British citizens. The French attitude was different, which helped to make the process of disentanglement more difficult. The British approach, born of long enjoyment of a superior position in the world, easily carried over from peoples who were ruled by Britain to others who were not. Vulgarly the thought is conveyed by the colloquialism, "Wogs begin at the channel." [78] It finds many other expressions. William Pickles of the London School of Economics, for example, properly paying attention to the French, German, and Italian history of political instability, cast aside the argument that Britain should enter Europe in order to provide a steadying influence. "The way to reduce instability in Europe," he argued, "is to give whatever help we can from outside, not to sacrifice Britain to it. The sensible missionary does not jump into the cannibal stewpot in order to reduce its temperature. Besides, if the argument were valid for us, it could equally well—or better—require the U.S.A. to merge her stability into South-American instabilities, but nobody seems to have suggested that. The U.S. prefers to exercise its stabilizing influence from outside, and we can quite well do the same for Europe." [79] Britain would, however, be more directly and more damagingly affected by instability in France, Germany, or Italy than the United States would be by upheavals in any Latin American state, and less able to do anything about it. The notion that Britain stands in relation to Europe as the United States does to Latin America embodies a disturbing disregard for Britain's interests and a gross exaggeration of her importance and power.

Pickles and many others, fearful of Europe's instability, would have Britain remain disentangled. The conclusion is sometimes turned in the opposite direction by the argument that because European countries are politically unstable, Britain should enter in order to help them.[80] A third attitude, still more commonly displayed, is found in Britain's unsurprising preference for working with the countries of the Commonwealth and, in Europe, with the Scandinavian and Low Countries. Gaitskell, urging that any EFTA members who wished to enter EEC should be permitted

[77]Strachey, *The End of Empire* (London: Gollancz, 1959), p. 55.

[78]The term "wog" is derived from "westernized Oriental gentleman," used in the 1920's to describe a native of India, especially a native laborer. During World War II, the RAF and the Flying Tigers shortened the phrase and adopted the conveniently brief composite. Eric Partridge, *A Dictionary of R.A.F. Slang* (London: M. Joseph, 1945).

[79]Pickles, *Not With Europe: The Political Case for Staying Out* (Fabian Tract 336 [London: Fabian Society, 1962]), p. 29.

[80]Cf. Roy Pryce, *The Political Future of the European Community* (London: Marshbank, 1962), p. 93.

to do so, mentioned that "the Scandinavian states have a very special relationship with this country and with this Party particularly; for social democracy has prospered in Scandinavia as it has nowhere else in the world. It is important to us that we should have these friends with us if we go in. I do not say that they will always vote with us, but there is a fairly good chance that they will, and it might be very important." [81] Surely it is easier and more pleasant for Britain to deal with the relatively small and weak countries of the Commonwealth and with her Scandinavian neighbors than to adjust her policies to a sometimes recalcitrant France or to work with West Germany, whose larger production and more useful military contribution to European defense have put in jeopardy Britain's position as first among states of the second rank. The habit of dealing with lesser states from a position of power is for Britain an old one. Though the habit may not enter consciously into decisions about policy, it is nevertheless an important influence.

A final example of the unconscious projection of attitudes is the distinction almost always made between empirical Britain and doctrinaire Europe. The "empirical" approach to Europe has led Britain to fall into a position that can legitimately be called doctrinaire. G. D. N. Worswick, economist of Magdalene College, Oxford, mentions that Englishmen are put off by the "almost mystical fervour" of European bureaucrats and economists. As an example, he cites from the EEC's first General Report: "If European integration is to make fresh advances it must become a reality both in practice and in the will of the individual." [82] The statement does not seem to be a very good example of anything in particular, but one can think of many British slogans, clichés, and catchwords that illustrate the fervor of her commitments and the doctrinaire quality of her thought: "The strength of sterling," "Commonwealth ties," "Colonial responsibilities," "outward-looking," "Atlantic Community," "special relation," "international cooperation without federation." [83] The question really has less to do with European ideology versus British empiricism than with one set of beliefs, habits, and commitments versus another. Europeans, and especially Frenchmen of the early and middle 1950's, have been inclined to economic integration, free movement of the factors of production, coordination of economic policies, and the construction of

---

[81] *61st Annual Conference of the Labour Party*, p. 160.

[82] Worswick, "European Economic Community and the Free Trade Area Negotiations, 1956–58," in G. D. N. Worswick, ed., *The Free Trade Proposals* (Oxford: Blackwell, 1960), p. 93.

[83] Cf. the criticisms of British attitudes by Harry G. Johnson, "The Common Market: The Economists' Reactions," in *ibid.*, pp. 135–42.

institutions. The British have been wedded, in the words of A. C. L. Day, another British economist, to "an idealised version of nineteenth-century free trade and national sovereignty." [84]

In looking at Europe, Britons early developed the habit of fastening upon the supranational or federal goals sometimes proclaimed, rather than of noticing what was actually going on. Surely Hallstein, in contrast, was right in emphasizing, as he did in his Clayton Lectures at the Fletcher School of Law and Diplomacy in April of 1962, that the EEC has been consistently, vigorously, and often ingeniously pragmatic. Adopting a habit of President de Gaulle's, Hallstein turned a British notion against them by describing Britain's application for membership as a testimonial to EEC's success and "a vindication of the 'pragmatic' approach which the Community adopted at the failure of the negotiations for an OEEC-wide free-trade area." [85]

The glorification of British empiricism raises a cloud that obscures the commitments upon which policy is based. A love for empirical procedures is joined, in British thinking and feeling, with a cherishing of sovereignty. European supranationalism and federalism, which are not very clearly distinguished in England, then become distasteful. The sovereignty of Parliament must not be sacrificed; indeed, according to William Pickles, it cannot be.[86] The statement would be amusing if the matter were not politically important. In almost every other context, the worry expressed is that Parliament has lost control of the government and its policy, which leaves one wondering what the sovereignty of Parliament may mean in practice. It is anomalous to proclaim the independence of Commonwealth countries along with the inviolability of Parliament's sovereignty and then not even blink when, as is customary, a Minister replies to a question by saying: "I cannot answer that question because our policy on the matter is determined in consultation with the Commonwealth." That is, the decision will be presented to the House of Commons as a *fait accompli*.[87] That worries about losing sovereignty come into play only when arrangements with European states are in question indicates that political attitudes are more important than regard for constitutional proprieties.

[84]Day, "The Case for British Entry into the European Economic Community," in *ibid.*, p. 111.

[85]Walter Hallstein, *United Europe: Challenge and Opportunity* (Cambridge, Mass.: Harvard University Press, 1962), p. 81.

[86]Since there is no written constitution, the constitution cannot be amended, for, as Sir Ivor Jennings has written, the "supremacy of parliament *is* the constitution." Thus argues Pickles, "Not With Europe," p. 13. But, of course, one could put this the other way around. Since Parliament is supreme, it is constitutionally able to hand over some of its powers to another organization.

[87]For one of many examples, see *H.C. Deb.*, Vol. 635 (February 21, 1961), col. 308.

Opinion and Policy

Throughout the 1950's, the British Institute of Public Opinion asked questions that touched upon Britain's relations with Europe. Relatively favorable responses were secured whenever the questions emphasized general cooperation, left Britain's role undefined, or played upon her interest in trade. For example, in October of 1952, 62 percent favored Western European unity; in January of 1957, 58 percent wanted a closer British-European partnership; in March of 1959, 54 percent wished to join the Common Market for trade. Tying England to Europe by institutional arrangements, however, always repelled. In January of 1952, 47 percent opposed British participation in ECSC, with only 23 percent in favor. In a poll taken in July of 1960, the long-prevailing pattern is clearly illustrated. Some 49 percent indicated they would support a governmental decision to join the Common Market, with 13 percent opposed. If joining were to have "political implications," however, only 22 percent indicated they would approve, with 35 percent dissenting. In the period preceding the government's decision, a pattern of general doubt and of distaste for specific and binding arrangements is evident.

The favorable response of the public to Macmillan's initiative was noticeable without being overwhelming. Approval of Britain's joining Europe stood at 46 percent in June of 1961, fell to 38 percent in mid-July, but rose after Macmillan's announcement to 48 percent in August, 52 percent in September and November, and 53 percent in December. Only in those three months is a majority recorded in favor of the government's policy. Most of the momentary increase came from self-declared supporters of the Conservative Party. Opinion was responsive to leadership but not enough so to change the earlier pattern of instability and confusion, ignorance and doubt. Twenty-six times, between June of 1961 and August of 1962, the British Gallup Poll asked the following question: "If the British Government were to decide that Britain's interest would best be served by joining the European Common Market, would you approve or disapprove?" From the public at large support never exceeded 53 percent, opposition never fell below 18 percent, and those uncertain were never fewer than 26 percent of the total. The more general questions continued to elicit relatively favorable responses, with opposition more clearly in view whenever possible meanings and effects of entry were suggested.

In April and July of 1962, when asked the standard question on Europe as recorded in the preceding paragraph, 47 and 42 percent approved, 27 and 25 percent did not. But in April, asked if they would support Britain's joining Europe if Australia and New Zealand were to look elsewhere for trade, support dropped to 35 percent and opposition rose to 38 percent. In July, 53 percent indicated they would prefer to stay out of the Common Market if going in meant forming a political union with France and Germany, while only 21 percent would have joined anyway. In the same month, on the related question of sharing British nuclear secrets with France, 50 percent indicated opposition, with only 28 percent taking a favorable view of such collaboration.

As domestic voices of opposition rose in volume and the concerns of Commonwealth countries became increasingly 'clear, opinion began to turn against the government. The Meeting of Commonwealth Prime Ministers, from September 10 to 19, 1962, and the Labour Party Conference in early October helped to focus discontent. In October, November, and December—the months immediately preceding President de Gaulle's veto—support for Macmillan's policy had dwindled to 41, 29, and 32 percent, respectively.[88]

Surely no government under these conditions could think that its policy was widely and firmly popular with the public at large. Beyond public-opinion polls, there were indications of uneasiness and dissent within both major parties in Parliament. From the Conservative benches Derek Walker-Smith and Robert Turton (both ex-Ministers), Sir Anthony Fell, and Lord Hinchingbrooke spoke sharply against joining the Common Market. On August 3, Fell voted against the government's motion. Approximately twenty-two other Conservative MP's abstained. Those who abstained represented a larger number who were disturbed in mind and uneasy in spirit. Indications of dissent are all the more impressive since Parliament was being asked only to support an intention to negotiate and was hearing promises that British internal interests and external position would be carefully guarded by the negotiators.[89]

Opinion was uncertain and interests confused. Opponents, skeptics,

[88]The question, one should note, had been changed to the following: "On the facts as you know them at present are you for or against Britain joining the Common Market?"

[89]A study of back-bench opinion based on Early Day Motions in the period from 1955 to 1959 led the authors to conclude that of 270 Conservative MP's, 104 could be described as "Europeans," while 127 members, who were evenly divided between "Stalwarts" and "Moderates," put the Commonwealth first. S. E. Finer, H. B. Berrington, and D. J. Bartholomew, *Back-Bench Opinion in the House of Commons, 1955–1959* (Oxford: Pergamon Press, 1961), p. 89.

and "don't know's" most often formed the majority. Public opinion was neither enthusiastically for joining the Six nor firmly against doing so. The Prime Minister's position was unclear, with many believing that Macmillan's government would, despite its many contrary statements, go in on the best terms it could get whether or not they would be widely accepted as being good enough. To some extent, the government's technique could be expected to succeed within the Conservative Party. Only if Britain were able to secure entry on favorable terms would negotiations be completed within months, and if terms were favorable, domestic political difficulties would be small. If, on the other hand, negotiations were to take very long, they would not end until the time for a general election drew near. Terms might then be less favorable, but the inclination of Conservatives to oppose their government would be dampened by the importance of maintaining unity preceding an electoral struggle.

The chief executive in a democratic state may be tempted to scatter stardust in order to becloud his people's vision while he pursues a policy of hidden meaning and objective. The freedom of citizens to examine and criticize and a competition of parties that puts a political premium upon exposing the inconsistencies and weaknesses of the government's policy may at once cause the chief executive to wish for a larger sack of stardust and make it more difficult both at home and abroad for him to distribute it. Promising more than he could reasonably get, Macmillan sought to allay domestic doubts by describing the arrangements that would be negotiated as being compatible with Britain's international commitments. The statements of Ministers were designed to convey the thought that from the government's policy all good things would follow. Macmillan would get Britain into Europe on terms that he would describe as acceptable and, with a triumphant foreign policy, carry his party into power for an unprecedented fourth term.

In November of 1956, preparing the way for free-trade negotiations with Europe, Macmillan had emphasized, as noted above, that agreement across parties was necessary since any international arrangement that might be made would require a continuity of British policy over a period of twelve to fifteen years. In 1956, the government had secured Labour's assent to its European policy. In 1961, the government proceeded alone. Earlier the parties were united on European policy. From 1961 to 1963 they drifted fitfully apart. In June and July of 1961, support for a positive approach to Europe differed according to the respondent's commitment to the two major parties by from 1 to 7 percent. In August,

September, and November of 1961, and in April and July of 1962, supporters of the two major parties were separated by a gap of from 16 to 20 percent, with Labour voters always lagging behind Conservatives in support of the government's policy.

If the government's policy were successful and the Labour Party suffered still another electoral defeat, it might well turn upon its leader and disappear in an ensuing war among factions. Beyond victory for the Conservative Party was the dazzling prospect of a transformation in British politics. Among the politicians of Britain, Macmillan had earned a reputation for being ruthless, unflappable, highly skilled, and inclined to gamble. In his European policy, the dangers were great, but because the domestic political stakes were high, risks were worth taking. Macmillan's technique, possibly serviceable at home, easily awakened doubts abroad. His policy was a bold one; that is, it was a gamble. It was not based on a frank and straightforward position taken by Macmillan and his principal Ministers from which they could educate and lead the nation. British leaders, it is said, move by degrees and blandly announce at each step that their policies have not changed. In the customary fashion, Macmillan sought to make it appear at home as though the new policy were compatible with old ones. At the same time, it was said to the Europeans that there had been a fundamental change in British policy.

De Gaulle's Veto

Macmillan had been unable to maintain, let alone increase, the mildly favorable public response to his European initiative. Many have nonetheless said that Macmillan's European policy collapsed because of de Gaulle's capricious opposition to Britain, which his European associates did not share, rather than because of weaknesses in Britain's European policy. The abrupt manner in which de Gaulle pronounced his veto is censured even by those who sympathize with his position.[90] More often the content of the decision is criticized as well. Multilateral negotiations that might have succeeded were brought to a halt by the will of one nation or, perhaps, of one man. "Of all those concerned," according to Paul-Henri Spaak, "only the French believed that the negotiations would fail."[91] De Gaulle, by taking upon himself the responsibility for ending

[90]Cf. Stanley Hoffmann, "De Gaulle, Europe, and the Atlantic Alliance," *International Organization*, XVIII (1964), 14.
[91]Spaak, "Hold Fast," *Foreign Affairs*, XLI (July, 1963), 615.

the negotiations, left the other five Continental countries and Britain herself free to exaggerate the chances that outstanding problems would have been solved had negotiations been allowed to continue.

In a speech at Strasbourg following de Gaulle's press conference of January 14, 1963, Walter Hallstein described the difficulties encountered in negotiations. Having done so, he reached the modest conclusion that the chances of success were great enough to justify further efforts.[92] However, comparing the ground covered to soil still virgin and the difficulties untouched to the position the British government had taken since negotiations began, one may easily be more impressed by what was not accomplished than by what was accomplished in the negotiations that had been going on for a year and a half. Acceptable arrangements had been found for industrial products from Canada, Australia, and New Zealand; agreement had been reached on rules that would apply to the trade of India, Pakistan, and Ceylon. But no way had been found to cope with agricultural imports from temperate-zone countries, especially from New Zealand, nor had any way been found of accommodating British domestic agricultural policy, though there were indications of possible progress. Failing agreement on those two major problems, a third, the question of the Community's relations with the other members of EFTA, had not been considered in any detail.

For de Gaulle the question of Britain's admission was not just a question of terms. To him, the matter of Britain's commitment was more important. Had her international orientation changed, or would she, under new conditions, pursue her old objectives? Tendencies toward unity in Western Europe or toward domination by any one state had for centuries past called forth British intervention. To play off one power against another—to keep Europe weak in order to make England secure and permit her to act elsewhere if she wished to—was both elementary good sense and a deeply ingrained national habit. Conversely, English weakness vis-a-vis Europe had meant entanglement in Continental affairs. Winston Churchill's consistent appreciation of the fact heightened his insistence before World War I upon maintaining England's naval preponderance in the face of Germany's challenge. It led him, before World War II, to dwell on air power as well, and after it to emphasize the necessity of remaining closely associated with the United States in order to buttress England's strength and increase her influence. At the

<hr />

[92]"Suspension of U.K.–Community Negotiations: Community Executives Speak Out," *Bulletin from the European Community*, No. 60 (February, 1963), pp. 1 ff.

same time, it was in his view important to develop England's nuclear power, lest association with the United States become dependence upon it. Prime Ministers and Foreign Secretaries of both parties persistently followed the traditional policy, at least until the summer of 1961. By then Germany had revived, France had been rejuvenated, and Western Europe seemed firmly set upon a course that would lead to its unity.

British traditions in foreign policy would have led her to seek to pry a uniting Europe apart. Many in the United States and England were startled by a report in the spring of 1960 that Macmillan, visiting Washington, had warned of the dangers a united Europe would present. Recalling that Britain had allied with Russia to prevent the Continent's consolidation under Napoleon, he raised the specter of revived German nationalism.[93] Bewilderment over his words and doubt that he had pronounced them would have been decreased by remembering that Macmillan, fond of historical analogies, had used this one before. "All through our history," he had written early in the 1950's, "we have fought long and destructive wars to prevent the unification of Europe under the control of a single Power." [94] In Europe, rumors of the words he had spoken found a readier, though angrier, credence. As evidence of consistency of attitude, they would hardly occasion surprise. England, if she could not remain aloof from European organizations, could be expected to attempt to disrupt them.

British policy in the negotiations of 1957 and 1958 had been to try to get the Six to join the United Kingdom and others in a Free Trade Area. Officially the Six would continue in form but become part of a larger grouping. Actually, it could only have appeared to the Six that Britain, fearing competition from a bloc that she was unwilling to enter, had attempted to destroy its separate existence. By 1961, Macmillan had reluctantly concluded that if you cannot divide your competitors, then it is better to join them. In view of the long record of British relations with Europe, some skepticism could be expected. In politics as in religion,

[93]There are various reports, and there seems little doubt that Macmillan, speaking to Secretary of State Herter and/or Under Secretary Dillon, made statements very close to those reported above. See, for example, *Daily Telegraph* (London), March 31, 1960, and April 1, 1960; *Observer* (London), April 3, 1960; "Mr. Macmillan's Map of Europe," *Economist*, CXCV (April 9, 1960), 130–32; Edwin L. Dale, Jr., "Macmillan Angry over Trade Split," *New York Times*, March 31, 1960; Thomas P. Ronan, "Macmillan Talk Held Misquoted," *New York Times*, April 1, 1960.

[94]Harold Macmillan, "The Commonwealth and Europe," *Daily Telegraph*, May 28, 1951. Cf. David Eccles, who in the late summer of 1958, remarked that the Common Market is objectionable because it is designed "to do exactly what for hundreds of years, we have always said we could not see done with safety to our country." Harold Callender, "Politics a Factor in Free Trade Bid," *New York Times*, August 10, 1958, p. 19.

sudden conversions are not unknown, but a wary wisdom will lead one to test the firmness of the convert's new belief carefully.

The orientation of Macmillan's foreign policy had quite naturally been disturbing to de Gaulle. Following the abortive Suez venture, Macmillan had moved quickly to mend ruptured relations with America. While the French followed a more independent course, British policy became more closely related to American policy and more dependent upon it. The moment of close cooperation with France, or of conspiratorial action, passed with indecent speed, as it must have seemed to de Gaulle, confirming his impression that in Britain's view the Atlantic is narrower than the Channel. At the time of the free-trade negotiations, de Gaulle's proposals for a three-power directorate of NATO had been coldly received by the British. When Macmillan met de Gaulle at the Château de Champs on June 1 and 2, 1962, the question of nuclear weapons was raised by neither of them. Macmillan was apparently unwilling to suggest nuclear collaboration, and de Gaulle was too proud to request it. When next they met, at Rambouillet in December, the United States had already canceled the Skybolt missile. A few days later, at Nassau, Macmillan asked for and got Polaris missiles as a substitute weapon in Britain's nuclear arsenal. The sequence of events raised doubts about the sincerity of Macmillan's dealings with de Gaulle. After France had blocked Britain's entry, Macmillan publicly affirmed that he had told de Gaulle at Rambouillet of his determination to obtain a substitute weapon. "I explained to him in some detail," Macmillan informed a Liverpool audience on January 21, 1963, "my view of the relations between interdependence and independence, and said that we must have a British deterrent available for independent use if need be. I am sure he fully understood our position." [95]

Insincerity is a blemish upon a statesman's record; lack of skill is a more serious offense. De Gaulle's view was clearly established. Britain must choose between giving priority to her interest in Europe or perpetuation of her "special relation" with the United States. It is possible, de Gaulle said in delivering his veto message, "that Britain would one day come round to transforming itself enough to belong to the European Community without restriction and without reservation, and placing it ahead of anything else, and in that case the Six would open the door to it and France would place no obstacle in its path. . . . It is also possible that England is not yet prepared to do this, and that indeed appears to

[95]Quoted in Miriam Camps, *Britain and the European Community, 1955–1963* (Princeton: Princeton University Press, 1964), p. 487.

be the outcome of the long, long Brussels talks." [96] As French Premier Pompidou was quick to point out, Britain at Nassau had chosen the United States over France and Western Europe.[97] And, one should add, without quite knowing she had done so.

"Europe must be European," according to the Gaullists.[98] Speaking to the Western European Union in April of 1962, Heath had said that the British government "quite accept . . . that a European point of view on defence will emerge. What is essential, however, is that any European point of view or policy on defence should be directly related to the Atlantic alliance." [99] In the very British view of Harold Wilson, "not only Britain's interest but the cause of world peace would be immeasurably impoverished if we were corralled in Western Europe, forced to look at the world through European eyes." [100] The true distinction between the terms "outward-looking" and "inward-looking" has little to do with trade and tariff, aid to backward countries, or pieties about the Commonwealth. It is instead a question of whether or not Britain's view of the world is to prevail. If Western Europe develops as a third force, it will by traditional British definition be inward-looking, for it will be "detached from liberal and progressive forces in North America and the world outside." [101] If Western Europe sees the world through British eyes, it will perforce be looking outward. The obvious difference of view was apparently appreciated by the British, but, strangely, they failed to connect it with their efforts to secure the six votes needed in order to bring them into the Common Market.

Entering Europe on the wrong terms, Prime Minister Wilson has subsequently written, would have cost Britain "the unique influence" she

[96]"Seventh Press Conference Held by General de Gaulle as President of the French Republic in Paris at the Elysée Palace on January 14, 1963," *Major Addresses, Statements and Press Conferences of General Charles de Gaulle: May 19, 1958–January 31, 1964* (New York: French Embassy, 1964), p. 215.

[97]French Press and Information Service, *Speeches and Press Conferences*, No. 189 (February 5, 1963). Cf. Michel Habib-Deloncle, speaking to the Council of Europe on September 23, 1963: "If Great Britain conceives her future as being within the European community, she can find in this nuclear field an opportunity for a real contribution—taking into account the vital choice which such a decision would entail." Quoted by Sidney Gruson, "Britain Disdains French Proposals on Nuclear Force," *New York Times*, September 25, 1963, p. 1.

[98]"Foreign Policy Statement made by M. Maurice Couve de Murville, French Minister of Foreign Affairs, Before the French National Assembly," *Speeches and Press Conferences*, No. 223 (June 16, 1965), p. 6. Cf. the statement of Premier Georges Pompidou, *Speeches and Press Conferences*, No. 224 (June 17, 1965), p. 2.

[99]*European Political Union*, Cmnd. 1720 (London: HMSO, 1962), p. 5.

[100]Wilson, *Purpose in Politics*, p. xvii.

[101]Iain Macleod, "Britain's Role in 1965," *Spectator* (April 23, 1965), p. 531. A similar distinction of course prevails in the United States. Cf. Senate Committee on Foreign Relations, Staff Study, *Problems and Trends in Atlantic Partnership*, II (Doc. No. 21 [88th Cong., 1st sess., 1963]), pp. 4, 8.

still in his view possesses "in world affairs." [102] Entry in the view of many others would have permitted Britain to mold Europe and lead it back into the center of Atlantic affairs, with England as its natural spokesman. In the course of negotiations, the British had let it be privately known that, in their view, "the Community would, in fact, be a 'different animal' once they were inside and that the agricultural policy would almost inevitably break down." [103] Publicly, in his speech at the mass meeting after the Conservative Conference of October, 1962, and in his pamphlet on *Britain, the Commonwealth, and Europe,* Macmillan had emphasized that, remaining outside, Britain would be able to "do nothing to influence" a "political solution in Europe which ran counter to our views and interests." Once a member of European institutions, Britain would be able to affect their development. And entering Europe was the only way for Britain to gain not only "a new stature in Europe, but also increase its standing and influence in the councils of the world." [104]

Britain wished to enter Europe in order to influence its development, which in turn would enable her to play her role in the world more effectively. De Gaulle needed no competitor in that game. Britain wished to play a European role without much modifying the other parts she was playing. Whether or not British preferences were wisely formed, they accorded uneasily if at all with the effort to join a European club in which the French member, along with others, had a "blackball."

Conclusion

The *New Statesman* in the summer of 1961 found it almost incredible that the decision to negotiate for entry was being taken without preceding debate in the country.[105] As noted above, the political institutions and habits of Britain encourage such a procedure. Decision had been delayed until the desirability of entry had impressed itself upon larger and larger numbers within the government, among civil servants, and in the business community. That the government should "give a lead to the country," or Britain to the world, is a cliché of British political rhetoric. The importance of leading is heightened by the fact that a lead is so seldom given.

[102]Wilson, *Purpose in Politics*, p. xvii.

[103]Camps, *Britain and the European Community*, p. 399. For a careful and sensitive account of the British negotiations, see *ibid.*, chaps. 11–12, 14.

[104]Quoted in *ibid.*, pp. 437–38. Cf. Younger, *Changing Perspectives in British Foreign Policy*, pp. 109–10, 123; and Michael Shanks and John Lambert, *The Common Market Today—and Tomorrow* (New York: Praeger, 1962), p. 242.

[105]"Collapse into Europe," *New Statesman*, LXII (July 14, 1961), 37.

At the last Conservative Party Conference held before the government's decision was announced, Edward Heath was the principal spokesman on the European question. Lord Home, then Foreign Minister, in preceding him had mentioned that Britain "must show the flag" in Europe, but without of course doing "anything to weaken our Commonwealth association." Macmillan, addressing the mass meeting after the Conference, dwelt on Britain's worldwide interests and suggested that her influence under the second Elizabeth might compare to her "influence in the days of the first." He made no mention of Britain's relations with Europe. Heath, in between, put two questions. One to Europe: "Do you want us to take part?" If Europe should say yes, that answer must come with full knowledge of Britain's traditional stance: "We are here with our Commonwealth, with our agriculture, with our well-known Parliamentary system and our known attitude to supra-national institutions." The second question he put to his fellow citizens: "Do we really want to take part by joining their institutions?" He did not suggest what the answer might appropriately be, but, well illustrating the nonleadership qualities of British governance, left the question to be mulled over by members of the party. To make it easier for the public to come to the conclusion he preferred, he did assert that if the decision were to join Europe, suitable arrangements for the Commonwealth, for agriculture, and for EFTA could surely be made.[106]

Not until the late summer and early fall of 1962, with his forthright speech at the opening of the meeting of Commonwealth Prime Ministers, his broadcast to the country, his speech at the Conservative Conference, and his pamphlet on *Britain, the Commonwealth, and Europe,* did Macmillan publicly paint a fairly realistic picture of the difficulties England faced and the reasons for the government's policy. The Conservatives, prior to the Conference at Llandudno in October, had managed to head off potential objections and silence some of the critics by working through internal party lines. Critics were mild in their censure, and the Conference, mindful of harsh statements recently made at Labour's similar meeting, appeared enthusiastic. By then, however, the meetings of the Commonwealth Prime Ministers and the Labour Party had revealed a close correspondence between the people's opinion and the government's critics. With Gaitskell more closely in touch with popular fears and

---

[106]National Union of Conservative and Unionist Associations, *Report of the 79th Annual Conference,* October 12–15, 1960, Scarborough (London, 1960), pp. 54, 151, 62.

aspirations than Macmillan, the government's inclination to equivocate was again reinforced.

Public opinion was not forced or formed; the people were not led. If the government's calculations were correct, they would not have to be. When speaking to the nation, Macmillan and other Ministers minimized the magnitude of adjustments that entry into Europe would require. They hoped apparently to present to Parliament and the nation a completed agreement which would shift the nation's attention from whether or not to join the Common Market to an examination of the details of negotiated provisions. These would surely be complex and their consequences for Britain impossible to apprehend with precision. If indeed the direction of Britain's foreign policy was to be markedly changed, the change would be contrived by elision, by a sidling movement proceeding by subtle degrees until finally a great change would have been worked without anyone being quite able to say just when it had occurred. Macmillan's attempt was to obscure or erase the moment for decision. The decision would emerge, and the necessary consent would not be within the politically reasonable power of Parliament to withhold.

In the absence of a firm majority opinion for or against a policy, political leaders can decide whether to attempt to lead the country or to maneuver among groups and try to outwit opponents. Politicians would quickly exhaust themselves and the nation if they moved forthrightly on all measures. Some decisions, however, are of such magnitude, so contrary to a nation's past, so important to its present well-being, so pregnant with its future, that the nation's interests can be served only by political leaders who are willing to lead. Macmillan had attempted a virtuoso political performance. Civic courage rather than political virtuosity on the part of the country's leaders would have helped to avoid the dangers, constant in pluralist polities, of the non-resolution of issues. The processes of politics in Britain do not readily result in a sequence of confrontation and resolution; rather, they tend toward evasion, confusion of issues, uncertainty, inactivity, and stalemate. Once a policy is announced by the government, the government's prestige depends upon its measures being pressed into legislation. Success in getting Britain into Europe was so important to the government's standing that the temptation to avoid public confrontation by stringing opponents along with technically true, or vaguely false, assurances was great. British governments act easily where a comfortable agreement on policy has formed, or they fumble along in its absence.

From the mid-1950's onward, a more forthright explication of Britain's situation and the limited choices open to her, and fewer words about Commonwealth, special relations, unique contributions, and how good one was having it, would have served the country better. Considerable strain would thereby have been put on the political system. It is the glory of England that in the present century her institutions have survived war and depression and war again, while those of Germany, France, and Italy did not. Constitutional instability is a characteristic of Continental countries. British institutions, however, have proved their resilience. Stanley Baldwin in the 1930's prided himself upon taming the Labour Party and fitting it for rule, and he was congratulated for the accomplishment.[107] That may have been good for Britain's political institutions, but it did little for a nation long and deeply depressed at home and dangerously threatened abroad. Institutions have endured while policy has failed or been inordinately long in the coming.

Macmillan's attempt to sidle into Europe was foiled by de Gaulle. But Macmillan's failure was larger than the failure of his immediate policy. A government's failure to secure its policy can be useful to the country. Woodrow Wilson did not carry the United States into the League, but he at least introduced his country to the twentieth century by waging a campaign that laid bare the issues. The radical reorientation of a nation internationally is sure to be difficult and is often traumatic. If the luxury of time to move leisurely is lacking, it may be better to force issues even at the price of some civic turmoil. Two decades after the War, Britain's international orientation is still uncertain; even the elements of the problems she faces are not clearly identified.

It is hard for the government to fool the people without obscuring the situation for itself—if only because so many public officials and civil servants are involved that many of the cues upon which they act must be taken from Ministerial conversations with the Commons and the people. And even Ministers, ineffectively challenged, lack the stimulus to face, first in their own minds, then among their counselors, and finally in their policies, the full force of problems. The people are not educated where issues are evaded, nor is the government. In its European policy, the British government, strikingly in view of the slow unfolding of events and its previous experience with Europe, never succeeded in accurately measuring the task it had undertaken.

Accurate measurement is not a guarantee of success; it is assurance of

[107]G. M. Young, *Stanley Baldwin* (London: Hart-Davis, 1952), p. 254.

relevance. In the 1930's, England was unable to bring her European interests and her worldwide concerns into balance. Whether as a spectator of European politics or a participant in them, her policies were disastrous. They have not been so since the war, for Western European countries have managed without her. England acted too weakly in the 1930's to serve her own interests and the cause of European stability. She had underestimated her importance to Europe. In the 1950's and 1960's, she made the opposite error. Macmillan's government had failed to reconcile its ends and bring the means to achieve them into accord. It is not that the government had chosen incorrectly. It had failed to choose at all. Reflecting upon the failure of Macmillan's European policy, C. Aubrey Jones, then a Conservative MP, perceptively made this point in the Commons: "de Gaulle differed from us in wanting to see Europe organised in terms of ultimate power apart from the United States. We took a different view, rightly, I think, and it was this difference which prompted the collapse of the talks. As I see it, the problem is to define the trans-Atlantic unit as a new centre of power, and in a way which, while it will not, I think, reconcile France in the short term, will, in the long term, keep the door open for her." The issue, he added, is one that the United States faced and tried to come to grips with, while Britain still had not done so.[108]

If there had been a change in the publicly and politically accepted definition of what British interests require, the government would have been able to enter negotiations with its hands free. Had the government in the absence of such change been able to maneuver freely in international negotiation, both its courage and its power would have been impressive. Neither of these conditional statements describes what actually took place. It cannot be said that British opinion changed fundamentally or that the government's policy went openly against notions long cherished by the nation. National notions, derived from the experience of Empire and Commonwealth, expressed themselves in attitudes of hauteur and skepticism toward Europe. Opinion was not overcome by the government but merely accommodated. The government did not so much attempt to lead as to manipulate both Parliament and the public. And little was gained from the venture.

[108]*H.C. Deb.*, Vol. 680 (July 2, 1963), col. 253.

Chapter 10

OPINION AND CRISES
IN
AMERICAN FOREIGN POLICY

The fear of public opinion impressing itself upon foreign policy is necessarily great if elections go far toward determining policy and if the outcome of elections is determined by the inclinations of ill-informed voters. The fears become greater still if the dread voice of public opinion is able to dictate policy between elections as well. On both counts Walter Lippmann has written democracy's indictment with a telling eloquence:

> The unhappy truth is that the prevailing public opinion has been destructively wrong at the critical junctures. The people have imposed a veto upon the judgments of informed and responsible officials. They have compelled the governments, which usually knew what would have been wiser, or was necessary, or was more expedient, to be too late with too little, or too long with too much, too pacifist in peace and too bellicose in war, too neutralist or appeasing in negotiation or too intransigent. Mass opinion has acquired mounting power in this century. It has shown itself to be a dangerous master of decisions when the stakes are life and death.[1]

All masters of decision are dangerous. Have the people been more dangerous than most of them? This question and many others are raised by Lippmann's statement. Does public opinion prevail in the Western democracies as Lippmann argues? If it does, has the mass voice in and between crises been simply wrong? If the great undifferentiated public, which he describes and assumes to be decisive, has indeed been wrong "at the critical junctures," have others—professors and pundits, political

[1]Lippmann, *The Public Philosophy* (Boston: Little, Brown, 1955), p. 20.

leaders and highly-placed officials—been more often and more nearly correct in their assessment of events and their estimate of policy requirements? If the democracies have erred consistently and disastrously as he says, have other types of modern government interpreted the world more reliably and acted more successfully upon their interpretations?

While Lippmann's harsh indictment is rejected by most students of politics, many would assent to a milder charge. Lippmann writes of democracy's inclination to "soft courses" of action, which are followed in order to "please the largest number of voters." Henry A. Kissinger finds that Americans have a "penchant for choosing the interpretation of current trends which implies least effort."[2] Lippmann writes of the public's impulsive commitment to appeasement and peace or to intransigence and war. Gabriel Almond, in a book first published in 1950, found that "an overtly interventionist and 'responsible' United States hides a covertly isolationist longing," that while interest in foreign affairs had increased, public responses remained "highly unstable."[3] Echoing the view a decade later, V. O. Key, Jr., doubted that "the new outlook toward the outside world has the same solidity and durability" as the isolationist opinion it had replaced.[4] Lippmann thinks of democratic leaders as followers. The ostensible leaders cannot actually lead, even though they may know what the situation requires, for the "great public" will impose its "massive negative" upon proposed new courses of action. Unable to act appropriately in times of crisis, leaders are deterred from preparing for trouble in moments of calm, for "with the massive veto" always latent, the political cost of doing so is likely to be high. Walt W. Rostow finds such a judgment borne out in at least one case, the Presidential election of 1956. "There can have been few elections," he writes, "which reflect less credit on the democratic process than the uncandid projection and the self-indulgent public acceptance of the slogan of Peace and Prosperity in 1956."[5] Hidden by the calm that prevailed, storm clouds had gathered, but Republican leaders told the people what they wanted to hear rather than what they should have been told. David Truman is inclined to spread the blame more evenly among a larger set of public figures. Presented with such challenges as the fall of China, the loyalty-security neurosis of the McCarthy era, and the Russians' first orbiting of

[2]Kissinger, *The Necessity for Choice* (New York: Harper, 1961), p. 7.
[3]Almond, *The American People and Foreign Policy* (New York: Praeger, 1960), pp. 67, 77.
[4]Key, *Public Opinion and American Democracy* (New York: Knopf, 1961), pp. 256–57.
[5]Rostow, *The United States in the World Arena: An Essay in Recent History* (New York: Harper, 1960), pp. 395–96.

a satellite, leaders of the press, of labor and business, and of other groups failed to respond boldly and courageously.[6] In replying to one of Lippmann's charges, Truman may be illustrating another: that leaders may be made timid by their fear of a hostile public reaction.

Three worries about the effect of democratic opinion on foreign policy are widespread. (1) Democracies will prefer the easy way. This is not to say that duties will always be shirked and dangers avoided. It is, for example, sometimes simpler to fight for a peace of "unconditional surrender" than to negotiate a limited settlement that is more likely to endure. (2) The public reaction to complicated international events is often unpredictable; feelings, whether of patriotism or fear, supplant reason and produce a response based on moods of the moment rather than on solid and sensible analyses. (3) The opinions of the many override the wisdom of the experienced; men of experience, by disguising their voices of wisdom when speaking to the untutored masses, compound the difficulty. Haunted by the memory of the democracies' failures to respond to the challenge of the totalitarian countries in the 1930's and dismayed by America's inability to adjust force to political purpose in and immediately after World War II, critics of democratic institutions found ample sustenance for a far-reaching pessimism. Although somewhat allayed by the rapidity and breadth of response to Soviet challenges in the period that began in 1947 and reached into the 1950's, pessimism reappeared in the Eisenhower years. Lippmann's critique, Emmet Hughes's description of the nation's plight as conveyed in the title of his book *America the Vincible*, the officially sponsored investigation by the Gaither Committee, and the unofficial but highly authoritative studies of the Rockefeller Brothers' Fund, all reflected the fear that the 1950's like the 1930's were years of the locusts.[7]

Does the common citizen, one must wonder, have the fortitude to sustain costly military programs, the benefits of which are necessarily uncertain? Will the public permit the government the flexibility it requires in dealing with a dangerous and changing world? Whether or not the citizenry is dogged and sensible, how closely is foreign policy controlled by the opinions of its citizens?

[6]Truman, "The American System in Crisis," *Political Science Quarterly*, LXXIV (December, 1959), 481–97.
[7]Hughes, *America the Vincible* (New York: Doubleday, 1959). The Gaither Report, which has not been published, was presented to the National Security Council in November, 1957. Rockefeller Panel Reports I and II, *The Mid-Century Challenge to U.S. Foreign Policy*, and *International Security: the Military Aspect* (New York: Doubleday, 1959 and 1958).

Political Leadership and
the Public Support of Programs

Often the person discussing the relation of opinion to policy is in the undignified posture of a dog chasing his tail. When it is charged that the people have been unduly complacent, the remedy prescribed may well be that their leaders should arouse themselves. Robert C. Sprague, Co-chairman of the Gaither Committee, businessman, and self-styled conservative Republican, expressed his belief before Senator Jackson's Subcommittee that the nation faced a threat to its survival to which it had not yet awakened. Who could awaken the country? In the opinion of Sprague, there was one man alone "in the United States that can do this effectively, and that is the President." [8]

The thought is perennial. It was Plato who said in effect: the people are sick; their rulers must be cured. The question of leadership lies beneath the problem of the people's willingness to sacrifice, and it directly affects the stability of their opinions as well. When Churchill sought to awaken his countrymen to mounting dangers in the 1930's, few of the leading men of any party followed him. Are the people at fault when Prime Minister, Foreign Secretary, military officials, and others who bear a national trust assure them that armaments are adequate and that military preparations are proceeding at the necessary pace? The correspondence of the people's opinion to the position taken by their governors is strikingly illustrated by the rapid reversal of opinion on the controversial introduction of conscription in 1939, the first time Britain had adopted such a measure in peacetime. Before conscription was adopted, 39 percent of the voters favored it, with 53 percent opposed and 8 percent doubtful. A week after the legislation was passed, 58 percent approved, 38 percent opposed, and 4 percent were uncertain. [9]

The survival of the nation depends not only on fortitude in reacting to a threat that has at last become obvious but also upon the people's willingness to pay and to serve when danger is not immediately visible. George C. Marshall, reflecting four years later upon his judgment of 1945 that the military force levels projected at that time were unrealisti-

[8]Senate Hearings before the Subcommittee of the Committee on Government Operations, *Organizing for National Security* (86th Cong., 2d sess., 1960), I, 55.
[9]Lindsay Rogers, *The Pollsters: Public Opinion, Politics, and Democratic Leadership* (New York: Knopf, 1949), p. 42.

cally high, explained in terms of public opinion the conclusion he had
reached:

> When it comes to [military] appropriations in piping times of peace, I
> don't think America will ever learn its lesson, because the political pres-
> sures are tremendous. In the next place, my associates haven't lived through
> the education I had had in the 1920's and the immediate problems I had
> inherited in 1938, 1939, and 1940, when our degree of poverty was very
> trying. I could well understand that. They just thought I underestimated
> public opinion in the United States.
>
> Well, I am a great respecter of public opinion, but, on the other hand, I
> am also a great respecter of the tremendous political influence of the budget
> and the fact that it almost gets beyond control when it relates to things
> that do not produce immediate results like good roads, agriculture matters,
> and such.[10]

Were American citizens, as Marshall thought, less willing to serve than
to pay and not sufficiently willing to do either?

Before and after Korea, the marked tendency of American defense policy was to substitute machines for men in the demanding task of containing the Russian and Chinese Communists. The Truman-Bradley "old
look" had meant reliance on air power and atomic bombs, with an army
of minimum size. The insufficiency of such an establishment was demonstrated by the invasion of the Republic of Korea from the north. With
the Korean War ended, military policy slipped back to the old basis with
a "new look" label attached. The Army Vice Chief of Staff, General
Bolté, along with many others, despairingly tried to drive home the lesson that events had failed to teach. "Recent history has shown—and
logic will sustain it—that the only way to defeat ground forces is by
ground forces. The lesson of Korea should ever be before us." [11]

A strong inclination to keep defense costs low as measured in manpower is often said to be the military attitude of democracies. That democracy is alone the cause of the attitude is doubtful. The democracies
that are thought to have this attitude are advanced industrial powers.
For such countries to emphasize equipment more heavily than men may
simply be an attempt to play from their strongest suit. In other fields,
such a practice is accepted as mere common sense. A few words on

[10]Warner R. Schilling, "The Politics of National Defense: Fiscal 1950," in Warner R. Schilling, Paul Y. Hammond, and Glenn H. Snyder, *Strategy, Politics, and Defense Budgets* (New
York: Columbia University Press, 1962), pp. 150–51.

[11]General Charles L. Bolté, "Speech to United States Armor Association," *Armor*, LXIII
(March–April, 1954), 27.

"economizing" will help to make the proposition clear. Counting savings in terms of money easily obscures the importance of the question: in terms of what factors of production shall savings be measured? If arable land and machines are scarce and manpower is plentiful, for example, a country can increase to the maximum its return for money expended and acreage employed by adopting a system of intensive hand cultivation. Precisely this is done, so long as there is no choice, in Indonesia, Japan, and China, where the yield of crops per acre is markedly higher than it is in the United States.[12] Economic rationality requires substituting plentiful and cheap factors for scarce and expensive ones whether in agricultural or in military matters. Soviet leaders, so long as Russia had no nuclear establishment, proclaimed that the "permanently operating factors" rather than military technology or strategic surprise would determine the outcome of any contest with capitalist countries. With the maturing of Russian nuclear capabilities, however, Khrushchev announced, as the United States had earlier, that the deploying of rockets would permit simultaneously a reduction in manpower and an increase in military strength.[13] It is no more unusual that America, Britain, and other industrial democracies should seek to substitute machines for men in their military establishments than that they do so in agriculture, in dam-building, or in any of a number of other endeavors.

The proposition that democracies are unusually reluctant to keep large armies is questioned from one direction by noting that societies other than democracies are pushed or lured into the practice. It can be questioned from another direction by pointing out that not all republics have engaged in the practice. Athens and the Roman Republic in antiquity, Israel and Switzerland more recently, have conscripted large numbers of their citizens. The consonance of such practices with republican or democratic theory is indicated by Machiavelli's and Harrington's conception of military service as a school for civic virtue and in Jaurès's idea of the nation in arms.

One may nevertheless fear that political economizing—in terms of votes—will complement economic rationality in such a way as to make the preference for the machine difficult to undo even when international conditions would indicate its folly. Public pressure for rapid demobiliza-

---

[12]Fred Cottrell, *Energy and Society* (New York: McGraw-Hill, 1955). His conclusion, supported by preceding analysis and data, is given on p. 143.

[13]N. S. Khrushchev, "Disarmament Is the Path toward Strengthening Peace and Ensuring Friendship Among Peoples," *Current Digest of the Soviet Press*, XII (February 10, 1960), 3–16.

tion in 1945 and 1946 was strong and apparently effective. The conclusion frequently drawn is that at the outset of the Cold War public opinion placed the American government at a grave disadvantage. Those who reach such a conclusion have failed to bear in mind that civil and military leaders did not themselves urge upon the public the importance of remaining militarily prepared. Nor have they made the important distinction between enthusiasm for "bringing the boys home" and willingness to support a sizable peacetime military establishment. The latter was not lacking.[14] The American public, in addition to supporting measures for improving our defenses in general, strongly favored the adoption of Universal Military Training. In nine surveys taken between December, 1945, and January, 1956, public support for the program, expensive in manpower, ran upwards of 65 percent on eight occasions and only once fell as low as 60 percent. Opposition to the measure never exceeded 33 percent and only once rose above 25 percent.[15] More generally, as Samuel P. Huntington has written and convincingly demonstrated, "Governmental policy and mass opinion on the level of military effort have frequently differed, but in every case the Administration has been in favor of less military effort and public opinion in favor of more." The statement applies, with variations that do not change the picture of broad and constant support, to all segments of the population and all sections of the country; and the pattern has been constant from at least 1937 onward.

When pollsters have asked where budgetary savings should be made, only small numbers of respondents have cited defense spending. As Huntington notes, one cannot say that the American people have put lower taxes or welfare programs ahead of an adequate national defense. At the same time the public in general, unsophisticated in matters of weaponry and strategy, looks to the administration for a definition of adequacy. "If the critics vigorously and articulately attack the Administration for reducing military strength, the Administration eventually is forced to make a public defense of its policies. The public listens to the Administration, not the critics, and the reassurances of the Administration induce mass acquiescence in its policies."[16] The attitude of support

[14]Samuel P. Huntington, *The Common Defense* (New York: Columbia University Press, 1961), pp. 33–39; H. Bradford Westerfield, *Foreign Policy and Party Politics* (New Haven: Yale University Press, 1955), pp. 196–202.

[15]Huntington, *The Common Defense,* p. 240.

[16]The above quotations and summary are from *ibid.*, pp. 234–48, where public-opinion data on questions of defense are set forth and closely examined.

and the implicit willingness to build the basis for a mass army have provided policymakers with a broad range of choice.

Electoral Punishment and International Crises

Democracies have often been thought defective not only in their ability to sustain costly military establishments in time of peace but also in their ability to move with speed and finesse in response to the shifting currents of international affairs. May one not say of the years since World War II that the close concern of the American people with problems of foreign policy has made it difficult for their government to conduct an international policy of feint and maneuver?[17] Is it not likely that the more people care about foreign policy the more closely their opinions will limit the government? Such an effect has not been noticeable, partly because the concern of the public has outpaced its knowledge.

An international event ordinarily does not disturb the nation unless it has first obsessed the government. In the face of such an event, the people rally behind their chief executive, as one would expect them to do in any cohesive country. William Gladstone long ago commented in a letter to the Duke of Argyll that if the justification for the continuation of the Crimean War by England was that the people approved of the war and supported it, then such justification could be given for any war that England ever waged within eighteen months of its commencement.[18] A comparable statement, adjusted for the speed with which events are now publicly registered, can be made of America's reaction to crises. Franklin Roosevelt's popularity fluctuated in accordance with the recurrence of crises in Europe.[19] The outbreak of fighting in Korea gave a lift to President Truman's low standing with the public. In June of 1950, immediately before the attack, 37 percent of those polled approved of the way Truman was doing his job, while 45 percent did not. In July of 1950, the corresponding figures were 46 percent and 37 percent.[20] The invasion of Egypt by Britain and France, coming late in the American electoral campaign of 1956, apparently added a little to Eisenhower's wide margin of victory. A year and a half later, in April of 1958, the deepening of an economic recession, following upon Russia's lofting her first

[17]See above, p. 66, n.
[18]Letter of October 18, 1855, reprinted in John Morley, *The Life of William Ewart Gladstone* (2 vols.; London: Edward Lloyd, 1908), II, 610.
[19]V. O. Key, Jr., *Politics, Parties, and Pressure Groups* (3d ed.; New York: Crowell, 1952), p. 596.
[20]*Public Opinion Quarterly*, XV (Spring, 1951), 177–78.

Sputnik, drove Eisenhower's popularity down to 49 percent, which for him was a low point. The following summer, a *contretemps* in Lebanon, which led the President to send American troops, boosted him to his 1958 high of 58 percent.[21] The Cuban missile crisis of October, 1962, worked similar wonders for Kennedy. In April of that year, 77 percent had approved of the way he was handling "his job as President." A gradual decline then set in, to 73 percent in May following April's crisis in steel, to 71 percent in June following a slump in the stock market, to 67 percent in September after federal troops were sent to Mississippi, and to 61 percent before the confrontation with Russia in October. In December, however, 74 percent expressed themselves as satisfied with the President's performance in office.[22]

The first effect of an international crisis is to increase the President's popular standing. One may wonder if this is so only when the response of the President is firm or when he otherwise gives the impression of being able to deal with the situation effectively and without inconvenience to the public. It is in fact not necessary to add such qualifications to the statement that so far as the public is concerned the President in a moment of crisis has the widest freedom of action. President Kennedy, facing threats to Berlin, sent additional troops to Europe and in the summer of 1961 called up 150,000 reservists, an act usually thought to be politically dangerous. The political costs, on balance, were nil. Several months earlier, the United States had unofficially sponsored an invasion of Cuba at the Bay of Pigs. In the wake of the ill-fated attempt, President Kennedy's popular standing reached its highest point ever, 83 percent, as compared with an average of 70 percent during his thirty-four months in office.[23]

At the moment of crisis, there is no time for dissension to develop. The public poses few problems for the President who acts deftly, or even clumsily, in a short and sharp encounter. If the crisis is prolonged and the blood of Americans is shed in carrying out the government's policy, should one not expect a different reaction? The experience of the Korean War seems to have led everyone to do so. In view of America's commitment of troops to combat on the mainland of Asia, questions debated since the early 1950's have once again become urgent.

[21]Richard E. Neustadt, *Presidential Power* (New York: Wiley, 1960), p. 205n.
[22]American Institute of Public Opinion (AIPO) release, December 5, 1962.
[23]AIPO releases, December 21, 1963, and November 30, 1963. The U-2 incident and the subsequent collapse of the summit meeting in May of 1960 were followed by a similar rise in President Eisenhower's popular standing.

America's military response in Korea had been prompt; it was also fairly effective. The North Korean and subsequently the Chinese invaders were met and thrown back; the line of the 38th Parallel was restored and improved upon slightly; the United States and the non-Communist world were stronger at the conclusion of the affair than they had been at its beginning. Still, as the war dragged on, public support dwindled. Polls taken by the American Institute of Public Opinion from June of 1950 to November of 1952 found anywhere from 81 to 35 percent supporting "President Truman's decision to send US troops to Korea," with 11 to 51 percent opposed. Polls of the National Opinion Research Center showed from 80 to 51 percent in support of the decision to send "American troops to stop the Communist invasion of South Korea," with from 13 to 40 percent opposed.[24] Different emphases in the wording of the questions may account for the discrepant results. No matter what poll one may look at, the line graph of President Truman's popular standing moved parallel to and consistently below the steadily declining popular support of America's fighting in Korea. In July, October, and December of 1950, 46, 39, and 36 percent of those polled approved of the way the President was "handling his job." After 1950 and to the end of his term, approval fluctuated between 32 and 23 percent.[25]

To take the full measure of the problem of executive leadership in a democracy, one must constantly bear in mind that a painful and costly policy may have to be long pursued, with the gains from the policy largely invisible. The rewards may be found mainly in preventing worse situations that might have arisen were the costly action not undertaken. It is clear that the decision to resist in Korea was widely approved and the execution of that decision over the next three years was not. If one dwells on the courage with which the decision was made to intervene in Korea, it becomes dismaying to notice that the party of the President who made it was punished in the subsequent national election. In the 1952 election, according to Key, "several million persons" voted against themselves "on domestic matters."[26] On grounds of domestic policy, these millions would have preferred a Democratic Administration. They

[24]AIPO releases: June, 1950; August, 1950; March, 1951; April, 1952; November, 1952. National Opinion Research Center (NORC): July, 1950 (100/287); September, 1950 (101/288); December, 1950 (105/295); January, 1951 (106/298); March, 1951 (107/300); April, 1951 (108/302); May, 1951 (109/307); August, 1951 (111/312); December, 1951 (115/315); March, 1952 (117/320); June, 1952 (121/327).
[25]*Public Opinion Quarterly*, XV (Spring, 1951), 177–78; Neustadt, *Presidential Power*, p. 96. Data in both of these sources are from AIPO.
[26]Key, *Public Opinion and American Democracy*, p. 173.

were impelled to vote for Eisenhower by confidence in him as a man who could make peace, which was matched by distaste for the Democrats as a party that had taken their country into a war that the administration was unable to bring to a conclusion.[27]

In the 1948 election, a bipartisan truce on foreign-policy questions had for the most part prevailed, while economic and welfare questions were sharply debated. In the campaign of 1952, the Democrats played upon the people's interest in prosperity and, as ever, attached the depression label to the Republican Party. Republicans drew political advantage from the higher taxes and prices that the war had brought and from the drafting of American boys to fight and die in a war that was said to be useless. The loss of China to the Communists, the Soviet threat to Europe, and corruption in government were also prominent issues.[28] According to University of Michigan surveys, foreign issues worked almost entirely in favor of the Republican Party. Twelve percent of self-declared Democrats criticized the handling of foreign affairs, especially the Korean War, by their own party, as opposed to 6 percent who had something good to say about the Democratic Administration in this field.[29] Twenty-two percent of respondents mentioned being favorably impressed with Eisenhower's ability to handle foreign problems and particularly the Korean War, as compared with 9 percent who spoke favorably of his ability to manage domestic affairs. The corresponding figures for Stevenson were 2 percent and 7 percent. In party rather than personal terms, 43 percent referred favorably to the Democrats on domestic policies and issues, 33 percent to the Republicans. On matters of foreign policy, preferences were reversed: 13 percent expressed approval of the Republican Party, while only 3 percent had kind words for the Democrats.[30] By a different measure, the Republicans led as the party more likely to keep the country out of war by a ratio of more than two to one in the spring of 1952, while the Democrats continued to find favor as the "party of prosperity."[31]

Out of the military and political experience of Korea a conviction de-

[27]Cf. the conclusion reached by Samuel Lubell: "the frustrations over Korea were the most important single propellent behind Eisenhower's sweep." *Revolt of the Moderates* (New York: Harper, 1956), p. 265.

[28]In the Republican slogan of "Corruption, Korea, and Communism," Communism at home did not become an important partisan issue; Korea and corruption did. Just as the Great Depression had stimulated many to vote for the first time, so the "Korean War appears to have activated several million people who had sat out the previous elections." Angus Campbell, *et al., The American Voter* (New York: Wiley, 1960), pp. 50–51, 164.

[29]Angus Campbell, Gerald Gurin, and Warren E. Miller, *The Voter Decides* (Evanston, Ill.: Row, Peterson, n.d.), p. 51.

[30]*Ibid.*, Table 4.12, p. 57, and Table 4.3, p. 45.

[31]AIPO release, September 3, 1964.

veloped, widely shared by officials, commentators, and students of politics, that America ought not or could not fight another peripheral action, costly in manpower and without "victory" in sight. Charles Wilson, Eisenhower's first Secretary of Defense, once said, "We can't afford to fight limited wars. We can only afford to fight a big war, and if there is one that is the kind it will be." [32] Either we should not fight at all, such reasoning runs, or, in fighting, we should take every advantage of the modern means of warfare available to us in order to strike for victory. Where Wilson thought that militarily the United States ought not to fight another "Korea," others concluded that politically America cannot. In 1951, following the Congressional hearings that were prompted by the relief of General MacArthur, a Republican minority report declared:

> We believe that a policy of victory must be announced to the American people in order to restore unity and confidence. It is too much to expect that our people will accept a limited war. Our policy must be to win. Our strategy must be devised to bring about decisive victory.[33]

Herman Kahn, drawing an electoral lesson from Stevenson's defeat, concluded *"that if there is another unpopular Limited War followed by the loss of the ensuing national election by the party in power, the ability of the United States to fight Limited War will be sadly impaired."* [34] For their Korean venture, it appeared that the Democrats were punished severely at home; Republicans as well as Democrats presumably learned the electoral lesson. Some commentators were therefore tempted to say dogmatically that no President would ever again be willing to take the nation into such a war. Irving Kristol, for example, carried Kahn's qualified conclusion to such an extreme when he wrote:

> The Korean War was unpopular to a degree that makes it inconceivable for any future Administration to contemplate that kind of limited, rigorously defensive military action. The scholars and the diplomats can continue to devise ingenious gradients of warfare, countering each enemy action with just so much (and no more) reaction. But they are indulging in a paper game. The American people cannot provide the kind of mercenary, professional soldiers such plans require.[35]

---

[32]Quoted by James M. Gavin, *War and Peace in the Space Age* (New York: Harper, 1958), p. 124.

[33]Quoted in Morton H. Halperin, *Limited War in the Nuclear Age* (New York: Wiley, 1963), p. 46.

[34]Kahn, *On Thermonuclear War* (Princeton: Princeton University Press, 1960), p. 418; italics in original.

[35]Kristol, "A Matter of Fundamentals," *Encounter*, XIV (April, 1960), 56–57.

Students of politics seconded the impressions of public officials and underscored the worries that military strategists and political pundits entertained. It will be sufficient to cite two of the weightiest. Some years after the event, Key advanced the opinion that "the failure of the Truman Administration to make plain the reasons for American involvement in the Korean episode—a novel sort of enterprise for the United States— may have made it impossible to drum up public support for American participation in brush wars and thereby restricted us to atomic wars. At any rate, the successful Republican exploitation of the issue in 1952 will give statesmen cause for the greatest reluctance to engage in comparable enterprises, no matter what the need or provocation." [36] Brzezinski and Huntington incline to a compatible conclusion: "The normal and generally healthy play of partisan politics continually restricts an Administration's freedom of action. In times of crisis, restrictions may be supplemented by mass demands for quick victories and simple solutions. For almost two years the Truman Administration found itself boxed into a position where it could neither win the Korean War nor extricate itself from the war." [37]

A political system that makes it difficult for the government to contrive appropriate responses may threaten the world with its erratic actions or may doom itself to a gradually disintegrating position in international politics. It is important to reexamine the Korean case to see if the conclusions that have customarily been drawn are as depressing as many people have thought them to be.

It is true, as Key noted, that the reasons for American actions in Korea were never clearly explained. It is also true that what should have been done and why were not wholly and consistently understood at any level: the President and his most intimate advisors, the executive branch generally, the Congress, the stratum of the public that is most concerned and best informed about public affairs, or the people at large. Scarcely anyone in the United States, and not very many people elsewhere, had tried to figure out under what circumstances a country might wish to fight a limited war and how it should go about doing so. After the event, President Truman observed that on the way north in the fall of 1950 the forces of the United Nations should have stopped "at the neck of Korea" as the British had urged. We knew, he said, that "the Chinese had close

[36] Key, *Public Opinion and American Democracy*, p. 261n.
[37] Zbigniew Brzezinski and Samuel P. Huntington, *Political Power: USA/USSR* (New York: Viking, 1964), p. 414.

to a million men" at the Manchurian border. But MacArthur was the President's man in the field, and as Truman himself remarked, he had to "back him up."[38] To make use of his own homely saying, Truman belonged in the kitchen because he was able to take the heat. His political courage was inspiring and his loyalty to subordinates admirable, but in this case a different and better response would have been possible. Why should the President's statement not have been: "Dean Acheson was my Secretary of State, and since military forces were fighting in Korea for political objectives, I had to back him up"? If Secretary Acheson had recommended and President Truman had then decided that the "neck of Korea" was the right place to stop, the appropriate orders presumably would have been issued. There may be many reasons why such reasoning did not prevail in the difficult autumn of 1950. Among them uncertainty is no doubt more important than civilian timidity. Not General MacArthur alone, but President Truman and Secretary Acheson as well, tended to seek broad goals in Korea. When asked in the early dark days of the war to describe America's and the United Nations' objectives, Truman and Acheson replied, in effect, to repel aggression and restore the *status quo ante*.[39] When the fortunes of war were reversed by the landing at Inchon and the route to the north lay open, however, official statements of purpose began to encompass the unification of all Korea by military force. In short, the goal was victory. Once Chinese troops entered the war in large numbers and the troops of the United Nations found themselves moving rapidly backward, the aim of the fighting was once again described as being to contain the enemy and limit the war. But this modest goal was immodestly combined with a desire to secure a propaganda victory by saving from repatriation those prisoners of war who did not wish to return to their Communist homelands.[40] Unwilling to commit the forces that would make victory possible, the United States was also reluctant to fit her ends to the military means made available. The lure of success is difficult to resist.

Even if the foreshortening of goals had been firmly accepted, it would have remained difficult to say just how far one side could have gone without provoking the other to an unwanted enlargement of the war. If

[38]Neustadt, *Presidential Power*, p. 128.

[39]Harry S. Truman, *Memoirs* (2 vols.; New York: Doubleday, 1956), II, 341, 359–60, 438–39; and McGeorge Bundy, ed., *The Pattern of Responsibility: From the Record of Secretary of State Dean Acheson* (Boston: Houghton Mifflin, 1952), pp. 251–52, 263, 284.

[40]Only about 70,000 of the 132,000 military prisoners agreed to return. Admiral C. Turner Joy, *How Communists Negotiate* (New York: Macmillan, 1955), p. 153. On the instability of American objectives during the course of the Korean War, see *ibid.*, pp. 173–74.

the Yalu bridges had been bombed on a line of flight parallel with them instead of perpendicular to them, would an important military advantage have been gained, or would the Chinese have retailated in way that the United States would have preferred them to continue to eschew? The Chinese and the North Koreans never bombed the ill-concealed and un-protected bases south of the 38th Parallel, nor did they interfere with America's shipping tons of materiel and thousands of men into Japan and Korea by sea. Should the United States have moved more daringly and imaginatively in the conduct of the war itself? Could she have used her superiority in materiel, her ability to produce grossly more than the Soviet Bloc countries, her atomic power, and her ability to increase dra-matically the extent of her mobilization in order to frighten the Chinese out of enlarging the war as the troops of the United Nations moved farther north? Should the United States have used the threat to enlarge the war earlier in order to persuade her opponents to agree to a truce? Even uncertain answers were difficult to come by, especially since so few officials were attuned to the delicate process of action and reaction that characterizes the fighting of a limited war.[41]

Under the circumstances it cannot be said that mass opinion tied the hands of officials. Instead, the mixture of firmness and vacillation in the government's policy was mirrored in the people's opinion. Military action was heartily supported at the outset. In the summer of 1950, upwards of 75 percent of those who were asked for their opinions approved of Presi-dent Truman's decision to send troops to Korea.[42] But what the decision might imply was wholly misunderstood. Just over half of those polled in July thought that they were "actually in World War III," while only 29 percent thought that the fighting in Korea would "stop short of another world war." [43] As one might have expected, there was little appreciation of the possibility of fighting a war within limits.

As the war dragged on, confusion grew and opinion broke into frag-ments. When people were asked to suggest a proper course of American action, doubt and bewilderment were displayed in their answers. In five polls taken in the year beginning in December of 1951, for example, from 16 to 24 percent of those polled thought that the government should pull the troops out and send the boys home. Thirty to 43 percent would have taken the offensive against the Chinese, while 27 to 37 percent were re-

[41]On the process of limitation, see Halperin, *Limited War*, esp. pp. 55–57.
[42]NORC: July, 1950 (100/287), and September, 1950 (101/288).
[43]AIPO release, July 28, 1950.

signed to carrying on the war while peace talks continued.[44] Early in March of 1951, 73 percent of those polled thought that if we pushed "the Chinese back to the 38th parallel," we then should "stop fighting if the Chinese agreed." But in the middle of the month 38 percent of all respondents thought that if negotiations were to produce a comparable result, the outcome would be unacceptable.[45] The American tendency was to think that settlement at or near the 38th Parallel would leave the Communists with greater gains from the war than the United States would enjoy. The idea of a truce nevertheless became increasingly attractive. The following question was asked in September of 1953: "As things stand now, do you think our government should have signed the Korean armistice, or should we have continued fighting?" Seventy-five percent approved of the truce, which apparently in their view was the best way out of an altogether bad situation; only 15 percent would have continued to fight.[46]

In sum, it can be said that the administration did not explain its political strategy in the Korean War because it did not itself have a clear understanding of it—and therefore neither did the people. The administration was constant in its determination to keep the war limited; it was at times uncertain about the relation of its military and diplomatic decisions to that one clear goal. Unwilling to settle for a modest peace after the brilliant stroke at Inchon, unwilling to risk enlarging the war by striking for victory after China became engaged, the administration appeared to be unable to wage war and equally unable to make peace.

Many have nevertheless thought that the Democratic Party suffered electorally for waging a war that became unpopular in the course of fighting it. If this was, rightly or wrongly, the lesson learned from Korea, then was it not to be expected that a future President would be reluctant to place restraints on the use of force in wartime? Wars that could be limited would then be made into big ones in the manner that the previously cited statements of Secretary Wilson and Professor Key suggest. Or, the small-scale use of force by an aggressive state might remain unresisted, with the territorial position of the non-Communist world slowly wearing away. The first possibility has lessened. Any Senator from Indiana who suggests now, as Senator William E. Jenner seemed to wish a dozen years

[44]NORC: December, 1951 (115/315); March, 1952 (117/320); June, 1952 (121/327); November, 1952 (125/333); December, 1952 (126/334).
[45]AIPO releases, March 1, 1951, and March 18, 1951.
[46]NORC: September, 1953 (134/348).

ago, that the United States go all out for victory will be inescapably aware that he may be arguing for a hydrogen bomb dropped on Gary.[47] Two can now play, with roughly equal ability, at the game of strategic nuclear retaliation, a condition that did not exist at the time of Korea. Without a system of defense effective against missiles fired in large number, the argument for keeping wars limited becomes politically as well as strategically much easier to make. But then why should the nation fight any wars at all? The other part of the argument becomes more difficult to make—namely, that it may sometimes be well to engage in small wars at considerable expense and with no prospect of "victory" in sight. No President and no party will wish to commit themselves to a difficult course of action with electoral punishment the likely result.

Even the policy that elicits a favorable response from a comfortable majority of the people may leave enough voters unhappy to tip the next election away from the incumbents. A dissident minority, bipartisan in composition, that finds itself badly put off by the policy associated with the party in power may cause the candidate of that party to lose the election. In controversial matters, even a policy popular with a majority of voters may be an electoral loser. The counsel of greatest caution may be to prevent issues from becoming prominent unless it is clear that action upon them will be overwhelmingly acceptable. One may then think that the habit that democracies will naturally develop is that of obscuring situations that ought to call forth vigorous responses in order to make those situations appear to be unimportant.

It is useful to take up the problem in its most difficult terms. The novelty of the Korean crisis was excuse enough for the vacillations of the Truman Administration. One can hope to learn from experience, and yet in international relations it must be expected that each succeeding experience will be novel. It is impossible always to act wisely. Even wise actions may not preclude a grueling and costly fight, and under such circumstances the clear explanation of policies will not keep internal recriminations from growing. A President who does what the moment seems to require can then often expect that he and his party will have to pay the domestic political bill, however unjustly it may be drawn. Here again foreign policy is not so very different from domestic policy. The Republi-

---

[47]Cf. the line of questioning persistently pursued by Senator Jenner in the Senate hearings held from August through December of 1954 by his subcommittee. A summary is found in the Report of the Subcommittee of the Judiciary Committee to Investigate the Administration of the Internal Security Act and Other Internal Security Laws, *The Korean War and Related Matters* (84th Cong., 1st sess., 1955).

cans, in office when the market crashed in 1929, still bear some onus as the party of depression. It would, of course, only be just to say that the crash and the succeeding depression were bigger than any party and that had Al Smith been sitting in the White House backed by an overwhelming majority of Democrats in both Houses of Congress, he would not have been able to prevent these disasters, either. And so the Democrats, in office during the wars in which America has fought in this century, long remained in the public mind the party of war. While this is not surprising, it may be rather discouraging.

Actually, for several reasons it should not be. First, the election of 1952 was more a personal tribute to Eisenhower than a triumph for the Republican Party, less a repudiation of the Democratic Party than a conclusion electorally expressed that the Republicans had found a man who could see the country safely through a difficult international situation. On questions of foreign policy, Republicans were publicly favored, but the personal preference for their candidate was even more marked. Eisenhower was thought of as the man who would bring peace with honor, who would end the fighting in Korea without weakening America's position in the world. Varied and clear-cut evidence, some of it cited above, indicates that Eisenhower was chosen as President largely on grounds of imputed personal ability rather than as a reflection of party preference.[48] The war had lasted for two years. During the electoral campaign, small-scale fighting sporadically continued. It was difficult to see what the purpose of such fighting might be. In these unpleasant circumstances, large numbers of people treated the Korean War as an important political issue and were led, in doing so, to prefer Eisenhower to Stevenson. One may quarrel with their judgment but scarcely with the inclination to treat the issue as a major one that should affect or even dominate the choice of a President. One might also think that the ability of the Republican Party to come forth with a man who seemed to measure up to the demands of the crisis was a tribute to it. That Korea was a dramatically effective partisan issue should not be taken as evidence of a national desire to be quit of the world, to avoid all painful efforts, and to withdraw from all costly commitments, even if that were to mean creating situations of weakness in the world. That the Republicans won an election by running Eisenhower and laying great stress on the Korean issue may be evidence of some impatience with sacrifice long sustained. Their victory was also

[48]Cf. Campbell, Gurin, and Miller, *The Voter Decides*, pp. 57–58, 175–76.

evidence of a feeling, which had some basis in reason, that someone could be found who would manage such difficult affairs with greater skill.

The second reason for not being deeply concerned that fear of being labeled the "party of war" will dissuade a party in power from standing firm in the face of aggression is that the reputations of parties are more fairly won and more easily lived down than is sometimes supposed. Traditionally, the Republicans have been viewed as the party of peace and depression. A Republican President, one must note, did conclude an honorable peace in 1953, which the Democrats for three years had been unable to do, and did avoid becoming militarily involved in Indochina in the following year. Republicans, at the same time, have been less willing to run a deficit in order to combat unemployment and less warmly in favor of social-welfare programs. Democrats have long been viewed as the party of prosperity, but also as the party of war. For a decade, from 1951 to 1961, only 15 to 25 percent of the public had thought of the Democratic Party as the "best" party to keep the country out of war, while from 26 to 42 percent had, on this ground, preferred the Republicans. It is not true, however, that only the good fortune of having Barry Goldwater to oppose them in the election of 1964 enabled the Democrats to shed the unwanted reputation for bellicosity. In July of 1962, presumably because of Kennedy's performance in office, Democrats found as much public approval on the peace issue as did Republicans; and in February and May of 1963, Democrats were favored over their rivals by margins of 32 to 23 and 31 to 26 percent.[49]

Finally, harsh criticism of the party that is trying to carry out a given action does not necessarily indicate unwillingness to support other parts of the President's foreign policy. It may not even imply a disavowal of the action criticized. A distinction must be drawn between critical attitudes, on the one hand, and the willingness or refusal to support policies, on the other. Republicans who in the 1950's criticized American policies in China, for example, were assigning blame for events that had already occurred. Their criticism did not indicate that they would withhold support from the President should he seek to undertake difficult international actions. Republicans in Congress did not deny the President the opportunity to carry out his policy. Indeed, because they had granted him the instruments he asked for, Republicans could more easily say that the ill-conceived policy of a Democratic President had opened the way for

[49]Data are summarized in AIPO releases of February 5 and May 7, 1963.

Communist conquest of China. Any party in opposition will try to lay the blame for national ills upon the party in power. It is then misleading to say that Truman erred in failing to associate the Republican Party with his Far Eastern policy, wrong also to argue that if he had woven a bipartisan net around his China policy as he did on European questions, his fall in popularity would have been cushioned.[50] No intelligently led opposition party would have bought shares in an American enterprise in China that looked as though it could be saved from bankruptcy only at a price that almost no one was willing to pay. In the very years when much political sport was had with the Truman Administration's troubles in the Far East, a majority of Republican legislators supported such radically new and far-reaching programs as the Truman Doctrine, the Marshall Plan, the Atlantic Defense Treaty, and such difficult actions as the Berlin Airlift and even the military effort in Korea.

Governmental Freedom of Action

The chances that a President will be unable to carry out a controversial policy are slight, nor is it at all likely that he will be dissuaded from pursuing a difficult and possibly unpopular line of policy by the fear that he and his party will thereby be electorally punished. Parties and Presidents must care about losing a little of their popularity on one issue or another if democratic government is to be responsive to the wishes and worries of the people. At the same time, in politics as in all human affairs, there are situations in which one is damned if he does and damned if he does not. No man and no party can govern without accepting this truth. If the United States disengages in Southeast Asia and North Vietnam sweeps to the tip of the Camau peninsula, the President in power and the party that he leads will be found to be at fault. But they will also be found at fault if the scale of American involvement is increased in order to hold what remains of the peninsula or to regain lost ground. In the most difficult matters, and international crises are certainly among them, there is no single policy whose widespread popularity would survive the test of action. If the world is a mess and the United States must act in it, then Presidents will often be in a position of deciding which of several unpopular policies they will follow. They will have no chance to pick a policy that will lose them no votes at all. If timidity and quiescence were truly and clearly more popular than boldness and action, then one

[50]Cf. Westerfield, *Foreign Policy and Party Politics*, pp. 266–68, 343–44.

would rightly worry that democratic countries would always fall prey to the aggressive thrusts of others. If belligerence were always more admired, then one would live teetering on the brink of nuclear war. If either condition prevailed, Presidents would always experience pressure to act in one way whether or not it was appropriate to the situation at hand.

Brzezinski and Huntington suggested that a President steadily losing public support may find himself boxed in, as to a considerable extent Truman did. After months of costly and inconclusive fighting, withdrawal would have been humiliating, and to threaten the use of unlimited means in order to achieve a limited end, as Eisenhower and Dulles did later, would have failed of acceptance at home and lacked credibility abroad. The box, however, was not built by "mass demands for quick victories and simple solutions." As data previously cited make clear, no such demands were made. Nevertheless, as the war dragged on, impatience grew, and the country lost confidence in the competence of the government. Kristol, Kahn, and others thereupon concluded that the constraints of political competition severely limit America's contrivance and conduct of policy. Since World War II, foreign policy has usually been the most prominent of issues, but its electoral effect has nevertheless been diluted by juxtaposition with other problems and policies when voters made their decisions. One who bases his vote in part on performance in office must also ask himself how the competing candidate and party are likely to do. Numerous surveys have indicated that both parties are looked upon as competent to manage foreign policy. Furthermore, most people continue to vote in the present as they have voted in the past, whether or not the policies and programs of their preferred party have pleased them. When such countervailing factors are borne in mind, the fear that electoral punishment will dramatically affect foreign policy loses most of its force. International affairs have gone badly while Presidents of both parties were in power. Neither party has suffered any very deep political damage as a result.

The competition of two parties for the people's favor is sometimes said to lead both of them to espouse policies and programs that they know to be bad. In contrast, George M. Trevelyan, giving the Romanes Lecture in the Sheldonian Theatre at Oxford forty years ago, strongly argued that the principal virtue of a two-party system is that where one party is weak, the other may be strong; where one party has failed, the other may succeed. "No one party," he asserted, "can cover all the ground." The party that reacted correctly to the French Revolutionary and Napoleonic

Wars could scarcely have approached the questions of Parliamentary reform with a proper attitude, "so powerful in the political mind is the instinct to associate ideas not logically connected with one another." If Fox and Grey in the 1790's had joined Pitt in opposition to the Jacobins, Trevelyan averred, there would have been no Whig reform bill in 1830.[51] In much the same way, it may well have appeared that the Democratic Administration, having begun the Korean War, was unable to end it either by military victory or diplomatic settlement. It is strange then that the Republican victory of 1952 has so often been described, in relation to the problem of limited war, as an indication of democracy's weakness rather than as a demonstration of its strength. "Weakness" would be an apt term only where the demise of the administration meant the loss of its policy, even though conditions had not changed sufficiently to make a policy of different intent appropriate to the national situation. "Weakness" would also apply if the political system provided no routine way of discarding a leader or ruling group when its policy, once popular, had taken on a sickly hue and when the people had lost confidence in the integrity and competence of the administration's leading members. Democracies permit a change of persons and parties to be easily and gracefully made. Because they do, policies that remain necessary though they have become unpopular can often more easily be continued. The situation found in a monarchy only upon the death of a king is the recurring condition of a democratic state. In the relation of crown prince to king, it was frequently thought by the people that the son would be saner and sounder and generally more pleasing than his father. In democratic countries, such a situation may be repeated every four or five years. It can then be said, and usually is by members of the opposition party, that the government has done everything wrong and that they, if elected, will do much the same things and, of course, do them much better.

One difficulty with Trevelyan's statement would seem to be this: it might just as plausibly be said that the constructive policies of one party may be lost later when a party of contradictory tendencies gains office or that the weakness and confusion of one party will be reinforced by the uncertainty and stupidity of the other. The mutual reinforcement of the virtues of parties for the benefit of the state depends upon their policy positions being sensible and upon their being separated only by a harmonious third rather than by an entire octave or some dissonant interval. When such is the situation of parties, their alternation can be the glory

[51]Trevelyan, *An Autobiography and Other Essays* (London: Longmans, Green, 1949), p. 197.

of democracy. The election of 1952 is a case in point. The Republicans stood for a policy of liberation, which was the administration's aspiration in North Korea and which was, in reference to Poland, the promise of any politician who happened to be speaking in Buffalo, Hamtramck, or Chicago. The responsible leaders of both parties and the vast majority of people in general wished to stand firm against the Soviet Union and Communist China, to set somebody free if that would not be too dangerous, and to avoid fighting and dying if that were at all possible. The Republican Party won the election on a platform that was different from the Democratic platform mainly in tone and in emphasis.

The American government had apparently decided before the event that it would not meet force with force in Korea.[52] But it did. Numerous statements by Eisenhower, Dulles, and others indicated that in Indochina in the spring of 1954 the United States would fight or somehow retaliate if the Communists continued to drive forward.[53] But this time, it did not do so. In neither case can it be said that fear of the people's opinion or of domestic political consequences noticeably affected the final decision. Nor had weariness with the war in Korea persuaded the public that giving way in other parts of the world would be preferable to fighting. Asked in May and September of 1953 and again in April of 1954 whether the American air force should be used if necessary to prevent the Communists from taking over all of Indochina, from 52 to 60 percent agreed that it should. In all three polls, a larger percentage still, that is from 59 to 65 percent, favored sending American troops, with always about a third of the sample opposed to either alternative.[54] For the next decade, as economic and military commitments grew, American policies in Indochina were viewed with a mixture of mild disinterest, mature skepticism, and judicial calm, with never an inclination to force the government's hand. Following the naval incidents of Tonkin Bay early in August of 1964, President Johnson proposed and the Congress overwhelmingly accepted a resolution that practically gave the President a

[52]John W. Spanier, *The Truman-MacArthur Controversy and the Korean War* (Cambridge, Mass.: Harvard University Press, 1959), p. 17; Trumbull Higgins, *Korea and the Fall of MacArthur: A Précis in Limited War* (New York: Oxford University Press, 1960), pp. 10–14.

[53]Cf. John Foster Dulles, who in September of 1953 said, "There is the risk that, as in Korea, Red China might send its own army into Indochina. The Chinese Communist regime should realize that such a second aggression could not occur without grave consequences which might not be confined to Indochina. I say this soberly in the interest of peace and in the hope of preventing another aggressor miscalculation." Address by Secretary Dulles to the American Legion at St. Louis, Mo., on September 2, *Department of State Bulletin*, XXIX (September 14, 1953), 342.

[54]NORC: May, 1953 (130/340); September, 1953 (134/348); April, 1954 (137/355).

free hand in Southeast Asia (Public Law 88-408). In February of 1965, the American bombing of North Vietnam began. In March of that year, 27,000 American troops were serving in Vietnam; in June, 54,000; in September, 128,500; by May of 1966, more than 250,000. Against the background of these events and in the presence of continued political unrest in South Vietnam, Americans, in their answers to pollsters, revealed themselves as being reluctantly willing to fight, amenable to settlement, anxious to negotiate, and, though obviously wary, worried, and confused, willing to give the President wide latitude.

Such a pattern of opinion persisted, even as the scale of American involvement increased and the toll of American lives rose. In the late spring of 1964, for example, of the 74 percent who then knew of the fighting in Vietnam, 53 percent opposed and 28 percent favored "the United States getting out of the Viet Nam war completely." At the same time, 46 percent favored trying for some such "compromise agreement with Communist China" as "making all Viet Nam neutral," with 29 percent against doing so.[55] In January of 1965, the respondents of the Gallup Poll affirmed by a margin of four to one their belief that the Vietcong were defeating the South Vietnamese, and by a margin of two to one their opinion that the latter would not be able to form a stable government. Still, by a margin of almost two to one they subscribed to the statement that the United States was right to have become militarily involved. At the same time, 81 percent expressed themselves in favor of President Johnson's calling an international conference with Chinese and Southeast Asian leaders to see if a peace agreement could be arranged, while only 11 percent dissented.[56] In February and March of 1966, a group of behavioral scientists, most of them located at Stanford University, sponsored a survey to find what the deeper attitudes were. Though the questioning, conducted by the National Opinion Research Center, was more detailed, the attitudes uncovered were much the same as those previously reported. For example, 52 percent would favor "a new government in which the Vietcong took some part," 36 percent would not. Offered three choices, 49 percent said they would continue to do in Vietnam as their government was then doing, 23 percent would prefer to fight a major war, and 19 percent would simply withdraw. Some 60 percent would fight a major war

[55]Council on Foreign Relations, *The American Public's View of U.S. Policy Toward China: A Report Prepared for the Council on Foreign Relations by the Survey Research Center, University of Michigan* (New York, 1964), Table 23, p. 42; Table 24, pp. 43–44. The survey was conducted, nationwide, in the late spring of 1964.

[56]AIPO release, January 31, 1965.

if the only alternative to it were withdrawal of American troops. At the same time, 88 percent favored "negotiations with the Vietcong if they were willing to negotiate," while 8 percent opposed them. In general, President Johnson's actions in Vietnam were endorsed by 61 percent and disapproved of by 29 percent, while 10 percent expressed no opinion.[57]

What thoughts lay behind the answers? Did the public perhaps entertain such notions as these—that delaying actions at low cost are worth mounting, that it is well to demonstrate that nothing is free for the taking, but that, all things considered, the time to leave had arrived if leaving could be gracefully arranged? While it is too much to attribute such intricacy, clarity, and precision of thought to the public mind, the state of the people's opinion permitted the President to fashion such an interpretation of America's position should he have wished to. It could not at any rate be said that public opinion constituted a pressing limit upon Presidential action, nor did the warning of the Korean experience lead the government to avoid military involvement. As difficulties in Vietnam multiply, criticism of the government will grow. Indeed, by the spring of 1966, disenchantment had begun to set in. In fairly steady progression, those approving of the way "Mr. Johnson is handling his job as President" declined from 69 percent of those asked in July of 1965 to 66 percent in early November and to 58 percent in March of 1966.[58] If the public standing and moral authority of the administration should gravely weaken, it will be time for a change, whether or not blame has been justly accorded. Obviously President Johnson has been keenly aware of the domestic political risks he was running. To have changed policies because of electoral fears for the future would not have been honorable. Examination of public opinion in periods of crisis has led us to the conclusion that it would not have been practical either. In their foreign policies, governments of all types have sometimes been fainthearted. One need not fear that pusillanimity is especially encouraged by the pressures of public opinion as it operates in the American democracy.

The fears born of the military and electoral struggles of the Korean era have faded. In the 1950's, it was fashionable to affirm that the American democracy would not sustain distant and indecisive military engagements firmly or long enough. In the 1960's it has become more common to suppose that the American government is impervious to criticism and given

[57]Sidney Verba, *et al.*, "Public Opinion and the War in Vietnam" (mimeo.; no place, n.d.), Appendix I, Tables 1, 2, and 12. The report was summarized by Wallace Turner, "Public Backs Negotiations With Vietcong, Poll Says," *New York Times,* March 15, 1966, p. 1.
[58]Gallup Poll, *Philadephia Bulletin,* July 11, 1965, and March 30, 1966.

too free a hand even during protracted periods of crisis. Both worries are important; each has in its day been exaggerated. Two dangers threaten especially. With multiplication internationally of the arenas of major contention, it will become more difficult to remember that American security interests require military engagement only where the adversary is of such strength that he is or may become a threat to the nation. Beyond that, though the margin of power that America enjoys over any other contender may be a source of comfort to her citizens, it may also worry the observer. Powerful nations have often abused their power to the detriment of themselves and of others. More than has been the case with any modern state, the restraint of the American nation must now be self-imposed. A nation as powerful as America may become impatient with the defensive pose it has struck and long maintained. Senator J. William Fulbright has detected in American foreign policy "signs of that fatal presumption, that overextension of power and mission, which brought ruin to ancient Athens, to Napoleonic France and to Nazi Germany." He has warned his country not to become "what it is not now and never has been, a seeker after unlimited power and empire." [59] Is Senator Fulbright premature in his pessimism and unduly alarmed by the experience of war in Vietnam?

In the case of Vietnam, spokesmen for the administration have asserted the vital importance of showing that insurgencies are costly, damaging, and doomed to defeat; they have argued that China must be contained for a time as the Soviet Union was earlier. One may wonder if the assertion and the argument do not rest on an overestimation of Chinese capability, a failure to appreciate the penchant for independence of the Indochinese whatever the political orientation of their governments, and an overlooking of the possibility that any increase in Chinese strength would be more of a worry to the Soviet Union than to the United States. The questions involved are, however, difficult ones on which no light can be shed by demonstrations and little by public debates. Nonetheless, with international restraints pressing less closely, internal correctives become all the more important. The American government is well supplied with them. To critics such as Senators Mike Mansfield, J. William Fulbright, and Robert Kennedy, the administration pays the closest heed; for institutionally and politically their positions are strong. Fulbright's eloquent

---

[59]"Excerpts from Fulbright's Speech on Vietnam War," *New York Times*, April 29, 1966, p. 32.

warnings are not misplaced. It is because of him and other powerful critics that the dangers of hubris are lessened.

One of the valuable qualities of the American political system is the persistence of effective criticism. Opposition to the President's foreign policy has most often since the war centered in the House of Representatives; on questions of foreign aid, for example, it lodged in the Appropriations Committee. In contrast, the Foreign Relations Committee, strong enough to influence the whole Senate, soon converted its members, even those once isolationist, to support of the country's new policies.[60] That was the pattern until recently. In his first years of office, President Johnson showed an unusual ability to keep issues closed, to prevent arguments from occurring in publicly conspicuous places. From February of 1965 onward, from the time when American military forces were first committed to battle in Southeast Asia, however, Senator Fulbright reluctantly permitted his Committee to begin to oppose the President's policies—in Vietnam, with regard to China generally, and on matters of foreign aid. The function of opposing, like the task of providing leadership, sometimes migrates from one political institution to another.

Conclusion

There is no end to one's worries. One who is not busily worried about a possible absence of support for waging limited wars is liable instead to fear that the United States is politically prevented from acquiescing in defeat on those occasions when losing would be the least unhappy of all the unhappy choices. The American reaction to the Chinese Revolution after World War II supposedly illustrates one type of recurrent difficulty: an unwillingness to acquiesce in "necessary" defeats. Unwilling (and sometimes wisely so) to expend the manpower and materiel that a drive for victory would require, the government is also reluctant to say simply that the goal is not worth its price. One may then fear that the American people will be overly eager to fight, ever unwilling to compromise, and thus be able to press a government to rashly adventurous actions. Denis Brogan created a phrase that caught on when he attributed the McCarthyite hysteria of the early 1950's to America's "illusion of omnipotence," understandable in view of her history but unforgivable

---

[60]David N. Farnsworth, *The Senate Committee on Foreign Relations* (Urbana: University of Illinois Press, 1961), pp. 151–55.

as the attitude of a country that stood as the leader of the "free world." [61]
Internal political criticism first focused on the "loss" of China, grew
with Representative Nixon's dramatization of the charges against Alger
Hiss, became still more widespread when McCarthy made his flamboyant
charges in February of 1950 that there were 205 or 57 or whatever number of Communists in the State Department, and reached a crescendo in
the years of the Korean struggle. The frenzied frustration and self-
indulgent hysteria of the McCarthy-Korea years could be interpreted
charitably as a momentary reaction, a relapse after the vigorous and
wholly unaccustomed activities in international policies that the Truman
Doctrine, the Marshall Plan, and the formation of NATO represented.
They could also be seen as the awkward and erratic responses of a par-
venu who did not know how to behave in the international arena. Finally,
of course, they could be and sometimes were taken as demonstrations of
the proposition that her political institutions and national character
make America unfit for a leader's role in the world.

Are the American people hopelessly naïve and in their naïveté a danger
to the world? Is America given to vacillation between the poles of international commitment and national withdrawal? Is the American political
system incurable without institutional surgery? Taking America's policy
toward China as a difficult last example will enable us to suggest answers
to these questions and at the same time make summary comments on the
present chapter.

Though opinion on the sensitive subject of China has often been contradictory, it has neither been rashly belligerent nor naïve about the
causes of American difficulties. Early in 1954, for example, the Gallup
Poll asked: "What, in your opinion, are the main reasons that China
went Communist?" Seventy-three percent of those polled thought the
reasons were to be found in the ignorance of the Chinese masses, the
skill of the Communists, and the corruption of the Nationalist regime;
10 percent blamed American policy and traitorous action; 17 percent
gave miscellaneous replies; and 23 percent did not know.[62] Though mul-
tiple responses to the single question cloud the finding, it is nevertheless
some evidence of maturity of political outlook that only 10 percent of
the replies ascribed to American officials responsibility for events in
China. Asked in April of 1955 whether we should "be friendly to Red

[61]Brogan, "The Illusion of American Omnipotence," *Harper's*, CCV (December, 1952),
21–28.
[62]AIPO release, January, 1954.

China and try to win her away from Russia," or should "treat her as an enemy," 47 percent preferred the first alternative and 40 percent, the second. At the same time, 78 percent opposed China's admission to the United Nations and 65 percent were against trading with her.[63] More recently, 53 percent of those who realize that China's government is Communist opposed her admission to the United Nations (31 percent were in favor); but 75 percent of the same sample would stay in the United Nations "if Communist China gets in," and only 5 percent would thereupon leave. While distaste for the Chinese Communist regime is deep and persistent, 62 percent oppose and only 10 percent favor "helping Nationalists to attack Communists." [64]

If the American people in general are more sophisticated than is sometimes supposed, are they not still in their inclinations dangerously unsteady? Paul Ramsey has recently written that "perhaps because of the Calvinism gone to seed in the atmosphere, and the lack of any doctrine of the Two Realms in which a human destiny is played out, the American people are ill prepared for the self-discipline necessary for the limitation of warfare." [65] His conclusion may once have been true, though not necessarily for the reasons he suggests. William C. Foster, a man of both business and political affairs, seems to have thought so. "We must," he once urged, "attempt to get away from the strange dichotomy with which we have traditionally viewed force, refusing to consider it except as a last resort, then approaching it in a crusading manner with a 'punish the bandit' view which has been prevalent in our recent conflicts." [66] While the religious beliefs of the general public have not changed noticeably since the Cold War began, America's notions of the place of force in foreign policy have evolved as her expectations of an easy international life have dwindled. Samuel Lubell, who is not the most scientific of pollsters but who may be the most perceptive, has drawn a sharp distinction between the typical American reaction of 1952 and of 1962. He reports that in 1952 he found people saying, "I'm against this idea that we can go on trading hills in Korea indefinitely." In other words, they implied, it may be well to strike at the enemy with all the power at our command. Early

---

[63]AIPO release, April, 1955.

[64]Council on Foreign Relations, *The American Public's View of U.S. Policy Toward China,* Table 16, p. 30; Table 13, p. 23; Table 10, p. 19. Of those interviewed, 28 percent were not aware that China is ruled by a Communist government (Table 1, p. 5).

[65]Ramsey, *War and the Christian Conscience: How Shall Modern War Be Conducted Justly?* (Durham, N.C.: Duke University Press for the Lilly Endowment Research Program in Christianity and Politics, 1961), p. 151.

[66]Quoted by Arthur Krock, "In the Nation," *New York Times,* December 20, 1957.

in 1962, in contrast, he reported the prevalent fear as being that "if we throw a nuclear bomb at them we'll get it back in this country." With the feeling that "all-out war" has become "unthinkable," acceptance of the likelihood of small wars has grown, and so has the willingness to fight them. "It's just a little country," Lubell found some people saying, "but if we let the Reds walk off with it we will be lowered in the eyes of the world." [67]

Ever since 1948, 80 percent or more of Americans polled have replied affirmatively to such questions about Berlin as this one: "Should we stay in Berlin even if doing so means war with Russia?" Should the audacity of the reply cause one to fear that the President may order shots to be fired so that by doing what the people seem to want he will look more like a leader? Or should one think of such responses as indicating a reluctant willingness to fight in situations of tremendous risk if the government should decide that other policies would be riskier still?

For several reasons, it is the latter question that merits an affirmative answer. (1) In an era of Cold War, the American people have not, despite what is frequently said, demanded either victory or withdrawal, though occasionally articulate minorities and a few highly placed public officials have done so. (2) Reluctance to retreat and willingness to fight in order to avoid having to do so are more the product of the international condition of bipolarity than of internally generated political pressures.[68] People *and* Presidents, the public at large *and* the dominant elites have united in their belief that the United States must stand firm in the face of aggression abroad. (3) One must ask what it means to "stand firm." The actions and words of the President, more than of anyone else, will define for the public this difficult term. To put it crudely: defeats will be described as unimportant and compromises, as triumphs, if it is at all possible to do so. The Cuban confrontation in October of 1962 was said to be an American victory over Khrushchev—he removed the Russian missiles. But Castro remained in power and a number of the Soviet Union's technicians remained in the country. Khrushchev was able to retreat, which is said to demonstrate that dictators enjoy freedom from internal constraint. But the United States, it should also be noted, was able to settle for something less than the achievement of ends that had earlier been widely proclaimed.

[67]Lubell, "Ideas Change about Small Wars," *Philadelphia Bulletin*, April 2, 1962, p. 5.
[68]Cf. Kenneth N. Waltz, "The Stability of a Bipolar World," *Daedalus*, XCIII (Summer, 1964), 881–909.

The people react to what the President does, and some of them at least form an opinion of how well he does it. If a President says that we need not fight, as Eisenhower in effect did when the French were besieged at Dienbienphu, no spontaneous rush to the colors is likely. Willingness to fight should not be identified with eagerness to do so. Reluctance to give way should not be confused with a stubborn unwillingness to compromise. It would seem from the record that the mass of the American people have learned to live with danger, to tolerate ambiguity, to accept setbacks, and to understand that victory is sometimes impossible or that it can be gained only at a price the wise would refrain from paying.

Chapter 11

FOREIGN POLICY
AND
DEMOCRATIC POLITICS

It is sometimes said with dismay that the British policymaking machine has broken down. It has not. Instead, conditions have changed, and in new circumstances the old machine, still running smoothly, no longer produces spectacular results. Perhaps it never did. Governments are praised when their nations are great. How much of the success of a nation is caused by the structure of its government and how much by other conditions is difficult to determine. During the Victorian age and earlier, British governments most often merely presided, while a virile and productive people pushed out in the world and colored the map red. The primacy of private life and the ineffectuality of the politician are recurring themes in nineteenth-century English literature. To cite one example, the young and inexperienced Endymion, who gave his name to one of Disraeli's novels, expressed his ambition to become a "public man" and shyly confessed that his ambition was grounded in a desire for power. "The most powerful men are not public men," he is thereupon advised. "A public man is responsible, and a responsible man is a slave. It is private life that governs the world." [1] George Eliot, to take another example, once described a father who was prey to his daughter's strategems and charms as having "as little of his own way as if he had been a prime minister." [2]

In an era of oligarchy and in a subsequent period of clashing political

[1] Earl of Beaconsfield, *Endymion* (London: Longmans, Green, 1882), p. 156.
[2] Eliot, *Middlemarch: A Study of Provincial Life* (New York: New American Library, 1964), p. 335.

powers and diffusion of governmental functions, the industrial and inter-national bases of modern British greatness were forged. In a third politi-cal period—of majoritarian democracy with parties disciplined ever more tightly—drift, decline, and decay at home and abroad have set in. Throughout most of the past century, Britain has appeared to be a state in which an institutionally strong ruler asserts his will when and as he may choose to. The joining of structure and performance explains why the appearance is misleading. The Prime Minister only appears to be strong, and the reason he appears so is that Parliament is inordinately weak. The contention of weak forces proceeds in an orderly fashion. Parliamentarians, who are political experts, remain amateurs in policy. They are, as a group, highly literate and pleasantly articulate; they talk of policy in broad terms and show a high regard for large issues. Intel-lectuals especially find the style of British government attractive. Beyond their aesthetic preference may lie a philosophic conviction that truth, the common interest, and the general well-being are better defined and served not by a contention of voices and a competition of interests but instead by the intellectual apprehension of each problem or issue.

Will a system of separated powers, one must ask, produce a better re-sult than will a majoritarian system? Neither aesthetic nor philosophic predilections are sufficient guides to an answer. The question of the coherence and adequacy of policy, since those attributes cannot be meas-ured objectively, resolves itself into a further question: namely, who de-cides that some policies are better than others? Partisans of Parlimentary government believe that a system of Cabinet or Prime Ministerial control based upon disciplined parties generates adequate political power and produces policies that meet the needs of the nation.

Attributes of British Government

Introducing a new edition of *The English Constitution*, R. H. S. Cross-man emphasized that Bagehot, understandably at his time of writing, re-lied upon a "solid centre of independent and independent-minded mem-bers" to ensure that party government would always be mild. Lingering uncertainty that sufficient votes would be available to support the Cabi-net's policy worked to restrain the government. The perfecting of party discipline has, in Crossman's view, completed the government's power and elevated the Prime Minister above his Cabinet colleagues. Crossman notes that yesteryear's collective decisions of the Cabinet have become today's Prime Ministerial decisions, some of which "are taken by the Premier alone, some in consultation between him and the senior ministers, while others are left to heads of departments, the Cabinet, Cabinet committees or the permanent officials."[3] This is fair enough as a description of how recent Prime Ministers have acted. But what indication of the government's power does the description of procedures give us?

Impatient with political constraints, Joseph Chamberlain once remarked to Balfour that it was England's misfortune "that we live under a system of government originally contrived to check the action of Kings and Ministers, and which meddles far too much with the Executive of the country."[4] It is nevertheless difficult to correct the impression of strength formed by seeing the Prime Minister leading his disciplined party. That the Prime Minister could do something bold if only he would decide to is a notion not easily got rid of. Even Crossman, who has so often been impatient of British governments, believes that "it is very much easier for a British than for a French or American statesman to initiate a new unpopular foreign policy."[5] Joseph Chamberlain was closer to the mark; the executive power of England is not too strong but instead is too tightly hobbled. With some amendments, Bagehot remains a better guide to the principles that prevail in present-day politics than does Crossman. The big error made by Crossman and by most interpreters of British government is to assume that the Prime Minister has an abundance of strength. They then seek to explain how it happens that the office is so powerful and concentrate their concern too narrowly upon the decline of Parliament. The concern is valid enough; the government, however, would function better if both Parliament and Prime Minister were stronger.

Proceeding in a different manner, Bagehot, having noticed that British rule is "moderate and mild," identified the means of restraining the government. Most of the restraints that he mentioned still work their effects, though not always in just the same manner. He described as mutual restraints upon Parliament and the Ministry not only the cautionary effects to be derived from the existence of independent members but also the Prime Minister's power of dissolution, the leaders being placed constantly "in contact with reality," and the characteristics of "parliamentary gov-

[3]"Introduction" by Crossman to Walter Bagehot, *The English Constitution* (London: Watts, 1964), pp. 43, 53.

[4]Arthur James Balfour, *Retrospect: An Unfinished Autobiography, 1848–1886* (Boston: Houghton Mifflin, 1930), p. 224.

[5]Crossman, *Planning for Freedom* (London: Hamish Hamilton, 1965), p. 208.

ernment" that set it apart from "constituency government" as it is practiced in America.

> Constituency government [he wrote] is the precise opposite of parliamentary government. It is the government of immoderate persons far from the scene of action, instead of the government of moderate persons close to the scene of action; it is the judgement of persons judging in the last resort and without a penalty, in lieu of persons judging in fear of a dissolution, and ever conscious that they are subject to an appeal.[6]

Parliament still acts as a powerful restraint, though no longer by virtue of the slack discipline of parties. Parliaments no longer make or unmake Prime Ministers; the parties in Parliament do so. In choosing a leader, members of a Parliamentary party will try to find someone who can lead them to victory; they will also look for a man who by their lights is sound and will be safe in the office. If responsibility is clearly and formally affixed, then the responsible person's tenure of office must be left uncertain. In the event of a fiasco, the person who by office is charged with responsibility cannot be permitted to continue. Prime Ministers of the mid-nineteenth century, while they had to manage their followers, were also concerned to impress Parliament and to influence those members who might waver between parties. The Prime Minister now, assured of formal backing especially in close divisions, must nevertheless worry lest between general elections his effective support dwindle and his position become politically insupportable. Prime Ministers must be, and must take pains to remain, acceptable to their Parliamentary parties. By the political system within which he operates, the Prime Minister is impelled to seek the support of his entire party, at the cost of considerably reducing his freedom of action.

The second restraint, dissolution, is now largely irrelevant. The third and fourth can be considered together. To judge "without a penalty" and without "fear of dissolution" is to be irresponsible. Members of the Parliamentary parties actually man the offices of state, or if in opposition, they aspire to. The Prime Minister and the other responsible men who make up the Cabinet are close to the affairs of state, "familiar with disagreeable facts," and cooled in their partisan ardors by the clearly affixed responsibility they bear for the conduct of government.[7] As discipline in England has tightened, responsibility has been more completely realized and more precisely fixed upon the Prime Minister. As Disraeli knew, and

---

[6]Bagehot, *The English Constitution* (London: Oxford University Press, 1928), pp. 124–29.
[7]*Ibid.*, pp. 126–28.

Bagehot apparently did also, "a responsible man," though he may appear to be powerful, is in reality "a slave." To be clearly responsible is to be highly visible. In the United States, the Congressional show detracts in some measure from the attention the President receives; in England, the public concentrates its gaze with single-minded intensity upon the Prime Minister. Fairly or not, he is praised or blamed for the good or ill health of the polity. Responsibility is concentrated rather than being diffused. The leader who is responsible then has to husband his power; the onus for the risky policy that fails to come off falls entirely upon him.

The Prime Minister is responsible for the government as a whole, and each Minister for his department. The restraint of responsibility, however, like others that operate in the system, is gross and external. It is for the Prime Minister himself to weigh the political forces at work in the nation. Though the Prime Minister is guided and restrained, he may not be effectively stimulated or controlled. This, the great paradox of British government, baffles most political observers; for it seems logically unsound and unduly subtle to distinguish between restraint and control, between guidance and stimulation. It is nevertheless essential to do so. In America, with a nearly unbroken string of strong Presidents reaching back thirty-five years, it is natural to think only in terms of limits that are imposed by strong institutions and to overlook the aspects of British government that in this book are emphasized—the recruitment of the leader and the effect of his having to manage a party so carefully. Indeed, in the two countries, the term "leadership" has different political meanings: in the United States, that strong men occupy the Presidency; in Great Britain that the will of the Prime Minister becomes the law of the land. To say that the will of the leader becomes law should not be taken to mean that the system is one of strong leadership in the American sense; instead everything will depend on the leader's identity and the forces that shape his decisions. The English system goes far to ensure that the leader is moderate and will behave with propriety. Power is concentrated in the hands of the Prime Minister and yet with great, though often informal, checks against its impetuous use: the apprentice system by which Parliamentarians rise to office; the subtle restraints of party that work upon the Prime Minister; the habit, institutionally encouraged, of moving slowly with events and of postponing changes in policy until their necessity is widely accepted.

Do these attributes describe the style of English government or merely of the Conservative Party? Those who write of the parties in England

302

tend to focus upon Labour, for with internecine battles openly fought and votes on issues and persons frequently taken, a large body of material is available to the student. In writing of British governance, one must concentrate more heavily upon Conservative policy, for since its birth at the turn of the century the Labour Party has commanded a majority in the Commons for less than a decade. Not all that we have said applies equally to governments of the two different parties. Embedded in Labour politics, for example, is the habit of looking upon Ministers less as gentlemen who occupy offices in order to preside over their affairs and more as men who are charged with tasks that require expert knowledge. Labour Ministers after the Second World War were intent upon making changes and carrying out new programs. They more frequently held a single Ministerial office for over two years than did succeeding Conservative Members. Consciously contrived innovation was more the mark of Attlee's first government than of later Conservative Governments. In foreign policy, the one clear peacetime case in this century of policy not muddled into or made simply in reaction to events was the firm decision to withdraw from India and to hasten the conversion of Empire to Commonwealth.

Is then the style of British politics merely the style of Conservative Governments? The Labour Party's long period of wandering in the political wilderness, the accumulated social and economic deficits of two decades of depression and unemployment, the unusual condition of an election following the upheaval of war without an election having been held for ten years preceding, the untypical circumstance of a woefully small party securing at one stroke a handsome majority: these factors combine to explain the greater than usual distinction in policy between what a Labour Government did and what a Conservative Government might have done. Given such special circumstances, one may all the more wonder at the quick depletion of energies in Attlee's first government. Roy Jenkins, long a Labour MP and presently Home Secretary, described the accomplishments of the postwar government as the climax of a century of social reform rather than as the opening of a new era of socialism.[8] The passing of its initial measures of social welfare and nationalization left the Labour Government without clear plans or purpose. Since 1964, in foreign as in domestic affairs, the policies that Labour has followed are strikingly Conservative in character. In economic matters, the "stop and go" policies of oft-condemned Conservative Chancellors con-

[8]Jenkins, *Pursuit of Progress* (London: Heinemann, 1953), p. 169.

303

tinue to be applied; in foreign affairs, the policies of a world power are still followed though material resources have long been insufficient to sustain them.

Massive continuity, painfully slow adjustment, response to crises only when they have almost hopelessly deepened: these characteristics are deeply ingrained in British politics and are scarcely affected by the identity of the ruling party. Robert T. McKenzie, more profound than his critics, saw the dominant point clearly. In crucial respects, the structure of government molds the political behavior of both parties and especially that of their leaders.[9]

Attributes of American Government

Though Prime Ministers are assumed to be in a strong position, British policy moves forward only after careful preparation of the ground upon which members of the governing party will be expected to stand. The fusion of powers and the concentration of responsibility encourage governments to avoid problems while broad accommodations are sought. In the United States, it is thought, government alternates between deadlock created by Congressional recalcitrance and dangerously dominant Presidential power, with the voters unable to apply an effective sanction because they cannot know which party or persons to blame. One should add, however, that where it is publicly unclear just who has done what, everyone can try to do something. The fragmentation of power and the confusion of responsibility encourage competitive political habits and in the twentieth century have more often than not produced governments of innovative zeal and vigorous leadership.

Because foreign affairs require such high degrees of flexibility and dispatch, Congressional participation in them becomes difficult. Many persons have feared that Presidential government will develop into Presidential dictatorship. Others have worried that the whimsical recalcitrance of Congress will discredit the nation by weakening and confusing its policy. That contrary worries simultaneously obsess the nation is itself of little comfort, for a true estimate of the situation may not rest on comfortable middle ground.

American government frightens and bewilders its friends and its enemies alike. Policy seems to depend on a chance constellation of forces

[9]McKenzie, *British Political Parties: The Distribution of Power within the Conservative and Labour Parties* (2d ed.; New York: Praeger, 1963), chap. 11.

rather than to result from calm deliberation and reasoned calculation. In a competition of particular interests, how can it be expected that the common interest will triumph? How reliably and how promptly the common interest can be expected to emerge will depend partly on the character of the society and the composition of the economy, partly on the structure of government and the adequacy of political management. Without examining the framework of competition and the identity of the competitors, it cannot be said whether competition will produce a good result or a bad one. Earlier chapters have therefore been occupied with the problems of relating political structure to process and of examining the institutional positions of political leaders.

In the United States, political struggles for office and arguments over policy take place among individuals and groups who openly clash and compete. Competition among interests and the clash of perspectives heightens issues and strengthens the institutions that express them. The Congressman, who is a political generalist, becomes an expert in one realm of policy or another in order to advance his career and forward his policy preferences. The executive official, who may be an expert in policy, schools himself in the political arts in order to protect his department and advance its programs. The American system is one of contention among strong institutions whose cutting edges have been honed in recurrent conflict. Within an economy, it matters whether competition takes place among inefficient firms or among firms that are well organized and managed. So also it matters in politics, though the point is less easily seen, whether the component parts of a system, in their varied relations of cooperation and opposition, are strongly constituted and suited to their tasks.

Should one say that the President is weak because Congress is strong, or should one say that the American government is powerful because its component parts are strongly constituted and active? Those who define power according to differences in the amount of force wielded by each of two entities—who think of power as a residue of strength—will surely reply in the negative. It is, however, more useful to think of the power of a government in terms of its effectiveness. May it not be that the government gains power from the strength of each of its component institutions?

The mild and moderate governments of Britain need not be closely reined, for the Prime Minister in his person and by his institutional position is weak. Because of the weakness of the component parts of the government, the quality of British policy has suffered. If one is worried that the power of the American President may become overwhelming and is at the same time concerned with the effectiveness of government, the British case suggests that the problem is not so simple as that of merely shearing the executive of some of its prerogatives. A strong President is needed, and yet the President must at times be curbed, corrected, and encouraged. The most obvious and important device, both for restraint and for stimulation, is a legislative body able to force the careful preparation, the full explication, the public defense, and finally the considered revision of executive programs. By the habit of scrutinizing details, by the function of passing upon appointments, by the power of granting or withholding money, the Congress—its political strength firmly grounded in the separate constituencies of its members—is able to accomplish these purposes. The virility and resilience of Congress has permitted the development of great strength in the Presidency without risk of Presidential dictatorship.

Reflections in Closing

Since foreign policy is fashioned by domestic institutions, we have sought to understand the political arrangements of the state and the style of the nation in order to assess its strengths and weaknesses in making and conducting foreign policy. Not surprisingly, British governmental arrangements and national temperament coincide and reinforce one another. The powerful are usually thought arrogant, a trait they may not recognize in themselves. Still, when Britain was the greatest of the great powers in the world, her preeminence was easily borne. Compared to most preeminent powers, her behavior was less damaging to others and to herself, the nation less given to hubris, her government and people less tempted by a string of successes to seek the victory that would place a seal upon her predominance and, in seeking it, to run grave risk of crushing and funereal failure.

The mirror of history reflects the same image; the world has changed more than Britain. Gracefully withdrawing from Empire, phasing out one base while jumping to another, muddling toward Europe, climbing summits in pursuit of a world influence for which the material basis is lacking, substituting the myth of Commonwealth for the reality of Empire: most of these are not inspiring ways of adjusting to decline in a country's international status, but they are benign. Quicker response and bolder movement have often produced worse results. External manner parallels internal procedure: though growth rates have lagged—whether in the economy generally, in the field of education, or in the construction of roads—employment is nevertheless full, the political system stable, and the administration of programs humane.

With the United States as with Great Britain, it is impossible to disentangle the internal from the external forces that work upon policy. The United States since the Second World War has conducted a series of blocking operations around the world, in Southeast Europe and Berlin, in Korea and the Taiwan Straits, in Cuba and Southeast Asia. Tasks that two decades ago were said to be beyond the capacities of the American democracy have been steadily performed. Difficult, dangerous, and costly policies have steadfastly been followed. Far corners of the world have been garrisoned by American troops year after year with no end in sight.

To what extent, one may ask, is the firmness of American policy to be explained by the nation's obsession with Communism? Exaggeration of Communist dangers did help to draw the nation from isolation to international involvement. For a number of reasons, however, a supposed obsession with an ideologically defined evil is an insufficient and misleading explanation of American foreign policy. If obsession there was, it was obsession with a very real danger. The external threat of Russia at the end of the Second World War and after did constitute an international menace, which only the United States was able to meet. Since the late 1940's, moreover, the United States has become more and more mindful of differences among Communist countries. Aid has been accorded to Yugoslavia and to Poland, as well as a measure of political acceptance. More generally, rather than trying to make the world over in the American image, America has aided governments of all political persuasions and has shown a higher regard for the independence of states than for the nature of their regimes. Devotion to the principle of national self-determination, which accords with America's interest, remains a better explanation of her policy than any new-found ideological fervor.

From the pages of this book, two general conclusions can be drawn. The one, analyzed, delineated, and illustrated at length, is that in matters of foreign policy (and of domestic policy as well) the American Presidential system is superior to British Parliamentary government. It was long believed that America's democratic institutions would prevent her from behaving effectively and responsibly in the world. The judgment should be reversed. American institutions facilitate rather than discourage the quick identification of problems, the pragmatic quest for solutions, the ready confrontation of dangers, the willing expenditure of energies, and the open criticism of policies. The second proposition, alluded to in the introductory chapter and sustained thereafter only by indirection, is that democratic governments of the Western type are well able to compete with authoritarian states. Enough has been said about democratic governments to demonstrate one half of the assertion, but a half-proved assertion is not proved at all. A direct comparison is required, of which only the outlines can be sketched here.

Students of American foreign policy, disheartened by the infelicities of their country's foreign policy, are inclined to emphasize inherent disabilities of democracy. At the same time, impressed by the difficult problems that the Soviet Union has sometimes posed, they too readily believe that Soviet rulers, because unencumbered by democratic restraints, are able to make and conduct their policies with unusual wisdom and cunning. Those who pay closer attention to the Soviet Union bring such views into balance. Adam Ulam, for example, has concluded that "in a totalitarian or authoritarian system foreign policy is much more intimately connected with internal politics than is the case in democratic and constitutional societies." He asserts, moreover, that "some of the most crucial shifts and puzzling decisions of the Soviet leaders make sense only if we keep in mind the internal conditions that accompanied them." [10]

Authoritarian states suffer many of the political disabilities of democracies; they also have other shortcomings, which though different are as damaging. Both types of handicap are indicated in the comments that follow.

Oswald Spengler suggested that the excellence of a ruler may be judged by his ability to construct a system that can be carried on and to create a tradition that will endure.[11] Are those who will succeed an authoritarian ruler, one may wonder, likely to be groomed for the responsibilities they must one day assume? It is difficult for the ruler to groom his successor

---

[10]Ulam, *The New Face of Soviet Totalitarianism* (Cambridge, Mass.: Harvard University Press, 1963), p. 122. For some other suggestions about the effect of internal politics on the external policy of the Soviet Union, see John A. Armstrong, "The Domestic Roots of Soviet Foreign Policy," *International Affairs*, XLI (January, 1965), 37–47; Zbigniew Brzezinski and Samuel P. Huntington, *Political Power: USA/USSR* (New York: Viking, 1964), chaps. 4, 5, 8, 9; S. I. Ploss, "The Uncertainty of Soviet Foreign Policy," *World Politics*, XV (April, 1963), 455–64; Marshall D. Shulman, *Stalin's Foreign Policy Reappraised* (Cambridge, Mass.: Harvard University Press, 1963), pp. 49–50; Robert M. Slusser, "The Role of the Foreign Ministry," in Ivo J. Lederer, ed., *Russian Foreign Policy: Essays in Historical Perspective* (New Haven: Yale University Press, 1962), pp. 236–38.

[11]Spengler, *The Decline of the West*, Charles Francis Atkinson, trans. (2 vols.; New York: Knopf, 1926 and 1928), II, 444.

without endangering his own power. Following a virtuoso performer, whether a Stalin or a Khrushchev, a Bismarck or a de Gaulle, one expects to find a period of political uncertainty and weakness of rule. While democratic elections give the impression that the continuity of policy is in question, the likelihood of discontinuity is higher in authoritarian states. The authoritarian ruler, if he dominates those who surround him, is, moreover, denied the corrective criticism and the honest reporting of events that are essential to the making of wise decisions. And with the advent of Freud it can no longer be said, if ever it could be, that running the affairs of a state according to the will of one man will ensure the unity of policy. The ruler is prey to the ills of the mind, perhaps the more so as his power approaches the absolute. In totalitarian states rather than in democracies are found the paranoid men of power surrounded by their bizarre coteries. The closed quality of rulership is itself a disability of authoritarian rule.

Because the making of policy is centralized, the foreign policy of an authoritarian state is assumed to be unified, integrated, and consonant with the ends of the state. To make decisions according to the merits of cases, however, requires information about them, an unclouded mind, and freedom from conflicting considerations. Can it at least be expected in authoritarian states that the last of these will be present? Whether authoritarian or democratic, governments merely because they are governments have much in common. Interests abound in any varied and extensive state. In democracies, their influence on government is palpable; in authoritarian states, for being less visible they are not necessarily less influential. Writing of German and American foreign policies, Alfred Vagts found imperial Germany as sorely beset by interests as was the United States.[12] Nor in the Soviet Union are interests aside from those of the Party and the central government lacking. The recurrent political role of the armed forces illustrates the point. Though it is true that the Party permeates and controls the military, it is also true that the Party is sometimes split at the top. On several occasions, military support has proved politically important and perhaps decisive.[13] The leadership of a totalitarian state may try to extinguish groups that present a challenge, or seek to play off some of them against others, or look for an accommodation. In the 1930's, Stalin was able to achieve unity only by eliminating everyone who

---

[12]Cited by Carl Joachim Friedrich, *Foreign Policy in the Making* (New York: Norton, 1938), p. 79.

[13]For a brief account, see S. E. Finer, *The Man on Horseback* (London: Pall Mall Press, 1962), pp. 106–8.

disagreed with him. One part of the price paid for the imposition of unity was reduction of the variety of views.[14]

The ruler is not given his power; power has to be gained by persuasion, bargaining, manipulation, and force. Once gained, it may be difficult to keep. In totalitarian and authoritarian states, as in democratic states, policy is one of the means to the securing of office. Until he put himself in power, Khrushchev opposed the policies of Malenkov, only to adopt them later. The pattern is a common one. Is a competitor for power, one may wonder, likely to follow a policy popular with those whose support he depends on and then return to reality as soon as he can afford to? Or is the leader's subsequent change in policy an effort to shake loose from his supporters and gain a wider freedom of action? Whatever the answer, one at least can say this: Indecision and stalemate, zigzags in policy produced by internal struggles for power, timidity abroad because of insecurity at home, and adventures in foreign policy for the sake of impressing a domestic audience are all familiar aspects of both totalitarian and authoritarian rule.

Totalitarian and authoritarian rulers, like others, face a choice that cannot be evaded. In order to buttress the security of the state, they can seek broader support from interests, organizations, segments of the society, and the people at large. But increase of support is gained at the expense of control or at the cost of freedom of action. The government that moves with grace and dispatch from one contradictory position to another demonstrates its control over policy and thereby indicates its weakness. Eighteenth-century diplomacy, for example, could be wondrously flexible because few were concerned with its conduct. The government that is strong in its foreign policy because it is widely supported at home will have difficulty in changing its course. One who thinks for a moment will see that the rapid alternation of Stalin's policy toward Germany in 1939 and his ultimate appeal to Russian nationalism after Hitler's attack in 1941 illustrate these propositions. Only when policy is divorced from the people's support are abrupt reversals easily possible. Only when policy is widely approved can the nation's resources be fully deployed. The conflict between the government's freedom of movement and the strength of its position, identified in discussing British government, is everywhere present.

Four major considerations, then, bring into question the assertion that in foreign policy authoritarian governments have a natural advantage.

[14]Cf. Slusser, "The Role of the Foreign Ministry," p. 231.

First, authoritarian rulers tend to blind themselves and stultify their successors' development. Second, authoritarian governments are no more immune to the politics of the interests and their pressures upon policy than are democracies. Third, rulers and would-be rulers in both types of state must worry about the relation of the policies they espouse to their own political fortunes. Finally, both authoritarian rulers and democratic politicians confront the dilemmas of control and security and must decide whether to strive for more of the one at the expected expense of the other.

In a world where military technology places a premium upon speed and opponents at times appear to be implacable, the flexibility, dispatch, coherence, and ruthlessness of authoritarian states have been thought to be decisive advantages. But the characteristics which, it is said, democratic governments cannot display are, despite the assertion, in part within their capacities and in part absent also in other forms of government. Disagreement about ends openly expressed in democratic states may cause some opportunities for gaining national advantage to be missed. But the running of risks foolishly is then also impeded. Democracies less often enjoy the brilliant success that bold acts secretly prepared and ruthlessly executed may bring. With the ground of action more thoroughly prepared and the content of policy more widely debated, they may, however, suffer fewer resounding failures. Coherent policy, executed with a nice combination of caution and verve, is difficult to achieve in any political system, but no more so for democratic states than for others.

INDEX

BOOKS WRITTEN UNDER THE AUSPICES OF THE
INSTITUTE OF WAR AND PEACE STUDIES
COLUMBIA UNIVERSITY

Defense and Diplomacy, by Alfred Vagts, 1956. King's Crown Press.
Inspection for Disarmament, ed., Seymour Melman, 1958. Columbia University Press.
Theoretical Aspects of International Relations, ed., William T. R. Fox, 1959. University of Notre Dame Press.
Man, the State, and War, by Kenneth N. Waltz, 1959. Columbia University Press.
The Common Defense: Strategic Programs in National Politics, by Samuel P. Huntington, 1961. Columbia University Press.
Changing Patterns of Military Politics, ed., Samuel P. Huntington, 1962. Free Press.
Strategy, Politics, and Defense Budgets, by Warner R. Schilling, Paul Y. Hammond, and Glenn H. Snyder, 1962. Columbia University Press.
Political Power: USA/USSR, by Zbigniew Brzezinski and Samuel P. Huntington (jointly with the Russian Institute), 1964. Viking Press.
Political Unification: A Comparative Study of Leaders and Forces, by Amitai Etzioni, 1965. Holt, Rinehart and Winston.
Stockpiling Strategic Materials, by Glenn H. Snyder, 1966. Chandler Publishing Company.
The Politics of Military Unification, by Demetrios Caraley, 1966. Columbia University Press.
NATO and the Range of American Choice, by Annette B. Fox and William T. R. Fox, 1967. Columbia University Press.
To Move a Nation: The Politics of Foreign Policy in the Administration of John F. Kennedy, by Roger Hilsman (jointly with the Washington Center of Foreign Policy Research, Johns Hopkins University), 1967. Doubleday and Company.
Foreign Policy and Democratic Politics, by Kenneth N. Waltz (jointly with the Center for International Affairs, Harvard University), 1967. Little, Brown and Co.

PUBLICATIONS WRITTEN UNDER THE AUSPICES OF THE
CENTER FOR INTERNATIONAL AFFAIRS
HARVARD UNIVERSITY

Books

The Soviet Bloc, by Zbigniew K. Brzezinski (jointly with the Russian Research Center), 1960. Harvard University Press.
The Necessity for Choice, by Henry A. Kissinger, 1961. Harper & Bros.
Strategy and Arms Control, by Thomas C. Schelling and Morton H. Halperin, 1961. Twentieth Century Fund.
Rift and Revolt in Hungary, by Ferenc A. Váli, 1961. Harvard University Press.
United States Manufacturing Investment in Brazil, by Lincoln Gordon and Engelbert L. Grommers, 1962. Harvard Business School.
The Economy of Cyprus, by A. J. Meyer, with Simos Vassiliou (jointly with the Center for Middle Eastern Studies), 1962. Harvard University Press.
Entrepreneurs of Lebanon, by Yusif A. Sayigh (jointly with the Center for Middle Eastern Studies), 1962. Harvard University Press.
Communist China 1955–1959: Policy Documents with Analysis, with a Foreword by Robert R. Bowie and John K. Fairbank (jointly with the East Asian Research Center), 1962. Harvard University Press.
In Search of France, by Stanley Hoffmann, Charles P. Kindleberger, Laurence Wylie, Jesse R. Pitts, Jean-Baptiste Duroselle, and François Goguel, 1963. Harvard University Press.
Somali Nationalism, by Saadia Touval, 1963. Harvard University Press.

The Dilemma of Mexico's Development, by Raymond Vernon, 1963. Harvard University Press.
Limited War in the Nuclear Age, by Morton H. Halperin, 1963. John Wiley & Sons.
The Arms Debate, by Robert A. Levine, 1963. Harvard University Press.
Africans on the Land, by Montague Yudelman, 1964. Harvard University Press.
Counterinsurgency Warfare, by David Galula, 1964. Frederick A. Praeger, Inc.
People and Policy in the Middle East, by Max Weston Thornburg, 1964. W. W. Norton & Co.
Shaping the Future, by Robert R. Bowie, 1964. Columbia University Press.
Foreign Aid and Foreign Policy, by Edward S. Mason (jointly with the Council on Foreign Relations), 1964. Harper & Row.
Public Policy and Private Enterprise in Mexico, by M. S. Wionczek, D. H. Shelton, C. P. Blair, and R. Izquierdo, ed. Raymond Vernon, 1964. Harvard University Press.
How Nations Negotiate, by Fred C. Iklé, 1964. Harper & Row.
China and the Bomb, by Morton H. Halperin (jointly with the East Asian Research Center), 1965. Frederick A. Praeger, Inc.
Democracy in Germany, by Fritz Erler (Jodidi Lectures), 1965. Harvard University Press.
The Troubled Partnership, by Henry A. Kissinger (jointly with the Council on Foreign Relations), 1965. McGraw-Hill Book Co.
The Rise of Nationalism in Central Africa, by Robert I. Rotberg, 1965. Harvard University Press.
Pan-Africanism and East African Integration, by Joseph S. Nye, Jr., 1965. Harvard University Press.
Communist China and Arms Control, by Morton H. Halperin and Dwight H. Perkins (jointly with the East Asian Research Center), 1965. Frederick A. Praeger, Inc.
Problems of National Strategy, ed. Henry Kissinger, 1965. Frederick A. Praeger, Inc.
Deterrence before Hiroshima: The Airpower Background of Modern Strategy, by George H. Quester, 1966. John Wiley & Sons.
Containing the Arms Race, by Jeremy J. Stone, 1966. M.I.T. Press.
Germany and the Atlantic Alliance: The Interaction of Strategy and Politics, by James L. Richardson, 1966. Harvard University Press.
Arms and Influence, by Thomas C. Schelling, 1966. Yale University Press.
Planning without Facts, by Wolfgang Stolper, 1966. Harvard University Press.
Political Change in a West African State, by Martin L. Kilson, 1966. Harvard University Press.
Export Instability and Economic Development, by Alasdair MacBean, 1966. Harvard University Press.
Contemporary Military Strategy, by Morton H. Halperin, 1967. Little, Brown & Co.
Foreign Policy and Democratic Politics, by Kenneth N. Waltz (jointly with the Institute of War and Peace Studies, Columbia University), 1967. Little, Brown & Co.

Occasional Papers, Published by the Center for International Affairs

1. *A Plan for Planning: The Need for a Better Method of Assisting Underdeveloped Countries on Their Economic Policies*, by Gustav F. Papanek, 1961
2. *The Flow of Resources from Rich to Poor*, by Alan D. Neale, 1961.
3. *Limited War: An Essay on the Development of the Theory and an Annotated Bibliography*, by Morton H. Halperin, 1962.
4. *Reflections on the Failure of the First West Indian Federation*, by Hugh W. Springer, 1962.
5. *On the Interaction of Opposing Forces under Possible Arms Agreements*, by Glenn A. Kent, 1963.
6. *Europe's Northern Cap and the Soviet Union*, by Nils Örvik, 1963.
7. *Civil Administration in the Punjab: An Analysis of a State Government in India*, by E. N. Mangat Rai, 1963.
8. *On the Appropriate Size of a Development Program*, by Edward S. Mason, 1964.
9. *Self-Determination Revisited in the Era of Decolonization*, by Rupert Emerson, 1964.
10. *The Planning and Execution of Economic Development in Southeast Asia*, by Clair Wilcox, 1965.
11. *Pan-Africanism in Action*, by Albert Tevoedjre, 1965.
12. *Is China Turning In?* by Morton H. Halperin, 1965.
13. *Economic Development in India and Pakistan*, by Edward S. Mason, 1966.
14. *The Role of the Military in Recent Turkish Politics*, by Ergun Özbudun, 1966.